# Nonalignment and Peace
## *Versus*
## Military Alignment and War

**About the Author**

Dr. Nihal Henry Kuruppu completed a doctorate in political science at Victoria University, Melbourne, in 2000. Research for his PhD., and this book, took him to Cambridge University, the Robert Menzies Centre for Australian Studies, University of London, the Commonwealth Secretariat, London and, the Nehru Memorial and Lok Sabha Libraries, New Delhi, among a number of other institutions and national archives.

He has written a number of articles and critiques on subjects ranging from international socio-economic trends to Greek philosophy and cricket. Before his present work as a university lecturer, he was a member of the senior executive group with General Motors Corporation's Australian subsidiary, Holden, and, prior to that, executive head of the corporate planning function with the Anglo-Dutch multinational giant, Unilever, at its subsidiary in Sri Lanka. In 1971, he was appointed to the UN (ILO) International Roster of Management Consultants, and in 1989, made a Bail Justice by the Government of Victoria. Nihal is married and has four children.

# Nonalignment and Peace
## *Versus*
# Military Alignment and War

NIHAL HENRY KURUPPU

ACADEMIC FOUNDATION

NEW DELHI

First Published in 2004 by

**A C A D E M I C   F O U N D A T I O N**

4772-73 / 23  Bharat Ram Road, (23 Ansari Road),
Darya Ganj, New Delhi - 110 002
INDIA

Phones : 23245001, 02, 03, 04
Fax : +91-11-23245005
e-mail : academic@vsnl.com
www : academicfoundation.com



*Nonalignment and Peace Versus Military Alignment and War*
by Dr. Nihal Henry Kuruppu
**ISBN 81-7188-363-X**

Designed and typeset by Italics India, New Delhi
and printed at Print Perfect, New Delhi.

*Dedicated to*

*Unie, Prins, Rohan, Ruvani, and Ranil*

# CONTENTS

# List of Abbreviations and Acronyms

| | |
|---|---|
| AA | Australian Archives |
| AFAR | Australian Foreign Affairs Record |
| AGPS | Australian Government Printing Services |
| ALP | Australian Labor Party |
| ANU | Australian National University |
| ANZAC | Australia, New Zealand Air Corp |
| ANZAM | Australia, New Zealand and Malaya |
| ANZUS | Australia, New Zealand and United States Security Treaty |
| APEC | Asia Pacific Economic Cooperation |
| ASEAN | Association of South East Asian Nations |
| CENTO | Central Treaty Organisation |
| CNIA | Current Notes on International Affairs (Australia) |
| CPD | Commonwealth Parliamentary Debates (Australia) |
| DEA | Department of External Affairs (Australia) |
| DFAT | Department of Foreign Affairs and Trade (Australia) |
| DLP | Democratic Labor Party |
| EAEG | East Asia Economic Grouping |
| EC | European Community |
| EU | European Union |
| HOR | House of Representatives |
| INC | Indian National Congress |
| IR | International Relations |

| | |
|---|---|
| MEA | Ministry of External Affairs, (Government of India) |
| MHR | Member, House of Representatives (Australia) |
| MP | Member of Parliament (India) |
| NAI | National Archives of India |
| NAM | Nonaligned Movement |
| NATO | North Atlantic Treaty Organisation |
| NGO | Non Government Organisation |
| NLA | National Library of Australia |
| NNRC | Neutral Nations Repatriation Commission |
| NSW | New South Wales, Australia |
| OAU | Organisation of African Unity |
| QLD | Queensland, Australia |
| SAARC | South Asian Association of Regional Cooperation |
| SCORE | Security Council Official Records |
| SEATO | South East Asia Treaty Organisation |
| TRT | The Roundtable (Journal) |
| UAR | United Arab Republic |
| UN | United Nations |
| UNCIP | United Nations Commission for India and Pakistan |
| UNESCO | United Nations Educational, Scientific and Cultural Organisation |

# Preface

Australia's interpretations of international relations have tended to reflect the dominance of the post-war realist orthodoxy. The behaviour of the non-aligned States in relation to the great powers (particularly the US, which under-pinned Australia's security) was the orthodox measure used to interpret a bilateral relationship with Australia. Any telling of the India-Australia story in the past has tended to be subject to this one dimensional approach, which was axiomatic of the times. The result has been a gap in the writings because of the restricted nature of the interpretations. This is the first analysis that seeks to present a stronger Indian perspective of the bilateral relationship with the primacy of peace and racial equality used as key measures in evaluating the bilateral relationship. This reflects a moral focus expressing India's psychological and operational responses to Australia and the world. It means an examination of the relationship in all its dimensions, enabling a fuller understanding.

This analysis of the India-Australia bilateral relationship (1947-1975) is based on empirical evidence and research material, both primary and secondary, and a range of interviews. It included research undertaken in the U.K. at Cambridge University's Commonwealth Studies Library; London University's Menzies Centre for Australia Studies; the Public Records Office, London; and the Commonwealth Secretariat Library, London.

In New Delhi, research was carried out at the Nehru Memorial Museum and Library. While a few of Nehru's personal papers of relevance to this study were available at this Library, the major part was not available to be examined during the research. The Government of India, Ministry of External Affairs (MEA) Library, the National Archives of India (NAI) and the Lok Sabha Parliament

Library, were other sources of the research. The Archives of the Government-owned Associated Newspapers of Sri-Lanka were also a source of research information, as was the Cultural Centre and Library of the Indian High Commission in Colombo.

The Australian National Archives (ANA) and the National Library of Australia (NLA) in Canberra provided the principal primary sources in Australia. India's Deputy High Commissioner in Australia, Mr B.B. Tyaji's assistance was sought particularly on gaining access to the research programme undertaken in India. Interviews were held with author and former Australian High Commissioner to India, Mr Bruce Grant and a number of other scholars and academics.

The book's aim is to interrogate the assertion that the changing nature and character of the bilateral relationship between India and Australia during the twenty-eight year period from 1947-1975, was, among other Cold War imperatives, a measure of the personalities and policies of the leaders on both sides. While scholars have recognised this as being an important influence in any analysis of the state of the bilateral relationship, the emphasis given to it has been too little. As a contributory factor, political changes at the Australian end had a greater bearing on the relationship because they not only involved a different leader with each new period (1947 - Chifley, 1949 - Menzies and 1972 - Whitlam) but also a different political ideology and some shifts in foreign policy positions. In India's case, although a change of leadership took place in 1964 and 1966, (Nehru to Shastri to Mrs Gandhi), a single political party, Indian National Congress Party (INC) committed to the broad Nehruvian philosophy of non-alignment, international peace, and racial equality, continued in office throughout the period examined in this book (1947-1975).

It should also be noted that in line with one of the principal arguments of the analysis, namely, the influence of personalities, the India-Australia relationship was favourably affected by the Whitlam view of the world, one which had much in common with Nehruvian philosophy and Australia's shift to a more regional focus. Yet, its impact on the India-Australia relationship was precursory, with any benefits from the mutual interest and accommodation accruing through subsequent decades of gradual activism, which is outside the scope of this book.

The analysis seeks to go beyond the empirical elements of the bilateralism in question to embrace International Relations theory, particularly in Chapter One. The resultant theoretical framework helps contextualise the overall examination and, it is hoped, will also be of use to future research on the bilateral links between India and Australia – links that, arguably, could be stronger to the mutual benefit of both countries.

# Introduction

There have been some excellent writings on the subject, India-Australia bilateral relationship. The case for a stronger Indian point of view springs from the impression that Australian scholarship has, understandably, had little reason to evaluate the relationship from other than a largely Australian view of the world. It should be stressed that the arguments here specifically set out to examine the Indian perspective and it is through this interpretive lens that the entire work is presented. For example, when analysing international issues that had Indian and Australian involvement in a participatory or mediatory capacity (e.g., Korean War, SEATO, Suez, apartheid and South Africa's Commonwealth membership, etc.) the interpretations have tended towards a wider understating of the Indian contribution and the thinking behind India's foreign policy, and of its implications for the country.

That is not to say that Indian case has been totally ignored. There is already a growing discussion among academics, writers and others about the importance of a better understanding of what went wrong with Australia's handling of the bilateral relationship and identifying the missing pieces: taking a look at the other side of the mountain too. In essence, it means seeking a view of the Cold War world as it affected the two countries but seen through a non-aligned Indian lens as well as from Australia's security-driven, 'White Australia' foreign policy orientation.

This is the basic premise of the approach taken in this book. It examines the changing nature and character of the relationship between India and Australia from 1947-1975, and the reasons for the peaks and troughs which characterised the relationship. Outwardly, the relationship between two former British colonies, with a number of shared experiences, seemed agreeable enough. Nonetheless, it masked a complex web of ideologically based alliances, pragmatic commitments and practical policy imperatives.

For the bilateral relationship, it often meant no more than mutual indifference for most of the twenty-eight year period covered in this analysis which examines newly independent India's relationship with Australia during three chronologically separate periods: the first under Chifley (Labor, 1947-1949), followed by Menzies and others (Liberal-Country Party Coalition, 1949-1972), and, lastly, Whitlam (Labor, 1972-1975). In India, the Indian National Congress (INC) under Nehru (1947-1964), followed by Shastri and Indira Gandhi, continued in office throughout this examination of nearly three decades of the relationship, although a split in the INC occurred in 1969. The responses of these and other key political figures of the two countries to the Cold War reveals as much about the shaping of their minds as it does about the key issues that determined the nature of the bilateral relationship. Consequently, a number of dominant themes emerged to underpin the hypothesis that the relationship moved from one of understanding and mutual respect in the first period, to indifference and inertia in the second, followed by mutual recognition, interest and accommodation in the reformist Whitlam period.

Some of the themes, a few stronger than others, represent common threads - such as colonialism, non-alignment, racial discrimination, and the personality factor - running through the book:

- The ideological rivalry of the Cold War and Australia's preoccupation with a perceived Communist threat, may have forced scholars to conform to a prevailing hegemonic realist ideological orthodoxy. Non-aligned India preoccupied dealing with priorities of poverty and related economic problems, and a foreign policy underpinned by its moral values was relatively free of ideological constraints imposed by the Cold War. Consequently, past interpretations of Cold War events and foreign policy premises of relevance to the bilateral relationship have been oriented largely towards the Australian realist view of the world. The result has been an understating of the Indian perspective.

- The bilateral relationship was shaped by the sensitivities of the Australian political party in government in Canberra, in particular the Prime Minister's (and key Ministers') personalities, their psychological and operational views of the world. The definition of 'personality' employed in this analysis is more than a simple catalogue of character traits, although these are important when considering such factors as arrogance, self-confidence and will-power. The definition includes personal political philosophy and ideological commitment of the main players in the game; the result, peaks and troughs in the relationship. While party politics was an influence on the bilateral relationship, the focus here is on personalities and policies and, hence, other influences are not explored to the same degree.

- The mainstream Australian view is that the relationship in the 1950s and 1960s suffered from Canberra's neglect of India. While this interpretation is without guile, in India (with its much higher international engagement and profile at the time) this was seen as presumptuous. Australia was somewhat outside India's international sweep and rather low on its list of international priorities, particularly when Menzies was Prime Minister with his British orientation and commitment to Western strategic interests.

- Australia's 'White Australia' policy and India's 'Non-alignment' Policy were pivotal to each country's external responses; they were also conflicting. India's deep sensitivity to racial discrimination meant Australia's 'White Australia' Immigration policy was a barrier to a stronger relationship. India's dramatic, although pragmatic choice of non-alignment, in its essence a moral force, influenced by its bitter experience of colonialism and the early Cold War rivalry, was criticised in Australia as naive and not in the West's global political interests. Australia did not seem to appreciate the multi-layered character of the doctrine, particularly during the Menzies period which was characterised by its preoccupation with security and alliance diplomacy.

- No study of the India-Australia relationship in the 1950s and early 1960s can profitably ignore the impact of the Nehru-

Menzies dissonance and differences, psycho-political in nature, which represented an impediment to a more constructive engagement between the two countries.

- There is evidence to suggest that Australia largely followed the British 'colonial' view of India in the 1950s.

- Given the Pakistan's conservatism, anti-Communism and friendly relations with Britain; Australia, with an inherited English approach to the subcontinent, felt more comfortable dealing with a pro-Western Pakistan than with the Hindu, non-aligned idealists in New Delhi. This is also seen in Australia's attitude to the Kashmir question during the Menzies period. At times, there was the impression of a trilateral balancing act rather than an India-Australia bilateral relationship.

- Australia's Treasury and External Affairs bureaucrats may have found India too large, too complex and too demanding of resources to handle.

- Nehru's disaffection (shared by other Indian leaders) with the West, including Australia, was largely a measure of his lack of admiration for the Americans with their blunt approach to International Affairs. In the view of some senior Indian bureaucrats, the graceless US national temperament tended to undermine the subtleties of diplomacy. As expressed by author Bruce Grant, a former Australian High Commissioner to India, this also was an English view of the US - one not shared by Australia. Australia's diplomatic shift from Britain to the US after World War II was a dominant paradigm shift in which India, itself a former British colony, was not involved.

- In strategic terms, the Pacific Ocean was viewed in Australia as commanding greater importance than the Indian Ocean which washed both Indian and Australian shores.

- There was little mutuality of economic and cultural interests between India and Australia, during the period covered in this study. Also, trade, normally a key determinant of bilateralism, was not a major factor in the relationship.

- From the time he entered Parliament in 1953, Whitlam's statements on India and Nehru, were positive. Particularly relevant was the closeness of his views in many areas with

Nehru's. This parallelism earned him admiration in India and made his affinity, when Prime Minister, with India's Prime Minister, Mrs Gandhi, a natural outcome. Whitlam's broader ideology transcended cultural limitations. His Government's decisive repudiation of the 'White Australia' policy in 1973, its resurgent independence in foreign policy, combined with Whitlam's visit to India (the first by an Australian Prime Minister in his first year in office) did much to change Indian perceptions of its regional neighbour with its previous unambiguously Western bias. Whitlam also supported the non-aligned countries' proposal for declaring the Indian Ocean a zone of peace.

- Another dimension to Whitlam's impact on the India-Australia relationship came about indirectly. Whitlam's reformist foreign policies and his dismantling of many symbols of the British link gave Australia a greater sense of pride in being a sovereign State. Coupled with the non-discriminatory immigration policy, this tended to make the idea of a multicultural society progressively more acceptable. It also meant less fear felt by Australians of its culturally different neighbours, which of course includes India, and therefore was of benefit to the future bilateral relationship.

The 1947-1975 period covered in this book, is examined by moving chronologically comparing personalities and philosophies in each period, together with policies and the role of public opinion as they influenced the relationship. Accordingly, the seven chapters examine the policy actions, themes of continuity and change (bilaterally and globally) in the two countries' direct and indirect foreign policy responses affecting each other in each of the three periods, 1947-1949, 1949-1972 and 1972-1975. It was not always possible, nor was it desirable, to maintain chronological precision when dealing with some of the important themes which relate to more than one period.

Chapter One considers the nature and determinants of bilateralism. It describes numerous types of bilateral relations and provides a framework for examining the India-Australia bilateral relationship. It continues with an analysis of the International Relations (IR) discipline and how it treats bilateralism. To understand the impact of the policy maker's mind on policies and therefore, relationships between States, the chapter includes discussion of realism in the two countries' foreign policies.

Chapter Two sets the stage for the rest of the book with a focus on the issues that stood in the way of greater bilateral engagement between India and Australia. It first considers the realist orthodoxy and its influence on writings of earlier years on Australia's foreign policies and interpretations of Cold War events. It then identifies the mutually exclusive Cold War imperatives for each country, such as the 'White Australia' policy, India's Non-alignment, the misinformed images, and the importance of the personality factor in understanding bilateral relations. It ends with a focus on the bilateral relationship in the 1947-1949 period characterised by the camaraderie and mutual respect that prevailed between Nehru, Chifley and Evatt with a snapshot of the relationship in the Nehru-Manzies (1949-1964) and the Indira Gandhi-Whitlam period (1972-1975).

While Chapter Two concludes with an examination of the fleeting convergence that prevailed in the bilateral relationship between 1947 and 1949, Chapter Three looks more closely at the reasons for the regression of the relationship between 1949 and 1964, while Nehru and Menzies were the Prime Ministers. It addresses the hypothesis that personalities, policies, ideologies and public opinion influenced the bilateral relationship by using an analytical framework to highlight the personality differences between Nehru and Menzies and how their views influenced foreign policy formulation, as well as their attitudes to each other. Examples of personal conflict at the Commonwealth over South Africa's membership of the Commonwealth, inspite of its Apartheid policy, as well as India's own admission to the organisation as a republic, the first to do so, are discussed for their impact on what was the major part of the bilateral relationship. Chapter Four continues the theme with examination of the two leaders' differences over policy on a number of international issues.

In Chapter Five, the enquiry is carried out in two sections: (i) Australia's 'White Australia' policy; (ii) India's Non-aligned policy. Both were crucial to each respective country's foreign policy responses and yet damaging in terms of the effectiveness of the bilateral relationship because of the dislike each had for the other's policy.

The discussion includes Menzies political support for South Africa, despite Apartheid and, the potential for focus on Australia's own racially based immigration policy.

Chapter Six starts with an examination of the complex factors that accompanied the 1947 partition of India followed by the India-Pakistan impasse over Kashmir. It then traces the existence of an inherited English view of India among some of Australia's policy makers and diplomats in the 1950s, resulting in what appears to be a tilt to Pakistan in Australia's international diplomacy. The Chapter ends with an examination of the effectiveness of Australia's Colombo Plan aid in relation to India for whom the issues of racial discrimination, decolonisation, fairness in world trade and non-alignment took precedence. Questions of the motives behind Australian aid as well as its apportionment showing a bias, in per capita terms, to Pakistan over India, are discussed.

Chapter Seven addresses the impact the Whitlam Government had on the bilateral relationship. It deals with this on two bases: first it considers Whitlam's broader ideology in foreign policy, including his interest in India, in contrast to what prevailed under the preceding governments of Holt, Gorton and McMahon. This includes Mrs Gandhi's own policies and expectations of greater engagement between the two countries during the Whitlam period. Secondly, it looks at the hitherto unexamined area of the parallelism of Whitlam's views (from the time he entered Parliament in 1952) and those articulated by Nehru (1947-1964) and its impact on the bilateral relationship after Whitlam became Prime Minister, given that the broad Nehruvian ideology was still influential in the 1972-1975 period of Mrs Gandhi's non-aligned government.

# 1

# What is Bilateralism?

The topic of this study - the relationship between India and Australia 1947-1975 - dissects bilateralism. An essential starting point in setting the stage requires throwing some light on the nature of bilateralism to contextualise the field of enquiry. However, bilateralism as a topic in its own right has been relatively unexplored. As a feature of international relations and foreign policy, scholars have given it some attention; but its limited treatment suggests it is almost taken for granted. This is odd given the wide range of bilateral relationships that exist in ordinary, everyday diplomacy. The fact that bilateralism is frequently mentioned in the conduct of foreign policy does not negate the view that the concept remains relatively unexplored in terms of academic analysis.

'Bilateralism', for the purpose of this book, is a condition where two States enter into a sustained relationship, the bases of which may differ from one situation to another. As a starting point, the following references to bilateralism and related issues may be of some use in revealing the nature and variety of this international concept:

- Viotti and Kauppi observe that 'good bilateral relations do not develop overnight. They require genuine, sustained efforts often over years, putting in place the building blocks that nurture the future diplomacy, and, consequently, the quality of the relationship.' They also note that: 'effective diplomacy is markedly easier to achieve when the parties have an established record of positive accomplishments over decades or longer.'[1]

- Kegley and Raymond argue that, 'bilateral relationships can either culminate in formal alliances or remain loosely defined informal friendships, with the degree of potential coordination subject to wide variation.'[2]

- Bilateral relations can and do change. O' Neill states that, 'the bilateral security relationship between Australia and the United States is constantly undergoing change. Perhaps, the most important recent development, a change of both perception and posture, is that the Australian Government now recognises explicitly a requirement to be more self reliant ...'[3].

- Finally, Holsti draws attention to the obligations of a weaker party in a bilateral relationship. A bilateral relationship can be constrained by a nation's obligations towards its more powerful partner. Holsti gives the India-Bhutan relationship as an example of this: Bhutan established a treaty with India in 1949 which required that India's guidance be sought in foreign relations and, despite Bhutan joining the UN in 1971, 'bilateral relations with others came very slowly indeed.'[4] He comments that Bhutan's ability to have bilateral relations with other countries was important 'because it touched upon the fundamentals of sovereignty, independence and international personality.'[5]

## Identifying the Determinants

Clearly, there are different ways of approaching bilateralism (limited though its analysis is). In practice there are different types of bilateral relationships (strong/weak, developed/undeveloped, one-dimensional focus - e.g., Australia-Japan bilateralism which is mainly based on trade).[6] These need to be considered to place the India-Australia relationship in its proper perspective. Of equal relevance is the question of the quality of a bilateral relationship: what constitutes a 'good' bilateral relationship? (Strong and equal?-strong and unequal?) Some are based on concrete national interests (defence, trade); others are based on less tangible qualities (kinship, shared values, cultural affinities).

Furthermore, the strength of a bilateral relationship can vary widely from indifference at the lower end of the scale, to warm and solid at the other with varying degrees of mutual interest between the two extremes. Then, again, does bilateralism assume the existence of a healthy relationship at all times? This, of course, is not the case: the capacity of a close relationship between two nations to endure, whatever the criteria underpinning it, is not assured. Its value to either country can change from being central in importance to one of peripheral status relative to others, even expendable, with changing domestic and/or external demands. For example, 'contemplating a post-Suharto succession crisis, the Howard Government's September 1997 White Paper on Foreign Affairs and Trade shifted Indonesia down the Coalition's hierarchy of bilateral relationships.'[7] Who now, apart from historians, speaks of the *Entente Cordiale* or the ANZAC (Australia New Zealand Air Corps) Pact?

It is also true to say that a strong bilateral relationship can sometimes withstand behaviour by one party considered prejudicial to the interests of the other, even if the misdemeanour is in a fundamentally important area such as trade. A recent instance involving Australia-America trade helps illustrate this. In order to protect the US lamb industry from Australian imports, the US authorities imposed a tariff-rate quota which had the effect of damaging the livelihoods of Australian farmers and the local economy. There was strong condemnation of the unfair measure by Australia's Prime Minister, John Howard; Minister for Foreign Affairs Alexander Downer; and the then Minister for Trade Tim Fischer, and 'yet other than rhetorical public statements to grapple politically with the bilateral relationship, there seemed little that this government would attempt, particularly as it was even less inclined to link security issues than the Australian Labor Party (ALP) had in the 1980s.'[8] It is useful to note that, in this case, 'because of the asymmetry in the relationship,'[9] Australia picked up the costs, but the relationship continues fundamentally unscathed. This underlines the truth that bilateralism in practice can be manifold and variegated.

Kelton and Leaver offer further insights into the complex nature of commercial bilateralism with their observation, relative to the above example, that 'bilateral relations received the lion's share of attention in the Coalition's formal trade policy position, ...' seen by the government as the 'appropriate route for dealing with Australia's rapidly escalating American trade deficit.' But, having assumed office, the policy approach "fell in line, behind the American penchant for 'aggressive bilateralism' ".[10] Then, of course, alliances come in many forms influenced by different factors. America's numerous types of alliances with other countries are good examples of this variation.[11]

## Bilateralism and the Concomitant Multilateral Network

Bilateral relations between two particular countries developed purely on the national interests of each (however understood) unaffected by external influences, do not exist in practice. In other words, a bilateral relationship, reflecting the unique objectives of two States, operates only as a part of a multilateral agenda:

> ... bilateral relations are not bilateral at all but part of a multi-layered international system of interlocking relationships, in which a States ability to pursue a bilateral relationship, is constrained by a multitude of factors external to both of the countries concerned.[12]

In a discussion of the character of multilateral diplomacy, the truism that bilateralism is intertwined with a country's web of multilateral links is also given credence by Gareth Evans and Bruce Grant with their observation that: 'the interests that have to be taken into account extend across the whole spectrum of Australia's relationships, with decisions rarely if ever being able to be made on calculations of their effect on relations with one country alone; ...' [13].

The objectives that underpin a country's interest in pursuing a bilateral relationship with another can vary widely, depending on needs. For example, India in the aftermath of independence saw economic factors as well as geo-political compulsions - bordered as it was by China, Pakistan and the USSR - as being central concerns. In Australia's case, fear of the spread of Communism and protection of an exclusively European population from an allegedly resurgent and over-populated Asia were central aims in its alliance-driven bilateral diplomacy. Such primary needs, which Modelski describes as 'core' interests, are the constituent parts of a country's foreign policy and are defined as:

> ... those kinds of goals for which most people are willing to make ultimate sacrifices. They are usually stated in the form of basic principles of foreign policy and become articles of faith that a society accepts uncritically.[14]

Australia's alliance with the United States, anchored by the ANZUS Treaty (trilateral in form but, for Canberra, bilateral in focus) which helped Australia contain the perceived Asian threat, exemplifies this type of bilateral fulfillment. The Minister for External Affairs in 1949/1950, Percy Spender, stated why the US relationship was special:

> It was almost an article of faith with me that the U.S.A. and
> Australia were the two countries which could 'in cooperation, make
> the greatest contribution to stability and democratic development of
> the countries of South East Asia ...'[15].

In addition, a country can also have subordinate interests which
are less critical as a determinant in the bilateral relations selection
process. Among the core and non-core interests, there are some
which have universal application. The objective of ensuring security
is clearly one of them and commands the highest priority in policy
makers' hierarchy of interests:

> ... most policy makers in our era assume that the most essential
> objective of any foreign policy is to ensure the defence of the *home*
> territory and perpetuate a particular political, social, and economic
> system based on that territory.[16]

## Infrastructure, Mechanisms and Diplomatic Proprieties

Apart from the assertion that bilateral relations do not operate as
a stand-alone entity, they also cannot succeed in achieving their
objective without the active support of governments. Diplomatic
activity is the instrument through which a country gives practical
effect to its expectations of a special bilateral relationship; it carries
the major burden of achieving the best possible outcome for the
represented country. A British diplomat, Paul Gore Booth, observed
that: 'foreign policy is what you do; diplomacy is how you do it.'[17]
The diplomat's work is also complemented by the efforts of Prime
Ministers and Foreign Ministers. It includes a country's policy aims
pursued at international forums such as the UN and its agencies and,
in the case of India and Australia, through the Commonwealth Heads
of Government Meetings and associated committees. As a basis for
bilateral cooperation, overseas aid and export-oriented support
programmes are also used.[18] Treaties are another useful mechanism
in bilateral initiatives and can serve as a measure of the strength of
a particular bilateral relationship. [19]

With a range of complex issues engaging the attention of policy
makers and diplomats, the importance of observing the proper
protocols is fundamental to effective bilateralism. Continually
operating in this demanding, often competitive environment, they
can make or mar bilateral relations by the degree and quality of the
commitment they bring to the task. Such things as mutual respect,

tolerance, recognition of religious and cultural sensitivities are the building blocks of good bilateral relations. Stephen Fitzgerald in a reference to East Asia (but which could equally apply to India) says 'relationships are the single most important thing about dealing with people ... They are therefore also the most powerful means of advancing or defending our interests.'[20]

This examination refers to occasions when perceived flaws in the conduct of diplomatic business between Indian and Australian personalities affected the bilateral relationship, particularly in the Nehru-Menzies era. A more recent example that helps highlight the importance of restraint concerns the former Australian Prime Minister Paul Keating's reference to the Malaysian Prime Minister Mahathir, as a 'recalcitrant'[21] on the latter's boycotting of the APEC summit in Seattle in 1993. Seen as offensive in Malaysia, this remark led to reprisals and Keating's expressions of regret in an attempt to settle the diplomatic row.[22]

Clearly, bilateral relations between two countries operating within the larger multinational canvas are, by their very nature, a test of the skills of those involved in the diplomatic process. This is made harder by the cultural differences that exist between countries. Distorted images, irrational argument and intransigence in decision making have led to many flawed, if not moribund, bilateral relationships:

> Whether conducted through trained diplomats or by heads of state, communications between governments representing widely diverse social, economic, and political systems is naturally liable to all sorts of distortion, due to cultural differences ideological cleavages, and plain misunderstandings.[23]

This is especially likely to arise in situations when national cultures are profoundly different or where surface similarities mask deeper contrasting realities. It is important to recognise that a country's core interests and values must find consonance with those of another country before a bilateral relationship of substance can be established. A good example of a strong bilateral relationship based on mutual interest is the one Australia is said to enjoy with America, described by Joseph A. Camilleri:

> Since the Second World War Australia's domestic policies as well as its external relations have been shaped to a large and increasing degree by its strategic, diplomatic and economic ties with the United States.[24]

This leads us to the different types of approaches to bilateral engagement adopted by States motivated by strategic considerations. For example, Australia used an alliance-based approach to secure its strategic objectives; India chose a philosophy of non-alignment, in line with its pacifism. Yet, among its multi-faceted purposes, the doctrine of non-alignment had a strategic component to it. This single aspect of the policy stood on the virtues of 'self reliance' and remaining outside great power rivalry (like Switzerland) as the basis for ensuring the country's security. In a discussion of the available options for international security strategies, Kegley and Wittkopf point to the 'choices to be made between *Unilateral* self help actions on one end of the continuum, *Multilateral* action with others on the other; and specialized *Bilateral* alliances and *ad hoc* partnerships in between.'[25] Common or complementary strategic interests are not the only grounds for a bilateral match. There are others: ideological, economic, cultural, geographic, institutional and many more that can represent coalitions of interest.

## The International Relations Discipline as a guide to Bilateralism

To attempt to understand the bilateral relationship between two nations like India and Australia, it helps to examine the complex subject of International Relations, particularly the conventional approaches taken to the discipline by Australian scholars. Although distinctions exist within their works, the emphasis given to the 'realist' orthodoxy by the leading scholars is based on a common positivist/empiricist approach. For example, Jim George in a critique of the leading scholars of the realism school states:

> ... the realism of Hedley Bull, J.D.B. Miller, T.B. Millar and Coral Bell, does not go beyond positivism even if it does appear to reject it altogether. Rather ... the realism of the leading figures in the Australian discipline is connected ... by a set of positivist/empiricist knowledge rules which shape and direct its attitude to study and to the real nature of the international relations 'object'. This is not to deny of course, some quite significant differences of style, insight and emphasis within the works of Australia's leading scholars.[26]

There is a growing body of literature which questions the reliance on a threat perception and balance of power approach of the realist orthodoxy in the interpretation of Australia's post-War foreign relations. The challenge represents a broader view of the study of the subject of International Relations.[27] ANZUS and alliance strategies are not treated as 'sacred cows' outside its reach. For example, it advocates inclusion of the political economy in an increasingly globalising world in which economic interactions transcend State boundaries. This contested approach is characterised by a sensitivity to the wider philosophical, economic and social issues as opposed to the State centrism of the traditional realist scholarship. For newly independent India, moral and ethical considerations together with its diverse heritage, comprising centuries of external influences absorbed through tolerance and synthesis, were of greater relevance.

The development of the Australian International Relations discipline in the early post-War years was heavily influenced by the European and American experiences. Consequently, interpretations of foreign policy and diplomacy affecting Australia-India relations may have, unwittingly, had a Western perspective. While such speculation gives rise to further questions, Campbell argues that 'confronting the practical problems that are the concerns of International Relations demands a critical perspective freed of the dichotomised and dualised traditions of Western thought.'[28]

The Indian commentator, J. Bandyopadhyaya, laments that the discipline has failed to be of relevance to the 'South' which he defines broadly as being made up of Asia, Africa and Latin America:

> ... its assumptions and postulates have arisen, almost without exception out of the rationalization of the historical experience of the North-West (Western Europe and North America) in particular and the North in general. Hence, the bulk of the literature of International Relations is irrelevant to the historical experience, present empirical environment, and futuristic perceptions of the peoples of the South who constitute the great majority of mankind.[29]

For the purpose, however, of understanding the India-Australia relationship between 1947 and 1975, it would not be necessary to do much more than consider broadly the International Relations discipline, its components and the contemporary discourses that challenge traditional realism. The aim is not to demonstrate how a modern approach, such as critical theory, in the contemporary debate on the International Relations discipline will provide a greater insight into Australia's past power politics-based foreign policy in its relationship with India. Rather, it is argued that a closer examination of the changing nature of the relationship, which takes in the Indian perspective and a more imaginative critical theory approach, leads to a better understanding. Such an exercise must include scrutiny of India's choice of non-alignment, a central plank of its foreign policy; its condemnation of colonialism, Apartheid and other forms of racial discrimination; Australia's commitment to the West's Cold War global strategies; the relatively greater political compatibility between the Chifley government and Nehru; and the Nehru-Menzies dissonance factor. It must also consider the convergence of the Whitlam Government's regional focus and greater independence in foreign policy under an Indira Gandhi led Government with a less rigid adherence to non-alignment.

To circumscribe the study within a chronological framework enabling a comparison of the Chifley-Evatt, Menzies and Whitlam periods of the bilateral relationship leads to a better understanding of the hypothesis that personalities and policies affected the relationship. The Holt-Gorton-McMahon period is also discussed, but figures less prominently in the analysis for historical reasons.

## Realism: the Core Orthodoxy

The discussion might appropriately begin with the views of Neeladri Bhattacharya who describes the realist perspective of International Relations as:

> ... a game of power in which each State pursues its national interest: ... All alliances and moves are to increase the security of the State, consolidate power and out maneuver the rival. ... Realists refuse to recognise the significance of other performers, other actors, other forces at play.[30]

The intrinsic preoccupation with military force and the politics of power implies, this and the belief that the great powers, as major players on the global theatre determine the destiny of the world, are characteristic of realism.[31] On the concept of "power politics", author Misra draws attention to the divergence of understanding this has generated.[32] Among the views held by Western scholars, Morgenthau saw international politics as essentially a trial of strength, a battle for power between States[33], while for Martin Wight it 'means the relations between independent powers.'[34]

The realists' approach, a Cold War prescription, is shared by an eminent collection of scholars, who saw International Relations and the behaviour of States being explained in terms of facts and events. It has difficulty in dealing with factors of uncertainty in inter-state behaviour determination. Here, the critique of Jim George is pertinent:

> ... J.D.B. Miller's realism is one which acknowledges a series of 'givens' or 'brute facts' which exist beyond theoretical boundaries, but which must be observed as part of an attempt to describe the way the world really 'is' in this or any other period.[35]

To amplify this definition of the realist approach based on an analysis of outcomes, their origins and effects E.H. Carr observes:

> In the field of thought, it places its emphasis on the acceptance of facts and on the analysis of their causes and consequences. It tends to depreciate the role of purpose and to maintain, explicitly or implicitly, that the function of thinking is to study a sequence of events which it is powerless to influence or to alter. [36]

In a stimulating critique of the nascent post-World War II International Relations discipline in Australia, Martin Indyk observes that the early practitioners of the discipline were influenced by a fear of Asia which 'predisposed Australian International Relations academics to a Realist approach to their subject.'[37] Strategic issues rather than Australia's regional engagement took priority as reflected in the writings of the 1950s.[38] Indyk also points to the lack of debate and the resultant homogeneity of the writings of the period:

> ... a common set of assumptions tends to underpin the work of almost all Australian scholars in the discipline. These assumptions about the nature of international affairs, the appropriate level of analysis, and the correct methodology ... are very rarely questioned by their practitioners.[39]

Furthermore, it may be argued that the narrow focus of the interpretations tends to operate in the more comfortable world of plausibility, with conclusions that are perhaps illustrative rather than exhaustive. However, with the India-Australia bilateral relationship, the topic of this thesis, the aim is to renew explorations, look again and offer new understandings which include the Indian perspective and to support the central hypothesis that the relationship between the two countries was influenced by personalities, their philosophies and policies on both sides, consequently, a relationship which was characterised by peaks and troughs. Foreign policy often has an ideological component to it but, of course, understanding the minds of the policy makers introduces an element of uncertainty to the task. This is handled not by presenting a probabilistic argument, but rather by contrasting the fear-driven and consequently Western focus in Australia's foreign policy under the Menzies and successive coalition governments, with those of the Chifley and Whitlam governments which came before and after Menzies respectively. They were generally characterised by greater respect for and understanding of regional aspirations which included a willingness to accommodate a non-aligned India.

Because of the orthodox views and influence exercised by realist theory, with security the policy makers' principal focus, potentially interesting underlying themes in international politics as they affected India-Australia bilateral relations, were, perhaps unwittingly, and in the absence of burning curiosity, not fully explored. A critical theory approach, with its greater flexibility, may have been more sensitive, enabling understanding of India's foreign policy premised as it was on a foundation of pragmatic idealism. These regional relationships were to prove invaluable to Australia's future, economically and politically.

Higgott and George explain:

> The lack of theoretical and methodological inquisitiveness that marked much of Australian scholarship over the years has been mirrored, since the cold war in particular, by a focus on the 'central balance' and the struggle between the super powers. While this approach has produced some fine works of the traditionalist-realist genre it has had an unfortunate side effect: insufficient attention has been paid to the evolution in Australia's relations with its own Asia-Pacific region. Yet, since the 1960s his region has become of major importance in the politico-strategic and economic order in general and for Australia, struggling to come to terms with the complexities of its regional location, in particular.[40]

Australian involvement in the Vietnam War exemplifies the inadequacy of the realist paradigm for providing an effective analysis of the merits of a balance of power, alliance-based foreign policy. Its commitment to the US objective failed to deprive the Vietnamese Communists of ultimate victory. Of greater relevance for theory, it did not help retain a continuing US role in Indo-China.[41] The limited interest in an analysis of the realist position on the Vietnam war may be explained as the response by an academic community, constrained by a Government clearly uncomfortable with disapprobation of its foreign policy, and also an expectation from within sections of the academy itself of a code of silence rather than open disagreement.[42] Lee and Waters in a similar view state, 'one of the major flaws in earlier writings on Australian foreign policy has been a narrowness of outlook and an intolerance of diverse viewpoints ...'[43]. It must be recognised however, that Australia's politicians and their advisers, working closely with their US and British counterparts, were operating within the US-managed Cold War framework. Realism was embedded in the structured bureaucracy of the Department of External Affairs; most scholars were at times constrained to conform in this demanding environment, or face official exclusion. There is a parallel to this in the distortion and inaccuracy that at times affects media reporting, for example of war. Matthew Ricketson, in his review of Phillip Knightly's *The First Casualty*, refers to the author's comments that in war 'the military acts as one, with one purpose; the media are a mass of competitors who can easily be divided and conquered... are often less interested in pursuing unpalatable truths than in protecting commercial and political interests.'[44]

Camilleri makes the relevant observation that the continuous existence of conservative governments in Australia in the 1950s and 1960s 'was another important structural factor helping to cement the ties of dependence.' His argument is based on the conservatives' ideological commitment to business and preoccupation with the alleged Communist threat, consequently they were better positioned to take Australia into the, 'global capitalist framework created by the United States at the conclusion of the Second World War.'[45]

In India's case, idealism and independence, rather than realism and dependence, imbued by Gandhi's credo of *Ahimsa* and *Satyagraha* provided the framework within which Nehru articulated India's post-colonial international relations, although Kashmir, Goa, briefly, and then the Sino-Indian Border War, tested this philosophical commitment. In the view of former Foreign Minister Gareth Evans and author-diplomat Bruce Grant, 'idealism and realism need not be competing objectives in foreign policy, but getting the blend right is never simple.'[46]

For the India-Australia relationship, Menzies' foreign policy, heavily dependent as it was on the US military linkage (ANZUS) in ensuring Australia's own sense of security and power, encapsulated the realist paradigm underpinning the foreign policy orthodoxy of the time. This realist orthodoxy also relies on the all-embracing role of the State. In a world of increasingly numerous and complex interactions a range of other factors influences inter-country political behaviour, for example, the linkage between the international political and economic systems, and consequently the impact of transnational organisations. Hedley Bull, who argued for a more discriminating orientation of realism, defines a transnational as an organisation, 'which operates across international boundaries, sometimes on a global scale, which seeks...to establish links between different national societies,'[47]. In India, for whom economic development was of the highest priority, the presence and impact of transnationals in the 1950s and 1960s was an experience of realism. If Nehru eschewed the realism of power politics and war, then the impact of transnationals on India was no less a manifestation of realism, something the International Relations discipline has not examined. Edward L. Morse comments:

> The politicization of economics and the creation of economic value
> for political goods are what transnational processes are all about.
> One can no longer be conceptualized independently of the other.[48]

Similar observations are made by Martin Indyk who point to the growing conflict of views on the dominant realism, in the post-war Australian International Relations discipline: 'as Realists or Rationalists, they have chosen either to examine the foreign policy process of individual states or the wider systemic relations between States - particularly the great powers.'[49] Indyk's point is that, regardless of the methodology used, the analytical emphasis has been on the State: 'but no-one has adopted a transnational approach, using non-state actors as the unit of analysis.'[50]

While the recognition of economic factors may have greater application for relationships in the world of the 1980s and beyond, they also have some relevance to understanding the forces that shaped relationships in the Nehru-Menzies era. One of Nehru's arguments for Afro-Asian solidarity and a non-aligned group was that the goal of greater economic equity for the poorer nations through international trade would be facilitated by their collective political voice, a form of pooled sovereignty. Poorer countries like India were undoubtedly vulnerable in their relative economic fragility to the effects of transborder operations. It is of pertinence to note that India assumed the Chairmanship of the UN panel assigned responsibility for examining the political and other implications of multi-national corporations with L.K. Jha elected its Head.[51] The panel was established in 1972 because, in the view of the UN Economic Division, 'multi-national corporations had the potential to challenge national sovereignty or precipitate an economic crisis at their will.'[52] India's concerns in this area are understandable, considering its experience of exploitation at the hands of foreign traders dating back to 1600,[53] followed eventually by the British who ruled from 1757 to 1947. India's Minister for External Affairs, delivering a speech on 'India's Foreign Policy Perspectives in the 1990s' had this to say on transborder operations:

> It is a world in which new communications technologies make possible instant movements of hundreds of millions of dollars across national boundaries. Never before have the economic fortunes of countries been more closely inter-linked.[54]

While this analysis is not concerned with the specific impact of transnationals, such as the World Bank, or multinational corporations such as Unilever and Proctor and Gamble (which operated in India, both before and after World War II), on the country's economic or political independence, it helps recognition of the argument that transnationals do play some part affecting sovereignty of the state. For understanding the India-Australia relationship in the 1950s and 1960s, this phenomenon may not be altogether irrelevant. With a rash of expropriations of Anglo-US multinationals (precursory transborder operations) sweeping Asia in the aftermath of decolonisation, India's own inflexible - even suspicious - attitude to offers of investment from the West was probably carried into the political arena affecting its foreign policy and choice of 'friends'. In India's defence, it may be said that centuries of commercial exploitation under colonial rule, referred to above, left it less enthusiastic about the presence of foreign business operations after independence. The substitution of two centuries of militaristic colonial intrusion with multi-national corporations continued to represent a form of realism, in conflict with Nehru's values of morality, economic justice and political independence.[55]

## The National Interest: Idealism *versus* Realism

For newly independent India, the dominant emphasis was rapid industrialisation engineered by the public sector. The national interest meant a decision to remain outside the Cold War; yet, as Misra argues, strenuously pursuing a mediatory role in easing international and regional conflicts.[56] The non-aligned approach to foreign policy was essentially a 'moralist'[57] ideology as distinct from a 'realist' one, its ethical underpinnings necessary for the country's pursuit of economic equity, racial equality and world peace. Holsti helps understanding of the relationship of ethical bases to policy making with this statement:

> ... conceive of ethics as a combination of cultural, psychological, and ideological 'value structures' which inhibit consideration of all possible policy alternatives in a given situation. They establish limits beyond which certain types of behaviour become inconceivable.[58]

Holsti's observation has relevance in relation to Nehru's conduct of India's diplomatic relations in the 1950s. Nehru's idealism was influenced by the 'Indian renaissance and the national movement under Mahatma Gandhi's leadership which propounded that right means are to be adopted to achieve right ends.'[59] In Australia, Evans and Grant argue that, on most issues, 'the ends remain clear, but it is a matter of tempering what we want to achieve with what we can deliver, and at what cost.'[60] Despite its early idealism there was one issue on which India's approach was more definitive: dealing with what it saw as threats to its western border from Pakistan over the Kashmir question. Australia's High Commissioner in New Delhi in 1950, Francis Stuart, in a despatch to Canberra, stated that Nehru 'is resolute against any extension of defence planning beyond what is needed to take care of the Pakistan and Kashmir situations.'[61]

Nehru's commitment, however, to an idealist foreign and defence policy was sorely tested at the time of the Sino-Indian Border War in 1962. Despite the five principles of peaceful co-existence (Panchsheel) established in Tibet between India and China in 1949 and reaffirmed at Bandung in 1955, Nehru was forced to compromise on India's rigid policy of non-alignment and accept military aid from the West, including Australia, giving credence to the observation that, 'the luxury of absolutism is very rarely available to the practitioners of this (foreign affairs) profession.'[62] Tellingly, Nehru, who was devastated by the unexpected Chinese behaviour, failed to read the Chou En Lai personality, a further illustration of one of the principal arguments of this analysis that personalities and policies do indeed influence the nature of bilateral relations. Of course, personalities do change in the light of experience, and a policy based on idealism may change to one of realism. There is also the view that 'in a sense the dichotomy between realism and idealism is a false one.'[63]

Holsti asks a hypothetical question which has relevance to Nehru's 1962 dilemma: "...is it ethically more correct to remain faithful to principle and endure certain invasion than to try to create an effective defense with which to deter the perceived enemy?"[64]

India's idealism, overshadowed by the Chinese threat, is something that India may have increasingly questioned in the post-Nehruvian years, albeit grudgingly; but Nehru himself was not altogether blind to the reality of Cold War tensions and arguments of the proponents of force and once observed that 'the paths to peace are difficult but pursue them we must. They alone enable survival and fulfillment.'[65]

For Australia, the contrasting picture that emerges is the realists' security focus that characterised much of its foreign policy regime in relation to Asia. Australia's core interests had more to do with quarantining itself from Asia, preservation of a 'White Australia', and the US-anchored military alliances (ANZUS and SEATO), reflected in the realist idiom of its International Relations interpretation:

> The Australian debate has continued to focus on a succession of "threat" scenarios, articulated increasingly in the contemporary period in the language and logic of the realist "security dilemma."[66]

With the pre-eminence given by the realist methodology to the dynamic of super power politics, and the State as the key player in International Relations, the ethical dimension of any disagreement between two nations was effectively ignored. India's non-aligned pacifism and Cold War ideology was in conflict with the realist paradigm. Consequently, Australia 'differed from India on practically every major issue since 1949.'[67] The problem then for the bilateral relationship was in Australia's attitude to India (a relatively weak country in economic and military terms) during the 1950s and 1960s. This realist approach was clearly unequal to the task of capturing the essence of the questions affecting India, a country renown for its doctrines of *ahimsa* (the sacredness of all life and therefore non-violence), *satya* (morality), and *satyagraha* (passive resistance) and the primacy of peace. As Hoffman argues:

> ... international relations as a discipline needed 'distance' away 'from the perspective of the superpower...toward that of the weaker...towards the peak which the questions raised by political philosophy represent.'[68]

That Australia was not in tune with India's philosophical view of the world is exemplified by an Australian diplomat in a despatch to Canberra from South East Asia which warns of India's propaganda efforts to create an environment 'in which ancient cultural primacy of India will once more be acknowledged' and goes on to say that, 'on a long term the effect of this attempt to create Indian hegemony may prove inimical to our own interests...'[69]. Seen through the eyes of this diplomat, India was an unwelcome competitor. Yet, Nehru was explicit from the beginning. Addressing the issue of the disadvantages of alignment with one power group, as opposed to the advantages of non-alignment, he said:

> What are we interested in world affairs for? We seek no domination over any country. We do not wish to interfere in the affairs of any country, domestic or other. Our main stake in world affairs is peace, to see that there is racial equality and that people who are still subjugated should be free. ... It is with this friendly approach that we look at the world.[70]

This not to say India was totally averse to the use of force in pursuing geo-political interests in Kashmir, wresting Goa from the Portuguese and defending itself against the Chinese. Also, Indian governments have not been reluctant to use force against political opponents such as the communists and to suppress dissent, e.g., Mrs Gandhi's emergency in June 1975.

While the traditional realist approach to International Relations analysis does not necessarily restrict interpretations within boundaries of strictly coded criteria, as exemplified by Hedley Bull's broader sensitivity, contemporary criticism of the realists' position with its disguised but primary focus on super power politics and security considerations, is not entirely irrelevant to the examination of the India-Australia relationship:

> The parsimony and neatness of realism falls away when the focus of our study is not a superpower. This is particularly the case when economic issues of openness and vulnerability are deemed to have as high, if not higher salience as politico-security issues.[71]

However, it is worth noting that realism and the primacy of security constitute a very small component of the totality of a bilateral relationship. Trade, tourism, aid, education and cultural issues easily represent the major activities. While trade and security were key factors in Australia's pursuit of bilateral relations, India was not seen as having much to offer in either area. Equally, in India, Australia was not exactly considered a cultural oasis.

Thus, the rigid State-centric approach to bilateral relations - the force that undoubtedly shaped Menzies' foreign policy - could well have had the effect of precluding closer political and cultural engagement with India.

## Critical Theory Approach

In contrast to the realist's position on foreign policy. the oppositional discipline, critical theory, offers an interesting, yet simple paradigm shift from the realist rigid methodology for International Relations analysis. It provides for more explicit definitions of factors appropriate to a broader approach to analysis and understanding of foreign policy. It challenges the single overriding power of the State and its unchallenged authority in foreign affairs as well as its ability to transcend questions outside the political strategic arena, such as in the economic sphere. Issues of money, pollution, popular culture and so on are now the new determinants of national economies and peoples' lives:[72] 'Even the most powerful States find the marketplace and international public opinion compelling them more often to follow a particular course.'[73] Thus, the wider approach used with critical theory, as opposed to the assumptions based approach of the traditionalists, compels attention, particularly when bilateral relations involving poorer nations like India are the subject of analysis.

Ideally, what would have helped the analysis is informative historically derived data on two countries such as Australia and India and how they responded on numerous international issues of Cold War conflict: it could represent the input for the development of a model, but 'traditionalists are usually skeptical of the effort to predict or to apply probability analysis to human affairs.'[74] In its absence, Australian scholarship - as well as the media with its relatively low priority coverage of India in the 1950s and 1960s - has tended to take an interpretive stance based on the power politics realist model in any discussion of the India-Australia bilateral relationship, resulting in unimaginative literalism however well-expressed. Trevor Taylor argues that:

> All views on and analyses of a political situation are based on hypotheses of some sort and International Relations, by concentrating on the explicit formulation of such propositions, can make a significant contribution to policy-making.[75]

The basic tenet then of the modern critical theory school is that, while the State's behaviour and influence are fundamental elements in International Relations analysis, a broader focus involving a number of additional factors, including economic, social and cultural in character rather than dependence on the primacy of the central balance of power politics, is advocated. The geo-strategic interests and economic well-being of a State, affected as they are by the international dimension of relationships, should not in their view be treated as separate entities. No one makes a better fist of the subtle distinction than Higgott and George who, in their critique on changes in the study of International Relations in Australia, define the definitive characteristic of the critical theory doctrine in its approach to analysing International Relations. This is of relevance to this examination which attempts to go beyond the primacy of the security dilemma that circumscribed Australian foreign policy, stultifying its relations with India, an ancient civilization. India's interests embraced a wider spectrum than the one of security, to include objectives that were international in character and conditioned by its past experience:

> The policy maker is concerned primarily with the pursuit of a given "national interest" (however defined) and the options available to best serve that interest. For the scholar, of greater considerations are the geostrategic, historical, cultural, socio-political and economic traditions that have conditioned the international relations of a given country.[76]

## International Relations Theory and
## the Mind of the Policy Maker

A central hypothesis of this study of bilateralism is the personality-impact on foreign policy and, thus, on the bilateral relationship. While foreign policy theory helps understand this, on its own it is not enough to understand the minds of personalities like Nehru, Menzies and Whitlam. Policy makers interpret situations in different ways and consequently act differently, particularly in those situations characterized by a multiplicity of factors: defence, economic, political, social and other.[77] Thus, an inventory of data derived from past International Relations literature on policy statements, less obvious assumptions and theories used in the political process, would considerably advantage policy makers in developing future actions, as well as being of value to students of past foreign policy behaviour.[78] For example, reaching new and unambiguous understandings of the minds of Nehru and Menzies, and of their policy advisers, more accurately revealed as they determined policy in a number of international situations of disagreement between the two countries, would certainly have been facilitated by such data. Dougherty and Pfaltzgraff make the point well:

> Such a matching exercise could provide insights into the theories, explicit or implicit, which guide policy makers, and would contribute to a better understanding of those theories of international relations which have had the greatest impact upon thought in the policy community.[79]

Brecher adds a cautionary note to this: 'while elite images will not provide the total data required for prediction, they can serve as the foundation for such projections.'[80]

Yet in the quest for understanding the impact of International Relations theory through the minds of personalities such as Chifley, Evatt, Menzies, Nehru, Menon, Whitlam and Mrs Gandhi on the bilateral relationship, the critical theory approach provides a better framework, a spur to the search for new understandings. The behaviour of policy makers to situations requiring foreign policy responses is often affected by psychological and operational environments. This may involve concepts such as moral values, attitudes and political ideology. Their perceptions of the reality of a situation are often influenced by these psychological influences leading to foreign policy responses unique to the policy maker. Holsti argues that 'there are both physical and psychological factors that can distort the information upon which policy makers' images of reality are based.'[81]

Applying International Relations critical theory to the analysis of leaders of the three periods, (1947-1949, 1949-1972, 1972-1975), offers some interesting examples of behaviour within the dichotomous scale of realism to idealism. The maiden India-Australia relationship (1947-1949) was characterised by the camaraderie between Chifley, Evatt, and Nehru; the personality of Evatt was unquestionably a factor in Australia's foreign policy formulation. Evatt, like those who shaped foreign policy before him, continued to regard the region as turbulent, even hostile; his support for the 'White Australia' policy as well as Australia's fear-driven security focus in foreign policy was unambiguous. Yet, this realism was tempered by his internationalism and sensitivity to Asian aspirations after centuries of colonialism, reflected in his enthusiasm for India's independence and, later, to it remaining in the Commonwealth even after it became a republic. As well, his acceptance of the reality of Indonesia's progress towards independence from the Dutch (who, in the end, were seen as incapable of resorting to peaceful negotiations) was evidence of Evatt's internationalism combined with his commitment to the UN Charter.

In Menzies' case, Chapter Three, examines how his personality was reflected in his foreign policy. A few examples of relevance to the theory are worthy of mention here. Menzies, with his insensitivity to Asian demands for freedom from colonial rule, and intimations of his sense of racial superiority, was opposed to the ejection of the Dutch from the East Indies (driven by a fear that it could lead to Britain's removal from Malaya and Singapore, and Australia's hold on Papua and New Guinea). His defence against criticisms that he failed to condemn South Africa's Apartheid policy, on the grounds that it was tantamount to interference in the domestic affairs of another country, was also related to self interest. He feared that it would invite criticism of Australia for its unimpressive record on the treatment of its indigenous people. It points also to a Menzies idealism, premised on the obsolete notion of the centrality of the Empire and the Crown to his view of the world, yet being capable of making discerning and even hard decisions about what was in Australia's interests, as he saw them. His version of realism also brought failures - such as with his decision to represent Britain on his failed mission to Cairo on the Suez impasse and his advocacy of force if negotiations failed. Some would argue that a clever realist would have taken the Nehru view and called for Anglo-French withdrawal given the opposition of the US (Australia's major ally) to the venture. Maybe Australia's involvement in Vietnam, in large part to cement further the United States' commitment to Australia's protection, was another of Menzies' policy failures, launched in the name of realism.

Nehru's nebulous pacifism was pitted against the hard-headed realism of China, forcing him to accept military aid from the West, including Australia, in order to secure India's defence capability against further Chinese aggression, demonstrating a leader's willingness to make compromises in very demanding circumstances. As Holsti observes:

> Leaders like Jawaharlal Nehru ... who stressed the importance of observing legal and ethical standards of conduct in international relationships, did not behave in practical situations very differently from other political leaders who claimed to be 'realists'.[82]

Not widely known about Nehru's Goa action, (explained by him at a Press Conference on 28 December 1961) is that his decision was influenced by the brutal nature of Portugal in its handling of anti-colonial movements in Angola and Mozambique, as well as the African nations' seeking of his leadership to end the Portuguese colonial Empire.[83]

Nehru, referring to foreign policy, once said that 'it should be idealistic ... and ... realistic. If it is not idealistic, it becomes one of sheer opportunism; if it is not realistic, then it is likely to be adventurist and wholly ineffective.'[84] In an interesting insight into Nehru's attitude to theory, Krishna Menon, discussing non-alignment and the balance of power, told Brecher that:

> He (Nehru) was not much interested in what he called theory but he did have more than a rudimentary knowledge of these things. Theories are often inferred from what statesmen do. He himself might have thought, "why should I go into theory?"[85]

Whitlam, like Evatt, was committed to internationalism while also giving Australia a renewed sense of nationalism through greater independence in foreign policy. His regional focus, including a new interest in India and recognition of China, was reflective of his long held view that Australia's geography, rather than its history, was important to its future. His broader view did not however permit withdrawal of Australia's commitment to the US alliance for its security. With Whitlam, too, his psychological environment tempered his realism in foreign policy expression, seen in his advocacy of support (from a very early stage of his political career), for Asia's independence from colonial rule and a more compassionate understanding of Asia's expectations of economic and political justice. His broader ideology allowed him to accommodate India's non-alignment policy, a major shift from the rigid approach to bilateralism under Menzies and his successors.

Critical theory despite its flexibility does not in itself provide answers to foreign policy behaviour, but the analysis is helped when it is supplemented by examination of the leaders' psychological (which, of course, includes personality) and operational environments, used in conjunction with policy:

> Theory helps us to order our existing knowledge and to discover new knowledge more efficiently. It provides a framework of thought in which we define research properties... Theory directs our attention to significant similarities and differences, and suggests relationships not previously perceived.[86]

It reinforces the central hypothesis of the thesis that understanding the impact of personalities and policies helps understanding of the reasons for the peaks and troughs in the bilateral relationship. It removes some of the cobwebs that blur the distinction between each of the three periods of the relationship.

## Balance of Power concept

A comment needs to be made about the term 'Balance of Power,' a strategic tool that had assumed primacy in Australia's politico-strategic thinking affecting its relationship with non-aligned India, through its US-aligned foreign policy for the Asian region. As a strategic notion, it meant the recognition of the reality of the Cold War and super power confrontation, a philosophy strikingly at odds with India's ethos: peace through international cooperation and not war. The balance of power as a concept has occupied a place in International Relations literature from Thucydides' Melian Dialogue (Peloponnesian war between Sparta and Athens) and in Indian (Kautilya) writings.[87] The term defies precise definition. One interpretation given to the balance of power as a system within international politics is provided by eminent scholar, Hans J. Morgenthau, who describes it as: 'the self regulatory mechanism of the social forces, which manifests itself in the struggle for power in the international scene, that is the balance of power.'[88] Morgenthau also imputes several other meanings to this belligerent war measure including one that claims 'the balance of power of that period, was amoral rather than immoral.[89] The emphasis given to balance of power in the Cold War confrontation between the superpowers in traditional International Relations scholarship is important to an understanding of the India-Australia relationship. Australia's approach to foreign policy under Menzies was, among other things, premised on power politics in a bipolar world dominated by the two super powers. Paul Hasluck, Australia's Minister for External Affairs in 1964, explained the reality of power politics:

> Force is being used and in such a world in which the possession of power is the main determinant of what happens, anyone engaged in foreign affairs must recognise and study the facts of power and also recognise the reality of power politics.[90]

In contrast to this, India's non-alignment, examined in Chapter Five, was both an instrument of military neutrality and pacifism, as well as an expression of justice in the quest for a more equitable global economic order. The postulate that war was somehow a necessary and natural element in the search for international order was inimical to the Indian ethos. The use of the 'balance of power' approach by States in the past as a deterrent or a tool for persuading others to positions of compliance, as a substitute for diplomacy, had varying degrees of approbation among scholars and politicians alike. McDougal observes that:

> ... critics ranging from Rosseau to Woodrow Wilson have argued that the balance of power was a factor which led to war; they tended to favour its replacement with a *community of power*, allowing for more universal arrangements as a means of upholding peace.[91]

While President Wilson's offerings on the subject were made in relation to the environment leading up to the First World War, they nevertheless represent an interesting empirical critique of the limitations of the balance of power doctrine as a means of achieving peace, or a just outcome. Wilson saw the balance of power system as stronger nations exploiting the weak believing that 'the little nations were always suppressed by the old alliances and by those who battened on the balance of power principle.'[92] Wilson was not alone in his disapproval. World leaders of the standing of Roosevelt and Churchill at times shared his strong misgivings about the balance of power principle and its adequacy as a safeguard against war.[93] Nehru too saw no virtue in the concept and expressed his distaste for the doctrine, thus:

> As a basis of international policy which would rid the world of war its impotence stands proven. For the last three hundred years, since the emergence of nation states in the modern world, nations have relied for survival or fulfillment on this process of mobilized antagonisms. All these years, the nations of the world have been engaged in wars with brief intervals during the greater part of which war clouds gathered on the horizon.[94]

Nehru emphasised 'the notion of a world order based on the equality of all States, rejecting the concept of balance of power ...' and predicted that China and India would give the poorer countries 'a sense of dignity and autonomy.' [95] Questioned on the concept, Krishna Menon, a key Nehru confidant and former Defence Minister, offered an interesting view of it:

> We are also a part of the balance of power both because we are its victim and because we are seeking to create our own balance. We were not playing the game of balance of power. But we were creatures or part of the complexes that can be described in terms of the balance of power.[96]

Indian writer, M.S. Rajan, cites Vietnamese scholar, Ton That Thieu, who saw India's role in the post-war decade as constituting a diplomatic "balance of power" approach: '... during the period 1947-60, ... Western might and Indian diplomacy combined to ensure a free and non-communist South East Asia and that India's policy " was perhaps nothing more, but certainly nothing less, than a policy of balance of power." '[97] Given India's successful role as peace maker in the 1950s, both the above interpretations of India's role, as having effectively provided a diplomatic balance of power, are not inaccurate.

In a bipolar polar world separated also by East-West and North-South divisions, the theory is that the realist saw world order achieved through restricting nationalism and radical change 'within the existing distribution of territorial borders, so that it does not upset a stable balance of power among the so-called "Great Powers." '[98] Thus, international stability, the theory continues, required the collusion of the big powers to maintain equilibrium.[99] Nehru had often himself suspected the foregoing premises, particularly after the Sino-Indian Border War and China's close ties with pro-West Pakistan; in the post-Nehru period, this phenomenon was seen in the Sino-US rapprochement forcing closer ties between India and the Soviet Union in 1971, all manifestations of balance of power manoeuvres through new alignments.

## Ideological Rivalry and Regional Competition

Cold War rivalry was not restricted to the superpowers but existed also between regional States such as India, Australia and China. Each strove to influence the Asian region, for its own reasons. China, through its ideology of communism and its formidable presence, while India, an advocate of freedom, peace and democracy, chose ethical persuasion to champion the cause of economic justice and racial equality for the rest of Asia as well as Africa. Australia with its commitment to the Western Alliance, strove to prevent the spread of communism in its region.

There is also the hypothesis that countries in a given region tend to share a common focus based on regional criteria, as occurred in the case of the European Union as a group from an institutional perspective, and Western Europe from a geographic and cultural perspective.[100] Both these groupings are regional in character although it could be argued that geographic proximity is not a mandatory requirement for the formation of regional groupings. Sri-Lanka's Foreign Minister, Lakshman Kadirgarmar, delivering the Krishna Menon Centenary lecture in Rajasthan, India, confirmed the view that compelling common interests, in spite of geographic dispersion, can and do provide the driving force for the creation of a regional group: 'today, across the globe, regional groupings tend to overlap because shared economic and political interests among discontiguous neighbours tend to converge.'[101] The contemporary unfolding of East Asia is another example. Noordin Sopie's argument is that, being heterogeneous (its mainland and insular states have enormous differences in factors of geography, ethnicity, language, religion, culture, economic systems, political way of life and historical experience), there should be no sense of regional consciousness at all; and yet an incipient sense of regional belonging within the East Asian States is clearly apparent.[102]

The point of the discussion of what fosters a spirit of regional bonding, is to show that none of the above criteria generated a degree of regional affinity in the case of India and Australia. The answer may be found in the argument that, while India and Australia were affected in different ways by the ideological rivalry between the great powers, the relationship between the two was further complicated by their divergent strategic interests. For India, the concerns were Pakistan and China; for Australia, the threat from Communism, which meant pursuing strategic interests in South East Asia in conjunction with the US, the UK and Japan. While Menzies saw Nehru's foreign policies (non-alignment, peace, racial equality and anti-colonialism) as providing grist to the Communist mill, *The New York Times* in 1950, saw it differently. Commenting on the battle for Asia between the Communists and the West, it referred to the crucial role of one man, Nehru:

> He is in a sense the counterweight on the democratic side to Mao Tse-Tung on the Communist side. ... to have him as an opponent, or even a critic could jeopardize the position of Western Democracy throughout Asia.[103]

Of course, there was no argument from any quarter on the importance of a democratic India to the region. For Australia this may be best gauged by the statement made by Evans and Grant in *Australia's Foreign Relations in the World of the 1990s:*

> The interest of Australia ... in seeing that India survives and prospers as a democratic entity means that we must be prepared to be as supportive as we can both materially and politically. India continues to be the most important test bed for democracy. ... If democracy works only for the rich and stable societies, it does not have much of a future.[104]

Unfortunately, for the bilateral relationship Australia's policy makers in the Menzies era, preoccupied as they were with the Chinese threat, failed to see the importance, both to Australia and regionally, of a strong democratic India.

## Divergence over Convergence

Given the fundamentals of bilateralism examined in this chapter, the question is how well did the India-Australia bilateral relationship measure up in the demanding Cold War environment of the period under discussion. Simply put, with little convergence of interest - core or secondary - between the two countries in the 1950s and 1960s, the essentials for a good bilateral fit were absent. To begin with, a common frame of reference, such as trade, cultural and ideological factors, did not apply in the India-Australia relationship. Also lacking was the essential of strategic interests that characterised Australia's relationship, for example, with Malaya or India's relationship with the Soviet Union. Convergence of the all-important strategic and economic interests is usually the underpinnings of successful bilateral relationships such as that which existed between Australia and the US. In this regard, author Dieter Braun observes that, 'there must be a minimum of parallel interest and priorities among potential partners regarding both domestic and foreign policies.'[105] Furthermore, Australia may have viewed India as competing with its interests in South East Asia, at least in the view of Australia's High Commissioner to Malaya who saw India 'as a more dangerous threat to peaceful development of South East Asia than China,' and also thought India's appeal to the region, and their response to it, meant 'India will be able to exert an influence which we cannot hope to equal,' if they succeeded in making South East Asia act in racial unity.[106]

This divergence of interests that characterised the India-Australia relationship is evident from the way they looked to other countries for fulfillment of their core and secondary needs. The India-Australia strategic maps below illustrate graphically this divergence and, while there was some overlap in a number of areas, the convergence did not mean shared interest in every case. Some factors such as China, South Africa, the Commonwealth, the UN, and, even the UK, were driven by different motives - the differences discussed in other chapters of this book - and, therefore, not mutually bonding. Those that did genuinely converge, such as shared democratic traditions, an independent judiciary, the love of cricket and the speaking of English, did not, unfortunately, constitute the essentials for building a strong bilateral relationship.

## FIGURE 1

### *India-Australia Strategic Map 1949-72*

### Cold War Imperatives and Interests

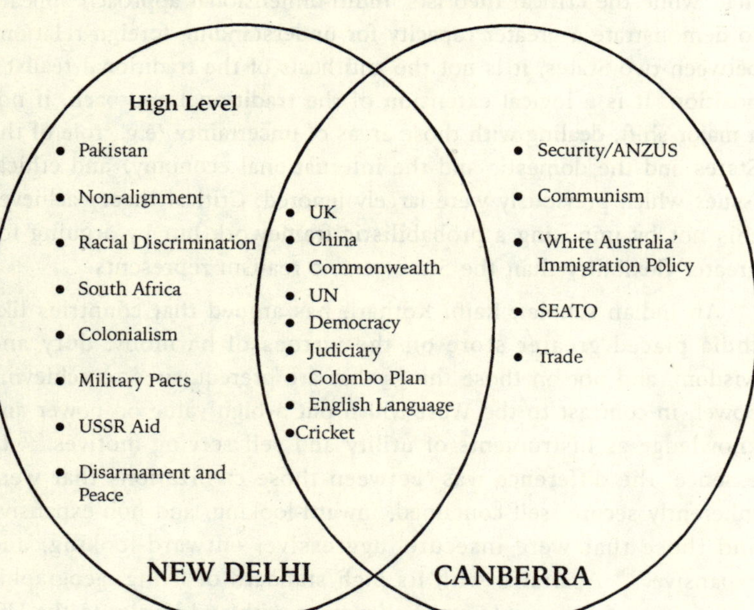


In the period following the end of World War II, interaction between governments on a wide range of interests were common. To begin to understand the bilateral relationship between India and Australia requires acceptance of the postulate that, while there was engagement between the two countries at both the State and non-state level, however minimal and even symbolic the interactions, they were relative to and part of an intricate structure of relationships each had with other countries. India-Australia relations were thus subject to numerous external constraints, not least the complex factors of foreign policy. While the discussion of the divergent and growing body of understanding of the International Relations discipline in Australia was, at times, theoretical, the multiple components and the influences of International Relations referred to, as well as its relationship with the personality factor, are of relevance to an understanding of the bilateral relationship.

In evaluating the benefits to understanding the India-Australia bilateral relationship through the traditional realist approach *versus* the modern critical theory in International Relations, suffice to say that, while the critical theorists' multi-dimensional approach appears to demonstrate a greater capacity for understanding foreign relations between two States, it is not the antithesis of the traditional realist's position. It is a logical extension of the traditional approach, if not a major shift, dealing with those areas of uncertainty (e.g., role of the States and the domestic and the international economy) and ethical issues which previously were largely ignored. Critical theory achieves this not by imposing a probabilistic framework but by arguing for greater flexibility than the State-centric realism represents.

An Indian scholar, Rajni Kothari, has argued that countries like India placed greater store on the virtues of harmony, duty and wisdom, and not on those things that are prerequisites to achieving power, in contrast to the West which put a high value on power and knowledge as instruments of utility and self serving motives.[107] In essence, the difference was 'between those civilizations that were inherently secure, self contained, inward-looking, and non-expansive and those that were insecure, aggressive, outward-looking, and expansive.'[108] Australia, with its high standard of living, geographic insecurity and its unambiguous alignment with and loyalty to the US, fell into the latter category in the 1950s and 1960s, both by its own interest reflected in foreign policy actions, as well as by proxy through association with US strategic aims. Bandyopadhyaya sees the weakness of the International Relations discipline with its emphasis on military and economic power:

> Another serious limitation of the discipline of International Relations, as it has developed in the West, is that the concept of power (which, underneath all the verbiage, is defined essentially as military and economic power) is the nucleus round which its fabric is almost exclusively built. ... As an academic discipline it is thus

loaded in favour of the North, which possesses and has historically exercised military and economic power, and against the South, which does not possess such material power, ...[109].

India by virtue of the low priority it gave to military power was a victim of this exclusion.

Accepting that International Relations theory does help understanding of relationships, the relative merits of the empirical and theoretical approaches taken to the International Relations discipline in understanding the India-Australia relationship are not significant factors. In a review of two books on realism, Francis Fukuyama sees it as one means of being informed on International Relations in appropriate circumstances:

> Rather than providing a comprehensive framework for understanding international relations, realism is one of several possible tools, better applicable in certain times and places than in others.[110]

But then there is also no pure realist nor an uncompromising idealist, as noted in the above analysis, of the minds of Nehru and Menzies. Critical theory, it may be argued, offers a better approach to understanding the Indian ethos with all its moral values. The debate should be viewed as comprising concepts which have areas of difficulty, but contributing to a more insightful understanding of the complex question of bilateralism in the Cold War. Political scientist Don Aitkin sums it up:

> But the best research and scholarship, it is right to say, make theory and data fuse in 'a satisfying way,' so that the empirical research directs itself to a point of importance, and theory is subsequently modified.[111]

Given that it is more accurate to understand international politics within the context of International Relations theory, by itself the discipline is not a comprehensive tool for explaining bilateral relationships. What does help is the relationship between the personality factor, foreign policy and international relations, and evaluating its impact on the India-Australia relationship through a contrasting of the nature of each period, 1947-49, 1949-72, and 1972-75; in effect, a conscious break with the purely traditional realists' methodology and interpretations. For instance, taking Menzies as an example, the difficulty for the analyst is that his policy responses were, on occasion, incapable of cold analysis and may have lacked judgment. This could be said of Nehru too in relation to his early attitude to China.

The view canvassed here, that the earlier International Relations scholarship with its rigid adherence to realism, was constrained in its interpretation of international politics for reasons either of loyalty to the Australia-Anglo-US Alliance, or fear of open dissent with the official stance of the policy makers, is not an unreasonable one. After all, for Australia in the 1950s and 1960s, the Cold War realist approach reflects the primacy of the bipolar superpower confrontation. As has been discussed above, both Nehru and Menzies were realists and idealists at different times in relation to different issues, though the emphasis in each case differed. In the 1970s, under Whitlam realism was not the sacred cow of Australian foreign policy it previously was. Whilst there was the dynamic of the personality impact, the cold war climate too had changed allowing greater flexibility in foreign policy, both in Australia and India, with convergence over divergence this time.

However, despite the lack of convergence, superficially at least for most of the 1947-1975 period, the two former British colonies shared a number of experiences, common values and British forms of administration. These included a Westminster model of parliamentary democracy, with an upper and lower house (Rajya Sabha and Lok Sabha respectively in India's case), and an independent judiciary with the structure of the court system in India similar to the Australian model. Both countries were members of the Commonwealth and, before India's independence, both served as part of Britain's imperial forces in World Wars I and II. Their love of cricket was another shared interest; the twenty sixth of January is celebrated by both, in India as Republic Day and as Australia Day in Australia.

What kept these two neighbours from nurturing a warmer relationship? The answer is, primarily, ideological differences which shaped their divergent views of the world of the 1950s and 1960s. From the moment of independence, sovereign India declared its distaste for great power dominance of international politics, as well as its commitment to political and economic justice for the poorer nations. Its early advocacy of non-alignment was a manifestation of this. Furthermore, 'India's economic weakness and the basic goal of development provide powerful inducements to the policy of non-alignment'[112] Facilitating aid from both camps and enhancing the prospects for maintenance of peace, this policy helped India avoid alienating its formidable neighbours, the Soviet Union and China.[113]

In contrast to India, Australia's commitment to the US-led Western alliance, underpinned by ANZUS (and SEATO), created the conditions for a sustained level of political conflict with India, which also found expression in confrontation at the Prime Ministerial level in the 1950s and early 1960s. There were numerous other reasons, discussed in later chapters, that contributed to the mutual uninterest and deserve to be briefly mentioned here: the 'White Australia' Policy; the absence of trade, the lack of a real interest in India at Australian educational institutions; the negative treatment of India by Australia's media; a divergence of views on major international political issues; scant discussion of each other in Parliamentary forums; the cultural interests of each channeled into directions other than towards each other. Other features were the Nehru-Menzies dissonance; India's distance (5,500 kms.) from Australia; Australia's strategic interests focused more in the Pacific than the Indian Ocean; and, while India's security focus was on Pakistan and China, it was buttressed by its relationship with the Soviets, much to Canberra's displeasure.

There was some convergence of course but much divergence too. The defining difference was the primacy of security and trade for Australia, while for India, independence, peace and moral considerations were paramount. Nevertheless, some would argue, and not unreasonably, that there was enough equivalence in the two countries' colonial backgrounds for a better bilateral match than has been the case. But then, personalities, their philosophies and policies (combined with some shifts in international circumstances in the early 1970s) did impact on the quality of the relationship.

# Endnotes

1. Viotti, Paul R. & Kauppi, Mark V., *International Relations and World Politics: Security, Economy, Identity*, Prentice Hall, New Jersey, 1997, p 127.

2. Kegley, Charles W. & Raymond, Gregory A., *Multipolar Peace: Great Power Politics in the Twenty First Century*, St Martin's Press, New York, 1994, p 156.

3. O'Neill, Robert 'Diplomacy and Defence', *Agenda for the Eighties: Contexts of Australian Choices in Foreign and Defence Policy*, Coral Bell, (ed.), Australian National University, (ANU), Canberra, 1980, p 50.

4. Holsti, K.J. 'From Isolation to Dependence: Bhutan 1958-62', *Why Nations Realign: Foreign Policy Restructuring in the Postwar World*, K.J. Holsti *et. al.*, (authors) Allen & Unwin, London, 1982, p 34.

5. *Ibid.*, p 32.

6. See Yoshide, Soeya, 'Common Interests, Common Objectives', *Look Japan*, June 1997, Vol. 43, Issue 495, p 19, 1p, 1c. for commercial agreement signed between Japan and Australia to initiate, 'the most successful economic relationships in Asia Pacific.' It also focuses on the development of a bilateral relationship. Also see, Leigh Purnell, 'Australia Reviews Foreign Policy Priorities' *Asian Business Review*, November 1996, for an examination of Australia's foreign policy priorities and the basis for bilateral cooperation.

7. Kelton, Maryanne and Leaver, Richard, 'Issues in Australian Foreign Policy', *The Australian Journal of Politics and History*, December 1999, Vol. 45, Issue 4, p 526.

8. *Ibid.*

9. *Ibid.*

10. *Ibid.*

11. See Arnold Wolfers, (ed.) *Alliance Policy in the Cold War*, John Hopkins University Press, Baltimore, 1959.

12. Gurry, M. 'No Will or No Way? Australia's Relations with India 1947-1993', Ph.D. Thesis, Latrobe University, Victoria, 1993, p 2. For a discussion on the future of international relations affected more by interdependence rather than the traditional sovereignty see, Michel Girard *et. al.*, (eds.), *National Perspectives on Academics and Professionals in International Relations: Theory and Practice in Foreign Policy Making*, Pinter Publishers, London, 1994.

13. Evans, Gareth and Grant, Bruce, *Australia's Foreign Relations in the World of the 1990s*, Melbourne University Press, Victoria, 1991, p 61.

14. G. Modelski, *A Theory of Foreign Policy*, p 86 in K.J. Holsti, *International Politics: A Framework for Analysis*, Second Edition, Prentice Hall, New Jersey, 1972, pp 136-137.

15. Spender, Percy, *Exercises in Diplomacy: The ANZUS Treaty and the Colombo Plan*, Sydney University Press, Sydney, 1969, p 195.

16. Holsti, K.J., *International Politics: A Framework for Analysis*, Second Edition, Prentice Hall, New Jersey, 1972, p 137.

17. Gore-Booth, Paul *With Great Truth and Respect*, Constable, London, 1974, p 15, in Bruce Russett and Harvey Straw, *World Politics: The Menu for Choice*, 5th Edition, W.H. Freeman & Co., New York, 1996, p 138. Also see, Harold Nicholson, *Diplomacy*, 2nd Edition, Oxford University Press, London, 1950 for an incisive examination of the process and development of diplomacy.

18. Purnell, Leigh 'Australia Reviews Foreign Policy Priorities' *Asian Business Review*, November 1996, p 66.

19. 'Treaty Actions' *US Department of State Dispatch*, Subject: United States Foreign Relations/ Treaties, 12 December 1994, Vol. 5, Issue 50, p 827, 2/3p, 1bw.

20. Fitzgerald, Stephen, *Is Australia An Asian Country?* Allen & Unwin, NSW, 1997, p 171.

21. Maslen, Geoff, 'Reprisals Follow Keating's Slur', *Times Higher Education Supplement*, 12 October 1993, Issue 1101, p 16, 1/2p, 26w; Michael Vatkiotis 'Case Closed', *Far Eastern Economic Review*, 23 December, 1993, Issue 51, p 13, 2p. Also see, 'The Keating Files, Don't Call Me Recalcitrant', an extract from Paul Keating, *Engagement: Australia Faces the Asia Pacific*, for his explanation of the issue, in *The Australian*, Wednesday, March 15, 2000, p 15.

22. Malaysian action included demands for the banning of government sponsored students coming to Australia; a 'Buy Australia Last' campaign including a threat to Australia's sale of defence equipment. See Paul Keating, *Engagement: Australia Faces the Asia Pacific*, Pan Macmillan, Sydney, 2000, pp 170-172.

23. Holsti, *op. cit.*, p 178.

24. Camilleri, Joseph A., *Australian-American Relations: The Web of Dependence*, Macmillan, South Melbourne, 1980, p 135.

25. Kegley, Charles W. and Wittkopf, Eugene R., *World Politics: Trend and Transformation*, 7th Edition, Worth Publishing, New York, 1999, p 410.

26. George, Jim, 'The Study of International Relations and the Positivist/Empiricist Theory of Knowledge: Implications for the Australian Discipline,' *New Directions in International Relations? Australian Perspectives*, R. Higgott (ed.), ANU, Canberra, 1988, p 70.

27. For interesting critiques on the widening nature of the International Relations discipline see *inter alia:* A. Vanaik, *India in a Changing World*, Orient Longman, New Delhi, 1995; J. Bandyopadhyaya, *North Over South*, South Asian Publishers, New Delhi, 1982; R.A. Mortimer, *Third World Coalition in International Relations*, 2nd Edition, Westview Press, Colorado, 1984; James E. Dougherty & Robert L. Pfaltzgraff, *Contending Theories of International Relations*, Second Edition, Harper & Row, New York, 1981.

28. Campbell, David, 'Recent Changes in Social Theory: Questions for International Relations', *New Directions in International Relations? Australian Perspectives*, R. A. Higgott (ed.) ANU, Canberra, 1988, p 51. Also see, Richard A Preston, *Canada in World Affairs: 1959-1961*, Oxford University Press, Toronto, 1965, pp 200-208; F.A. Mediansky 'Conservative Style in Australian Foreign Policy', *Australian Outlook*, Vol. 28, No. 1, April 1974, pp 54-56.

29. Bandyopadhyaya, J., *North over South*, South Asian Publishers, New Delhi, 1982, p 3.

30. Battacharya, N., 'Editorial Preface' in Achin Vanaik, *India in a Changing World*, Orient Longman, New Delhi, 1995, p vii.

31. *Ibid.*

32. K.P. Misra, 'Power Politics *versus* Influence Politics in International Affairs and Nehru,' *Journal of Afro-Asian and World Affairs*, Vol. 2, 1965, pp 9-18, in K.P. Misra, (ed.) *Studies in Indian Foreign Policy*, Vikas Publications, New Delhi, 1969, p xi.

33. Morgenthau, Hans J., *Politics Among Nations*, 5th Edition, Alfred A. Knopf, New York, 1973, p 27.

34. Wight, Martin, *Power Politics*, London, 1946, p 7, in K.P. Misra, (ed.) *Studies in Indian Foreign Policy*, Vikas Publications, New Delhi, 1969, p xi. For an useful examination of power and its role in relation to a country's domestic and international policy implications, see Fred Greene, *Dynamics of International Relations*, Holt, Rinehart & Winston, New York, 1964 pp 145-165.

35. George, Jim, 'The Study of International Relations and the Positivist/Empiricist Theory of Knowledge: Implications for the Australian Discipline,' *New Directions in International Relations? Australian Perspectives*, R. Higgott (ed.), ANU, Canberra, 1988, p 115.

36. Carr, E.H., *The Twenty Years' Crisis: 1919-1939*, Macmillan, London, 1962, p 10.

37. Indyk, Martin, 'The Australian Study of International Relations', *Surveys of Australian Political Science*, Don Aitkin (ed.), George Allen & Unwin, Sydney, 1985, p 269.

38. *Ibid.*

39. *Ibid.*, p 266.

40. Higgott, Richard A. and George, Jim, 'Tradition and Change in the Study of International Relations in Australia', *International Political Science Review*, Vol. II, No. 4, 1990, p 433. Also see, Note 11, p 433. 'There is in Australia a very strong tradition of fine scholarship on the states of the Asia-Pacific region. Such work, however, has been carried out mainly by researchers who would all too often be considered "area specialists" rather than scholars of international relations. This is an unfortunate and narrow exercise in labelling. In many ways "Asian studies" can legitimately lay claim to being perhaps the strongest component of the wider disciplines of political science, sociology and anthropology in Australia.'

41. *Ibid.*, p 428.

42. Miller, J.D.B., 'The Development of International Studies in Australia 1933-83', *Australian Outlook*, Vol. 37, No. 3, December 1983, p 140. Also see, Jim George, *Discourses of Global Politics, A Critical (Re) Introduction to International Relations*, Lynne Rienner Publications, Colorado, 1994; Martin Hollis & Steve Smith, *Explaining and Understanding International Relations*, Clarendon Press, Oxford, 1991; Steve Smith *et al.* (eds.) *International Theory: Positivism and Beyond*, Cambridge University Press, Cambridge, 1996.

43. Lee, David and Waters, Christopher (eds.), *Evatt to Evans: The Labor Tradition in Australian Foreign Policy*, Allen and Unwin, NSW, 1997, p 2. (Introduction)

44. Ricketson, Matthew, 'Military is winning its battle with the media',(Book Review, *First Casualty*, updated Edition) *The Age*, July 31 2000, p 13.

45. Camilleri, J.A., *Australian American Relations: the Web of Dependence*, Macmillan, South Melbourne, 1980, p 18.

46. Evans, Gareth and Grant, Bruce, *Australia's Foreign Relations in the World of the 1990s*, Melbourne University Press, Victoria, 1991, p 35.

47. Bull Hedley, *The Anarchical Society*, Macmillan, London, 1977, p 270.

48. Morse, Edward L., 'Transnational Economic Processes', *Transnational Relations and World Politics*, Robert O. Keohane and Joseph S. Nye (eds.) 2nd printing, Harvard University Press, Massachusetts, 1973, p 47.

49. Indyk, Martin 'Australian Study of International Relations', *Surveys of Australian Political Science*, Don Aitkin (ed.), George Allen & Unwin, Sydney, 1985, p 267.

50. *Ibid.*

51. Sharma Shri Ram *Indian Foreign Policy Annual Survey: 1973*, Sterling Publishers, India, 1977, p 162.

52. *Ibid.*, p 163.

53. George, T.J.S. (ed.) *India at 50:1947-1997*, Express Publications, Chennai, India, 1997, p 23.

54. Solanski, Madhavsinh (Minister for External Affairs), 'India's Foreign Policy Perspectives in the 1990s', Speech delivered at the India International Centre, 13 August 1991, New Delhi, pp 1-2.

55. Hedley Bull, a sensitive exemplar of the realist scholarship, argues that a globalist doctrine that transcends the state system is an ideology of the dominant West and consequently, removal of state sovereignty means the loss of 'barriers that they, the weaker countries, have set up against Western penetration: the barriers that protect ... Third World countries from imperialism.' See Hedley Bull, 'The State's Positive role in World Affairs', *Towards a Just World Order*, Richard Falk, *et al.* (eds.), Westview Press, Colorado, 1982, p 69.

56. Misra, S.N., *India: the Cold War Years*, South Asian Publishers, New Delhi, 1994, p 30.

57. See Bajpai, G.S., 'Ethical Stand on World Issues: Cornerstone of India's Foreign Policy', *Studies in Indian Foreign Policy*, K.P. Misra, (ed.), Vikas Publications, New Delhi, 1969, pp 25-31.

58. Holsti, K.J., *International Politics: A Framework for Analysis*, Second Edition, Prentice Hall, New Jersey, 1972, p 428.

59. Misra, S.N. *op. cit.*, p 38.

60. Evans, Gareth. and Grant, Bruce., *Australia's Foreign Relations in the World of the 1990s*, Melbourne University Press, Victoria, 1991, p 43.

61. AA, Report from F. Stuart 10 August 1950, to DEA, Series A1838/278 Item 3123/7/13.

62. Evans, and Grant, *op. cit.*, p 41.

63. *Ibid.*, p 43.

64. Holsti, *op. cit.*, pp 437-438.

65. Nehru, Jawaharlal ' Foreword', *Paths to Peace: A Study of War: its Causes and Prevention*, V.H. Wallace, (ed.) Melbourne University Press, Victoria, 1957, p xx.

66. Higgott, Richard and George, Jim, 'Tradition and Change in the Study of International Relations in Australia,' *International Political Science Review*, Vol. II, No. 4, 1990, p 425.

67. Neale, R.G., 'Australia's Changing Relations with India', *India, Japan, Australia: Partners in Asia?* J.D.B. Miller (ed.), ANU, Canberra, 1968, p 84.

68. Hoffman, Stanley, 'An American Social Science: International Relations' *Daedalus*, 1977, p 59, in R. Higgott (ed.),'The State and International Politics: Of Territorial Boundaries and Intellectual Barriers', *New Directions in International Relations? Australian Perspectives*, ANU, Canberra, 1988, p 180.

69. AA, Despatch 22 March 1948, from the Australian High Commissioner in Malaya to DEA, (Department of External Affairs) Series A1838/283, Item 382/4/1.

70. Appadorai, A. *Select Documents on India's Foreign Policy and Relations, 1947-1972*, Vol. 1, Oxford University Press, New Delhi, 1964, p 12.

71. Higgott, R. 'The State and International Politics: Of Territorial Boundaries and Intellectual Barriers' *New Directions in International Relations? Australian Perspectives*, R. Higgott (ed.), ANU, Canberra, 1988, p 196. For a cross section of views on the subject of International Relations also see: K.N. Waltz, *Theory of International Politics*, Addison Wesley, Massachusetts, 1979; K.N. Waltz, *Man, the State and War: A Theoretical Analysis*, Columbia University Press, New York, 1959; A. Wolfers 'The Actors in International Politics' *Discord and Collaboration: Essays on International Politics*, A. Wolfers (ed.), Johns Hopkins Press, Baltimore, 1962; Trevor Taylor, 'Introduction: The Nature of International Relations', *Approaches and Theory in International Relations* Longman, London, 1978; Inis L. Claude *Power and International Relations*, Random House, New York, 1962.

72. Mathews, Jessica 'Power Shift' *Foreign Affairs*, January/February, 1997, p 50.

73. *Ibid.*

74. Dougherty, James E. and Pfaltzgraff, Robert L. *Contending Theories of International Relations*, Harper & Row, Second Edition, New York, 1981, p 35.

75. Taylor, Trevor (ed.) 'Introduction: The Nature of International Relations' *Approaches and Theory in International Relations*, Longman, London, 1978, p 3.

76. Higgott, Richard and George, Jim, 'Tradition and Change in the Study of International Relations in Australia,' *International Political Science Review*, Vol. II, No. 4, 1990, p 423.

77. Holsti, *op. cit.*, p 291.

78. Dougherty and Pfaltzgraff, *op cit.*, p 564.

79. *Ibid.*

80. Brecher, Michael *India and World Politics*, Oxford University Press, London, 1968, p 336.

81. Holsti, *op. cit.*, p 361.

82. *Ibid.*, p 437.

83. J. Nehru's Statement at Press Conference on 28 December 1961 in B.N. Pandey, *Nehru*, Macmillan, London, 1976, p 402. Also see S.M.S. Chadha's statement on Territories under Portuguese administration, MEA, *Foreign Affairs Record*, Vol. XIV, June 1968, No. 6, Government of India New Delhi, pp 134-135.

84. Congress Bulletin, No. 5, June-July 1954, p 246, in Michael Brecher, *Nehru: A Political Biography*, Abridged Edition, Oxford University Press, London, 1961, p 217.

85. Brecher, Michael, *India and World Politics*, Oxford University Press, London, 1968, p 299.

86. Dougherty and Pfaltzgraff, *op. cit.*, p 40.

87. McDougal, D. J., *Studies in International Relations: The Asia Pacific, the Superpowers, Australia*, Edward Arnold, Melbourne, 1991, pp 136-137; Also see, R. Pettman, *International Politics: Balance of Power, Balance of Productivity, Balance of Ideologies*, Longman Cheshire, Melbourne, 1991, Thucydides, *A History of Peloponnesian War*, (Trans.) Rex Warner, Penguin, Middlesex, Book 111 1954; Thucidydes, *Peloponnesian War*, (Trans.) Crawley, Modern Library, New York 1951; George Modelski, 'Kautilya: Foreign Policy and International System in The Ancient Hindu World', *American Political Science Review*, 58, 1964, p 553.

88. Morgenthau, Hans J., *Politics Among Nations*, 5th Edition, Alfred A. Knopf, New York, 1973, p 24.

89. *Ibid.*, p 190. Ernest B. Haas offers eight definitions to further illustrate the ambiguity of meaning attached to the term. 1) any distribution of power; 2) an equilibrium or balancing process; 3) hegemony or the search for hegemony; 4) stability and peace in a concert of power; 5) instability and war; 6) power politics in general; 7) a universal law of history; and 8) a system and guide to policy makers. See 'The Balance of Power: Prescription, Concept or Propaganda?' *World Politics*, V, July 1953, pp 442-447, in James E. Dougherty and Robert L. Pfaltzgraff, *Contending Theories of International Relations*, Harper & Row, New York, 1981, p 24

90. Harper, Norman, 'Australia and the United States', *Australia in World Affairs 1966-1970*, Gordon Greenwood and Norman Harper, (eds.), Cheshire Publishing, Melbourne, 1974, p 271.

91. McDougal, D. J., *Studies in International Relations, The Asia Pacific, the Superpowers, Australia*, Edward Arnold, Melbourne, 1991, p 137.

92. Bonsal, Stephen, *Suitors and Suppliants*: Prentice Hall, Englewood Cliffs, 1946, p 275.

93. Weigert, Hans W. and Stefanson, V. (eds.), 'The Balance of Power' *Compass of the World*, Macmillan, New York, 1944, pp 59-60.

94. Nehru, Jawaharlal, 'Foreword' in *Paths to Peace: A Study of War its Causes and Prevention*, V. H. Wallace, (ed.) Melbourne University Press, 1957, p xv.

95. Kothari, Rajni, *Footsteps into the Future*, Free Press, New York, 1974, p xxi.

96. Brecher, Michael, *India and World Politics*, Oxford University Press, London, 1968, p 227.

97. Rajan, M.S., 'India in World Politics in the Post-Nehru Era', *Studies in Indian Foreign Policy*, K.P. Misra (ed.) Vikas Publications, New Delhi, 1969, p 263.

98. Griffiths, M. and Sullivan, M., 'Nationalism and International Relations Theory', *The Australian Journal of Politics and History*, Vol. 43, No. 1, 1997, p 56.

99. *Ibid.* p 57.

100. Dougherty, and Pfaltzgraff, *op. cit.*, p 168.

101. 'Regional Cooperation and Security', *The Daily News*, Sri-Lanka, 9 January 1997, p 6. (The Krishna Menon memorial lecture, delivered by L. Kadirgarmar, Minister for Foreign Affairs, Sri-Lanka, at Rajasthan, India on 15 December 1996.)

102. Sopie, Noordin, 'The Development of an East Asian Consciousness', *Living with Dragons*, Greg Sheridan, (ed.) Allen & Unwin, NSW, 1995, pp 184-186.

103. Ramachandram, G., *Nehru and World Peace*, Radiant Publishers, New Delhi, 1990, p 63.

104. Evans, Gareth and Grant, Bruce, *Australia's Foreign Relations in the World of the 1990s*, Melbourne University Press, Victoria, 1991, p 246.

105. Braun, Dieter, 'New Patterns of India's Relations with Indian Ocean Littoral States', *The Indian Ocean in Global Politics*, L.W. Bowman and I. Clark (eds.) Westview Press, Colorado, 1981, p 22.

106. AA, Despatch 22 March 1948, to DEA from the Australian High Commissioner in Malaya, Series A1838/283 Item 328/4/1.

107. Kothari, Rajni, *Footsteps into the Future*, The Free Press, New York, 1975, pp 21-22.

108. *Ibid.*, p 21.

109. Bandyopadhyaya, J. *North over South*, South Asian Publishers, New Delhi, 1982, pp 4-5.

110. Fukuyama, Francis Book Review, (*Roots of Realism* and *Realism: Resentments and Renewal*, Benjamin Frankel (ed.), Frank Cass, Portland, 1997) *Foreign Affairs*, July/August 1997, p 147.

111. Aitkin, Don, 'Political Science in Australia: Development and Situational' *Surveys of Australian Political Science*, Don Aitkin, (ed.) George Allen & Unwin, Sydney, 1985, p 32. Richard Higgott and Jim George argue that, future developments in the discipline should not be expected to lead to logical replacement of one approach by another, 'nor as a chaotic field of incommensurable "paradigms." ' See 'Tradition and Change in the Study of International Relations in Australia', *International Political Science Review*, Vol. 11, No. 4, 1990, p 431.

112. Brecher, Michael, *Nehru a Political Biography*, Abridged Edition, Oxford University Press, London, 1961, p 213.

113. *Ibid.*

# 2

## Setting the Stage

This chapter first considers the issue of interpretations of events and orientations in writings on bilateral relations. It then deals with some of the basic issues of divergence that separated the two countries and ends with an examination of the 1947-49 period that was characterised by the mutual respect and camaraderie that prevailed between Nehru and the Chifley government in which Dr Evatt was such a powerful figure.

The chapter also offers an introductory snapshot of the bilateral relationship during the Nehru-Menzies and Mrs Gandhi-Whitlam periods in office. These are of course given substantive treatment in subsequent chapters.

The importance of bilateral relations between Australia and other countries has not gone unrecognised in the past. Indeed, bilateralism continues to constitute a major tool in contemporary Australia's complex mix of international relations. An Australian Government white paper states, 'effective bilateral relationships are the building blocks for Australia's foreign and trade policies. They contribute to and complement regional and multilateral efforts.'[1]

While this is amply reflected by the existence of numerous bilateral studies,[2] the writings of earlier years on Australia's international relations have mostly been articulated within the prevailing realist theoretical frameworks, 'the Australian discipline (being) identified predominantly with the "hard headed" realist power politics approach ...'.[3] Consequently, the interpretation of cold war events and foreign policy premises of relevance to the bilateral relationship have been oriented towards the Australian view of the world. Besides, for a Westerner, an understanding of Indian foreign policy requires understanding a complex India and interpreting the Indian way of thought, no mean task. Casey understood this problem well. In *An Australian in India,* he states: 'We have not spent much time trying to understand the Indian mentality; nor to become friendly enough with them to enable them to speak their minds freely.' Probably speaking as a British representative in India (Casey was Governor of Bengal 1942-1944), he added, ' "how odd" we tend to say when confronted with the natural behaviour of "foreigners" and turn back to our comfortable familiar circle.'[4]

In his Ph.D. thesis entitled, 'The Buddhist Crisis in Vietnam: 1963-1966', Phan Van Lun argued that writers from the West 'did not know Vietnamese or had insufficient knowledge about the culture, civilization and history of these people. Thus, through the lens of Western models, their work sometimes did not reflect the real ideas and feelings of the Vietnamese.'[5] Lun's lament could well apply, albeit to a different degree, to Western writings on the India-Australia relationship which provide some, but not total, illumination. Another example of the problem of different interpretations between India and Australia is seen in Dr. Nasir Tyabji's observation at an India-Australia Round Table discussion in 1995 that 'part of the problem lies in our different historical perceptions of the major political events after 1945,' identifying South Africa, Palestine and Vietnam as three issues on which there is continuing disagreement.[6]

The hermeneutic end-points reached by scholars and political analysts can, of course, be shaped by the political climate and academic environment of the day, in which the personalities of the political leadership can be a key determinant. To reach, therefore, historically specific and factually incontestable conclusions from the literature, about international relations and how political leaders and their foreign policy affected inter-country relationships, is unquestionably difficult but not impossible.

## Regional Orientation and India Knowledge

Australia's lack of sensitivity towards emerging Asian aspirations led to early relations with many of the countries of Asia being insubstantial if not sterile, shaped as they were, by Australia's Western orientation in foreign policy. In the specific case of India, left with a British imprint (an inevitable legacy of centuries of a British commercial presence and colonial rule), the lack of interest shown in the 1950s and 1960s by Australian scholars and political analysts in the world's largest democracy is a cause for lament. Understanding foreign policy requires understanding contexts and in the case of the Indian relationship this also meant greater sensitivity to, and inclusion of, India's circumstances and foreign policy principles. It leads to a more contextualised understanding of policy as well as relationships. Mediansky argues for greater attention being paid to the context within which foreign policies were developed. While much of the scholarship has focused on content of foreign policy, he argues that this has been at the cost of context which is essential to gaining a better understanding of policy:

> Yet, public policy cannot be fully understood without some knowledge of the contextual factors within which it is formulated and executed. Content and context are interacting dimensions of a single process.[7]

In his review of '*Evatt to Evans: The Labor Tradition in Australian Foreign Policy*', Dave Cox takes a similar view when he states that, 'for many years Australian foreign policy analysis had been largely confined to the study of particular events and issue areas rather than contexts and frameworks.'[8]

At a fundamental level, the critique of Indian writer, P.C. Mathur, is pertinent to understanding the bilateral relationship. He makes the point that, except for infrequent interest in India's economy shown by Western scholars, usually undertaken on behalf of international agencies, 'for a variety of reasons, India has always remained on the periphery of Western social science academia despite its remarkable success in absorbing a lot of Western ideas, institutions...'[9]. He refers to the lack of India-expertise in most Western academic institutions; for instance, the absence of someone who has studied 'the dynamics of India's development, specially the ... extraordinary resilience shown by the retrogressive forces of social customs and cultural traditions.'[10] Australia's High Commissioner to India, in a letter to Casey in 1954, argued for the learning of Hindi at the High Commission: 'we should encourage the right attitudes, including that one or two of the Diplomatic Officers learn Hindi. (In five or ten years this knowledge will in any case be unavoidable if the mission is to work efficiently.)'[11] Author and academic Ian Copland importantly observes that 'the first substantive undergraduate courses on South Asia came only in the 1960s and the schools didn't embrace India until the 1970s. ... But the subject of South Asia, and Indian Studies in particular, quickly caught on.'[12] On the lack of Asian knowledge generally, Judith Brett states, 'Australian academics with deep knowledge of Asian societies are not a dime a dozen' and proceeds to suggest a *modus vivendi* (in the present inter-university competitive environment) for producing graduates literate in Asia.[13] In another different assessment of the Indian studies puzzle, Roger Peacock of the Asian Studies Council asserts that the absence of South Asia studies in Australia's education system is traceable to the 'Colombo Plan hangover. ... Most Australians still see Asia as a place we give help. It also remains a frustrating aspect of the view of most academics, including Asianists.'[14]

A Report of the Inquiry into the Teaching of Asian Studies and Languages in Higher Education in Australia says, ' the study of Asia and its languages matters because we are Australians, located in a specific geopolitical environment and linked through trade, migration, investment and tourism to Asia in a way probably different from other Western countries.'[15] The Asian Studies Council put it more bluntly when it argued that 'the proper study of Asia and its languages is about national survival in an intensely competitive world.'[16] Marika Vicziany, (Director of the National Centre for South Asian Studies based at Monash University), whose work in promoting educational, business and cultural understanding of South Asia has been highly commended,[17] laments the diminishing nature of South Asia expertise within Australia's universities when she observes that, 'it is generally understood that South Asia is a fairly low priority.'[18] Roger Peacock in a similar view deplores the lack of attention given to South Asian cultural studies in Australian tertiary institutions:

> Knowledge of their rich influence on other down stream Asian cultures is important to a full understanding of the values and norms of many contemporary societies. I suspect it would also help to change Australian attitudes towards Asia, and South Asia in particular, if we learnt more as children about the rich legacies generated by the rubbing of the British and Indian cultural tectonic plates over a number of centuries. This goes far deeper than scouting the culinary influences and the common expression in our vocabulary.[19]

Australia's poor attitude to learning about India is further exemplified in this reference by Associate Professor Jim Davidson to a visit to India in the early 1960s by a group of students:

A third year student from the University of Tasmania, a member of the second AOST (Australian Overseas Student Travel) tour to India in 1962-1963, arranged to see the President, Dr Radhakrishnan. On granting the interview - which was to assist her honours thesis - he was amazed to find that she had done no preliminary reading.[20]

Davidson adds that Prime Minister Nehru found the time to meet with a group of these students at his residence (Teen Murti House) for twenty minutes in February 1963.[21]

Despite Australia's lack of curiosity about India, Australia's interest in the 1950s and 1960s in a number of nation states, notably Indonesia, Japan, Malaysia and even Pakistan, (SEATO) led to greater attention being paid to relations with them, albeit driven by trade and or strategic imperatives, the usual key determinants of foreign policy. Greenwood states:

> ... the Australian Government failed to give high priority to a rapprochement with India and was disinclined to give serious weight to Indian attitudes on international questions. ... the lack of success here was all the more regrettable since for Australia, India undoubtedly constituted the most important area.[22]

## India's Global Interests Exclude Australia

It is equally true to say that non-aligned India, with its major international stature at the time and its sheer size in population, was neither conscious of being neglected by Australia, nor particularly interested in upgrading the relationship. Australia did not excite the attention needed to figure in India's global interests. To say otherwise is to skirt the truth. In his insightful article 'Australia's Changing Relations with India', R.G. Neale states:

> The first thing to strike the inquirer into Australia's relations with India is, I think, the contrast between the tremendous importance attached by Australia to India's role in Asian and world affairs, and the insignificant extent to which Australia has figured in India's view of Asia and the world.[23]

Australia was seen as a European outpost, clearly a member of the Western alliance, and thus constrained by the Anglo-US strategic objectives in Asia, as well as by its own fear of communism and commitment to its containment, and, of course, to a 'White Australia'. The relatively junior ranking of diplomats assigned to Canberra by New Delhi is reflective of the low priority India gave to the bilateral relationship with Australia. High Commissioner to India, W.R. Crocker, in a despatch to Casey, states: 'it was symptomatic of the rather slight importance attached to Australia by the Indian thinking that when Shri Duleepsinjhi returned to India on the expiration of his appointment as High Commissioner in Australia, he was not invited to visit Delhi or to make any report.'[24] Crocker also refers to Mrs Pandit's (India's representative to the UN and later High Commissioner to the UK) attitude to R.G. Casey's invitation to visit Australia, which she accepted, but then cancelled twice. Crocker explains why: 'she cancelled one arrangement to visit Japan and another to fit her Indonesian trip into a time table suitable to the Indonesians.'[25] But, then, India's interests were directed primarily towards achieving freedom and economic equity for the poor nations of Asia and Africa, as well as being concerned with the implications of global superpower rivalry and world peace. India's commitment is exemplified in Malaya's Prime Minister Tunku Abdul Rahman's statement in 1958 that 'the people of Malaya are proud to acknowledge the debt which we and all freedom-loving people of Asia owe to the great leadership of India.'[26] Australia's and India's interests converged as well as diverged. Australia's strategic compulsions *versus* India's moral values constituted the defining difference.

## Mutual Indifference: Bilateralism without Engagement

Importantly, it helps to recognize that the indifference that apparently characterised the India-Australia bilateral relationship, in the Nehru-Menzies period, was mutual. India's economic focus was predominantly on the Soviet Union. With their broadly socialist approach to economic planning, the country opted for 'a mixed economy where a larger role was assigned for the public sector and lesser to a State-regulated private sector.'[27] Despite Nehru's attraction to the USSR's approach to economic planning, India's commitment to democracy was reflected in its choice of the British Westminster bicameral parliamentary model, with which the new nation was already familiar as an interim government one year before independence. But of course, Westminster type institutions were in use in India at least from the 1920s when the Montague-Chemsford Constitution came into operation. The constitutional framework under which India was governed between independence (1947) and 1950 was the Government of India Act of 1935, large parts of which were later incorporated into the republican constitution of 1950.

While India's approach did not represent a problem for the relationship in the Chifley-Evatt period, as the analysis reveals, it failed to help it in the Menzies period when anything socialist in character was seen as contrary to Australia's interests, aligned as they were with those of the anti-socialist West. Not everybody shared Menzies' narrow judgment. Australia's High Commissioner, James Plimsoll, for instance, in a wide ranging assessment of Nehru which he sent to Paul Hasluck, Minister for External Affairs, from New Delhi in 1964, spoke of Nehru's efforts to raise living standards of the masses and 'as a means of doing so, he fostered economic planning by the State but within a framework of Parliamentary democracy.'[28]

But the mutual apathy was more pervasive in its manifestations. For example, of seventeen cultural agreements between India and other countries made between 1951 and 1963, seven were with East European States and four with Arab States. None were with Australia. C.R.S. Rogers of the Australian High Commission in New Delhi commented that 'India directs much of her international goodwill towards these two groups.'[29] In the educational sphere, Britain, France, and the USA[30] were more frequently the source of India's interactions than was Australia. As a preferred country to migrate to, the UK, USA and Canada of the Western nations attracted significantly more Indians than did Australia.[31] In Australia's case, its political, economic and cultural interests were aligned with the Western nations with which it was ideologically in tune and, where Asia was concerned, the North East and South East, rather than South Asia.

In the area of trade, too, India and Australia looked primarily to others. B.N. Ganguli, in a report prepared for the Commonwealth Relations Conference in Lahore in 1954, indicated that, in the post-war period, the USA accounted for a significant increase in the share of India's import trade (raw materials) rising from 7 per cent in 1937-1938 to 30 per cent in 1947-1948, followed in importance by Iran (oil), Egypt (raw cotton), Italy (textiles, etc.) and Switzerland (high grade precision instruments).[32] The report also points to the importance of South East Asia with which India has established 'strong emotional and economic ties in recent years.'[33] Trade between India and Australia - an important dimension of any successful bilateral relationship - was of little consequence in the 1950s and 1960s. Australian exports to India were principally wheat, wool, tallow and metals while India sent Australia jute, cotton manufactures and tea.[34] In the period 1956-1971, Australia's imports from India in monetary value dropped by 30 per cent while imports from all other countries rose by 138 per cent.[35]

## Totally Ignored or Totally Distorted

The lack of mutual interest in each other was also marked by an absence of any discussion of each other in their respective Parliaments. The Australian media too rarely discussed events in the subcontinent with any relish and, when they did, occasionally betrayed a hint of superiority, with any reference to India usually made in terms that militated against the development of good bilateral relations. A patronising tone coupled with pessimistic expectations was often the impression conveyed. According to Greenwood, the press in Australia, despite its desultory and limited coverage of international issues, helped improve knowledge of developments in the Commonwealth and to stress the importance to Australia of the changes taking place in Asia. Yet, he observes, it had not 'satisfactorily fulfilled its obligations to assist in education of the Australian community in the realities of the international situation by the provision of extensive and unbiased information drawn from a wide range of sources.'[36] While this comment is not specifically in relation to India, it would not be an inappropriate description of the media's treatment of Indian issues in the 1950s and 1960s. In 1951, a question was asked of the Indian Prime Minister in the Lok Sabha about the 'prevailing anti-Indian propaganda' in the Australian Press. In reply, the Deputy Minister for External Affairs, Dr Keskar, said, 'I do not think there has been any organised and persistent propaganda but off and on there are spates of anti-Indian criticism ...'[37]. The comments though recent, of a prominent Indian official, Romesh Bhandari, illustrate further this gratuitous portrayal of India's image abroad:

> ... We continue to be viewed as a disorganised, strife torn, and caste ridden backward country. ... Much of this false impression is due to the way in which the international media is projecting us. Only negative events are highlighted and positive achievements ignored.[38]

Furthermore, the Australian media and policy makers had little interest in understanding India's policy of non-alignment, a principal component of India's foreign policy. This was also true with regard to Kashmir, where India was often seen by Australia and the West as the intransigent party. While Australia's attitude to non-alignment and Kashmir are examined in chapters Five and Six respectively, a writer to *The Round Table* saw India's predicament in these terms:

> Looked at from India, world opinion does seem greatly prejudiced and unduly unsympathetic; often disproportionately hostile. In all the attacks one sees in the foreign press, it is rarely mentioned that India has a case, that whilst there are questions that India cannot answer there are others which world opinion does not even attempt to answer.[39]

The Australian High Commission in New Delhi was not always accurate or balanced in its reporting of Indian issues to the Department of External Affairs (DEA), Canberra. For instance, in one report on India's attitude to the West, it points to an exaggerated sense of emotionalism shown by India on Western issues. It cites the example of the, 'current denunciation here of American bombing in Korea ... This is passionately denounced, while the original North Korean aggression is almost always treated apologetically ...'[40]. And, yet, the factual position is that Nehru himself did earlier condemn North Korea accusing it of being the aggressor which was correctly reported by Australia's Acting High Commissioner in an earlier despatch to DEA.[41] Nehru himself lamented the falsehoods that were written about India in the West because of India's 'anti-imperialist record' and, using the United Kingdom as an example, he said that they 'deliberately and offensively misrepresent us.'[42]

In a review of John Hohenberg's book, *Between Two Worlds*, which examines the 'relationship between foreign correspondence and foreign policy, particularly as it exists in Asia,'[43] Michael Donelan observes that, 'the treatment of India, no doubt, the most complex case, seems rather mechanical and flat.'[44] 'We are shown', he adds, 'how the vast American news network was rapidly dismantled after the last war, and how thereafter the American media were on the whole interested in Asia only in terms of war, crisis or picturesque trivia.'[45]

If all this suggests there was a need for moderation by Australia and the West in their portrayal of India, it is best illustrated by former Australian High Commissioner to India, W.R. Crocker, with his comments made in relation to Chinese Communism and Australia's handling of it, but could well apply to the Australian media's treatment of India in past years:

> ... our firmest commitment of all should be to patience and talk, ... and at the same time to de-dramatize and to lower the voice. The sensationalism of the mass media is a bigger peril and a worse betrayer than Communist enemies, imagined or real.[46]

Crocker's apposite advice to the media, however, is not reflected in the exaggerated tone used in his own despatch to Minister Casey in December 1954 in which, as High Commissioner to India, he refers to Nehru's impetuosity over nationalist and racial issues, and likens the Nehru government's attitude to Goa and Pondicherry to those of Hitler.[47] In the same despatch, Crocker also conveys, accurately, India's lack of interest in Australia when he says, 'it would be idle to claim that we occupy much space either in Mr Nehru's interest or that of the average politically minded-Indian.'[48]

Then, again, imbued by nearly two centuries of British rule, India's upper echelons of administration carried with them memories of British colonialism into the post-independent years. The Hindu Indian, (as distinct from the Muslim Indian) ever resentful of the British Raj, was understandably never going to be comfortable dealing with Australian diplomats whose approach to Indians was not unlike those of the British civil servants of the colonial period. Crocker himself recounts the story of how a prominent political leader, when news of his appointment to India as High Commissioner became known, is alleged to have said 'he's no Australian.'[49] Crocker who spent eight years with the British colonial service and the British army and six years with the League of Nations, comments that 'the eyes are indubitably Australian but through accidents of life they probably saw a little differently from average Australian eyes.'[50] Casey, who was liked by Indians when he was Minister for External Affairs, tells the story of India's initial reaction to the news of his appointment by the British government as Governor of Bengal in 1942: 'have we to become a colony of Australia? ... a country that prohibits Indians from even entering their country.'[51] During an interview with Australian foreign policy scholar Max Teichman, he expressed the opinion that Australia, in the 1950s and 1960s, followed a colonial British view of India.[52]

There are those who would point to India's own nonchalant attitude to Australia as also being unhelpful to a good bilateral relationship. Sandy Gordon compares the Australia-India relationship with Australia's relations with China. To those who believe Australia's treatment of India is anomalous, measured in terms of Australian resources committed to India as opposed to China, he has this to say: 'such a view ignores the fact that China has regarded Australia as far more important than India has, and has put greater resources into the relationship.'[53]

While there were many reasons that contributed to the lacklustre bilateral relationship, as the thesis reveals, the uninterest in, and lack of curiosity about each other in the Menzies era were also the result of the greater focus on the wide cultural gap that separated the predominantly young white nation of Australia (of mainly British origins) from India, an ancient civilisation steeped in tradition and history. Understanding this complex nation is a huge task for any country, but given that there is some truth in Australia's 'noted lack of imagination'[54] in understanding cultures foreign to its own, this was another reason for the poor relationship. Nehru himself had this to say on the West's inability to understand the Asian ethos:

> They (the West) are ... very able people and ... write books and magazines and newspapers full of articles about India, ... And yet sometimes I feel that they have concentrated on the essentials and not wholly looked into what lay inside the mind and heart of Asia.[55]

Indian scholar Ravinder Kumar's insightful analysis of Indian civilisation in all its historically rooted political, social and religious evolution - including the impact of British colonialism and the opposing Indian national movement on the country - makes a valuable contribution to understanding the vastly complex India.[56]

If there is an inference to be drawn from this seemingly labyrinthine web of mismatch, it is that no exclusive blame could be apportioned to either for the past mutual indifference except that personalities and policies on both sides were an influence. Here Gurry's admonitory warning is appropriate:

> A problem, it seems to me, for scholars and observers of the Australia India relationship is that they seek to allocate blame readily:... But understanding the complex set of factors which have led these two ... states to give each other scant attention will not be reached by pointing accusing fingers.[57]

## 'White Australia' Policy and Racial Discrimination

Another issue that sharpened the differences between India and Australia was the exclusion of non-Europeans ('White Australia') Immigration policy which came into legislative effect immediately after federation operating in a spirit of bipartisanship. It remained a statute, if not always practised policy, until it was finally abrogated by the Whitlam government.[58] In the intervening period, there was bipartisan support for its enforcement as this 1949 statement by Menzies makes clear:

> It becomes necessary for me to state, ... the attitude of my colleagues and myself towards Australia's national immigration policy and its administration. Ever since the legislative expression of that policy 48 years ago it has been administered and upheld without major amendments by Labor Governments for something like sixteen years and by non-Labor Governments for something like thirty two years. It will be seen that all political parties have stood in relation to this policy on completely common ground.[59]

Yet, the discriminatory immigration policy does not, by itself, explain the mutual indifference between the two countries. There were other factors as the narrative will show. This policy, offensive to Indian sensibilities, was vigorously defended by Australia to the detriment of projecting a better image of Australia in India. It triggered early doubts about Australia's interest in a genuine and independent regional role as an equal in its non-white neighbourhood. To Indians, the humiliation lay as much in its undisguised connotation as in its application and Australia's image became associated with the colour-based immigration policy, as attested to by an Australian journalist working in India in 1960: 'the first thing that an Indian thinks about Australia, and probably the last, is the White Australia policy.'[60]

Australia's High Commissioner to India, in the mid-1940s, Iven Mackay argued for a loosening of the policy he described as '... also racial and not merely economic and social ...'[61] to allay Indian sensitivities as well as for its potential economic benefits to Australia. There were others including Members of Parliament and writers who, in later years, returning from India spoke of their personal experiences of Indian resentment towards Australia's discriminatory policy. These are examined in Chapter Five where the discussion will reveal, India's moral outrage had more to do with self-respect and the affront to human dignity, than any deprivation of immigration opportunities imposed by Australia's exclusion of non-Europeans under the Immigration Restriction Act and related legislative measures. Nehru was relentless in his pursuit of the issue of South Africa's racialism and, despite the denials by Australia, its 'White Australia' policy was also seen in India as racially based. In a speech to the Lok Sabha, (India's lower House of Parliament), on 6 December 1950, Nehru said: 'if I may say so, it is the issue of racialism that is of paramount importance. ... we shall not submit to racialism in any part of the world.'[62]

The impact of the 'White Australia' policy on Indian sensitivities was even raised by Australia's Minister for External Affairs Casey when he briefed Prime Minister Menzies before one of the latter's visits to India: 'more than any other Asians ... educated Indians see evidence of racial superiority in our traditional immigration policy and are resentful of it.'[63]

Casey refers to a meeting with Krishna Menon during which Menon suggested Australia follow Canada's example of having a quota system for Asians. To Casey's response that few Indians had taken advantage of the Canadian offer, Menon said that 'the important thing was that the Canadian quota system ... had greatly improved the general Indian attitude towards Canada which was much better than the Indian attitude towards Australia.'[64] Casey's voice, however, was not the most influential in shaping the Menzies' government's policy, as will be made apparent in later chapters.

At a meeting in Canberra in 1962 with the Foreign Affairs Committee, a three member Indian team representing the Lok Sabha, Air India and the Indian Tourist Development Council raised the immigration issue. According to a record of the meeting, one member, Mr Alva (Lok Sabha) asked 'whether Australia was likely to follow Canada's example and admit for permanent residence "approved" Asians? He implied that future international situation would be influenced by current events and policies and that Australia's standing in the world five years from now could be effected (sic) by the attitude adopted now on the immigration question.'[65]

For Menzies, however, the 'White Australia' policy was central to his foreign policy, as did Nehru's policy of non-alignment underpin his fear of neo-colonialism and involvement in Cold War conflict. In Menzies' case, it includes his stand opposing the expulsion of South Africa from the Commonwealth Association, as well as his refusal to condemn the Sharpeville massacre, actions reflective of his self-interest based realism as he interpreted events - however short-sightedly. Both 'White Australia' and 'non-alignment', though opposites on a moral spectrum, had the common effect of seeking to protect national interests. Of course, the Indian perception of Australia as a colour conscious country, no longer holds true having progressively faded with the gradual easing of restrictions from the mid-1960s and Prime Minister Whitlam's decisive repudiation of the 'White Australia' policy in the early 1970s.

## Non-alignment: A Many-Strings-to-the-Bow Policy

Another issue of equal importance in its impact on the relationship was India's decision to steer clear of Cold War rivalry by not being aligned to either the West or the Soviet led bloc. Non-alignment was the central underpinning of India's foreign policy, an ideological construct. There were other aspects to its character which sought to fulfill some of independent India's core needs such as economic, geopolitical, national cohesion and world peace. Essentially, newly independent India's foreign policy had a strong moral dimension to it. Dr Suresh Chandra (MP), in an address to the Lok Sabha proclaimed the principles that underpinned it:

> that India supports the right of self-determination for all oppressed people of the world. ... The second principle is anti colonialism. The third is India's non-alignment with political blocs and the fourth is establishment of peace in the world ... The Fifth is the fight against racial discrimination.[66]

The achievement of these required that India had the freedom to make foreign policy independent of the great powers. Nehru therefore lost no time in announcing India's policies to the world giving a sharp edge to its non-aligned stance, an amalgam of pragmatism and caution in dealing with the outside world:

> In the sphere of foreign affairs India will follow an independent policy, keeping away from the power politics or groups aligned one against the other. She will uphold the principle of freedom for dependent peoples and will oppose racial discrimination wherever it may occur.[67]

To comprehend India's non-aligned policy in all its dimensions helps unravel some of the conjecture surrounding India-Australia relations. It reveals more about the reasons for, and nature of, the indifference that marked the bilateral relationship. Given that Australia's 'White Australia' policy had an impact on Indian attitudes to Australia even before it gained its freedom in 1947, Australia's failure in the Menzies era to appreciate the complex motives behind India's decision to adopt non-alignment as a central element of its foreign policy after independence compounded the earlier disquiet. Australia's preoccupation with the alleged communist threat and its commitment to the West's strategic aims meant trying to understand India's non-aligned philosophy was difficult and of little interest anyway. For a country where security and trade commanded greater primacy in the nurturing of bilateral relationships, India's doctrine was seen as naive and even pointless. Bandyopadhyaya tries to explain the difficulty the West had in understanding the concept: 'the Western perception of the Cold War as a mortal struggle of the West in defence of "freedom" clouded the Western understanding of the nature of non-alignment.'[68]

Ironically, though, Australia actively sought to strengthen its relations with non-aligned Indonesia. Obviously, India's democracy, which posed no threat to Australia, accounted for little when measured against the criterion of security.

## Misinformed Images and Mutual Indifference

In the complex world of bilateralism, images too are crucial to relationships. Dipesh Chakrabarty observes that:

Until the Salman Rushdie arrived on the scene and made the intellectual ferment of modern India more visible to the outsider, India remained, in the dominant grids of Western perceptions, a place of 'heat and dust' where the Europeans had once founded a resplendent *Raj*. To 'heat and dust' was often added another familiar list: of crowds, dirt and diseases.[69]

A perception also has existed of India as a country of restrictive trade barriers, poor telecommunications, transportation and infrastructure, and, of course, red tape. Exaggerated images of instability created by sporadic religious and sectarian violence and India's links with the former Soviet Union, conveying an impression of tight socialist controls contributed to the negative stereotyping of India. These negative stereotypes largely represented Australia's limited, uninstructed view of India. The US Ambassador to India in the early 1950s, Chester Bowles, was critical of this shallow view:

> Some Western visitors to India, for instance, still see only the Rudyard Kipling, Katherine Mayo land of tiger hunting maharajas, sacred cows and cobras, against an endless backdrop of tradition bound, poverty stricken humanity. But for the visitor who looks below the surface there is a new and immensely exciting India.[70]

Geoff Heriot of Radio Australia takes the view that the Western media's assessment of Indian affairs has been formed through an English language and democratic system based perspective. The benchmarks were Western and assumed to be superior:

> The perceived authority symbols of India on which Australian and other western journalists have always relied were judged according to the fairly smug assumptions of our own society. Democracy was the natural order, reinforced by English as an instrument of culture....The event orientation of the news centred very much on challenges to that supposed natural order,- bound together by the Nehrus - whether it was political chaos, Indira Gandhi's emergency, poverty or communal strife which provided the drama. Perhaps there's been a racist element to news judgment about many non-western, non-developed countries.[71]

Casey, in his book, *An Australian in India*, speaks of the confining stereotyped generalisations about India made by the outside world, an image rooted more in preconceived notions than factually based.[72] Yet, Casey, as Australia's Minister for External Affairs (1951-60), received a report from his own High Commissioner to India, W.R. Crocker, whose admiration for Nehru in the despatch is mixed with comments that may be explained as close to reflecting the Oxbridge-educated civil service paternalism that existed in British India:

> ... Mr Nehru now has a better and more balanced knowledge of the international situation than he had two or three years ago; ... But his judgment is still too apt to be upset by impetuosity, especially by nationalist and racial prejudices, as illustrated by such affairs as US aid to Pakistan, ... his government acts not unlike Hitler over Pondicherry or Goa ... [73].

Crocker however, was far less conservative in his attitude to India than Menzies was.

In a memorandum to the Secretary, DEA, J. Oldham, (Special Adviser on Commonwealth Relations), refers to the need for improving Australia's propaganda services in India but cautions that 'any sign of official superiority or officialdom on the part of our various missions there, of course would undo the ends to which we are striving.'[74] It could be argued perhaps, ironically, it also has something to do with a residual colonial image India reflected; then there may be an explanation buried in past racism.

Questions about some obstacles on the Indian side too have to be faced. Not all the criticism of India is misinformed. Doing business with India has always been a problem and the situation does not appear to have changed. Protracted delays have been experienced by prospective investors, frustrated by the Indian bureaucracy, (perhaps no worse than that of Indonesia or China), as this comment suggests: 'simple tasks have been made so awesome, so gigantic, so convoluted, that once investors get into the procedural whirlpool, it is virtually impossible to get out.'[75] Colin Ward, a Director of Atlas Air, a Sydney-based company, comments on the five years it took him to establish a joint venture agreement after the Indians were convinced of the Australian company's capability of meeting India's specifications for an air-conditioning technology business project:

> I had many trials and tribulations ... But as the obstacles came our way, as they did from the bureaucracy at that time, it made me all the more determined to win that prize. ...It's going to take a lot more than the six years' experience I've had to understand India, ...[76].

On the other hand, there are those attributes, which Neerja Jetley highlights, that makes India more attractive than China, *viz.*, a good legal system, democracy and an ' English speaking technically qualified workforce...'[77]. The automotive giant General Motors

Corporation and Microsoft, among others, have in recent times, looked to India for business opportunities. For example, John Smith, the President of General Motors said in New Delhi in November 1997 that the country's 'democracy with its belief in the rule of law, ... along with the huge market, make for a very powerful combination.'[78] An Indian writer, S.P. Gupta, attributes some of the early failures to selection of poor policy courses: 'policy direction left them inward-looking and dominated by an inefficient public sector, in a highly regulated and controlled market.'[79] This is a view shared by Indian economist, Jagdish Bhagwati, who, according to David Dodwell, 'admires India's democratic vitality but deplores its economic ineptitude.'[80]

It should be remembered that the mutual mood of indifference between the two countries in the two decades after India's independence in 1947 was not entirely of Australia's making. It was also characterised by India's interest being channeled into two separate directions. Its political-economic relationship was predominantly with the former Soviet Union, whose centralised approach to management of the economy India adopted with emphasis on the public sector (but within a democratic framework), much to the chagrin of the West, including the Menzies-led pro-Western conservative Australian governments of the time with their anti-Communist fervour. Its cultural and trade links were more with Britain, the US, the Middle East and Eastern Europe than with Australia. Trade, of course, is fundamental to inter-country relations, but here too, not much happened between India and Australia. India's exports to Australia of jute goods, tobacco, tea and textiles, were matched by exports of wheat, flour, milk products and tallow from Australia; in value, however, the trade factor was of little significance. In a letter to Casey, Crocker offers an explanation:

> The paucity of economic relations is in keeping with the small part played by Australia in Indian consciousness. Until not long ago Australia was thought of by the average Indian, if it was thought of at all, as the country from where the horses used in the Army before mechanization, the rancid butter served in up-country hotels, and the jockeys for the Calcutta and South India race meetings, came from.[81]

More evidence of Australia's lack of significance to India is seen in the absence of Australia in the last three sections of an Indian

Government publication on foreign policy between 1946 and 1961; it deals with India's relations with 36 individual countries of Asia, Africa, Europe and America. Australia fails to merit inclusion.[82]

Yet, for Australia and the Western mind, understanding this hugely complex, country was a towering challenge. There is no sameness, in India, no standardisation to facilitate understanding, and enlighten the outsider. Shashi Tharoor attests to this:

> Everything exists in countless variants. There is no single standard, no fixed stereotype, no "one way." This pluralism is acknowledged in the way India arranges its own affairs: all groups, faiths, tastes and ideologies survive for their place in the sun. ... One result is that India strikes many as maddening, chaotic, inefficient, and seemingly unpurposeful. ... Another, though, is that India is not just a country but an adventure, one in which all avenues are open and everything is possible.[83]

Midway into its Second Five-Year Plan, this was how Nehru saw the contradictions:

> India today presents a very mixed picture of hope and anguish, of remarkable advances, and at the same time of inertia, of a new spirit and also the dead hand of the past and of privilege, of an overall and growing unity and many disruptive tendencies.[84]

Better than most, Nehru understood the Indian puzzle with all its uncertainties, and once observed, 'to endeavour to understand and describe the India of today would be the task of a brave man, to say anything about tomorrow's India would verge on rashness.'[85] Yet, as Tharoor argues, nothing about India remains permanently valid. It is at once static and dynamic. There is no single defining characteristic. This patternless, yet alluring, quality about India's character is best captured in Nehru's own words cited by Tharoor: 'About her there is an elusive quality of a legend of long ago; ... she is a myth and an idea, a dream and a vision, and yet very real and present and pervasive.'[86]

## A Question of Resources and Commitment

There is another explanation for Australia's indifference to the India bilateral relationship. While all the inflexible stamping, the distorted images were clearly unhelpful the mutual indifference also had something to do with questions of priorities and resources to undertake a more penetrative understanding of each other.

Economics indeed does come into it. In Bruce Grant's view it is not unreasonable to assume that Australia's Treasury and External Affairs departments found India too large, too complex and too demanding of resources to handle; it was relatively easier, he observed, to concentrate on relations with smaller nations, a few with great powers (UK and US) and regional neighbours (Indonesia and Japan), adding that a few attempts by Australian diplomats in New Delhi to change Canberra's attitude to India, resulted in inflated political rhetoric but little else beyond that, in the 1950s and 1960s.[87] Then, again, a country's interests and efficient use of resources must come into the calculation. Evans and Grant for instance point to the unavoidable requirement of allocating scarce resources to achieve what is possible - in Australia's interests - when pursuing relations with another State.[88] From India's perspective, while the economic argument would have been equally, if not more compelling, it did not see the building of relations with Australia as a high priority at the time; with its international mediatory role[89] (disproportionately impressive considering its newly independent nation status) occupying the country's policy makers, such as Nehru and Menon, Australia, as an Anglo-US dependent nation of European migrants, hardly figured in India's general foreign policy sweep.

## 1947-1949: Maiden Bilateralism, Fleeting Convergence

Despite these impediments to bilateral engagement, there was every promise of an effective relationship being developed in the 1947-1949 period. Sovereign India's foundational relationship with Australia commenced, of necessity, in 1947, the year in which it became independent from Britain. For the purpose of this analysis and one of its postulates that the relationship was influenced by personalities, policies, philosophies and public opinion at both ends, the Nehru/Chifley-Evatt period, represents a 'peak' as opposed to a 'trough'. That said, the question of foreign policy convergence between the two countries is a good starting point for explaining the affinity that existed between the Nehru-Chiefly governments between 1947-1949. It is useful, however, by way of background to consider briefly the way foreign policy formulation evolved in Australia up to the point at which, for the first time, it had to deal with an independent India.

Australian governments, both Labor and Liberal Coalition had little interest in formulating foreign policy on their own, much before World War II. T.B. Millar explains the reasons:

> A combination of apathy, remoteness and a lingering sense of dependence on Britain gave Australia few national attitudes in foreign affairs, little policy and almost no independent voice (other than trade) until World War II. A separate Department of External Affairs dealing with foreign policy was not created until 1935, and Australia's first diplomatic post was set up in Washington in 1940.[90]

Camilleri describes Australia's early external responses as 'a whole series of attitudes towards the outside world,' and refers to 'a number of recurring themes' that have characterised Australia's international responses. As for any changes that have taken place in Australia's attitude to the outside world, he argues that they are more the consequence of 'unavoidable adaptations to a changing world rather than a conscious and deliberate revision of accepted values and assumptions.'[91]

This view of the existence of 'recurring themes' in Australia's foreign policy is shared by a number of political scientists who have studied the period. For instance, Andrews draws attention to the similarity in Australia's support of Britain's 'policy of appeasement' in the 1930s with its strong espousal of the US-Vietnam policy of the 1960s.[92] Pointing to Australia's unflinching commitment in each case, he concludes: 'there does indeed seem to be a pattern in our foreign policy since the first World War.'[93]

The period leading up to World War II provides valuable insights into Australia's inchoate and dependent mentality in the area of foreign policy development. For example, Menzies, on October 5, 1938, as Attorney General, responded to Opposition Leader Curtin's charge that the government had no foreign policy of its own, and specifically to Curtin's question as to whether a Dominion should formulate foreign policy and announce it, whether or not it was in line with Great Britain's policy, with this warning: 'to adopt such a line of conduct would be suicidal, not only for us, but also for the British Empire as a whole, ...'[94]. Limited mainstream political interest and the lack of a strong national identity had allowed Australia's politicians *carte blanche* running on international relations. In practice, this meant acquiescence with British dictates on foreign policy, except for intermittent periods when an independent stance was taken. Prime Minister Curtin's refusal, during World War II, to yield to Churchill's demands that Australian troops be moved from the Middle East to Burma in defence of Rangoon, rather than returning to Australia's defence as Curtin wanted, was an example of this.[95]

This dependence on Britain up to World War II as a main source of foreign policy information is further underscored by the fact that notwithstanding the outbreak of the Second World War and its significant implications for Britain and its allies, Australia had no diplomatic representation in France, Italy, Germany, the United States, the Soviet Union or Japan.[96] Eurocentric Australia's unimaginative and self-imposed isolation meant little interest in maintaining a dynamic foreign affairs function. Keith Suter concludes that there have been several themes in Australian foreign policy for the past two centuries:

> The first has been a fear of enemies. One of the earliest moves made by the colonials ... at Sydney Cove in 1788 was to build an earthen redoubt and put a cannon in it. ... The second theme has been the belief that Australia cannot be defended unaided. ... This ... led to the belief that Australia needs a protector. ... The final theme has been, ironically, a lack of interest in foreign policy.'[97]

Foreign policy used effectively in its own economic and strategic interests could have secured for Australia a valuable role in the Asia-Pacific region.

In contrast to Australia's lack of any real interest in independent foreign policy framing, Nehru's attitude towards the great powers and India's external affairs policy was marked by a determination to remain free to make independent judgments on every issue. He said unequivocally: 'I am not prepared to surrender my country's judgment to any other power or any group of powers.'[98] Against Australia's security-driven, Western alliance-dependent foreign policy, shaped by its European history rather than its geography, India, even as a British colony, displayed a determination to adopt an independent stance. In 1927, two decades before independence, Nehru was a participant at the Brussels Conference on anti-imperialism,[99] and, in the same year, the Indian National Congress opposed the use of India by Britain as a base from which to interfere with the freedom struggles of other people.[100] In an inaugural address to the Asian Relations Conference on 23 March 1947, under the auspices of the Indian Council of World Affairs, Nehru expressed his feelings on the need for independence in foreign policy:

> For too long have we of Asia been petitioners in Western courts and chancelleries. That story must now belong to the past. We propose to stand on our own legs and to co-operate with all others who are prepared to co-operate with us. We do not intend to be the playthings of others.[101]

Indian diplomat and historian K.M. Panikkar observes that: 'up to 1946 it was an axiom of international diplomacy that the affairs of Asia were dependent upon a conference of Western powers.'[102] Not surprisingly then, having just emerged from nearly two centuries of colonial rule, India, through Nehru, confronted what it saw as its wider obligation to champion freedom movements in Asia and Africa. Nehru told the UN General Assembly in 1948, just one year after independence that 'countries like India who have passed out of ... colonial stage do not conceive it possible that other countries should remain under the yoke of colonial rule.'[103] This attitude of Nehru to colonialism was the antithesis of Menzies' (and some of his colleagues') view of it.

## Stirrings of Independence

Returning to Australia's progress in the field of government responsibility of external affairs, a conscious process of foreign policy development for Australia, by Australians, commenced during and after the War. But central to Australia's external relations policy was the continued protection of Australia's European society from Asia's 'teeming hordes', reinforced by the 'White Australia' Immigration Act. Camilleri explains the motivation underlying this self absorption:

> ...her (Australia's) self-imposed estrangement from the interests, aspirations,... of her Asian neighbours, ... and the increasingly favourable performance of her economy combined to produce in Australian political elites a singular determination to maintain the *status quo* in her external relations. Economic self-interest, cultural conformism, racial prejudice and intellectual laziness ... provided the basis for a philosophy aimed at preserving and extending the existing pattern of relations almost at any cost.[104]

With Britain preoccupied during World War II with its own defence, the fall of Singapore in 1942 not only made Australia more aware of its vulnerability but it was also, as Millar puts it, 'paying the penalty for twenty years (since Versailles) of neglect of international relations, twenty years of substantial acquiescence in British foreign policy decisions.'[105] In the theatre of war, Australia like India, made its contribution as a part of the Empire's forces in both World Wars, yet, its opportunity for influencing Britain's policies in relation to Australia, its neighbourhood and beyond, was minimal. In this 'follow-Britain' approach since federation, the first signs of the need for Australia to exercise some responsibility for determining a foreign policy free of British dictates emerged with the Chifley government of the 1940s. Christopher Waters in his discussion of Australia's decolonisation process of the 1940s and the conflict between 'Anglo Australia' and 'Nationalist Australia' observes that:

> It is crucial to understand that the hold of Anglo-Australia over the institutions of the Australian state was partially broken during the 1940s. ...The Curtin/Chifley Labor governments viewed the world through different eyes from the pre-war Anglo-Australian elite. ... They (the nationalists) had a different conception of Australia's international status, of the possibilities of internationalism and of Australia's relations with Asia. Evatt and Ben Chifley, the Australian Prime Minister, in particular, were prepared to take policy decisions that their predecessors would not even have considered.[106]

Given the ferment and accompanying demands for freedom sweeping through the region, changes that led Casey to tell Parliament that 'instead of living in a tranquil corner of the globe, we are now on the verge of the most unsettled region of the world...'[107], the response of the Chifley government to the turbulent external environment is noteworthy for its courage and sensitivity relative to the fear and self-imposed isolation that existed previously. Sir Zelman Cowan, (former Governor General of Australia) while on a lecture visit to Sri Lanka in 1987 offered this view of Australia's foreign policy changes in the aftermath of World War II to Quadir Ismail of *The Sunday Times*:

> The Australia I grew up in... didn't exercise many independent initiatives in foreign affairs. Culturally it belonged to Europe and more specifically belonged to Britain. It was not a time when Australia was in any significant sense aware of its geographical position in the world.[108]

His additional comments that there were the post-war beginnings of an independence in Australia's foreign policy and a realisation of its location in the Asian region,[109] are reflective of the greater assertiveness of the Chifley-led Government. Much of the credit for this unshackling goes to the Chifley Government's Minister for External Affairs, Dr H.V. Evatt. While there has been considerable debate about Evatt's contribution in his role as Minister, and later as Leader of the Opposition, few would disagree that his international outlook led to a distinctively Australian foreign policy:

> Foreign policy was given special emphasis by the performances of Dr H.V. Evatt, the first Australian foreign minister to emerge from the shadow of Prime Ministerial control and British official surveillance and to present an alternative view of the world.[110]

In a more recent assessment, Gareth Evans, is no less complimentary in his acknowledgment of Evatt's pioneering contribution to Australian foreign policy:

> The creation of an Australian foreign policy, and the identifiable beginning of a distinctive Labor tradition in foreign policy, came only with Evatt. He was not Australia's first Foreign Minister ... but he was certainly the first to deserve that title.[111]

David Lowe in his review of a collection of ten essays entitled *A Brave New World: Dr. H.V. Evatt and Australian Foreign Policy* states: 'the Evatt who emerges here is one who can stand the test of significant others intruding on and contributing to his foreign policy patch, without surrendering his pioneering status.'[112]

Illustrative of Evatt's independence was his determination during the framing of the UN Charter - to which he made a significant contribution - to minimise dominance of the resolution of international issues by the permanent members of the Security Council. He was criticised for this by Menzies and Hasluck who felt he offended Britain and the great powers with his assertive stand.[113] It is also worth noting that at this time, John Burton, as Secretary of the Department of External Affairs (1947-1950), felt that Australia's interests were not threatened by Communism, arguing that it had strong popular support, and that it was widely seen as far better suited to under-developed countries in Asia than existing regimes, which he called 'feudal and colonial.'[114] On this and other issues such as the West's mistaken military strategies for Asia, Burton was closer to India's own thinking. Because of the influence his position had on external relationships, Burton's view of the world was another positive for the bilateral relationship in the 1947-1949 period.

As Minister for External Affairs, Evatt made clear the underpinnings of the Chifley government's foreign policy in a debate in the House of Representatives on 9 February 1949. The three main principles, he claimed, that had guided Labor Governments since 1941, were:

1.  Steady and unwavering support for the United Nations and especially for the purposes and principles declared in the Charter of the United Nations.

2.  The closest co-operation with all members of the British Commonwealth of Nations.

3.  Co-operation with the United States of America.[115]

The relevance of this to discussion of the bilateral relationship is two-fold: first, Australia's commitment to the first two of these principles led to a strengthening of relations with India, which also used the UN and the Commonwealth to seek redress for a number of its grievances. Secondly, as a basis for contrasting the quality of the bilateral relationship of the Chifley-Evatt period with that of Menzies' which followed, these core elements of foreign policy are useful indicators even if the differences on the surface appear to be marginal. To this end, the comparison with Menzies' response on foreign policy in the same debate, shows that, while he acknowledged the UN Charter as 'a background and the ultimate ideal of our international policy ...'[116], Menzies saw Australia's immediate priorities differently:

>  ...first, to build up strength of the British Empire and the United States; secondly, to press on with the restoration of France and Western Europe generally; and, thirdly, to promote such special pacts and alliances as will make clear to the Soviet Union that aggression will not pay.[117]

In his consistency of respect for Nehru's views, Evatt, during the debate on the Suez Canal crisis, told Parliament there was the need for 'mediation and conciliation, by skilled people, and not by people who wish to humiliate one party to the transaction, ...' and then mentioned that the Prime Minister of India has 'suggested a Plan.'[118]

The 1947-1949 cordiality between Evatt and Nehru is also confirmed in retrospect by E.G. Whitlam when he addressed the international seminar to celebrate the hundredth birth anniversary of Jawaharlal Nehru, *viz.,* 'I met him only once in June 1962. I was struck by his first question: " How is Dr. Evatt?" '[119].

Chiefly and Evatt were also committed to the ending of colonialism in Asia, ' giving priority to political and economic support for nationalist movements ahead of the military suppression of genuine or supposed communism.'[120] With Nehru a consistent and strong voice against colonialism in Asia and Africa, the Chiefly-Evatt commitment strengthened the friendly relations that existed between the two countries. Nehru was also clearly impressed with the Chiefly government's interest in Asia as well as its independence in stating its views. Australian journalist and writer Donald Horne refers to the 'UN Committee member' approach to Evatt's involvement of Australia in international problems and observes that:

> This ... was the period when the Labor Party Government saw Australia as one of the consciences of the world, the literate vote of the smaller powers and an opponent of colonialism in South East Asia - where Australia assisted in the destruction of Dutch rule in Indonesia.[121]

An insight into how India's High Commissioner to Australia perceived Labor's attitude to Australia's foreign policy development is reflected in his 1952 Political Report to New Delhi from Canberra in which he cites Evatt's (Leader of the Opposition) reaction to ANZUS:

> I welcome this Pact but regret the price that has been paid for it. ... Australia should have its own independent foreign policy. It should recognize US leadership but not the domination of the policy of Australia by the US or any other country.[122]

Then there was the emotional issue of India's independence. The dissimilarities of the reaction between Labor's pleasure and Menzies' disagreement, if not disappointment, on receiving the news could hardly have gone unnoticed in New Delhi. Soumyendra Mukherjee of the Australia India Council, addressing a discussion on India-Australia relations in February 1995, had this to say of Evatt:

> ... in the last 45 years those among us who have done some work on Australian history know that Dr Evatt was very close to the ideas

of Jawaharlal Nehru. If Evatt had succeeded (in becoming Prime Minister of Australia) the Australian policy would have been quite different. We would have seen another Scandinavia in the Southern Hemisphere which could have changed the whole perspective of Australia and its relationship with Asia. ... But it took the Whitlam Government to bring those things and turn the situation around. Until Whitlam came Evatt's dreams were never fulfilled.[123]

## Common Interests and Mutual Admiration

The background of Australia's foreign policy development of the 1940s, important as it might be, does not, by itself, provide the basis for describing the 1947-1949 period of the relationship as an example of highly successful bilateralism. One test of effective bilateral relations is the existence of common ground and shared objectives between two countries in the area of foreign policy. This leads logically to those questions on which there was convergence between India and Australia in the Nehru-Chifley (1947-1949) period of the relationship. There were, of course, several areas of compatibility between the two governments as well as some of divergence, which stood as obstacles to even greater promise for the future of the bilateral relationship. Two areas of significance, however, for India were the ending of colonialism and the right to independence for subject peoples, and greater economic equity for the poorer nations. The passion with which Indian leaders denounced colonialism before and after independence is exemplified in this indictment of the practice by Krishna Menon:

> It is not possible either to restore the economic imbalances or to establish peace, co-existence and, cooperation in this world, or indeed to restore the dignity of human beings, so long as there are subject peoples.[124]

For Nehru, too, these questions were fundamental to his whole outlook and were themes he persisted with, in his fight for the emancipation and dignity of those subjected to colonial rule. A good example of this was the concern he showed in relation to Indonesia. At the 18 nation conference, held in January 1949 in New Delhi, and initiated by India, it urged the UN to 'take immediate steps towards independence of Indonesia. This was the first concrete manifestation of Asian solidarity and also of India's support to national liberation movements.'[125] In his opening address to the Conference (attended also by Australian representatives) Nehru, said:

> We meet today, because the freedom of a sister country of ours has been imperilled and a dying colonialism of the past has raised its head again and challenged all the forces that are struggling to build up a new structure of the world. That challenge has a deeper significance ... for it is a challenge to a newly awakened Asia which has so long suffered under various forms of colonialism.[126]

Lamenting the dominance of the United Nations by Europe and America, and their problems as opposed to those of Asia, Nehru had this to say in March 1949 at the Council of World Affairs about India's concerns on the Indonesian issue:

> ...if some kind of colonial domination continues in Indonesia ... it will be a danger to the whole of Asia. ... obviously it can only continue with the passive or active acquiescence of some of the great powers, ... it is not merely a political game of chess for us in India;[127]

The Chifley government, like the new India under Nehru, was committed to decolonisation, demonstrated by its support for Indonesia's freedom from Dutch rule. It was also nominated to the UN 'Good Office Committee' by Indonesia as the country which it felt could best help its independence cause.[128] It went further to support India's call for expulsion of The Netherlands from the United Nations.[129]

Despite Australia's foreign policy aims being primarily concerned with security characterised by ambivalence, the Chifley government was seen as having an enlightened approach to its regional realities. This is reflected also in Nehru's address to the eighteen member Conference on Indonesia's independence, when he said, 'ours is ... a regional conference to which we invited both Australia and New Zealand, whose interest in the tranquillity and contentment of Indonesia is as great as that of any of us.'[130] This support for the Indonesian struggle and in particular Evatt's championing of the republican movement at the UN in the late 1940s is a further illustration of not only Australia's contribution to Indonesia's ultimate freedom, but also Australia's sympathetic engagement with Asia.[131] Like Nehru, Chifley held the view that communism was not the cause of all the world's ills. He told Parliament 'there could be no greater fallacy than that.' He also added that 'Lord Mountbatten, Lord Killearn and other eminent British diplomats' were of similar mind.[132] In contrast, the Liberal Coalition, in Opposition at the time but destined to win government later in the same year, saw the issue as coming within the domestic jurisdiction of the Netherlands. Menzies was unambiguous in his criticism of Australia's stand:

> In plain terms, we have been assisting to put the Dutch out of the East Indies. If we continue to do that the same problem will no doubt, in due course eject the British from Malaya and the Australians from Papua and New Guinea.[133]

In the Australian Senate the Opposition's Neil O' Sullivan was more blunt in his dissent arguing that the Dutch were the 'one white hope standing between us and the hundreds of millions of coloured peoples to our north.'[134]

Then there was the seemingly controversial issue of India's Commonwealth membership, in which the Chifley government's support for India went beyond what it saw as a morally just issue to include India's strategic value to Australia; both Chifley and Evatt not only felt India's independence from Britain was highly desirable, they also wanted a sovereign India to remain in the Commonwealth despite its decision to become a Republic. Chifley's feelings on the issue conveyed to Canada's Prime Minister, L.S. St Laurent, (prior to a conference in London in 1949 to discuss the India-Commonwealth relationship question), were a good example of the Chifley government's interest in India during this time, contrasting sharply with Menzies who, despite his obsessive fear of the spread of Communism, objected to democratic India's membership in the Commonwealth as a Republic. The Chifley rationale was:

> ... I feel the question to be decided is of very great importance and I think that we should do all that is possible to retain India as a friendly power. ... I feel that India must certainly be the leader of the Asian peoples and provide a bulwark against any onward rush of Communism through that area.[135]

Then, again, Nehru and Chifley were able to get on well, both at the official and personal levels. In his insightful political biography of Chifley, L.F. Crisp reveals that 'from Nehru in 1949 Chifley seems to have received both stimulus and at the same time confirmation of many of his own conclusions about Asian affairs. He warmed to the charm and the swift, shrewd wit of the man.'[136] In 1951, Chifley, then Leader of the Opposition, told Parliament that:

> India and Pakistan, and particularly India, have become very great and influential dominions in the British Commonwealth of Nations.

...Furthermore, it may be said with confidence, and without casting reflections on anybody else, that Pandit Nehru has the most influential voice in Asia today.[137]

The admiration of course was mutual. Nehru probably liked the direct manner of the amiable Chifley admiring his sensitivity to the aspirations of India and Asia in general. Years, later, remembering his earlier meetings with Chifley, Nehru described him in these words: 'an outstanding personality ... simple and straight forward, ... whatever he said in the Prime Ministers' conference made an impression.'[138]

The Chifley governments' felicitations expressed to India on the threshold of its gaining of independence from Britain, cemented the cordiality that existed from the beginning. The Nehru-Evatt friendship was no less a reflection of the warmth that characterised the bilateral relationship during this brief two year period. In fact, their camaraderie started a decade before India's independence when the two men met in England in the company of Atlee, Bevin, Morrison and Cripps.[139] Australia's High Commissioner to New Delhi Iven Mackay, records that, besides being asked by Evatt to 'pay a special call on Pandit Nehru and give his (Evatt's) remembrances to Nehru,' Evatt wanted it conveyed, 'that the Australian government desired to help the national government in every way they could ...' and 'they wished to continue and extend the friendliest relations with India.'[140]

Evatt was also keen that Nehru be given assurances of Australia's independence of thought and action and conveyed through Mackay, 'that it was the policy of the Australian government, while adhering to the British Commonwealth, to express its own views when necessary and that Australia had exercised independent rights at all recent international conferences and transactions.'[141] This can be seen as an important message as far as the Indian relationship was concerned, because Australia up to that stage was seen in India as a European outpost in the Asia-Pacific and, up to World War II, as an unquestioning and loyal ally within the Anglo-US strategic alliance. On the question of India's future in the Commonwealth, the High Commissioner observed that Evatt 'reiterated that Australia did not want India to leave the British Commonwealth and that she would feel it a great loss if India ever did. A foreign country in the geographical position of friendly India was not to be contemplated in the Australian viewpoint.'[142]

Nehru's response to the generous declarations of support for the imminent new Government of India was conveyed by Mackay in a Despatch to Evatt: 'Called on Nehru. ... Obviously gratified receive your message expressed grateful thanks ... Nehru invites you to visit Delhi in the near future.'[143] The Nehru response also included a comment by him on 'the freedom with which Australia expressed her views' and that India would be pleased to have Australia participate in future meetings on 'the peoples of Asia and the Indian Ocean.'[144] The closeness between the two men is also reflected in Evatt's strong commitment to the UN as an instrument for international justice. With his activism within the UN, Evatt argued that the body should protect the interests of the weaker nations and saw peace as dependent on equity and justice being achieved at a global level.[145] Nehru, like Evatt, was committed to the UN and used it to advocate such causes as greater economic equity for the Third World countries, and world peace through negotiated settlement of disputes rather than the use of force, with the UN being the arbiter of ultimate policy on resolving international conflict.

Naturally, this convergence of interests between two Ministers for External Affairs (Nehru was both Prime Minister and Minister for External Affairs) led to close relations between the two countries. Nehru too did not hide his admiration for the Chifley Government and its Minister for External Affairs. He once applauded an Evatt speech (made in the House of Representatives, Canberra, on 26 February 1947), in which Evatt called for India's cooperation in establishing a regional body committed to the interests of South Eastern Asia and the West Pacific:

> That was a wise speech of Dr. Evatt, and the general policy that the Australian Commonwealth has been following in regard to foreign policy has been a wise policy because it is thinking in realistic terms of the present; it is thinking of these areas which are tied together. ...because the economic factor, and even the defence factor override these political boundaries and other considerations.[146]

Evatt like his predecessor Chifley continued in Opposition (as Leader) to pay tribute to Nehru seeing him as important to world peace. During a debate in Parliament on external affairs, he acknowledged approvingly Minister Casey's tribute to Nehru, while he himself described Nehru in these words: 'the great Prime Minister of India, Mr Nehru, the conciliator, the man who, of all the leaders of the world to-day has done most for conciliation in a troubled world.'[147]

This portrayal of Nehru-Chifley/Evatt affinity is important to this analysis because of one of its postulates that there were peaks and troughs in the bilateral relationship influenced by personalities and policies and also by the political party of the government in Canberra.

## 1949-1964: Dissonance and Regression

True, the normal bilateral communications that take place between two countries like India and Australia with the change of government in 1949 continued but, for most of the Menzies-led period, the bilateral relationship was hamstrung by the indifference, even hostility, that characterised the relationship between Nehru and Menzies. It lacked the friendly spirit that marked the earlier Nehru Chifley engagement. The often embittered confrontations between the two in the United Nations (Suez crisis and Five power resolution), and at Commonwealth Prime Ministers Conferences, (Apartheid and South Africa's membership), did nothing to help raise the bilateral relationship to an effective level. Driven by differing world views, each held divergent policy positions on the international conflicts that arose during their Prime Ministerial terms. Racial equality, morality in international behaviour and a refusal to be engaged in the Cold War, were cardinal tenets of Nehru's philosophy. In contrast, notions of white superiority, an obsession with the Empire and royalty, a fetishtic fear of Communism, and dependence on the Anglo-US attachment for protection of a predominantly European Australia, underpinned Menzies' persuasion. While Nehru's belief in international peace was genuinely held, Menzies condoned the use of force in the settlement of conflict and the containment of communism. In a sense, it was a case of internationalism *versus* national self-interest.

This dissonance between the two leaders constituted a substantial barrier to better bilateral relations. An early example of the roots of dissension were Menzies' comments in the House of Representatives in March 1951 on the Kashmir issue and Pakistan's importance to

Australia's position in the Middle East,[148] The two men were also divided on the question of South Africa's expulsion from the Commonwealth Association in 1961 on account of its policy of Apartheid. Menzies failed to come to terms with Nehru's philosophy of non-alignment. The doctrine sprang from, among other things, Nehru's love of freedom after nearly a century of being under imperial Britain, and a fear of neo-colonialism, as well as the formidable presence of two communist giants in India's neighbourhood. Menzies, however, saw it as providing solace to the communist camp and, unlike his External Affairs Minister Casey, showed little interest in trying to understand a country not aligned with the West. Concepts of imperialism, the love of freedom after centuries of colonialism, and international peace efforts (rather than military-power alliances), meant little to Menzies. Yet, they were the issues of primary interest for Nehru. An address by him to the Lok Sabha, perhaps best illustrates India's Cold War concerns:

> As peace was said to be indivisible in the present day world, so also freedom was indivisible. ... If freedom was to be established, in the world ... imperialism had to be completely liquidated.[149]

## Casey, External Affairs and the Menzies Factor

Where was Casey, Minister for External Affairs, during this period of relative regression? Unlike Menzies, who had difficulty dealing with non-Europeans, Casey's credentials in India were impressive. There was not even a hint of racism in his attitude to Indians, right from the start of his term as Governor of Bengal in British India. Britain's Prime Minister Atlee, in a letter to Casey on the termination of his assignment in India, wrote ' you have both been an inspiration to Europeans and Indians in most difficult times.'[150] *The Times of India,* at the time, praised Casey's 'great patience ...'[151]. Crocker, in a detailed account to Casey on Indo-Australian relations which he describes as 'slight', refers to a few positives, (which includes Casey's good image) and states 'you yourself are well known in India and continually get a good and favourable coverage in the press; ...'[152]. Then there was the radio broadcast in New Delhi to the Indian people by Casey which marked the difference between him and Menzies on their attitude to Nehru, an illustration of the effect of personalities and policies on the bilateral relationship. In contrast to

Menzies who had difficulty accepting Nehru's refusal to condemn communism, Casey in the New Delhi broadcast, praised Nehru as:

> a man who, while making his rejection of the communist way of life so plain, can yet win the confidence and friendship of the leaders of Communism is obviously a great man ...[153].

Despite Casey's sympathy for India's broad political philosophy, ultimately his influence in foreign policy determination was limited by the presence of the domineering Menzies. That the two men had little in common and no affection for each other is exemplified by this Crocker observation: 'it was clear that he (Casey) and Menzies hate one another and that Menzies would sack him if he could. (n.d.)'[154] Casey's disagreement with Menzies over the use of force to settle the Suez crisis was, in his view, the reason for his (Casey's) defeat in the ballot for the Deputy Leadership of the Liberal Party. About this he wrote to Crocker that Menzies' 'speech in the party room ... appeared to me to be almost entirely directed against me, although without mentioning my name.'[155] Casey himself confronted Menzies on one occasion to tell him that 'it was essential that the Prime Minister and Minister for External Affairs should be on terms of easy confidence with each other and that it was very difficult to do my work in the absence of this sort of relationship.'[156]

In an assessment of Casey's performance, *The Sydney Morning Herald,* in February 1956, applauded his contribution to improving Australia's understanding of Asia, but added that the lack of interest in Asia at the 'higher reaches of Cabinet' had hindered Casey's work, although the paper also concluded that he was not a strong man.[157] A stifled Australian Minister for External Affairs (a key portfolio in any bilateral relationship) did little for the cause of the India-Australia bilateral relationship in the Menzies era.

In Chapters Three and Four a closer examination is carried out of the Nehru-Menzies dissonance, their roles in the Cold War, including an attempt to understand the impact of their personalities on the bilateral relationship.

## 1972-1975: Foreign Policy Reform and a New Beginning

The arrival of the Whitlam government in 1972, saw the start of a fresh approach to Australian foreign policy. It was imbued with greater sensitivity to India's own political ethos, and created the climate required for change in the relationship, from indifference to mutual interest and accommodation. While Australia remained within the broad Anglo-US alliance, a number of Whitlam initiatives, including wider consultations on regional issues, are illustrative of a degree of independence in foreign policy, untrammeled by conventions, something that did not go unnoticed in India. Viviani makes the point that: 'Whitlam made the adjustment for Australia to the changing Cold War politics, and laid the foundation for the shift from the alliance and towards the region.'[158]

Claire Clark captures the impact of the Whitlam government's 'bold and rapid initiatives in foreign policy'[159] in what was a dynamic international environment - a period of dramatic change - by suggesting that Australia's earlier foreign policy 'in this ferment ... had seemed sterile, unable to move out of its established ideological mould.'[160] The friendly links and warmth that characterised the India-Australia relationship (at the leadership level) during the Chifley-Evatt-Nehru period, but progressively allowed to dissipate in the subsequent Menzies era, had returned. The first step, *une entente cordiale* between the two nations, had been restored with Whitlam's visit to India in 1973 to be warmly received by Mrs. Gandhi, delighted by his early interest in India. For instance, in an interview on the Australian Broadcasting Commission on 26 May 1973, she was asked why the new Prime Minister of Australia, was visiting India before Australia's 'traditional areas of interest in Asia - Singapore and Malaysia.' Expressing her pleasure at the imminent Whitlam visit to India, Mrs. Gandhi responded with, 'well, Mr. Whitlam has broken many traditions, hasn't he? And I saw in one of his statements that he wants to give greater importance to relationship with India, which we certainly welcome very much.'[161] After her meeting with Whitlam, Mrs. Gandhi said the talks 'have enabled us to have a clearer understanding of the direction which Australia is taking under your dynamic leadership.'[162] Whitlam, who in his speech spoke of Nehru's pioneering role in promoting peace, said, 'I profoundly believe Australia has everything to gain by the closest possible cooperation with India.'[163] *The Statesman*, a prominent Delhi newspaper, wrote: 'Mr Whitlam assured today that he intended to "amend thoroughly" the anomaly that, though India and Australia had much in common, they had not forged "very close" relations between themselves till now.'[164]

Furthermore, Whitlam's decisive repudiation of the 'White Australia' policy removed a lingering Indian concern about Australia, existing from the early Nehruvian years if not before; as well, the more sophisticated Australian diplomats of the Whitlam period, such as Bruce Grant (High Commissioner to India), were better able to deal with Indian sensitivities, as well as a post-Nehru Indian polity, still wedded to non-alignment, but tempered with pragmatism.

Other Whitlam initiatives that had the effect of loosening Australia's constitutional and traditional ties with Britain, so zealously guarded by Menzies, impressed an India reminded of her own ultimate release from the shackles of colonisation and the British Monarchy. There is also the impact of the remarkable convergence of the Whitlam views (1953-1975) with those of Nehru's, extant even after his death in 1964. Conspicuous for little reference to this in any of the earlier writings, it is examined in Chapter Seven of this thesis along with the substance of the Whitlam government's influence on the India-Australia relationship. For the purpose of setting the stage in this Chapter, suffice to say the election of the Whitlam government in 1972 was welcomed in New Delhi by Mrs. Gandhi's government with more than ordinary enthusiasm, raising expectations of an improvement in relations with Australia.

## The Personality Factor

Another supposition of the study concerns the existence of a correlation between personalities, policies and relationships. Australia's foreign policies, old and new, and their effect on the country's image among its regional neighbours, India in this case, underpin one of the postulates of this study of bilateralism that there were distinguishable differences in the three periods identified by the Chifley, Menzies and Whitlam government's attitudes towards India, influenced by individual personalities. While this impact of personalities and policies on the bilateral relationship is examined in Chapters Three and Four below (through an analysis of the Nehru-Menzies Dissonance and Differences), it is necessary to define the concept here as a preliminary to the broader discussion. As a central hypothesis, it is used throughout the thesis to validate its importance.

Both Nehru and Menzies were regarded as arrogant, self-confident and having strong will-power. It was perhaps inevitable that two such strong minded individuals would clash because of competing egos and rival ambitions and, not least, opposing political philosophies. The historical fact that Nehru was an idealist and socialist and Menzies a conservative and pragmatist cannot be overlooked in the general interpretive scheme of things. On the question of policy, it was unlikely that Nehru the internationalist and architect of non-alignment would have much in common with Menzies the British imperialist, Cold War crusader and defender of the 'White Australia' policy.

In the case of Whitlam, his arrogance was legendary but was tempered, in philosophical and policy terms, by his democratic socialist credentials (not unlike Nehru's) and his final abolition of the 'White Australia' policy. In a broad discussion of Whitlam's character, Freudenberg refers to two aspects: 'the pursuit of personal excellence and his contempt for race pride or prejudice.'[165] Moreover, he personally demonstrated a genuine interest in India and its history and culture. James Walter who argues that 'politics is politicians; there is no way to understand it without understanding them ...', refers to the, 'propensity towards contradictory and paradoxical interpretations of Whitlam, ...'[166] and asks:

> How free was our man to interpret his role in his own way, and to what extent did he? How much did such idiosyncratic interpretation affect political outcomes and how much were they shaped by the contingent factors of time and circumstance or the forces of history and society? [167]

Casey, who was appreciated in India and was far more urbane and sophisticated than the provincial Menzies, lacked the strength of personality and political skills to secure a more enlightened policy towards India. Krishna Menon, a major influence in Indian foreign policy between 1947 and 1962, was a complex personality. An internationalist like Nehru, Menon mobilised public opinion in England and allied countries to secure India's independence.[168] Brecher observes that 'he possessed and articulated a comprehensive image of the operational environment' and, on his attitude to the Americans, Brecher adds 'the tone and sweep of Menon's derisive comments on "American imperialism" suggest an intense emotional antipathy,...'[169]. With his strong ideological motivation, Menon held negative images about many issues, notably, colonialism, Apartheid and American hegemony. He was unwavering in his steadfastness on these questions throughout his political life even though some changes to the external environment may have occurred in that time. Yet, in Ramachandram's opinion, 'no Indian, other than Menon, could match Nehru's intellect and the grasp of world events.'[170]

Evatt was a powerful political figure who shared Nehru's socialism and his internationalist world view, but not his anti-racism fervour. Author and diplomat Alan Renouf describes him as 'an internationalist as well as a great Australian nationalist.'[171] In any case, Evatt's period on the international stage with Nehru was too short to have had a major impact on the India-Australia relationship.

The 'atmospherics' of the relationship were conditioned by four variables and combinations within that range. The political personality is a combination of the individual, his or her character traits, historical experiences and a chosen philosophy or ideology which leads to party affiliation. Most are prisoners of their history; few escape from the cage of the past. Donald Horne in *The Lucky Country*, refers to Menzies as a 'frozen Edwardian', [172] for his awkwardness in dealing with aspects of international change; Nehru, it was said, could never divest himself of the political habits and responses he acquired in the anti-colonial struggle against the British.

In terms of policy orientations, it must be remembered that the political leaders of both India and Australia, however dominant within party or cabinet, had to operate in their respective democratic systems and respect the mood of the electorate - as Menzies had learned to his great cost in 1941. The general tenor and thrust of Nehru's foreign policy were certainly consonant with the aspirations of the people of an independent India. Fiercely anti-colonial and proudly nationalistic, they supported the idealistic policy orientation of their revered leader; in particular, the Non-alignment policy was regarded as an expression of India's moral and political leadership in world affairs. In the case of Menzies, his pro-Western stance, his anti-Communism and his advocacy of the 'White Australia' policy were all good domestic politics in that they represented the deeply-held convictions of the vast majority of Australians of the time. Anti-communism paid huge political dividends for Menzies and his successors in helping to rout a demoralised and divided Labor Party and keeping the Coalition in office for a record period.

While public opinion, as reflected in the popular media, was not measurable with any degree of precision that sophisticated methods of polling offer today, they were however, used as a guide to informed opinion. Given the settled political mood of both the Indian and Australian peoples, it was unlikely that Nehru or Menzies would risk the enormous political advantages gained by respecting public opinion, by major policy shifts to accommodate their antagonist's different world view. It was in reality these different world views, sincerely held and diametrically opposed as they were, which prevented any real political convergence between the India of Nehru and the Australia of Menzies.

An aspect of politics in democratic countries which needs to be considered in this context is the role of the Press, first as an instrument in the shaping of public opinion and, second, as a player in the political game with its own agenda, the first often used to secure the second. In Australia, both popular newspapers and magazines were pro-Western, anti-communist and regarded Third World neutralists as dupes and fellow travellers, reflecting the political beliefs and prejudices of owners and editors. Menzies had been forced to recognise the power of the press barons of Australia (especially Fairfax) in 1941 and was determined not to be wounded again. After 1949, the relationship was a symbiotic one. Hocking argues:

> Menzies dominance of Australian domestic politics was, with the telling exception of the Fairfax press, bolstered by media support. In many respects he was the first Australian Prime Minister to understand the media - and radio in particular, to his electoral success.[173]

Nehru, from the beginning, commanded the enormous respect of the domestic media not least because of the depth of his personal involvement and capacity to galvanise a nation during the freedom campaign. Frank Moraes, one time editor of the prestigious *Times of India*, was an admirer of Nehru. But Nehru was not unaware of the importance of an independent media to the young democracy. He cautioned it against exaggerated claims about India's importance in world affairs. He was sensitive to the electorate and criticism from the Left of politics; but it would not be inaccurate to say that, on most foreign policy issues, he carried the media and public opinion with him, the exception being in 1962 when an ill-prepared India was subjected to an attack in its northern border territory by China.

Given the historical shift in the international focus to Asia, bringing regional turbulence to what was once a situation of order, (taken for granted under colonialism), the India-Australia relationship was at its warmest, flourishing briefly under the post-War Chifley government in which both the Prime Minister and the Minister for External Affairs were staunch friends of India and great admirers of Nehru. Labor's voice and choice of words, in Government and in Opposition, were also different to the didactic outpourings of the Menzies era that followed. Evatt saw India 'as the linchpin of Asia' with Asia's future linked to the future of the Indian subcontinent, a bulwark against the communist bogey.[174] Both Chifley and Evatt obviously enjoyed a warm relationship with Nehru, evident from their meetings and exchange of messages.[175]

Despite Labor's genuinely held views about the value to Australia of good relations with India, the Chifley Labor government shared the conservative Opposition's fear of the external threat. Both Chifley and Evatt viewed the security question as of supreme importance to Australia's interest. Evatt, as Minister for External Affairs, was to say ' the primary problem of the post-war world will be that of freedom from fear ... in short the problem of security ...'[176]. Furthermore, as Camilleri argues, the Labor Party's support for decolonisation was also motivated by a fear of the alternative social unrest, a potentially fertile ground for communism taking root.[177]

Last, there was the issue of racial discrimination which Nehru would not compromise on, particularly his resentment of Apartheid. Labor's commitment to a 'White Australia', a policy that enjoyed bipartisan support, did not go unnoticed in India. While Nehru himself may not have made specific mention of Australia's discriminatory Immigration policy, the Indian political elite was aware and resentful of its presence, as revealed in Chapter Five. Australian public opinion was strongly in favour of the 'White Australia' policy and the Chifley government simply could not have acted to remove this barrier to a more developed bilateral relationship without suffering political and electoral damage. Christopher Waters in his book *The Empire Fractures,* suggests that the predominantly (over 90 per cent) Anglo-Irish ancestry of the Australian population in 1947 'was another element that ... constrained the freedom of the Chifley government to act with total independence.'[178]

The media in Australia at the time, would have condemned any government which sought to modify or reform Australia's racist immigration policy. Moreover, the media largely conservative, if not reactionary, in opinion were extremely critical of India's policy of non-alignment which was widely interpreted as aiding and abetting the march of communism. Despite this one blot, Mackay, in a despatch to Evatt, while drawing attention to India's sensitivity on the racially based Immigration policy, expressed optimism about the bilateral relationship:

> Apart from her 'White Australia' policy, Australia's stock in India stands high today. A tone of friendliness and goodwill runs through practically all references to Australia in the Press.[179]

If this says anything at all, it is that, despite the undoubted mutual respect and warmth that characterised the briefly formed positive connection between India and Australia during the Nehru/ Chifley-Evatt period, Australia's commitment to security, and consequently, the US for its protection, taken together with its non-European exclusion immigration policy, were factors that stood in the way of the relationship achieving its full promise. Officers of India's Ministry of External Affairs interviewed in New Delhi in 1997, did not disagree with this conclusion.[180] The meagre two year period of the relationship, before its abrupt termination with the Chiefly government losing office in December 1949, was also unhelpful to the cause of a more fruitful, enduring bilateral relationship.

Menzies' assumption of the Prime Ministership fundamentally altered the nature of the relationship. While outwardly the relationship seemed cosy enough at the diplomatic level, closer examination reveals an illusion of simplicity in the relationship and masked a deeper conundrum. The contrasting perceptions each had of the other tell the story. T.B. Millar captures the essentials:

> To India, Australia has probably appeared reactionary, unduly influenced by Western policies, imbued with a sense of racial superiority, wealthy, brash, a little Britannia, firmly clasping the-coat tails of Uncle Sam. To Australia, India has seemed hypocritical,

> demanding, sanctimonious and obstructive, much readier to accept
> the good faith and to promote the interests of a communist than
> of a Western state.[181]

Furthermore, a number of international policy issues of the Cold War period on which the two countries took diametrically opposing positions, reflecting basic differences in the way each viewed the world, offer illuminating historical insights into the prevailing mood of indifference between India and Australia in the 1950s and 1960s. Equally abundant are the records of the spirited, occasionally irascible, exchanges that took place between Prime Ministers Nehru and Menzies, whose leadership of their respective nations ran parallel for fifteen consecutive years from 1949. The foreign policy direction provided by the two men, through consistent application of their respective doctrinal politics (and personalities) to international situations, is therefore pivotal to the analysis of the relationship between the two countries in the 1949-1964 period, where the difference was real-politik *versus* morality. It also represents the major part of the span of the period covered in this examination.

Ironically, there were personalities such as Casey and Crocker in the Menzies period who were capable of a better relationship with India but who lacked the strength or authority of Menzies. Crocker, for instance, said of India-Australia relations:

> ...one fact will always remain beyond dispute and that is the
> nearness of the two countries to one another. ... While as for
> outlook, inspite of all differences it is nearer to us than is any other
> Asian country.[182]

Another indicator of the mutual indifference that characterised the relationship is that the economic and cultural interests of both countries found fulfillment through being channeled elsewhere, not with each other. Yet trade and cultural interactions are important determinants of successful bilateralism. Besides these and other differences that marred the relationship in the Menzies era, which represents a low ebb, the research for this book, points to the positive impact of the 1972 Whitlam government. With Whitlam's broader ideology capable of transcending India's non-alignment and racial sensitivities, it became a precursory turning point in the post 1970s development of the relationship giving it a new future. Hence, the hypothesis is advanced that the India-Australia relationship moved from mutual respect and understanding (1947-1949) to indifference (1949-1972) and then accommodation and mutual interest in the Whitlam period (1972-1975). The comparison of the three periods makes sense in the context of the relative differences obtaining in the quality of the relationship in each; particularly at the psycho-political level, it enables a personality impact comparison that provides a valuable basis for examining the bilateral relationship over the whole period, 1947-1975.

# Endnotes


1. In the National Interest - Australia's Foreign and Trade Policy, White Paper, DFAT, AGPS, Canberra, 1997, p 53.

2. See *Inter alia*, David Anderson (ed.), *Australia and Indonesia: A Partnership in the Making*, Pacific Security Research Institute, Sydney, 1991; Ravinder K. Varma, *Australia and Southeast Asia: The Crystallization of a relationship*, Abhinav Publications, New Delhi, 1973; H.A. Dunn, and Edmund S.K. Fung, (eds.) *Sino-Australia Relations: the records 1972-1985*, Centre for the Study of Australia-Asia Relations, Griffith University, Qld. 1985; Norman A. Harper, *Great and Powerful Friend: A Study of Australian American Relations between 1900 and 1975*, University of Qld. Press, Qld. 1987; Z. Marshallsay, (ed.), *Australia-Malaysia relations: New Roads Ahead*, Monash Asia Institute, Victoria, 1996; D. Phillips, *Ambivalent Allies: Myth and Reality in the Australian American Relationship*, Penguin, Victoria, 1988.

3. Higgott, Richard A. and George, Jim, 'Tradition and Change in the Study of International Relations in Australia', *International Political Science Review*, Vol. II, No. 4, 1990, p 431.

4. Casey, R.G., *An Australian in India*, Hollis & Carter, London, 1947, p 103.

5. Lun, Phan Van, 'The Buddhist Crisis in Vietnam 1963-1966', Ph.D. thesis, in Nguyen Ngoc Tan 'The Miracle of Vietnam: The Establishment and Consolidation of Ngo Dinh Diem's Regime 1954-1959', Ph.D. thesis, Monash University, Melbourne, 1997, p 2.

6. Tyabji, Nasir, *A Round table Discussion on Australia-India Relations*, held at the Nehru Memorial Library, New Delhi, on 14 February, 1995, published by the Australian High Commission, New Delhi, March 1995, p 108.

7. Mediansky, F. A., 'The Conservative Style In Australian Foreign Policy,' *Australian Outlook*, Vol. 28, No. 1, April 1974, p. 50.

8. Cox, Dave, (Book Review-*Evatt to Evans: The Labor Tradition in Australian Foreign Policy*, Allen & Unwin, 1997.) *Australian Journal of Political Science*, Vol. 33, No. 1, March 1998, p 133.

9. Mathur, P.C., *Political Contours of India's Modernity*, Aelekh Publishers, Jayapur, India, 1994, p 27.

10. *Ibid.*

11. AA, Despatch No. 23, 6 December 1954 from W.R. Crocker to R.G. Casey, Series A1838/263, Item 169/10/1, Part 2.

12. Copland, Ian, Seminar discussion, *Australia And India: The Next Ten Years*, South Asian Studies Group, Melbourne, 1991, p 47. (See under Conference Papers category in Bibliography)

13. Brett, Judith, 'A small nation like our's needs its Asian friends,' *The Age*, Melbourne, 19 June 1997, p A17.

14. Peacock, Roger Seminar discussion, *Australia And India: The Next Ten Years*, South Asian Studies Group, Melbourne, 1991, p 55. 'It is not an accident that French was the second language taught in Australian schools up to the sixties. Australia's British heritage remained strong it seems in those who determined education policy with France next door.' See David Lee and Christopher Waters, (eds.), *Evatt to Evans: The Labor Tradition in Australian Foreign Policy*, Allen & Unwin, NSW, 1997, p 2.

15. 'Asia in Australian Higher Education', Report of the Inquiry into the Teaching of Asian Studies and Languages in Higher Education, the Asian Studies Council, January 1989, p 33.

16. 'A National Strategy for the Study of Asia in Australia', Asian Studies Council, 1988, p 2.

17. See Don Plimer Consultancies Report, 'Performance evaluation of the National Centre for South Asian Studies', 1996, p ii.

18. Vicziany, M., Seminar discussion, *Australia And India: The Next Ten Years*, South Asian Studies Group, Melbourne, 1991, p 57.

19. Peacock, Roger Seminar discussion, *Australia and India: The Next Ten Years*, South Asian Studies Group, Melbourne, 1991, pp 54-55. (See under Conference Papers category in Bibliography) Examination of AA, Series A1838/1, Item 553/1/14/1, Part 1, reveals the existence of 17 cultural agreements (from 1951-1963) between India and countries of Asia, Eastern Europe, USSR, Greece, the Middle East etc. Australia was not among them.

20. Jim Davidson, (personal communication) 7 March 2000, at Victoria University of Technology, Footscray Park, Melbourne.

21. *Ibid.*

22. Greenwood, Gordon, 'Australian Foreign Policy in Action', *Australia in World Affairs 1956-1960*, Gordon Greenwood and Norman Harper, (eds.) *F.W.* Cheshire, Melbourne, 1963, p 95.

23. Neale, R.G., 'Australia's Changing Relations with India', *India, Japan, Australia: Partners in Asia?* J.D.B. Millar, (ed.), ANU, Canberra, 1968, p 67.

24. AA, Despatch 23, 6 December 1954, from W. R. Crocker to R.G. Casey, Series A1838/283, Item 169/10/1, Part 2, p 2.

25. *Ibid.* For Crocker conversation with Mrs Pandit and his opinion of her see, AA, A1838/283, Item 169/10/4.

26. *The Hindu*, Madras, 8 December, 1958. Also see, *Foreign Affairs Record*, Government of India, New Delhi, Vol. 8. No. 10, October 1962, for Tunku's complimentary references to Nehru.

27. George, T.J.S. (ed.), *India at Fifty 1947-1997*, Express Publications, Chennai, India, 1997, p 41.

28. Australian Archives, (AA), Despatch No. 2/64, 2 June 1964, from J Plimsoll, Australian High Commissioner, New Delhi, Series A1838/272, Item 169/1/3, Part 3.

29. AA, Document, subject: 'Cultural Agreements', Series A1838/1, Item 553/1/14/1, Part 1.

30. East Asia Analytical Unit, *Australia's India Strategy: India's Economy at the Midnight Hour*, Department of Foreign Affairs and Trade, (DFAT), Australian Government Printing Service, (AGPS), Canberra, 1994, p 205.

31. Gordon, Sandy and Henningham, Stephen (eds.) *India Looks East: An Emerging Power and its Asia Pacific Neighbours*, Strategic Defence Studies Centre, ANU, Canberra, 1995, pp 18-19.

32. AA, Report - prepared for the Commonwealth Relations Conference in Lahore, 1954, 'India and the Commonwealth' Part II, Economic, by B.N. Ganguli, Series A4311, Item 174/1.

33. *Ibid.*

34. See AA, Report-'Trade Relations with India', CP 554/1, Item 2/174/B/1 for an analysis of India's exports to Australia from 1956-1971. A.L. Lougheed and K.C. Roy, 'India's Export Trade With Australia: Problems and Prospects,' *Australian Outlook*, Vol. 28, No. 2, August 1974, pp 179-186.

35. Lougheed, A.L. and Roy, K.C., 'India's Export Trade With Australia : Problems and Prospects,' *Australian Outlook*, Vol. 28, No. 2, August 1974, p 180.

36. Greenwood, Gordon and Harper, Norman (eds.) *Australia in World Affairs 1956-1960*, F.W. Cheshire, Melbourne, 1963. p 11.

37. Lok Sabha Debates, 4 June 1951, Vol. VIII, Col. 4898-4899. Also see, National Archives of India, (NAI) Anti-Indian propaganda - Australian press, File No. 12/11-XPP; File No. 23/1/10-XPP (1951); File No. 7/2/25-XPP (1950).

38. Bhandari, Romesh, 'India's Sun in the Ascendant,' *New India Digest*, Vol. 1, No. 25, May-June 1996, p 10.

39. 'India: Retreat from the West,' *TRT*, No. 177, December, 1954, p 70. Also see, NAI, 'American Press Comments on India 1948-49', File No. 45(347) AMS; 'World Press', File No. 111/52/55610/41-70.

40. AA, Report from the Australian High Commission in New Delhi to DEA, 28 August 1950, Series A1838/283, Item 382/4/1.

41. AA, Report from Acting High Commissioner Francis Stuart to DEA, 27 July 1950, Series A1838/278, Item 3123/7/13.

42. *Jawaharlal Nehru's Speeches, Sept. 1946-May 1949*, Vol. I, Ministry of Information and Broadcasting, Government of India, 1949, p 220. Also see, NAI, 'Anti Indian False report, UK' File No. PIII/52/55658/41.

43. Donelan, Michael Book Review, (John Hohenberg, *Between Two Worlds: Policy, Press and Public Opinion in Asian- American Relations*, Praeger New York, 1967) *International Affairs, A Quarterly Review* Vol. 44, No. 1, January 1968, p 168.

44. *Ibid.*

45. *Ibid.*, p 169.

46. Crocker, W.R. *Australian Ambassador: International Relations at First Hand*, Melbourne University Press, Victoria, Australia, 1971, p 205.

47. AA, Despatch from W.R. Crocker, to R.G. Casey, Minister for External Affairs, Canberra, 23 December 1954, Series A4534/1, Item 44/6/2. Goa was taken from Portuguese control by the Indian army in December 1961.

48. *Ibid.*

49. Crocker, W.R. *Australian Ambassador: International Relations at First Hand*, Melbourne University Press, Victoria, 1971, p v. (Foreword)

50. *Ibid.*

51. Casey, R.G., *An Australian in India*, Hollis & Carter, London, 1947, p 13.

52. Interview with Max Teichman, 9 October 1999, at Clifton Hill, Melbourne.

53. Gordon, Sandy, *The Search for Substance: Australia-India Relations into the Nineties and Beyond*, ANU Canberra, 1993, pp 2-3.

54. Gordon, Sandy and Henningham, Stephen (eds.) 'India: Australia's Neglected Neighbour,' *India Looks East An Emerging Power and its Asia Pacific Neighbours*, ANU, Canberra, 1995, p 233.

55. Lok Sabha Debates, Vol. V, Part II, 1950, Col. 232.

56. See Ravinder Kumar, *The Making of a Nation: Essays in Indian History and Politics*, Manohar Publications, New Delhi, 1989, pp 174-192.

57. Gurry, Meg Book Review, (India's Economy at the Midnight Hour, AGPS, 1994), *South Asia: Journal of South Asian Studies*, New Series, Vol. XVII, No. 2, December 1994, pp 140-142.

58. For a comprehensive listing of all remaining restrictions applying to non-European migrants and preferential treatment of Europeans, removed by the Whitlam Government, see, Gough Whitlam, *The Whitlam Government: 1972-1975*, Viking, Victoria, 1985, pp 501-502.

59. AA, Statement by R.G. Menzies, Series A1838/278, Item 169/10/7 part 1.

60. McInnes, N., 'To Indians Distant, Insignificant,' *The Bulletin*, 28 December, 1960, p 25.

61. Hudson, W.J. & Way, Wendy (eds.), *Documents on Australian Foreign Policy 1937-1949*, Vol. X, July-December 1946, DFAT, AGPS, Canberra, 1995, p 534.

62. *Jawaharlal Nehru's Speeches*, Vol. II, August 1949 - February 1953, Ministry of Information & Broadcasting, Government of India, New Delhi, 1954, p 248.

63. National Library of Australia (NLA), M S 4936, series 8, box 329 in Meg Gurry 'No Will or No Way, Australia's Relations with India 1947-1993,' Ph.D. thesis, Latrobe University, Victoria, 1993, pp 165-166

64. Millar, T.B. (ed.), *The Australian Foreign Minister: The Diaries of R.G. Casey*, Collins, London, 1972, p 155.

65. AA, Record of meeting of the Foreign Affairs Committee with an Indian team on 11 May 1962 in Canberra, Series A1838/275, Item 1531/99, Part 1.

66. Parliamentary Debate, Vol. II, Part II, 6-25 March 1954, Col. 2827.

67. Josh, Harcharan Singh (ed.) *India's Foreign Policy: Nehru to Rao*, Indian Council of World Affairs, Surjeet Publications, Delhi, 1994, p 36.

68. Bandyopadhyaya, J. *North Over South*, South Asian Publishers, New Delhi, 1982, p 204.

69. Chakrabarty, D. 'Open Space, Public Place: Garbage Modernity and India', *South Asia: Journal of South Asian Studies*, New Series, Vol. XIV, June 1991, p 15.

70. Bowles, Chester, 'New India', *Foreign Affairs*, Vol. 31, October-September 1952-1953, p 79.

71. Heriot, Geoff Seminar discussion, *Australia And India: The Next Ten Years*, South Asian Studies Group, Melbourne, 1991, p 61.

72. Casey, R.G., *An Australian in India*, Hollis and Carter, London, 1947, p 115.

73. AA, Despatch 23 December 1954, from W.R. Crocker to R.G. Casey, Series A4534/1, Item 44/6/2.

74. AA, Memorandum 12 December, 1955, from J. Oldham, to DEA, Series A1838/283, Item 169/11/52, Part 3.

75. Jetley, Neerja Pawha 'Political see-saws, red tape, plain hostility: foreign investors run scared,' *Outlook*, India, October 13, 1997, p 54.

76. Ward, Colin Seminar discussion, *Australia And India: The Next Ten Years*, South Asian Studies Group, Melbourne, 1991, p 31.

77. Jetley, Neerja Pahwa 'Political see-saws, red tape, plain hostility: foreign investors run scared,' *Outlook*, India, October 13, 1997, p 54.

78. 'GM will diversify role in India, Invest US$ 1 billion in 3 years', *The Times of India*, New Delhi, 11 November 1997, p 15. Also see, *The Times of India*, 12 November 1997 for John Smith interview with T. Dasgupta and B. Mukherji, p 13.

79. Gupta, S.P., 'India's Increasing Eastern Orientation in Trade and Investment: Context and Challenges', *India Looks East: An Emerging Power and its Asia Pacific Neighbours*,

Sandy Gordon and Stephen Henningham, (eds.), ANU, Canberra, 1995, p 79. Also see, East Asia Analytical Unit, 'Impediments to Growth and competitiveness of Indian Industry to Date', *India's Economy at the Midnight Hour: Australia's India Strategy*, DFAT, AGPS, Canberra, 1994, p 49.

80. Dodwell, David Book Review, (Bhagwati Jagdish, *A Stream of Windows, 1998*), *Far Eastern Economic Review*, 24 June 1999, p 48.

81. AA, Despatch No. 23, 6 December 1954, from W.R. Crocker to R.G. Casey, Series A1838/283, Item 169/10/1, Part 2. For principal imports from India to Australia, see, AA, CP 554/1/1, Buss 2/174/8/1, Appendix B, and CP 554/1/ 1 Buss 2/174/01. Trade was also affected by difficulties obtaining import licences for shipment of goods to India and concerns over Australia's wheat infestation. For these and other trade enquiries including interest in uranium imports, see AA, Report on India-Trade Enquiries, Series A1838/1, Item 169/ 10/2/1.

82. *India's Foreign Policy, Selected Speeches, September 1946-April 1961*, Ministry of Information & Broadcasting, Government of India, New Delhi, 1961. For further evidence of India's uninterest in Australia see, *Foreign Policy of India: Texts of Documents 1947-64*, Lok Sabha Secretariat, New Delhi, 1966, listing Treaties, Agreements, Resolutions, Proposals and Joint Communiqués with 44 countries. Australia is not mentioned once.

83. Tharoor, Shashi, *India: From Midnight to Millennium*, Arcade Publishing, New York, 1997, pp 8-9.

84. 'India Today and Tomorrow,' extracts from the Moulana Azad Memorial Lecture, delivered by J. Nehru, *The Times*, Ceylon, 14 September 1959, p 6.

85. Nehru, Jawaharlal, *Vision of India*, Indian Council for Cultural Relations, New Delhi, 1981, p 191.

86. Tharoor, *op. cit.*, p 7. Also see, Sadhiv Kakar, *The Indian Psyche*, Viking, New Delhi, 1996.

87. An interview with Bruce Grant, 9 May 1999, at Domain Street, South Yarra, Melbourne.

88. Evans and Grant, *op. cit.* p 32.

89. For India's mediatory role in international crises and Nehru's impact on the world, see G. Ramachandram, *Nehru and World Peace*, Radiant Publishers, New Delhi, 1990, pp 59-97.

90. Millar, T.B. *Australia's Foreign Policy*, Angus & Robertson, Sydney, 1968, p xiii (Introduction).

91. Camilleri, J.A. *An Introduction to Australian Foreign Policy*, Fourth Edition, The Jacaranda Press, Qld., 1979, p 10.

92. Andrews E.M., 'Patterns in Australian Foreign Policy,' *Australian Outlook*, Vol. 26, No. 1, April 1972, p 31.

93. *Ibid.*

94. CPD, (H of R), Vol. 157, p 429, in Alan Watt, *The Evolution of Australian Foreign Policy 1938-1965*, Cambridge University Press, London, 1967, p 20.

95. Andrews, E.M., *A History of Australian Foreign Policy*, Longman Cheshire, Melbourne, 1979, Documents 103.

96. Watt, Alan. *The Evolution of Australian Foreign Policy 1938-1965*, Cambridge University Press, London, 1967, p 20.

97. Suter, Keith. *Is There Life After ANZUS*, Pluto Press, Sydney, 1987, p 30.

98. ANA, DEA Listening Post, New Delhi, Series A1838/278, Item 3123/7/13.

99. Josh, Harcharan Singh (ed.) *India's Foreign Policy: Nehru to Rao*, Indian Council of World Affairs, Surjeet Publications, Delhi, 1994, p 11.

100. *Ibid.*

101. Appadorai, A., *Select Documents on India's Foreign Policy and Relations 1947-1972*, Vol. 1, Oxford University Press, New Delhi, 1982, p 6.

102. Panikkar, K.M., *France Observateur*, 21 April 1955, in Phillipe Braillard and Mohammad Reza Djalili, *The Third World and International Relations*, Lynne Rienner Publishers, Colorado, 1986, p 51.

103. Ramachandram, G., *Nehru and World Peace*, Radiant Publishers, 1990, New Delhi, p 102.

104. Camilleri, J.A., *An Introduction to Australian Foreign Policy*, Fourth Edition, Jacaranda Press, Qld. 1979, p 14.

105. Millar T.B., 'The Australia-Britain Relationship: Where Has It Come To?', *TRT*, No. 266, April 1977, p 195.

106. Waters, Christopher, *The Empire Fractures: Anglo-Australian Conflict in the 1940s*, Australian Scholarly Publishing, Melbourne, 1995. pp 11-12.

107. CPD, (H of R), Vol. 15, 27 October 1954, p 2382.

108. Cowan, Zelman, *The Sunday Times*, Sri Lanka, 13 December 1987, p 5.

109. *Ibid.*

110. Miller, J.D.B., 'The development of International Studies in Australia 1933-83', *Australian Outlook*, Vol. 37, No. 3, December 1983, p 139.

111. Evans, Gareth, 'The Labor Tradition: A View from the 1990s', *Evatt to Evans: The Labor Tradition in Australian Foreign Policy*, David Lee & Christopher Waters, (eds.) Allen & Unwin, NSW, 1997, p 12.

112. Low, David, Book Review, (*Brave New World: Dr. H.V. Evatt and Australian Foreign Policy*, David Day, ed.), *Australian Journal of Political Science*, Vol. 32, No. 1, March 1997, p 130.

113. Andrews, E.M. *A History of Australian Foreign Policy*, Longman Cheshire, Melbourne, 1979, pp 117-120.

114. Edwards, Peter and Pemberton, Gregory, *Crises and Commitments*, Allen & Unwin Sydney, 1992, p 152.

115. 'Australia: A Debate on Foreign Policy', *TRT*, No. 155, June 1949, p 281.

116. *Ibid.*, p 284.

117. *Ibid.*

118. CPD, (H of R), Vol. 12, 25 September 1956, p 830.

119. Whitlam, E.G., 'Nehru, Champion of freedom', address at an International Seminar on 'Nehru, the Man and his Vision', to celebrate the hundredth birth anniversary of Nehru, organized by UNESCO, Sydney, 27 -29 September, 1989. An Annual Report by India's High Commissioner in Australia, M.S. Duleepsinjhi, reflects India's more favourable attitude to Evatt and Labor. Commenting on the decline in popularity of the Menzies Liberal Country Party Government, the High Commissioner states, 'it is unlikely that he (Menzies) will come through the next general elections.' Duleepsinjhi proceeds to comment on doubts expressed early in the year about Evatt (then Leader of the Opposition) making a popular leader, and adds '... but he has during the year consolidated his position and now there is no doubt that he will be the next PM if Labor wins the next elections.' See NAI, Annual Political Report, (1st January 1952 to 31st December 1952), p 1.

120. Edwards, Peter & Pemberton, Gregory, *Crises and Commitments*, Allen & Unwin, Sydney, 1992, p 20.

121. *Foreign Affairs*, XLIV, April, 1966, pp 448-449, in Amry & Mary Belle Vandenbosch, *Australia Faces Southeast Asia*, University of Kentucky Press, Lexington, 1967, p 38.

122. NAI, Annual Political Report (1st January 1952 to 31st December 1952), M.S. Duleepsinjhi, High Commissioner for India in Australia, Canberra, pp 7-8.

123. Mukherjee, S., *A Roundtable Discussion on Australia-India Relations*, held at the Nehru Memorial Library, New Delhi on 14 February 1995, published by the Australian High Commission, New Delhi, 1995, p 108.

124. Reddy, E.S. and Damodaran, A.K., *Krishna Menon at the United Nations: India and the World*, Sanchar Publishing House, New Delhi, 1994, p 239.

125. *India 1993- A Reference Annual*, Ministry of Information & Broadcasting, Government Of India, New Delhi, 1994. Also see, Amiya Rao & B.G. Rao, *Six Thousand Days*, Sterling Publishers, New Delhi, 1974, p 245.

126. *Jawaharlal Nehru's Speeches*, Vol. 1, September 1946 to May 1949, Ministry of Information & Broadcasting, Government of India, New Delhi, 1949, p 324. For Australia-India involvement in the Indonesian independence issue see following documents in David Lee, (ed.) *Australia and Indonesia's Independence: The Transfer of Sovereignty, Documents 1949*, Vol. XV, DFAT, AGPS, Canberra, 1998. Doc: 350, p 361; Doc: 338, p 348; Doc: 309, p 321; Doc 308, p 321; Doc: 241, p 249; Doc: 242, p 249; Doc: 243, p 250.

127. *Ibid.*, p 257.

128. Edwards and Pemberton *op. cit.*, p 16.

129. UN Security Council Official Records, No. 133, December 23, 1948, p 11, in Amry and Mary Belle Vandenbosch, *Australia Faces Southeast Asia*, University of Kentucky Press, Lexington, 1967, p 36. Some believe that Chifley's decision to send the question of Indonesia's independence to the Security Council was probably affected by similar action proposed by India. See J.A.C. Mackie, 'Indonesia', in Gordon Greenwood & Norman Harper, (eds.) *Australia in World Affairs 1956-1960*, F.W. Cheshire, Melbourne, 1963, p 278.

130. *Jawaharlal Nehru's Speeches*, Vol. 1, September 1946-May 1949, Ministry of Broadcasting and Information, Government of India, 1949, p 328.

131. Dennis, Peter 'Australia and Indonesia: The Early Years,' *Australia and the end of Empires*, David Lowe, (ed.), Deakin University Press, Victoria, 1996, p 43. For the correspondence between DEA and the High Commission in New Delhi on the India-Australia involvement in Indonesia's independence from the Dutch, see David Lee (ed.), *Australia and Indonesia's Independence: The transfer of sovereignty, Documents 1949*, Vol. XV, DFAT, AGPS, Canberra, 1998.

132. CPD, (H of R), 7 March 1951, p 82.

133. Quoted by H.A. Wolfson, 'Australian Foreign Policy and the Indonesian Disputes' paper No. 2, Studies submitted by the Australian Institute of External Affairs, as preparatory papers for the Eleventh Conference of the Institute of Pacific Relations at Lucknow, 1950, in Amry & Mary Belle Vandenbosch, *Australia Faces Southeast Asia*, University of Kentucky Press, Lexington, 1967, pp 36-37. The contrasting attitude to colonialism between the Chifley Government and that of the Menzies' which followed. is also seen in Liberal MHR, Anderson's statement blaming the Labor Government's policy for Indonesia's premature independence from the Dutch and the risks of a Communist take-over. See, CPD, (H of R), Vol. 19, 1 May 1958, p 1378.

134. CPD (Senate) Vol. 201, March 2 1949, p 826.

135. Crisp, L. F., *Ben Chifley: A Political Biography*, Angus & Robertson, London, 1977, pp 284-285.

136. *Ibid.*, p 277.

137. CPD, (H of R), Vol. 212, 7 March 1951, p 82.

138. Crisp. *op. cit.*, pp 286-287.

139. Hudson, W.J. and Way, Wendy (eds.) *Documents on Australian Foreign Policy, 1937-49*, Vol. X: July-December 1946, DFAT, AGPS, Canberra, 1995, p 146. Apart from

Atlee, who was Labour Prime Minister of Britain, Bevin, Morrison and Cripps were prominent political figures at the time.

140. *Ibid.*, pp 146-147.

141. *Ibid.*, p 147.

142. *Ibid.*

143. *Ibid.*, p 178. Also see, *ibid.* Note by Mackay of conversation with Evatt dated 26 August 1946, p 146.

144. *Ibid.*, pp 178-179.

145. Watt, Alan, *The Evolution of Australian Foreign Policy, 1938-1965*, Cambridge University Press, London, 1967, p 72.

146. *Selected Works of Jawaharlal Nehru*, Second Series, Vol. II, S. Gopal (ed.), J. Nehru Memorial Fund, New Delhi, 1984, p 582.

147. CPD, (H of R), Vol. 18, 15 April 1958, p 875.

148. 'Menzies View of Kashmir Issue,' a report on the Menzies Statement on Foreign Affairs in the (H of R), on 7 March 1951, *The Hindustan Times*, India, 10 May 1951, p 5.

149. *Jawaharlal Nehru's Speeches*, September 1957-April 1963, Ministry of Information & Broadcasting, Government of India, New Delhi, 1964, p 285.

150. Hudson, W.J. *Casey*, Oxford University Press, Melbourne, 1986, p 178.

151. *Ibid.*

152. AA, Despatch No. 23, 6 December 1954, from W.R. Crocker to R.G. Casey, 1954, Series A1838/283, Item 169/10/1 Part 2, p 2.

153. AA, Text of Broadcast by R.G. Casey on All India Radio, on 13 October 1955, Series A4534/1, Item 44/6/2.

154. Gurry, Meg, 'Whose History? The Struggle over Authorship of Australia's Asia Policies', *Australian Journal of International Affairs*, Vol. 52, No. 1, April 1998. p 81.

155. Hudson, W.J., *Casey*, Oxford University Press, Melbourne, 1986, p 276. For Menzies' statement on the imposition of sanctions against Egypt and support for Anglo-French intervention and Casey's opposition to it, see Neville Meaney, *Australia and the World*, Longman Cheshire, Melbourne, 1985, pp 619-622 (Docs. 331, 332 & 333).

156. *Ibid.*, p 265.

157. *The Sydney Morning Herald*, 6 February, 1956, in W.J. Hudson, *Casey*, Oxford University Press, Melbourne, 1986, pp 286-287.

158. Viviani, Nancy, 'The Whitlam Government's Policy Towards Asia', *Evatt to Evans: The Labor Tradition in Australian Foreign Policy*, David Lee & Christopher Waters, (eds.), Allen & Unwin, NSW, 1997, p 109.

159. Clark, Claire, (ed.), *Australian Foreign Policy: Towards A Reassessment*, Cassell, North Melbourne, 1973, p ix.

160. *Ibid.* Among the major events at this time were, admission of the Peoples Republic of China to the UN; President Nixon's visit to China; The breaking away of East Pakistan and birth of Bangladesh; the NAM proposal sponsored by Sri-Lanka, for treating the Indian Ocean as a neutral zone.

161. Prime Minister Indira Gandhi's Interview to Australian Broadcasting Commission, New Delhi, 26 May 1973, in Satish Kumar, (ed.) *Documents on India's Foreign Policy 1972*, Macmillan, New Delhi, 1976, p 216.

162. Ministry of External Affairs (MEA), *Foreign Affairs Record*, Vol. 19, July 16-22, 1973, Government of India, New Delhi, p 215.

163. *Ibid.*, p 217.

164. *The Statesman*, Delhi, 5 June 1973, p 1.

165. Freudenberg, Graham. *A Certain Grandeur*, Sun Books, South Melbourne, 1978, p 67.

166. Walter, James., *The Leader: A Political Biography of Gough Whitlam*, University of Queensland. Press, Qld. 1980, p xviii. (Preface).

167. *Ibid.*.

168. Sen, S.P. (ed.), *Dictionary of National Biography*, Vol. III, Institute of Historical Studies, India, 1974, pp 98-101. Krishna Menon was a member of the Lok Sabha in 1959 and 1962; was High Commissioner to the UK from 1947-1952; and Minister for Defence 1957-1962; he was also a local government councillor of St Pancras, London pre 1947.

169. Brecher, Michael., *India and World Politics*, Oxford University Press, London, 1968, p 301.

170. Ramachandram, G., *Nehru and World Peace*, Radiant Publishers, New Delhi, 1990, p 60.

171. 'Portrait of H.V. Evatt', Southern Cross Programme, Discovery Channel, Foxtel Television, 2.00-3.00 p.m. 18 June 2000.

172. Cited by Judith Brett, in *Robert Menzies': Forgotten People*, Macmillan, Sydney, 1992, p 2.

173. Hocking , Jenny (Book Review of A.W. Martin, *Robert Menzies: A Life*, Vol. 2, Melbourne University Press, 1999), *The Australian's Review of Books*, Vol. 4, Issue 10, November 1999, p 21.

174. Dalziel, A., *Evatt the Enigma*, Lansdowne Press, Melbourne, 1967, p 67.

175. See, Alan Watt, *The Evolution of Australian Foreign Policy 1938-1965*, Cambridge University Press, London, 1967, pp 220-221; W.J. Hudson & Wendy Way, (eds.), *Australia and the Postwar World: Documents 1947*, DFAT, AGPS, Canberra, 1995, pp 811-813.

176. Evatt, H.V., *Foreign Policy of Australia : Speeches*, Angus & Robertson: Sydney, 1945, p 121.

177. Camilleri, J.A., *An Introduction to Australian Foreign Policy*, Fourth Edition, Jacaranda Press, Qld., 1979, p 15.

178. Waters, Christopher, *The Empire Fractures: Anglo-Australian Conflict in the 1940s*, Australian Scholarly Publishing, Melbourne, 1995. p 10.

179. Hudson, W.J. and Way, Wendy (eds.), *Documents on Australian Foreign Policy 1937-49*, Vol. X, July-December 1946, DFAT, AGPS, Canberra, 1995, p 535.

180. Interview with V.K. Jain, Director, Library and Information, on 27 January 1999, at MEA Office, New Delhi.

181. Millar, T.B. *Australia's Foreign Policy*, Angus & Robertson, Sydney, 1968, p 103.

182. AA, Despatch No. 23, 6 December 1954, from W.R. Crocker to R.G. Casey, A1838/283, Item 169/10/1, Part 2.

**3**

# Nehru and Menzies: The Clash of Titans

## Preamble

The Nehru and Menzies parallel periods in office (1949-1964), constitute the major part (53 per cent) of the twenty eight year span of this thesis (1947-1975). Its analysis proportionately more extensive is therefore divided into two chapters. In relation to the claim that the relationship was characterised by peaks and troughs, this was the period it suffered the greatest strains and was at its lowest ebb in terms of bilateral effectiveness. There are principally two closely related reasons for this. The first, and probably the more important explanation for the troughs in the relationship, often easily overlooked, is the impact of personality on foreign policy development, affecting the nature of the bilateral relationship. The study comes to this question in this chapter by examining the Nehru-Menzies dissonance, seen in their rivalry played out at the Commonwealth of Nations over South Africa's membership of the body despite its policy of Apartheid and India's membership as a Republic. The second reason, examined in Chapter Four, concerns the differences of ideology and how they shaped each country's domestic and international interests. The rivalry was evident at the UN over the Suez crisis. The UN was also the stage for their heated clash over the Five Power Resolution. The lack of harmony is also seen in a number of third party international conflicts in which India and Australia were involved as mediators or participants.

Foreign policy, however, is developed within a national and international environment affected by complex factors operating at any given time. To help reach a contextualised understanding of the issues that shaped foreign policy and, consequently, the India-Australia bilateral relationship in the Nehru-Menzies period, a broad historical summary of political events, as background to the international environment of the period (1949-1964), is considered useful.

## The Indian, Australian and International Environment - A Summary

The period (1949-1964) opened with three important events of relevance to the India-Australia bilateral relationship. The first of these occurred when Robert Gordon Menzies became Prime Minister of Australia in 1949 with the Liberal Party and its coalition partner, the Country Party, winning the Australian Federal Election defeating Chifley's Australian Labor Party.[1] The second, which also took place in the same year, concerns India, independent since 1947, becoming the first former British colony to join the reconstituted commonwealth of Nations as a Republic.[2] The third, of international significance and one of Australia's Cold War preoccupations, was the gaining of power by the Communists in mainland China.[3] The year 1949 saw the Dutch finally surrender control of Indonesia to the Nationalists under Sukarno who became the country's first President after independence.[4] The period also witnessed conflict between the Netherlands and Indonesia over West New Guinea, and civil war in Laos. The Malayan insurgency, called the Emergency, had already begun in 1948.

The Colombo Plan was established in 1950.[5] The period was also identified with the Korean War which lasted for three years from June 1950. It drew Australia into the US-led UN forces supporting the South against North Korea, the latter backed by the Soviets and Chinese volunteers. India played a mediatory role throughout the war. In October 1950, the Chinese occupied Tibet, and in the following year, the ANZUS treaty (Australia, New Zealand and the US), representing the cornerstone of Australia's security strategy, was established, with the signing of the San Francisco Treaty of September 1951. The Geneva Accords, a settlement on Indo-China, were reached in July 1954 and brought a cease-fire covering Cambodia and Laos and a partitioned Vietnam.[6] Another international event of the period (which soured India's relations with Australia and the Western powers) was the formation of SEATO in 1954, whose membership included Australia, France, Pakistan, Philippines, Thailand, the UK and the US.[7]

In April 1955, Prime Minister Churchill resigned and Anthony Eden replaced him. In December of the same year, Clement Atlee resigned as Leader of the British Labour Party and H. Gaitskell replaced him. The decade was marked by the Soviet Union's march into East Germany in 1953 and Hungary in 1956. Another major crisis loomed with the Anglo-French invasion of Egypt in 1956 as a consequence of President Nasser's nationalisation of the Suez Canal Company, with India again taking a mediatory role in preventing a deepening of the crisis.[8] The reform of the Commonwealth, enabling admission of a number of newly independent states, took place in this period with several former colonies gaining independence including Malaya and Ghana in 1957 and Nigeria in 1960. The inauguration of the West Indian Federation took place in 1958. A significant development occurred in the UN, with the increase in Afro-Asian membership bringing radical shifts in voting patterns on international issues.[9]

For Australia, security and the containment of Communist China were the key factors driving the foreign policy of the Menzies' government, with Spender, and later Casey, in charge of the External Affairs Ministry; Menzies himself took a strong interest in external affairs.[10] The failed referendum on the banning of the Australian communist Party and the split in the Australian Labor Party (ALP) resulting in the formation of the Democratic Labor Party (DLP), occurred in 1951 and 1954 respectively.[11] The Labor opposition led by Dr H.V. Evatt, known for his significant contribution to the drafting of the UN Charter in the 1940s, showed greater sensitivity than the Menzies government to Asia's political and economic aspirations, (including India's membership of the Commonwealth) irrespective of the ideological leanings of the individual country, except on the 'White Australia' policy which had bipartisan support.[12]

For India, the period was characterised by the substantial role the country played in the easing of international conflict with its avowed quest for world peace.[13] Nehru, aided by Krishna Menon, was dominant in the formulation of India's foreign policy. The non-aligned movement, was born in 1955 at the Bandung Conference attended by leaders from 29 nations, including India's Nehru, Yugoslavia's Tito, Egypt's Nasser, Chou En Lai of China, Sukarno of Indonesia and U Nu of Burma. This enhanced India's international stature in view of the leadership role Nehru took in its formation.

In India, Indira Gandhi was elected leader of the Congress Party in 1959. The Sharpeville massacre took place in March 1960 precipitating the debate on South Africa's membership of the Commonwealth. In the same year Prime Minister Macmillan made his 'Winds of Change' speech in Cape Town. The Kennedy-Kruschev talks in Vienna took place in June 1961 as did the sealing of the Berlin border and India's move on Portuguese Goa. The Cuban missile crisis took place in 1962. 1963 saw the Organisation of African Unity (OAU) founded; the creation of the Federation of Malaysia; and the establishment of the 'hot-line' between Washington and Moscow.

The period also marked continued tension between India and Pakistan over the disputed Kashmir territory, as well as India's concerns over the unexpected violation of its northern border by China in 1959 culminating in the war with China in 1962. The 1960 Five Power Resolution presented to the UN to ease prevailing Cold War tensions saw a bitter clash between Nehru and Menzies in the ensuing debate. Nehru died in May 1964. Menzies retired two years later. The period 1949-1964 was, as the Chinese say, interesting times.

## Nehru and Menzies - Conflicting Personalities, Divergent Policies

It is a truism that the character of leaders, and the time in which they hold political power, often influence the prevailing nature and direction of events, large and small, domestic and foreign. Central to the argument of this study is the impact of the personality on policies and consequently the bilateral relationship. As well, the particular philosophy they bring to their political role, and the level of public support they receive on policy, especially foreign policy, are other influences. Nehru and Menzies, two very different personalities, had this effect. The mutual indifference and at times, hostility that characterised what could hardly be considered a productive bilateral relationship, is attributable, in no small measure, to their personality differences; and while the two countries were at no time seen even remotely as military rivals, the Nehru-Menzies rivalry was very real. However, the root of dissension is not traceable to any single issue, although for Nehru anti-racialism was a leitmotiv and for Menzies devotion to an outmoded concept of Empire was all consuming. Ironically, there were as many similarities in the background of the two as there were differences, but the differences predominated. As it turned out, they adversely affected the relationship between the two nations in the 1950s and 1960s. In evaluating the impact these had on the India-Australia relationship, the similarities provide a useful point of entry.

Both Nehru and Menzies were strong willed, obstinate and did not lack confidence, easily commanding the compliance and respect of their contemporaries. Brecher describes Nehru's dominance as Prime Minister as "more the giant among pygmies" than "first among equals."[14] On the day Nehru left India on a historic twelve day visit to China, 'a newspaper thought nothing of reporting ... that everything in the Government of India would be a in a state of suspended animation "for the duration" of Mr Nehru's absence. It was a reflection on his colleagues which they did not seem to mind.'[15] Stanley Wolpert shares this view when he speaks of the shift from, 'what at times seemed to be one-man rule ... to something more closely resembling national management by an administrative board of equals (after Nehru), clearly reflects the gap in personality, power, and ability between Nehru and his successors.'[16] Australia's one time High Commissioner to India, W.R. Crocker, in a despatch to Casey in 1954, says as much: 'no discussion of India today or of India in the foreseeable future, is possible without a discussion of Mr Nehru. He wields more power than most dictators, and, unlike most dictators he has the people behind him.'[17]

Menzies was no less a towering political figure in the Australia of the 1950s and early 1960s. In Perkin's words, 'Menzies was not a loved leader; he was feared, he was a one man band, waiting to control everything that went on around him ... as a human being he towered in his powers of persuasion, in his sense of overriding authority, ...'[18]. Paul Hasluck, a Minister in the Menzies government, made the observation, that, 'in Parliament, the cabinet and in the party room, Menzies had immense authority ... the simple explanation and the one nearest the truth is that Menzies was the best man there.'[19] Both had a great love of the English language and its literature. Nehru, his English education gained at Harrow, Cambridge and the prestigious Inner Temple, practised law under his successful lawyer father, Motilal Nehru, but with little enthusiasm for it: 'there was little that was inviting in that legal past of mine, and at no time have I felt the urge to revert to it ...'[20], he was to say later of this period. Menzies' education took him from state school to Wesley College in Melbourne, and from there to the University of Melbourne where he gained a First Class Honours degree in Law. Menzies was outstanding as a lawyer, becoming a King's Counsel in 1929, eleven years after entering the Bar. As skilled public speakers, both Nehru and Menzies had few equals among their political contemporaries, a skill that was to serve them well during their virtually unchallenged hold on the prime ministership, for seventeen years in each case during the period.

The stamp of approval each enjoyed was no less impressive, though their electorates were distinctly different. Nehru's support was among the masses of India, as well as internationally with the emergent Afro-Asian states which saw him as a champion of liberation from colonialism. In Menzies' case, it was essentially a symbiotic relationship with Australia's middle class, whose support ensured his continuity in office. Academic Robert Manne says Menzies was 'an almost uncanny intuiter of that peculiar, genial, provincial optimism that settled over "middle Australia" in the increasingly prosperous post-war-years.'[21] Their reliance on Menzies' foreign policy judgment for protecting Australia against the unpredictable and alien neighbours to the north underpinned their loyalty to him. Each leader authored several books and have inspired many biographies and political assessments of their periods in office. This is particularly true of Nehru where the writings on his impact on both post-independent India and the global political climate during the first two decades of the Cold War had an international dimension to its authorship.[22]

Their entry into the political arena was marked by different dynamics. Menzies' motivation was no different to that which drives most would-be politicians: ambition, the power of office, being on center stage, to serve one's ideals and country, among other reasons. There was no single dramatic event that inspired his decision. Brett, writing on Menzies' early political ambition and commitment to his ideals, describes him as, 'a young man in a hurry, impatient to test his skills against the demands of high office, very conscious of his own considerable gifts, and not too tolerant of the inadequacy of others.'[23] For the comparison with Nehru and the impact on the India-Australia relationship, it helps to realise that Menzies' political ambition, arguably his strongest characteristic, 'led him into actions which were seen by contemporaries as expressing his own competitive urge to succeed rather than as the principled actions he pretended them to be.'[24] In the event, only five years younger than Nehru, Menzies entered Parliament at the age of thirty four. He became Prime Minister in 1939 (aged forty five) for two years, returning to the helm in 1949 for his second and substantive Prime Ministerial reign of seventeen years.

With Nehru, it was different. There was a *coup de theatre* to his entry. His instinctive sense of justice led him to sacrifice his privileged social position (Nehru belonged to a wealthy aristocratic Brahmin family) to enter the political fray in the early 1920s, drawn to it by the national cry 'swaraj' (self-rule for India) at the time gathering national momentum under the leadership of Mahatma Gandhi. Nehru stated: 'I became wholly absorbed and wrapt in the movement, ... I gave up all my other associations and contacts, old friends, books, even newspapers, except in so far as they dealt with the work in hand.'[25] Nehru's abilities and commitment to India's independence were recognised early when he was elected to the crucial post of President of the Indian National Congress in 1929. He was 40 at the time. If there was self interest driving Nehru at that particular stage of his political life, there is no evidence to support it. Rather, Nehru was consumed by his passion: freedom for India, India for the Indians. This is reflected in his comments to Brecher about this period of his life: 'at that time I didn't think very much about myself ... We were so involved in the struggle, so wrapped up in what we were doing that I had little time or inclination to give thought to my own growth.'[26] Professor S.S. Bhatia observed that Nehru's interest in Indian politics was premised 'on sheer human considerations. He could not stand poverty and sufferings of the Indian people, who were being crushed under foreign yoke.[27] Consequently, the years spent in the struggle for liberation – including nearly a decade in prison - denied Nehru the opportunity of being of direct service to his country till he was fifty seven, at which age he became the first Prime Minister of independent India in 1947.

Nehru's bond with the Indian masses was strong. It provided him with the *raison deter* for his looming political undertaking, the inspiration he needed to face the intractable challenges that independent India faced. These included problems of poverty, of social and economic division, communal strife, caste and religious bigotry and, the tragedy of India's partitioning and the consequent seemingly endless *impasse* with Pakistan over Kashmir. His ability to reach out to his fellow Indians was easily his most valuable asset. He thrived on it:

> I go out and see masses of people, my people, ... and derive inspiration from them. There is something dynamic and something growing with them and I grow with them. I also enthuse with them.[28]

Former Australian High Commissioner to India, James Plimsoll, confirms Nehru's credibility with the Indian people when he observed that, 'in my travels around India I have seen that the ordinary people remained trustful of him and had a genuine regard for him.'[29] Wolpert thought it impossible to predict when another Nehru (or Gandhi) would appear who could 'win the affection and allegiance, to spark the imagination, of so vast and varied a population as India's - ....'[30].

Clearly, Nehru struck a responsive chord with the people of India from the outset. His popularity was as genuine as it was India-wide. The abiding public perception was that he was the man to see the new India through its difficulties. Mahatma Gandhi thought so too. When questioned as to why he preferred to anoint Nehru as his political successor rather than someone more in sympathy with his own philosophy, Gandhi replied, 'Jawaharlal is a pure soul. His heart is pure as crystal. He can make mistakes but the interests of the poor masses of India are safe in his hands.'[31] Brecher, who spent time in 1956 travelling across India with Nehru stated, 'to observe Nehru talking *with* his people, makes it possible to penetrate the intangibles of his popularity ... Candor and spontaneity are the outstanding qualities of his speech.'[32] There were other reasons for the great trust he enjoyed. T. Zinkin, for instance, believed Nehru 'has the rare gift of saying what the average Indian feels; as soon as he says something, people recognise that, that is what they have been thinking but did not quite know how to express it.'[33] This ability for a strong rapport with his people was noticed elsewhere too. *The San Francisco Chronicle* paid tribute to the unparalleled skill Nehru had of winning the minds of people: 'no one in history has ever enjoyed the uncoerced political trust, allegiance and leadership of more human beings than Jawaharlal Nehru.'[34]

Menzies too had this gift of communication. Shedden, who accompanied Menzies on his ten week visit to London in 1941, would attest to this in words, the similarity of which with those used by Zinkin above in relation to Nehru, is uncanny:

> His crystal-clear mind and beautiful English explain difficult things that worry the ordinary citizen (in such a simple manner that he feels they are the very things he has been feeling but unable to express himself).[35]

Also, like Nehru, Menzies used this skill to his advantage. Brett, in an insightful analysis of Menzies' 1942 address, 'The Forgotten People', to war-time Australia describes this skill as, 'his single most important asset in his successful career,' adding that, 'language for Menzies ... was central to the way he conceived of democratic politics.'[36]

The two enjoyed remarkably successful political careers, although, in Menzies' case, after a chequered start. And here the similarities end to focus on their differences which, after all, are of greater relevance to an understanding of how these two men influenced not only the substance of the India-Australia relationship during their periods in office, but also how and why they strove to influence Cold War events of the period in the way they did. This, of course, means looking at their personality differences and how they influenced their view of the world and consequently their foreign policy actions.

## Anglophilia *vs* Nationalism

Menzies' early period in politics was the personification of Anglophilia. He built up an image of himself as 'an imperial rather than a colonial personality'.[37] About this attachment to Britain, Menzies wrote: 'an interviewer once asked why I am an Anglophile. "Because", I said, " I have a great respect for my ancestors. But for them I would not be here. So why should I not be an Anglophile?" '[38] Menzies was also unsparing in his praise of British institutions: 'think of any British institution that matters: the authority of

Parliament, the rule of law or responsible government. These are tremendous concepts. We have them in Australia.'[39] But how did Menzies' performance measure up against these British political traditions? Perkins gives us an insight into one aspect, namely, Menzies the Parliamentarian, and the 'unfortunate legacy' left: 'he towered to such an extent that he regarded Parliament as a rubber stamp for decisions made secretly in government departments or the Cabinet room.'[40]

Menzies' arrogance was highlighted by Arthur Calwell, when he criticised Menzies in Parliament for his refusal to 'consult the House before leaving to attend a Prime Ministers' Conference or a meeting of the United Nations and does not bother to report to the Parliament when he returns, unless he is pressed to do so.'[41]

Obviously, Australia's colonial attachment to Britain - notwithstanding its strong commitment to the US alliance - was all embracing for Menzies. He rationalised it on the grounds of the racial character of the relationship. Australia was an extension of Britain as far as he was concerned and preserving the Empire was therefore an important aim. He did not attempt to mask this extraordinary ingratiation with Britain and the Empire. For example, returning to Australia after an extended stay in London, he showed his early preference for the British environment, when on arrival, he observed, 'I come back to Australia with just one sick feeling in my heart - that I must come back to my own country and play politics.'[42] To be aware of this side of Menzies' personality is important. The contrast with Nehru, schooled and imbued with British ideals, was stark. Not only did Nehru fight hard to evict the English from India but he also strove to shed any trace of Englishness (in manner and outward bearing), he may have acquired in the seven formative years he spent in England where his intellectual interests and political ideas were to develop. Casey, who had met Nehru and most of the others of the Indian Congress Party, describes him as:

> '...by far the most anglicised of the members of ... the Congress.
> ... But, on the other hand, there is no one in India who speaks in
> such unmeasured and unbridled terms in fierce condemnation of the
> British.'[43]

This is not to say Nehru did not have an admiration for British institutions and traditions. On the contrary, he was unsparing in his praise of such things and once said, 'personally I owe too much to England in my mental make up - ever to feel wholly alien to her.'[44] In fact, his English experience was a not insignificant influence on his attitude to many things. Wolpert observes that Mountbatten, during his awesome task of preparing India for independence, dealing with the disparate Indian personalities involved, 'would never have been able to work as closely with any Moulana, Mahatma or Sardar as he did with Jawaharlal, for they spoke the same language and shared that ineffable experience of proper public schooling.'[45] Yet, Nehru's admiration for England did not extend to British rule in India. He was fiercely nationalistic and India's dignity and self respect were involved in the struggle to rid the country of British rule. His resentment of the British period included regret at India's isolation in its own region, conveyed in this remark: 'Do you realise that one of the principal results of the coming of the British to India was the cutting off of India almost completely from all its neighbours in Asia.'[46]

With India's representation abroad totally in British hands, he lamented the fact that India ' became nearer to some places in Europe than to our neighbours. That is an extraordinary thing to happen ...'[47]. Once free of the rigours of colonialism, Nehru, spoke passionately about India's resumption of its Asian links as well as its geographic perspective:

> ... you find now a big change and a transformation happening, that is, we are developing our old contacts with Asian countries ... and India, by virtue of its geographical position, is inevitably connected with the whole Indian ocean region, with South East Asia, Australia, New Zealand and right up to the Persian Gulf ...[48].

Again, the two men had different images of their regional geography and cultural heritage. Nehru emphasised India as 'the central point of the Asian picture,' adding that 'We cannot escape various responsibilities that arise out of our geography and history.'[49] In contrast to this, Menzies appeared to show little sense of Australia's geography as this Brett assessment suggests:

> Menzies became the supreme representative of Imperial Australia, of those whose geographical, cultural and political imaginations were essentially imperial and whose sense of personal significance depended on being part of a political and moral order whose centre was London.[50]

## Personalities and Policies: The Imponderables

The narrative thus far seeks to throw some light on the differences and causes of the Nehru-Menzies dissonance and its negative impact on the bilateral relationship. In its essence, the differences represent their view of the world, a set of images that ultimately reflect their foreign policy actions. But, of course, the views and images held by political leaders are by no means easy to analyse. Influenced by a compound of time and place, background, class ramifications, the full emotional spectrum and the prevailing internal external political milieu, including a complex web of alliances within which bilateral relationships operate, the picture becomes obscured. This is no less valid in its application to the personalities of Nehru and Menzies. Indeed, their power was in many ways a measure of their personalities. Author Lloyd Jensen, in his treatment of the impact of idiosyncratic factors on foreign policy framing, makes several interesting observations some of which are of relevance to this study. The first of these concerns the policy makers level of interest on which Jensen argues, 'the higher the interest of a decision maker in foreign policy matters, the greater the impact of personality upon foreign policy.'[51] Jensen also says that 'personality factors are more important the higher the level of the decision making structure at which a decision is made.'[52] As Prime Ministers, both Nehru and Menzies were not only interested in foreign policy, but had a virtual monopoly on the framing of it.

Brecher, in his analysis, offers a valuable paradigmatic approach to the understanding of particular foreign policy actions, which helps unravel the labyrinthine task for the analyst. Having defined the variables in a system of foreign policy as consisting of 'an environment, a group of actors, structures ... and processes ...', Brecher argues that, 'it is possible - indeed it is necessary for rigorous analysis of foreign policy - to explore the content and interrelations of the key variables...'[53].

One of the key variables in the personality analysis is the actor. Applying Brecher's analytical model to some aspects of Nehru's and Menzies' images of the world, which, for actors, are 'no less "real" than the reality of their environment and are much more relevant to an analysis of foreign policy flow ...'[54] allows a better understanding of their foreign policy behaviour, and its share of responsibility for the indifference that prevailed in the bilateral relationship during their periods in office in the 1950s and early 1960s. Thus, going on the personality hypothesis and applying it to the operational and psychological areas of both men, one element that emerges is evidence of a time lag; in Menzies' case, between his early experiences, the formative influences, and the world in which he found himself as Prime Minister in the 1950s, the one in which he strove to make his presence felt. His tenacious adherence to the notion of a pre-eminent West, with its North-South strategic view of the world, stood in the way of a more constructive bilateral relationship with India. There was also a stubborn consistency in Menzies' attitude to the new India. It did not fit into his 'old' world. The combination of an independent minded Nehru, non-alignment, India's role as a mediator in world conflicts at the time much more important than Australia's, the absence of significant trade with India and, perhaps, a sense of racial superiority, made India inimical to Menzies' personal and operational view of the world. His policy actions in the Suez crisis carried out in conjunction with Anthony Eden underscores this anachronism. Martin describes it:' "they shared a conception of cold war strategy shaped by the vision they had formed of the world when they and Britain were in their prime in the 1930s and 1940s" and sustained this vision with "a tendency to facile historical analogies." '[55]

This predilection to cling to the past is also evident in Menzies' reaction to the Korean War with his diary entry that 'all these Asian adventures are diversions by the Russians.'[56] Lowe interprets this as 'a classic expression of Menzies' construction of the Cold War as an international crisis analogous to that of 1940-41, an equation with which he was thoroughly familiar.'[57]

Nehru's personality, moulded from many influences, also had a significant impact on the way he responded to the world and India's place in the world of the 1950s. In Plimsoll's words, 'Nehru's authority rested on his great personality, his contribution to the independence movement and his recognition by Gandhi. He stood for things that have kept India in the modern world and on the side of parliamentary democracy, ...'[58] all of which were related to early influences. His foreign policy training was like that of Menzies', consistent, though different. Unlike Menzies, his image of the world and any suggestion of time lag associated with it, was, for the most part, not as damaging. If there was any inference of delay in Nehru's personality traceable to psychological origins, and having difficulty in adapting to the reality of change in the environment, it had to be his insistence that non-alignment continued to serve India's interests even after the unforeseen 1962 Chinese incursions into disputed territories in the Himalayan region which India regarded as its own. Of course, this persistence with the doctrine, seen as irrational in the West, has to be viewed in the context of his image of the world shaped primarily by his bitter colonial experiences as well as by Mahatma Gandhi's guidance towards non-violence. Also, non-alignment had deeper meaning for Nehru and was not simply a question of securing India's borders as revealed in Chapter Five.

Memories of colonialism for Nehru gave rise to a fear of neo-colonialism. He used Gandhi's non-violent moral force (*satyagraha*) not only to free India from colonial rule, but in the way he approached the outside world during the Cold War. All of this contributed to a resentment of the West which did not exist to the same degree in relation to China, an Asian country. Satyanarayan Sinha, who in 1952 warned Nehru that China would one day invade India [59] in his book *China Strikes*, points out that in India, 'at one time the slogan *Hindi-Chini, bhai-bhai* (India-China, brother-brother) was officially supported and generously patronised.'[60] Clearly the anti-West attitude transcended all else and at times may have defied logic. It may also have involved psycho-political concepts that surfaced in the aftermath of independence. Casey, who knew the Indian mind well, offers an explanation with this perceptive observation:

> Many politically-minded Indians had understandably developed an acute and bitter sense of resentment against Britain arising from the events in the last decades of Britain's suzerainty including social discrimination practised by the British and what was regarded as commercial exploitation.[61]

And yet, unlike Menzies, Nehru was acutely conscious of the time lag phenomenon and its negative implications as early as 1939, when he spoke for greater cooperation in the world. He said:

> One of the tragedies of history is the slowness with which people's minds adapt themselves to a changing environment. The world changes from day to day, not so our minds which are peculiarly static and insist on imagining that today is the same as yesterday

and tomorrow will not differ greatly. This lag between our minds and reality prevents us from solving the problems of the day and produces war and revolution and much else that afflicts the world....'[62].

Some critics, saw Nehru's constant reference to colonialism as remarkably simplistic and devoid of international realism. For example, a correspondent to *The Round Table,* in a critique on Nehru's foreign policy, describes this preoccupation with the West's culpability, linking every unsavoury global situation or change to the West, as an outlook 'astonishingly narrow, static and inflexible, for it reduces every conflict to the outworn formula of his pre-1947 agitating days.'[63] But, then, Nehru was an idealist, a weaver of dreams, from his early days; in Ramachandram's words, 'his life was a perpetual battle, a continual conflict between what is and what ought to be. He strove hard to bring reality and idealism closer.'[64] Nehru's role at the NAM conference in Bandung in 1955 was an example of his willingness to sacrifice his own importance in the interests of the larger objective which included the recognition of China. As one writer observed, he showed this by allowing Chou En Lai to get as much of the running as possible and intervened only when it seemed that the conference proceedings were threatened in some way.[65] The writer goes on to state that 'he (Nehru) had to show the world that the resurgence of Asia he speaks of is not merely the resurgence of Mr. Nehru.'[66]

That Nehru was a visionary there was no doubting, influenced as he was by his English education and early interest in Fabian Socialism. M.H. Heikal, the Egyptian writer who travelled with Nehru and interviewed him over a twelve year period, observed that 'the Fabian intellectuals - dreamers of socialism and democracy - weaved the threads of bright futuristic prospects ...', [67] but they also knew, that the intellectual needed more than a dream to succeed in the political sphere even if their object was to educate the people [68] which, of course, Nehru often set out to do. According to Heikal, Nehru failed because the 'experiment imposed the two roles (intellectual and demagogue) on him but he found no self-fulfillment in either of them.'[69] Australia's Minister for External Affairs, Percy Spender, who worked with Nehru at the Colombo Plan conference in May 1950, described him as,. 'a. complicated. man, capable of great compassion, ruthlessness, and personal courage. ... A philosopher rather than a man of action, his mind was slanted to forensic performance. He was an adept politician.'[70] What Spender does not mention is Nehru's quick temper.

## The Commonwealth: a Change of Flags, Faces and Races

Membership of the Commonwealth and Prime Ministerial Conferences were other theatres where the sharp differences between Nehru and Menzies were aired. Events that preceded India's decision to become a republic and remain within the Commonwealth, were grounds for dissension between the two men.

The granting of independence to India in 1947 meant the country was free to join the Commonwealth as a sovereign nation. India, however, was bent on becoming a republic because 'for psychological purposes, there is something in a Republic which makes independence complete ...'[71]. Nehru's determination that India becomes a republic predates independence, with his resolution put to the Indian Constituent Assembly in 1946, an interest that goes back even further into the past. For instance, in an address to the Indian National Congress, he said: 'I must frankly confess that I am a socialist and a republican and am no believer in kings and princes, ...' but, importantly, he went on to point out that this choice of a socialist approach necessary to alleviate India's poverty and remove inequality, would, however, be of a kind developed for India through its 'own methods.'[72] While his preference for socialism may have been construed by some as representing a fundamental difference in ideology between the two men, (Nehru and Menzies) it must be recognised that Nehru was firmly committed to democratic processes, but stressed that 'as far as I can visualise, there cannot be full democracy without socialism.'[73] Nehru's distaste for communism as a system of government with its rigid authoritarianism was equally well known. His love of democracy, is best exemplified in Lord Butler's endorsement of Nehru when he observed that 'at the bar of history, Nehru will emerge as a great Indian and a great world figure ... as a man whose *contribution to the cause of effective democracy ranks as high as those Himalayan mountain peaks*'.[74] (emphasis in original) But, Menzies saw socialism as being akin to Communism and used it effectively to influence the Australian electorate.

India's decision to become a Republic in 1948, yet opting to remain in the Commonwealth, altered the nature of the bonding that prevailed within the Commonwealth. However, there was opposition to India's republicanism. In the ensuing search for a solution to the problem, Pakistan's Prime Minister, Liaquat Ali Khan, muddied the waters further when he asked, 'what about the king; we cannot have a Declaration of the Commonwealth without a king!'[75] As to whether this was a precursory reflection of Pakistan's greater compatibility (relative to India), with the British and the West (including Australia) during the Cold War, is a question of relevance to the India-Australia bilateral relationship. In Krishna Menon's view of the delicate negotiations, 'it was Pakistan that made the difficulty. They tried to push us out.'[76] He also saw the Australians as being more 'Kingish'[77]. Nehru too was intent on ensuring the King had only a symbolic relationship with the Commonwealth. As for independent India's direct relationship with the Monarchy, he observed that: 'as far as the Constitution of India is concerned, the King has no place and we shall owe no allegiance to him.'[78]

In the end, a formula[79] was found that was acceptable to all concerned and satisfied the constitutional ramifications. The Commonwealth underwent a transformation from that point. Whereas previously it was a small group of members with common interests brought together under the British Empire with allegiance to the Crown, the Commonwealth Constitution changed to accommodate Republican India, followed by other newly independent Asian and African states, joining it in the decolonisation surge of the 1950s. It became a less formal but more politically sensitive forum for the heads of member nations to pursue their interests. *The Sunday Times* (London), commenting on the impact of the new membership, defined the change taking place as where a 'group of nations closely connected by blood ... all sharing a European attitude towards people of different continents, colours or races ...' to an organisation to which now was, 'suddenly added three Asian nations whose history was one of submission to and revolt against European imperialism, and whose culture, though deeply affected by European contacts, had deep roots in their own soil, ...'[80]. The change was not without some disquiet. The contrast between India and Australia with regard to the future of their relationships with the new Commonwealth institution, and their attitude to republicanism, is a measure of the gulf that existed between the two leaders. Nehru's attitude to the transformation of the Commonwealth from an imperious overlordship to the humbler Commonwealth of Nations was a positive one but not without some reservations:

> ... we all want a Commonwealth of nations ... but if we think in terms of an empire gradually being transformed into a commonwealth, almost retaining its own structure, economically and politically, then it seems to me we are likely to delude ourselves very greatly. We cannot have a real commonwealth of nations born of empire. It must have different parents.[81]

## Tradition *versus* Nationalism

In London, a memorandum issued by the Secretary of State for Commonwealth Relations summarised Commonwealth press and public reactions to the new declaration enabling republic India to retain membership. Menzies' (then, Leader of the Opposition) negative attitude to the decision, was that it 'damaged considerably the family relationship under the Crown,' and '... was indicative of a process of retreat and disintegration and was disturbing to millions of British people.'[82] This view of Menzies was not only poorly premised but was contradicted by subsequent events which showed that the Commonwealth not only endured but by 1973 70 per cent of Britons wanted it strengthened as the narrative reveals below. Expressions by Menzies of his disappointment with India's republican status continued. At Cambridge to deliver the first Smut's Memorial Lecture, he scoffed at India's republican status and the consequent downgrading of status this meant for the monarchy in India. Speaking about the change in the character of the Commonwealth, Menzies referred to Smut's view that it 'violated every concept of the Commonwealth' and proceeded to tell his audience of his agreement, at the time, with Smut's view. He also showed his preference for the 'old Commonwealth' when he then admitted to having 'prepared what I thought to be a powerful and pungent speech' to Parliament on the historic change, but was thwarted from doing so by Prime Minister Chifley 'who ... guessed my intentions and, ... left the item at the bottom of the Notice Paper.'[83] Besides being disappointed at the transformation of the Commonwealth from the 'old-club' to the new expanded grouping, Menzies held exaggerated fears for its future. As for his attitude to a republican form of government, it is best seen in his unequivocal comment on the question of its applicability to Australia at a time when support for a Republic in the country had grown to an estimated quarter of the population:

> ... in spite of the dilution of the Australian population in terms of British stock, it is still true that the vast majority of the people of Australia have their roots well down British history, which, of course, is royal history. [84]

Like Menzies, his Cabinet colleague Alexander Russell Downer held little hope for the future of the Commonwealth unless the new members acknowledged the Queen as sovereign, and there was convergence on foreign policy. Addressing Parliament he said:

> If the touchstone of membership cannot be allegiance to the sovereign ... then at least it ought to be a community of interest and an adherence to the grand design of a common foreign policy. [85]

Menzies' also underscored his commitment to the *status quo*, a Monarchy, with his rhetorical question whether a President of a Republic of Australia would be 'the chief executive of the nation, as in the United States, or is he to occupy an honorific post, like the President of India, ...' and proceeds to answer it with 'given that choice, I am all for a monarch; ...'[86]. If further evidence is necessary of Menzies' obsession with things royal, then take his comments that 'the Governor General is the Queen's representative. I am the Queen's Prime Minister, my Ministers and I are the Queen's servants, our statutes are enacted by the "Queen's Most Excellent Majesty"...'[87]. In *Afternoon Light*, Menzies proclaims: 'to have seen the Queen is something, to know somebody in her entourage is something better, to have spoken to the Queen is to enter, though unofficially, the ranks of the nobility.'[88] Not surprisingly, then, a UK Cabinet meeting with Churchill in the chair had the Chancellor of the Exchequer express his 'appreciation of Mr Menzies' offer of an Australian contribution towards the cost of using the vessel (SS Gothic) ...'[89] to bring the Queen and Duke of Edinburgh on a visit to Australia. About this tenacious attachment Menzies had for the Crown and the regal trappings that went with it, as well as his ability to make political capital out of it, Bruce Grant argues:

> The master of the politics of royalty was prime minister Menzies, who was more responsible than any other Australian of his time for

promoting and prolonging the link with the Crown, with the most genuine of romantic intentions and with the connivance, or indulgence, of the electorate.[90]

In *Australia and the Monarchy*, Harris carries out what he describes as a 'psychoanalytic diagnosis' on Menzies (and colleague Downer) who he states, 'have given public demonstrations of an intense fixation on the idea of the British Monarchy. ... In neither ... is the obsession basically an intellectual or an ideological one, but rather purely an emotional response.' [91]

India's contrasting attitude to this is exemplified in Krishna Menon's comments that India (and Canada) were not impressed all that much by royalty, but thought 'Australia is, but she doesn't count much in terms of making any impact .'[92] In an interview with Brecher, he stressed that, while India's ties to the Commonwealth were not like Australia's, it took steps to retain the Commonwealth links after becoming an independent Republic, and the reasons for this had more to do with being 'rational, pragmatic and sensible ...'[93] than with India's earlier ties with Britain and the Commonwealth. Nehru himself was no less realistic on this question: 'We join the Commonwealth, obviously, because we think it is beneficial to us and to certain causes in the world that we wish to advance.'[94] When questioned by an interviewer about his earlier advocacy of severing all ties with Britain after independence, Nehru replied:

> Why should we break off a relationship? ... we are a republic and they are a Monarchy ... Canada and Australia are also free countries but of their own will they have accepted the Queen of England as their Queen. We have broken off even that relationship.[95]

India's wish, however, to remain in the Commonwealth after becoming a Republic was to be unfettered by conditions which would mean a dilution of its total independence as a sovereign nation. This is unambiguously conveyed in the Resolution [96] passed by the Congress Party before Nehru's visit to London in 1949 for the Prime Ministers' Conference, which eventually approved India's republican status within the Commonwealth. Of course, there were other reasons for the decision, seen as beneficial to India such as in trade, educational opportunities, and technical aid, but the commitment was also politically sensitive to the Nehru government. According to Chanchal Sarkar, Nehru and his Civil Service, though supportive of the Commonwealth link, were conscious of the residual

' psychological resentment against a relationship with the former rulers ...', particularly in the Left among India's political parties, who saw 'it as a guise for retaining British domination.'[97] But Nehru, defending India's decision to continue membership, asked his critics the question:

> ... does a nation lose its independence by an alliance with another country? Alliances normally mean mutual commitments. The free association of sovereign Commonwealth nations does not involve such commitments.[98]

While India's reasons for remaining in the Commonwealth are seen in the above views of Nehru and Krishna Menon, its attitude to the future of the Commonwealth relationship provides further evidence of the distance separating Nehru from Menzies. For instance, on the viability of the relationship, Krishna Menon stressed that it 'depends a lot upon mutuality of interests. Britain will throw Canada ... and us overboard if she cannot survive, shall we say, without the Common Market, as well as on any future positive role Britain might play in the ...erasement of racial discrimination,'[99] a concern for India that is a persistent theme running through this thesis. For Nehru, racialism was a key factor. He said 'there are few natural links between India and England, ... In many parts of the Empire there is racial ill-treatment and a policy of exclusion of Indians.'[100] Maintaining the *status quo* was not made easy for the Nehru government as a conversation between well known Indian editor of *The Times of India* and staunch critic of the West, Frank Moraes, and a representative of the Australian High Commission, suggests. During the discussion, Moraes stressed that 'the real issue was why India should remain in association with the Commonwealth while countries like South Africa and Australia practised outright discrimination against her.'[101]

## Menzies' *Cri de coeur*

It is doubtful that Menzies ever appreciated the degree of opposition Nehru faced from the Communist party and others of the Left within India on its membership of the Commonwealth, as well as on his determination to preserve democracy at this early but crucial period of nationhood for India. It is not as if Menzies was unaware of Nehru's problems considering the information provided to DEA, Canberra from the High Commission in New Delhi. For example, in a despatch to Casey on the 1953 Coronation celebrations in India, Crocker states, 'the display might have been extremely cautious on the part of the present rulers, who keep an alert eye on Communist and Socialist criticisms of their remaining in the Commonwealth ...'[102].

Paradoxically, the importance of India being a democracy appears to have not counted for much in Australia's bilateral interests, despite there being only a few others with claims to democratic forms of government in the region. That democracy and poverty could co-exist in a populous and complex mix as India was testimony to Nehru's influence across the many and diverse levels of the Indian polity. Then, again, for Menzies the Commonwealth bonds and his concerns for its future were premised on entirely different imperatives as this lament suggests:

> When I first attended a Commonwealth Prime Ministers' conference, 33 years ago, the leaders present representing Britain, Canada, Australia, South Africa, and New Zealand - understood each other fairly well and could approach together something that closely resembled a common foreign policy. In 1949 it was agreed, however, that a country could become a republic and remain in the Commonwealth.[103]

Menzies went on to describe the bonding that held these former members of the Commonwealth together as being one 'based on common allegiance to the crown', arguing that such relations between these countries which 'contain the greatest volume of political experience, judgment and moral influence in the world are ... absolutely essential.'[104] What he fails to mention is that these countries, as far as India was concerned, were also drawn together by their European heritage as well as the economic and political power they enjoyed through their colonial possessions. Furthermore, Menzies failed to appreciate that there were strong reasons for the newly independent nations joining the Commonwealth. In his article, 'Overhaul of the Commonwealth,' James Eayers makes the valid comment that:

> Each new member of the Commonwealth joins to further some particular objective of foreign or domestic policy. ... Their's is a political commitment to a political association. They have not joined a church. They have not taken holy orders.'[105]

India's T.N. Kaul makes the interesting observation that the Commonwealth terminology (often emphasised by Menzies) requiring member countries to show 'allegiance to the British Crown ' and the principle of 'free association' are contradictory terms because, he argues, 'if members are bound by allegiance to the Crown, the voluntary character of the association is in doubt.'[106]

Menzies had little interest in using the Commonwealth Institution and the Prime Ministers Conferences to develop new relationships and improve others, such as with India, difficult for a man who, when referring to the important relations between the older members, and not without a note of nostalgic regret, says 'our relationship was organic and internal; ...' but, when he refers to the new republicans, the relationship 'is in a sense functional and certainly external.'[107] Clearly, Menzies was not happy with the transformation that took place: a Commonwealth club of a handful of White members to one in which the majority was Asian and African and republican to boot. *The National Herald* (Lucknow) writing about Menzies' dissatisfaction with the composition and value of the Commonwealth, had this to say in relation to his comments about the conference decision: 'Mr Menzies does not seem to be happy over the presence in the Commonwealth of countries like India and Ceylon, which have their own outlook and their own independent foreign policies ...'[108]. As Pemberton observes, 'it was Dominion leaders such as Menzies who were appalled, (at the transformation) wishing to preserve the empire in much of its original form, ...'[109]. The old Commonwealth gave the imperially minded leaders such as Menzies a sense of global power in belonging to the empire. Menzies' lack of interest in other members of the Commonwealth, in particular the Asian members, was exemplified further in his critique of Britain's wish to join the European Common Market and its impact on Australia:

> Britain goes on and on as if it is 'Europe or nothing.' But it is not Europe or nothing. There is the whole wide world and it is a world that is made up of a series of countries. One is Australia. One is New Zealand. One is Canada. And one is the United States.[110]

The possibility that Britain's entry might hurt other Commonwealth nations like India fails to enter Menzies' calculations. As a fellow member of the Commonwealth, Menzies could not have been unaware of the negative impact of Britain's decision on India's preferential trade (as a member of the sterling area) with Britain.[111] Menzies also states that, while he accepts the more recent members of the Commonwealth, he is 'not half as interested' about their relationship with Britain as he is about relations 'between Britain and my own country.'[112] Helpful also for the insight it gives to Menzies' personality is his refusal, despite his great love of Britain, to help Macmillan overcome any opposition in the Commonwealth, as well as domestically, to Britain's intentions to join the European Economic Union.[113]

Unambiguously, the difference between the two men is revealed here: Nehru the internationalist, concerned with greater equity for India and Third World countries, *versus* Menzies, the traditionalist, concerned more with Australian interests and the preservation of British-Australian links and a version of British imperialism in world affairs.

## Nehru's Relentless Crusade: Anti-Racialism

What is clear from the discussion so far is that India was not only 'the pioneer of modern Asian nationalism,'[114] through its success in winning independence from Britain, but also, by remaining in the Commonwealth as a Republic, it 'established the *bona fides* of the new Commonwealth, based less on blood than on will,'[115] it enabled many other Afro-Asian states to follow suit, undeterred by the experience of racialism and colonialism.

That said, an issue of fundamental importance to India was the presence in the Commonwealth of South Africa, whose Apartheid policies were not only at odds with the Commonwealth ideal of equality of its members, but also strenuously opposed by India's Nehru who was constrained to comment that 'If there is no solution to this problem very soon, the whole of Africa may be ablaze.'[116] . This issue is of particular significance to any discussion of the Nehru-Menzies dissonance. The declaration of Commonwealth principles, to which member nations were signatories at the Singapore Conference, is an important starting point. It states, *inter alia:*

We recognise racial prejudice as a dangerous sickness threatening the healthy development of the human race and racial discrimination as an unmitigated evil of society. Each of us will vigorously combat this evil within our own nation. No country will afford to regimes which practice racial discrimination assistance which in its own judgment directly contributes to the pursuit or consolidation of this evil policy. [117]

## Apartheid the Bone of Contention, Sharpeville the Turning Point

Racial equality was undoubtedly the underpinning to a successful Commonwealth grouping, evident from a part of the Singapore Declaration cited above. Consequently, South Africa's presence, with its racially based policy of Apartheid, became more than a trifle inconvenient. It was a growing sore, and particularly irksome to Nehru (who spoke out against the practice of racialism everywhere), his concerns not only related to the treatment of Africans, but also the Indians in South Africa, as seen in this statement:

> ... it is well to remember what is happening in one part of the Commonwealth today. In South Africa racialism is the state doctrine and our people are putting up a heroic struggle against the tyranny of a racial minority. [118]

Yet, much had been said in praise of the Commonwealth institution and its success, 'in keeping diverse governments and peoples in amity and mutual understanding,' [119] despite the South African question. But this congenial atmosphere was dramatically tested with the Sharpeville shootings and the worldwide condemnation that followed; it brought the Nehru-Menzies conflict, *vis-à-vis* South Africa and its membership, into the hitherto tranquil atmosphere of the Commonwealth Prime Ministers' meetings, where discussion of the internal affairs of the member nations were studiously avoided, (e.g. the Kashmir dispute and the rights of Aboriginal people in Australia), with both Menzies and Nehru committed to the principle. Menzies, who had previously shown no interest in criticising South Africa's repressive authority imposed on Africans, Indians and mixed races, commenting on the Sharpeville incident, (not long after it occurred) at Cambridge told his audience that 'Apartheid which has been the accepted policy of South African governments ... never previously been brought up at a Prime Ministers Conference, flared into the news and into debate.' [120] To a call from Labor's Calwell (Leader of the opposition) for inclusion of the question for discussion at the next Prime Ministers Conference, Menzies responded with what was often used by him in defence of Australia's inaction on international questions, (such as decolonisation), the principle of non-intervention in the internal affairs of other nations, in this instance 'a domestic problem for the Union of South Africa.'[121] Menzies' seemingly insensitive and cavalier attitude to the Sharpeville massacre provides a further insight to his character. His tendency to underestimate, if not remain impervious to, the international community's ability to make discerning judgments about his attempts to mask, or give some legitimacy, to the reasons for his policy stance is, in this case, a measure of his overriding loyalty to South Africa and his willingness to disregard Commonwealth colleagues such as Nehru. This tendency to seek shelter is exemplified in the explanation he offers when challenged in relation to Sharpeville:

> One of the inhibitions that is laid upon the man who is the head of the Government of Australia is that his personal feelings are a luxury in which he cannot publicly indulge ... This is a great responsibility. It requires calm judgment ... [122].

Logically, then, such onerous restraint must apply equally to leaders like Nehru who did not hesitate to condemn South Africa's behaviour. Besides, if by his argument Menzies meant that there were political constraints placed on his ability to give full expression to his feelings on Sharpeville, then his gratuitous correspondence with Verwoerd [123] on South Africa's almost certain expulsion from the Commonwealth after Sharpeville, (compounded by its defiance of the United Nation's decision on South West Africa), is an action difficult to understand and gives rise to doubts about Menzies' defence. But, then, Menzies' efforts to help Verwoerd, someone who, he says, 'was not personally known to me, ...'[124] and Verwoerd's description of Menzies in his letter of reply 'as perhaps the best friend South Africa has, ... '[125] suggests motives other than the demands of restraint felt by a Head of Government to express genuine feelings on an issue like Sharpeville. This becomes evident in Menzies' subsequent explanation of his soft stand on Sharpeville, which included the self- interest argument that Australia needs to be wary of providing any grounds for others in the future to 'discuss our aboriginal policies and claim as a precedent whatever action occurs in relation to South Africa ...'[126].

At the Commonwealth Prime Ministers meeting held in London after Sharpeville, Nehru, and other Asian and African Heads, some of whom had already severed trade and diplomatic relations with

South Africa, warned that the Sharpeville issue could 'shake the very foundations of the Commonwealth'.[127] Menzies, however, persisted with his defence that, 'it is a matter of domestic jurisdiction as migration is a matter for us.'[128] Little wonder then, that even after India continued as a republican member of the Commonwealth, 'many Indians still saw the Commonwealth as a "White man's Club." '[129] But Menzies' unyielding attitude on the issue resulted in the limits of their endurance being reached and, for South Africa, the beginning of the end of its membership.

## Nehru Diary: The Majority Mood

Nothing reflects the mood that prevailed at the Commonwealth Conference better than Nehru's Diary notes (hand-written in shortened sentences) of the conference held in mid-1960. It reveals a growing impatience among Commonwealth leaders with South Africa. Extracts from it, tell the story:

May 3, 1960 11.20

Macmillan (UK Prime Minister)

- Regret absence of Dr Verwoerd.(PM of South Africa)

  Transient nature of our authority

Tunku Abdul Rahman (Malaya)

- Commonwealth stands for equality - black, white or yellow

  ...What has happened in South Africa has gone beyond the barriers of domestic - has shocked whole world - expectations of people everywhere that we should do something. Attitudes of white supremacy

R. Menzies (Australia)

- accepts proposal of Macmillan for informal talks about S.A. (South Africa)

  Louw (Minister representing South Africa in the absence of Verwoerd)

- Agreeable to meeting small groups informally. But would not agree to whole conference discussing this (South Africa's policy) informally.

May 9, 1960 10.30 a.m.

- Louw refers to Tunku's statement to which he had taken strong exceptions. ... Reference to Diefenbaker- Reference to Nehru's press conferences or speeches where he attacked S.A. Racial policies.

Nkrumah (Ghana)

- I have personally restrained myself on this question of apartheid inspite of strong feelings. ... To us apartheid isa burning ? (question)

Ayub Khan (Pakistan)

- No doubt (about) this. World opinion shocked as result of events in S.A. ... Now feelings roused. Human dignity and self respect involved. ... No good saying that F.M. Smuts had drawn this policy 1928-29. World changes. Tremendous human tragedy.

Welensky

- Fuller appreciation of S.A. problems - neighbours - Still I understand world reactions - headlines. Responsibility to our parliaments. ... We must not hasten too quickly - Let us hasten slowly. I recognise difficulties of new members of C (Commonwealth) and also those of Mr. Luow. No personal attacks.

Cooray (Ceylon - now Sri Lanka)

- Our Govt. - completely opposed to racial discrimination - We do not subscribe to statement by Louw that this is entirely a local matter.

Diefenbaker (Canada)

- ... We cannot ignore an issue of such importance? How can we deal with it without interfering with rule of non-interference?

  ? (question) of racial discrimination is one which goes beyond confines of civil rights. Commonwealth cannot stand for less than what UN stands for.[130]

Later in page 88 of the Diary notes, Nehru continues:

Diefenbaker

> Agrees with J.N. (J. Nehru). Commonwealth standing for human dignity and sacredness of individual. This Commonwealth cannot exist if there is this rigid attitude of Louw. Obdurate...

Nehru's Diary notes end with a final statement by Louw.

Years ago it was decided here two things cannot be discussed:

> 1. Disputes not to be discussed here -
>
> 2. Local Affairs not to be discussed -
>
> ... I cannot too strongly warn against breach of these two rules.[131]

## Natural Justice: The Axe Falls

Menzies' support for South Africa with his legalistic arguments and consequent conflict with Nehru continued in the Commonwealth, as the membership issue took a decisive turn. In London to attend the Commonwealth Prime Ministers meeting on South Africa's membership, (this time attended by Verwoerd himself), Menzies - in a cable to his deputy John McEwen sent during the meeting - made little effort to disguise his disappointment about South Africa's prospects for remaining in the Commonwealth. For instance, on the unexpected approach taken to the discussion of the South African question, (which was at variance with what he thought was previously agreed with Macmillan), Menzies complains, 'I can only assume that this change in approach by Macmillan came from the meeting he had last night at Chequers (British Prime Minister's country residence) with Nehru.'[132] Then, on Verwoerd's defence of South Africa's racially based policies at the meeting, Menzies writes: 'this he did with a great deal of competence and some effectiveness and ... made a certain number of digs at aspects of internal policies in Ghana, Nigeria, Malaya, Ceylon and India.'[133] Menzies gives the impression here that he derived some pleasure from Verwoerd's performance. In contrast to Nehru, 'who left the conference (1961) in no doubt as to India's detestation of Apartheid ...'[134], and warned of the consequences of South Africa's membership on the future existence of the organisation, Menzies was uncompromising in his stand. On Macmillan's draft statement from the meeting on South Africa's position in the Commonwealth, Menzies comments, 'nobody seems ever to define these terms, racial equality and racial discrimination. They have become slogans.'[135] This was despite having signed off on the Declaration of Commonwealth Principles at the Singapore Conference (referred to above) which was, explicitly, a statement of the centrality of racial equality to the Commonwealth and within the member nations.[136] Menzies concludes his cablegram to McEwen with the message that the writing was on the wall for South Africa's membership and adds, 'in view of our plainly discriminatory immigration policy we have a good chance of being the next in line.'[137] This revelation of Menzies' hidden motive was another example of the personality factor and its impact on policy and the India-Australia bilateral relationship.

In the event, South Africa withdrew from the Commonwealth in the face of overwhelming opposition from the new members of the Commonwealth in particular. Crocker, Australia's High Commissioner in New Delhi at the time in a cable to Australia's Department of External Affairs concerning Verwoerd's decision to leave the Commonwealth, says the departure of South Africa was well received by the Indian media, and adds that the 'Australian Immigration Policy has been noticed unfavourably in this connection in several papers including *The Times of India'* and ends with the comment that 'few papers published Mr. Menzies' statement'[138] which of course, was about his expression of regret at South Africa's departure. The withdrawal of South Africa from the Commonwealth at the meeting was a triumph for Nehru, whose response was that it 'has strengthened the Commonwealth' and on the historic nature of the Commonwealth decision, he said:

> this very tenuous and vague association has developed certain basic formulae ... one of them is equal treatment of races, equal opportunities, no racial suppression and certainly no segregation.'[139]

Author M.S. Rajan observes it was only after the withdrawal of South Africa from membership of the Commonwealth that the new members were confident that the old members (with the exception of Australia) also accepted the principle that 'the promotion of racial equality (both within and without their territories) is a new and additional Commonwealth obligation.'[140]

Menzies' reaction to the historic departure of South Africa is best conveyed in his address to Parliament on his return from the Commonwealth Prime Ministers Conference in London:

> Under inexorable pressure, South Africa is out of the Commonwealth. It is not the Verwoerd government that is out. It is the Union of South Africa; the nation evolved by the great liberal statesmanship of 1909; the nation of Botha and Smuts; ... The nation ... which recently voted to remain within the direct allegiance to the Throne; ... [141].

Menzies concludes his announcement with an appeal to his fellow Parliamentarians 'to share in my sorrow at these unhappy circumstances.'[142] Yet, annoyed at the suggestion that he was keen to help South Africa remain in the Commonwealth, and also seen as having been indifferent to the Sharpeville shootings, he finally spoke out against Apartheid and admitted to being 'against some of the modern manifestations and practices (of Apartheid) because they offend the conscience; ... But we are a fair minded people, I hope, and we should try to understand how the basic policy came to be adopted, ...'[143]. It could be asked whether these were just new words for old meanings? He proceeds with a didactic explanation to Parliament of the reasons for Apartheid, quoting Smuts,[144] and consequently his condemnation, long withheld, appears to be grudging when it was delivered, and more an attempt to compensate for his mild and defensive previous response to Apartheid, Sharpeville and South Africa's continuing membership.

J.K. Galbraith, one time US Ambassador to India, writes about a pre-dinner chat he had with Nehru who, discussing South Africa, spoke of his (Nehru's) gratitude to Diefenbaker for his support on the South Africa issue at the Commonwealth conference and, in reference to Menzies, said that, while he was 'once a friend of *apartheid*, (Menzies) had now heard enough from home to be opposed.'[145] Academic Robert Manne observes that 'there was, unhappily, one great lesson from the Second World War - the evil of racism - which Menzies stubbornly refused to learn.'[146]

It is also instructive to note Nehru's contribution to preserving the Commonwealth by his actions on South Africa, it sharpens further the differences between him and Menzies. Bimal Prasad in his article, 'Nehru and the New Commonwealth', describes it as 'a crucial role in giving a new shape to it after the end of the Second World War', pointing also to Nehru's 'refusal to countenance India's withdrawal from it, ...' when Britain's invasion of Egypt during the Suez crisis threatened the break up of the Commonwealth.[147] Gopal observed that 'his patience gave the Commonwealth time to surmount the strain. Nehru was not just the creator and leader of the new Commonwealth; he was also its saviour.'[148] Nehru himself valued highly the institution of the Commonwealth and used it to launch the new sovereign India to the world. Reporting to the Lok Sabha on his return from attending the 1956 Commonwealth Prime Ministers Conference, Nehru spoke enthusiastically about such conferences describing them as 'a good thing for the world, beset as it is by the sectional outlook and much intolerance-ideological, racial and other.'[149] Rajan pointedly comments that all the Prime Ministers would agree with Nehru's view, 'perhaps with the lone exception of the Australian Prime Minister ... '[150]. Another difference, perhaps less noticed, between the two men is that Nehru's decision to remain in the Commonwealth and advance its causes, despite the colonial experience, despite the presence of South Africa, (till 1961) and India's nemesis Pakistan (with its membership of SEATO), and despite Britain's inexorable march towards the European Union (EU), has been vindicated in contrast to Menzies' pessimism about its future. One writer puts the case for India's faith:

> India represents, more perhaps than any other nation, free and uncommitted opinion in Asia and Africa, so membership of the Commonwealth has enabled India to reach out and influence opinion in all parts of the world.[151]

Another incident that alarmed Menzies, worsening his dislike of Nehru, occurred when Prime Minister Macmillan called on Nehru to chair a Commonwealth Prime Ministers' conference in his temporary absence. David Goldsworthy, writing about this, cites a record of a subsequent meeting between Sir Eric Harrison, (Australia's High Commissioner in London) and Duncan Sandys (Britain's Secretary of State for Commonwealth relations) to show that Menzies was 'much put out by Mr Macmillan's apparent preference for a brown face. He had now got the idea firmly fixed in his head that compared with the "brown" Commonwealth countries, Australia did not "count for a row of beans" '[152]

That Macmillan and Nehru got on well is due more to the former's personality rather than Menzies' ungracious speculation. First of all, Macmillan 'presented himself as a more ardent champion of the "new" Commonwealth' and, secondly, he 'made himself known to the Commonwealth and its peoples in a manner wholly pleasant to the hosts, and this without displaying either of the complexes that bedevil international relations today- ...'[153]. Unhampered by Britain's diminished international stature, Macmillan was the antithesis of Menzies, who seemed to cling to the notion of a British Empire at its zenith.

## Indo-Canadian Links: An Object Lesson

To understand the impact of personalities on policies and bilateralism, it helps to contrast the India-Australia relationship under Menzies with that which India enjoyed with Canada and its post World War II leaders. It is worth noting here that India's relations with Canada (like Australia, a member of the old Commonwealth and the Western alliance) were remarkably warm with the two finding common ground on foreign policy issues. Also, Canada's aid to India, more generous than Australia's, included assistance in establishing India's atomic energy programme for peaceful purposes and not, according to Nehru, for 'nefarious and destructive purposes.'[154] But then Canada's leaders like St Laurent, Pearson and Diefenbaker (the last named supporting Nehru on the question of South Africa's membership of the Commonwealth)[155] had a broader view of the world more capable of understanding Nehru's concept of the Commonwealth as a dynamic body for international cooperation based on racial equality. According to James Eayers, these men also played key roles in enabling Commonwealth members to remain honorably in the Commonwealth in several close-to-the-brink situations of disintegration, such as, the Suez crisis, South Africa and Rhodesia.[156] Apart from the economic aid Canada gave India, one writer ascribes the strong Indo-Canada friendship to the fact that:

> ... India found Mr St Laurent, Mr Pearson and Mr Diefenbaker (all of whom have visited the country) sympathetic personalities. Party politics in Canada have had no influence on Indo-Canadian relations. With Australia and New Zealand relations have never attained the same intensity.[157]

There were others, such as Lord Garner, who commended Canada for its Commonwealth contribution. In his article 'Commonwealth Under Strain', he refers to '... the good fortune that the interests of Canada included the Commonwealth relationship as an essential element ... ' and credits Pearson for his valuable contribution during the Suez crisis.[158] That the Canadian link with India was stronger and more capable of withstanding greater strain - even on the sensitive issue of restrictive barriers to immigration - than the Australian relationship is evident from an Australian High Commission despatch to Canberra. It concerns the Ontario Supreme Court's rejection of an Indian family's appeal in 1954 against deportation orders. The despatch from Crocker, observes that, 'the item was published in an obscure part in the Indian press in small print ...' and then adds that had it occurred in Australia, 'it would have been on the front page and with headlines.'[159] But, then, Nehru too became increasingly friendly towards Canada and got on well with its leaders so much so that, according to Gopal, as the Indo-Canadian links grew in strength for Nehru, 'as the years passed, the axis of the Commonwealth became more and more not India's old link with Britain but the new relationship with Canada.'[160]

Gopal describes the essential difference in the India-Canada Commonwealth environment: 'it became multi-racial, held together, as Nehru saw it, not by kinship or by common allegiance but by a shared sense of values.'[161] He makes the further point that the previously held view 'that all who have grown up under the Union Jack are in their hearts devoted to it,' is no longer a supportable argument.[162]

In the Whitlam-Mrs Gandhi period of the bilateral relationship too, (1972-1975) Canada continued to collaborate with Commonwealth members under prime Minister Trudeau. He viewed the Commonwealth as giving Canada a 'separate identity on the American continent',[163] adding to the high regard New Delhi had for the independence with which Canada has expressed its views and supported India's initiatives of the Nehru period and continued by Mrs Gandhi's government.

Given Menzies' pessimism about the future of the Commonwealth, Praful Bidwai and Kuldip Nayer in their article, 'Is there any common weal in the Commonwealth?', provide two different, though incisive assessments, of what the Commonwealth institution has meant to India and others over the decades but, also as importantly, its relevance for the future. Bidwai sees it as 'a forum without function', one that needs, he says, to 'reinvent a useful role for itself: a North-South forum to promote an equitable economic and ecological world order, ...'. On the other hand, Nayer believes its 'relevance today lies not in its economic or political clout, but in `terms of cohesiveness and contacts, attitudes and agreements.'[164] Britain too, like Nayer above, saw the Commonwealth as useful and enduring, and not an obstacle to Britain's integration with the European community. A poll conducted in 1973 on usefulness of the Commonwealth found seven out of ten people in Britain disagreed with any question of it being wound up and, on the contrary, thought it should be made even stronger.[165] The relevance of this British-Canadian sharing of Nehru's optimism is that it presents a picture that is in sharp contrast to Menzies' earlier pessimistic view of the future Commonwealth and his extraordinary concerns for the people of Britain made in the aftermath of India's republican membership.

## Endnotes

1. See Martin, A.W., *Robert Menzies: A Life*, Vol. 2, Melbourne University Press, Victoria, 1999, Chapter 5.

2. See Wolpert, Stanley, *Nehru: A Tryst with Destiny*, Oxford University Press, New York, 1996, Chapter 29.

3. See Ladamy, Laszlo, *The Communist Party of China and Marxism*, Hoover Institution Press, Stamford, 1988, Chapters IX and XI.

4. See Hall, D.G.E., *A History of South East Asia*, Macmillan, London, 1966, pp 804-810.

5. See Watt, Alan, *The Evolution of Australian Foreign Policy, 1938-1965*, Cambridge University Press, London, 1967, p 197.

6. See Edwards, Peter and Pemberton, Gregory, *Crises and Commitments*, Allen & Unwin, Sydney, 1992, pp 143-150.

7. See Mackerras, Colin (ed.) *Eastern Asia: An Introductory History*, Longman, Melbourne, 2000, pp 439-441.

8. See Hobsbawm, Eric *Age of Extremes: The Short Twentieth Century, 1914-1991*, Pantheon Books, New York, 1995, pp 220-222.

9. *Ibid.*, Chapter 7.

10. See Martin, *op. cit.*, Chapters 7 and 8.

11. See Lowe, David, *Menzies and the 'Great World Struggle': Australia's Cold War, 1948-1954*, University of NSW Press, Sydney, 1999, Chapter 4.

12. See Albinsky, Henry, *Australian External Policy Under Labor*, Queensland, University Press, Qld. 1977, Chapter 1.

13. See G. Ramachandram, *Nehru and World Peace*, Radiant Publishers New Delhi, 1990, pp 4, 20, 83; S.N. Misra, *India: the Cold War Years*, South Asian Publishers, New Delhi, 1994, p 126; S.N. Varma, *Aspects of India's Foreign Relations, 1954-1957*, Indian Council of World Affairs, New Delhi, 1957,  p 18; Michael Brecher, *Nehru: A Political Biography*, Abridged Edition, Oxford University Press, London, 1961, p 218.

14. Brecher, Michael, *Nehru a Political Biography*, Abridged Edition, Oxford University Press, London, 1961, p 14.

15. 'India Retreat from the West', *TRT*, No. 177, December 1954, p 73. Besides carrying Prime Ministerial responsibility in the new Indian Government, Nehru had responsibility for Foreign Affairs, Defence, Commonwealth Relations and Planning to contend with at the time.

16. Wolpert, Stanley *India*, Prentice Hall, New Jersey, 1965, p 9.

17. AA, Despatch, 23 December 1954, from W.R. Crocker, Australian High Commissioner, New Delhi, to R.G. Casey, Series A4534/1, Item 44/6/2.

18. Perkins, Kevin *Menzies: Last of the Queens Men*, Rigby, Adelaide, 1968, p 184.

19. Lowe, David 'Menzies Memory and Britain', *Working Papers in Australian Studies*, No. 88-96, Kate Darian-Smith, (ed.) Sir Robert Menzies Centre for Australia Studies, London, 1994, p 120.

20. Nehru, Jawaharlal *India and the World*, George Allen & Unwin, London, 1936, p 130.

21. Manne, Robert, 'Revisiting Menzies', *The Age*, 29 November 1999, p 15.

22. See Nehru Memorial Museum & Library, *Jawaharlal Nehru: A Bibliography*, Vikas, New Delhi, 1989.

23. Brett, Judith, 'Robert Menzies and England', *Political Lives*, Judith Brett (ed.) Allen & Unwin, NSW, 1997, p 76. 'Menzies was not a loved leader; he was feared. He was a one man band waiting to control everything that went on around him. ... he towered in his powers of persuasion, in his sense of overriding authority, over people who were less aggressive, articulate, and lacked strength in the presentation of their views.' See, Kevin Perkins, *Menzies, last of the Queen's Men*, Rigby, Adelaide, 1968, p 184.

24. *Ibid.*

25. *Jawaharlal Nehru: An Autobiography*, John Lane, The Bodley Head, London, 1936, p 77. For a comprehensive study of Nehru's personal and political life see Marie Seton, *Panditji: A Portrait of Nehru*, Dennis Dobson, London, 1967.

26. Brecher, *op. cit.*, p 21.

27. Nehru Memorial Library, Manuscripts Section, New Delhi, S.S. Bhatia, (Director, Indian Institute of International Understanding, New Delhi) 'Jawaharlal Nehru-An Internationalist: Apostle of Peace', Accession No. 49.

28. *The Indian Express,* Bombay, 18 November 1952, in Michael Brecher, *Nehru a Political Biography*, Abridged Edition, Oxford University Press, London, 1961, p 4.

29. AA, Despatch No. 2/64, 2 June 1964, from J. Plimsoll, to Paul Hasluck, Minister for External Affairs, Series A1838/272, Item 169/1/3, Part 3.

30. Wolpert, *op. cit.*, p 9.

31. Chaudary, Ramanarayan, *Nehru: in His Own Words*, Navajivan Publishing House, Ahmedabad, India, 1964, p 94.

32. Brecher, *op. cit.*, pp 8-9.

33. Zinkin, T., 'Indian Foreign Policy: An Interpretation of Attitudes' *World Politics*, Vol. 7, 1954-55, p 180.

34. Ramachandram, G., *Nehru and World Peace*, Radiant Publishers, New Delhi, 1990, p 5.

35. Martin, A.W., *Robert Menzies a life*, Vol. 1, Melbourne University Press, Victoria, 1993, p 355.

36. Brett, Judith, *Robert Menzies: Forgotten People*, Macmillan, Sydney, 1992, p 21.

37. Brett, Judith, 'Robert Menzies and England', *Political Lives*, Judith Brett (ed.) Allen & Unwin, NSW, 1997, p 80.

38. Menzies, Robert, 'Australia and Britain Drift Apart: the Need for Common Purpose', *TRT*, No. 232, October 1968, p 366. Also see, Gregory Pemberton, 'An Imperial Imagination: Explaining the Post-1945 Foreign Policy of Robert Gordon Menzies', in Frank Cain (ed.) *Menzies in War and Peace*, Allen & Unwin, NSW, 1997.

39. *Ibid.*

40. Perkins, *op. cit.*, p 256.

41. CPD, (H of R), 6 December 1966, p 3576.

42. Movietone News, 1941 in J. Brett 'Robert Menzies and England' *Political Lives*, Judith Brett (ed.) Allen & Unwin, NSW, 1997, p 82.

43. Casey, R.G., *An Australian in India*, Hollis & Carter, London, 1947, p 66.

44. Narasimha Char K.T. *The Quintessence of Nehru*, George Allen & Unwin, London, 1961, p 15.

45. Wolpert, Stanley, *Nehru: A Tryst with Destiny*, Oxford University Press, New York, 1996, p 384. Moulana Asad, Mahatma Gandhi and Sardar Patel were prominent leaders with Nehru in the negotiations with Mountbatten for independence, and except for Gandhi, the other two served as Ministers in Nehru's first Cabinet of independent India.

46. Gopal, S. (ed.), *Selected Works of Jawaharlal Nehru*, Vol. 15, Orient Longman, New Delhi, 1982, p 518.

47. *Ibid.*

48. *Ibid.*

49. *Inside America*, pp 54-55, in Michael Brecher, *Nehru: A Political Biography*, Abridged Edition, Oxford University Press, London, 1961, p 227.

50. Brett, Judith, *Robert Menzies: Forgotten People*, Macmillan, Sydney, 1992, p 174.

51. Jensen, Lloyd, *Explaining Foreign Policy*, Prentice Hall, New Jersey, 1982, p 14.

52. *Ibid.*, pp 14-15.

53. Brecher, Michael *India and World Politics*, Oxford University Press, London, 1968, p 295.

54. *Ibid.* p 298. Also see, Judith Brett, 'Robert Menzies and England' *Political Lives*, Judith Brett (ed.) Allen & Unwin, NSW, 1997, pp 71-84, for a comprehensive analysis of the Menzies' personality.

55. Martin, A.W., 'R.G. Menzies and the Suez Crisis', *Australian Historical Studies*, 23, 2, p 183, in David Lowe, 'Menzies Memory and Britain', *Working Papers in Australian Studies*, Nos. 88-96, Kate Darian Smith (ed.), Sir Robert Menzies Centre for Australia Studies, London, 1994, p 128.

56. Menzies Papers, MS 4936, Box 397, Series 13, in David Lowe, 'Menzies Memory and Britain' *Working Papers in Australian Studies*, Nos. 88-96, Kate Darian Smith (ed.), Sir Robert Menzies Centre for Australia Studies, London, 1994, p 117. While there is some evidence of Soviet involvement in the Korean War, it was not merely a Russian 'dimension'. The war had its own set of complex causal factors.

57. Lowe, David, 'Menzies Memory and Britain' *Working Papers in Australian Studies*, Nos. 88-96, Kate Darian Smith (ed.), Sir Robert Menzies Centre for Australia Studies, London, 1994, p 117.

58. AA, Despatch No. 2/64, 2 June 1964, from J. Plimsoll, Australian High Commissioner in New Delhi to DEA, Series A1838/272, Item 169/1/3, part 3, p 1.

59. Sinha, S., *China Strikes*, Blandford Press, London, 1964, p vii.

60. *Ibid.*, p 122.

61. Casey, R.G., *The Future of the Commonwealth*, Frederick Muller, London, 1963, p 68.

62. Gopal, S. (ed.), *Jawaharlal Nehru: An Anthology*, Oxford University Press, New Delhi, 1980, p 346.

63. 'The Foreign Policy of Mr Nehru', *TRT*, No. 176, September 1954, p 365.

64. Ramachandram, *op. cit.*, p 5.

65. 'India: Bandung Balance Sheet', *TRT*, No. 179, June 1955, p 278.

66. *Ibid.*

67. Nehru Memorial Library, Manuscripts Section, New Delhi, M.H. Heikal interview, 'A Dialogue with Nehru', at the Embassy of India, Cairo. Information Service of India, Accession No. 1097.

68. *Ibid.*

69. *Ibid.* Also see, Rafiq Zakaria (ed.) *A Study of Nehru*, Times of India Publication, Bombay, 1959.

70. Spender, Percy, *Exercises in Diplomacy: The ANZUS Treaty and the Colombo Plan*, Sydney University Press, Sydney, 1969, p 203.

71. Brecher, Michael, *India and World Politics*, Oxford University Press, London, 1968, p 20.

72. Nehru, Jawaharlal, *India and the World*, George Allen & Unwin, London, 1936, pp 27-28. Casey, who was more familiar with the Nehru personality than most Australians, writes about Nehru's dislike of the monarchy concept and his preference for the 'republican form of government with its authority deriving from the people.' See *The Future of the Commonwealth*, Frederick Muller, London, 1963, p 64.

73. Chaudary, Ramanarayan, *Nehru: in His Own Words*, Navajivan Publishing House, Ahmedabad, India, 1964, p 106.

74. Lord Butler, Jawaharlal Nehru Memorial Lectures, Jawaharlal Nehru Memorial Trust, London, 1973, 15, in G. Ramachandram, *Nehru and World Peace*, Radiant Publishers, New Delhi, 1990, p 147.

75. Brecher, Michael, *India and World Politics*, Oxford University Press, London, 1968, p 24.

76. *Ibid.*

77. *Ibid.*, p 27.

78. *Nehru: The First Sixty Years*, Dorothy Norman, (ed.) Vol. II, John Lane The Bodley Head, London, 1965, p 473.

79. Brecher, Michael, *India and World Politics*, Oxford University Press, London, 1968, p 24. The words that secured the break through were ' We are a free state, the Crown is a *symbol* of this Union and, *"as such"* Head of the Commonwealth ' Also see, T.N. Kaul, *My Years Through Raj to Swaraj*, Vikas Publishing, New Delhi, 1995, pp 258-259 for the *communiqué* issued after the April 1949 meeting approving India's republican membership of the Commonwealth.

80. Hodson, H.V., 'Problems Before the Commonwealth', *International Relations and Foreign Policy of India, Great Britain, Commonwealth*, Verinder Grover (ed.), Deep & Deep Publications, New Delhi, 1992, p 349.

81. Narasimha Char, *op. cit.*, p 96. Also see, NAI, India's Continuation in Commonwealth - Speeches, File No. 35(56)-AMS.

82. Public Records Office, London, Memorandum by the Secretary of State for Commonwealth Relations, dated 16 June 1949, 'The Commonwealth Relationship: Reactions to the Commonwealth declaration of 27 April, 1949', C.P. (49) 139,

copy No. 31, p 156. Also see, *ibid.* p 157, Appendix 1, Summary of Commonwealth press and public reactions to the Commonwealth Declaration as received in London at 11th May 1949.

83. CNIA, 'The Changing Commonwealth,' the first Smuts Memorial Lecture by R.G. Menzies, at the University of Cambridge, 16 May 1960, Vol. 31, 1960, p 258. Jan Christian Smuts, was the South African Union Premier from 1919-1924 and 1939-1948, and a contributor to the Commonwealth Charter.

84. Menzies, Robert, 'Australia and Britain Drift Apart: the Need for Common Purpose', *TRT*, No. 232, October 1968, p 365.

85. CPD, (H of R), Vol. 14, 21 March, 1957, p 159.

86. Menzies, Robert, 'Australia and Britain Drift Apart: the Need for Common Purpose' *TRT*, No. 232, October 1968, p 365.

87. CNIA, 'The Changing Commonwealth,' the first Smuts Memorial lecture by R.G. Menzies, at the University of Cambridge, 16 May 1960, Vol. 31, 1960, p 257.

88. Menzies, R.G., *Afternoon Light*, Cassell, Melbourne, 1967, p 233.

89. Public Records Office, London, Royal Visit to Australia, Minute of UK Cabinet meeting dated 17 June 1952, cc 60 (52), Item 2, p 161.

90. Grant, Bruce, *The Australian Dilemma: A New Kind of Western Society*, Macdonald Futura, NSW, 1983, p 30.

91. Harris, Max, 'Monarchy and the Australian Character', *Australia and the Monarchy: A Symposium*, G. Dutton (ed.) Sun Books, Melbourne, 1966, p 115.

92. Brecher, Michael, *India and World Politics*, Oxford University Press, London, 1968, p 30.

93. *Ibid.*, p 31.

94. *Jawaharlal Nehru's Speeches*, September 1946 to May 1949, Vol. I, Ministry of Broadcasting and Information, Government of India, New Delhi, 1949, p 282. Also see, Lok Sabha Debates, 23 July 1957, Col. 4747 and 9 December 1958, Col. 3965 for Nehru's arguments about the benefits of Commonwealth membership to India; *The Hindu*, Madras, 18 March 1953, in S.C. Gangul, *India and the Commonwealth*, Shiva Lal, Agarwala, India, 1970, p 70.

95. Chaudary, *op. cit.*, p 63.

96. For the text of the resolution see R.G. Casey, *The Future of the Commonwealth*, Frederick Muller, London, 1963, pp 69-70.

97. Chanchal, Sarkar, 'Heart Searching in India about the Commonwealth link' *The Times*, (Ceylon), 4 December 1958, p 8.

98. *Nehru: The First Sixty Years*, Vol. II, Dorothy Norman (ed.) John Lane The Bodley Head, London, 1965, p 473.

99. Brecher, Michael, *India and World Politics*, Oxford University Press, London, 1968, p 32.

100. Gopal, S. (ed.) *Jawaharlal Nehru: An Anthology*, Oxford University Press, New Delhi, 1980, p 342.

101. AA, Confidential memorandum, 14 May 1954, from W.R. Crocker to DEA, Series A1838/2, Item 169/11/1 part 3.

102. AA, Despatch, 6 June 1953, from W.R. Crocker to R.G. Casey, Series A1838/2, Item 169/11/1 part 3. Also see, *ibid.* Crocker Memorandum to DEA, dated 2 August 1954, for reference to Nehru's strong defence of India's membership of the Commonwealth against attacks from Communists and socialists.

103. Menzies, R.G., 'Australia and Britain Drift apart', *TRT*, No. 232, October 1968, p 368.

104. *Ibid.*

105. Eayers, James, 'The Overhaul of Commonwealth', *TRT*, No. 225, January 1967, p 48.

106. Kaul, T.N., *My Years through Raj to Swaraj*, Vikas Publishing, New Delhi, 1995, p 242.

107. Menzies, R.G., *Afternoon Light*, Cassell, Melbourne, 1967, p 188.

108. *The National Herald*, Lucknow, 31 July 1956, p 5.

109. Pemberton, Gregory 'An Imperial Imagination: Explaining the Post-1945 foreign Policy of Robert Gordon Menzies', *Menzies in War and Peace*, Frank Cain (ed.) Allen & Unwin, NSW, 1997, p 157.

110. Menzies, R.G., 'Australia and Britain Drift Apart: the Need for Common Purpose', *TRT*, No. 232, October 1968, p 367.

111. Gangul, S.C., *India and the Commonwealth*, Shiva Lal Agarwala, India, 1970, p 39. For a discussion of the impact of Britain's entry into the EUC on the economies, culture and politics of other Commonwealth countries see Raymond Aron, 'The Commonwealth and the European Community' *TRT*, No. 244, October 1971, pp 447-454; Dharma Kumar, 'The New Community and the Developing Commonwealth-Problems of Trade and Aid', *TRT*, No. 244, October 1971, pp 475-484.

112. *Ibid*. p 368. Also see, Gordon Burns, 'An Australian View of British Entry: Economic Gains, Political Dangers', *TRT*, No. 244, October 1971, pp 527-532. Britain first made known its decision to apply for entry to the European Economic Community in July 1961.

113. Goldsworthy, David, 'Menzies, Britain and the Commonwealth: the Old Order Changeth', *Menzies in War and Peace*, Frank Cain (ed.), Allen & Unwin, NSW, 1997, pp 105-106.

114. 'The Commonwealth An Indian View: The Pioneer Republic,' *TRT*, No. 200, September 1960, p 371.

115. *Ibid*.

116. 'Commonwealth Relations: the Coronation Conference', *TRT*, Vol. XLIII, December 1952- September 1953, p 362.

117. Ingram, D., 'Prospects for Ottawa: the Prime Ministers prepare,' *TRT*, No. 250, 1973, p 177. Also see, D. Ingram, *Commonwealth for a Colour-blind World*, Allen & Unwin, London, 1965, and *The Commonwealth at Work*, Pergamon Press, New York, 1969.

118. *Jawaharlal Nehru's Speeches, September 1946-May 1949*, Vol. 1, Ministry of Information and Broadcasting, Government of India, New Delhi, 1949, p 3.

119. 'Commonwealth Relations: The Coronation Conference' *TRT*, Vol. XLIII, December 1952- September 1953, p 359.

120. CNIA, 'The Changing Commonwealth', the first Smuts Memorial Lecture, by R.G. Menzies, delivered at the University of Cambridge, Vol. 31, 1960, p 261.

121. *Ibid*.

122. *Ibid*.

123. *Ibid*., pp 198-210, for exchange of letters between Menzies and South Africa's Prime Minister Verwoerd who was represented at the London Conference by his Foreign Minister, Eric Louw.

124. *Ibid*., p 198.

125. *Ibid*., p 202.

126. *Ibid*., p 192.

127. 'Prime Minister Nehru's Visit to London', *Indian Panorama*, V. 1, 8 June 1960, in Sean Brawley, *The White Peril*, University of NSW Press, Sydney, 1995, p 287.

128. Private Papers of A.A. Calwell, Australian National Library, Box 143, 'Extracts from a Press Conference Given By Mr Menzies in London, March 19th 1961,' in Sean Brawley, *The White Peril*, University of NSW Press, Sydney, 1995, p 287.

129. Nanda B.R., *Indian Foreign Policy: The Nehru Years*, Vikas Publishing, New Delhi, 1976, p 7.

130. Nehru Memorial Library, Manuscripts Section, New Delhi, Diary of Jawaharlal Nehru, Commonwealth Prime Ministers Conference, 1960, Accession No. 1423, pp 1-2, 40-44.

131. *Ibid.*, p 88.

132. AA, Cablegram, 14 March 1961, Australian High Commission, London, R.G. Menzies to J. McEwen, Series A1838/2, Item 169/11/128, pt 1, p 1.

133. *Ibid.*, p 2.

134. *The Hindu*, India, 14 March 1961; *Daily Telegraph*, London, 18 March 1961, in S.C. Gangul, *India and the Commonwealth*, Shiva Lal Agarwala, India, 1970, p 38.

135. AA, Cablegram, 14 March 1961, Australian High Commission, London, Menzies to McEwen, Series A1838/2, Item 169/11/128, pt 1, p 3.

136. D. Ingram, 'Prospects for Ottawa: the Prime Ministers Prepare', *TRT*, No. 250, April 1973, p 177.

137. AA, Cablegram, 14 March 1961, Australian High Commission, London, Menzies, to McEwen Series A1838/2, Item 169/11/128, pt 1, p 3. This last statement of admission on the 'White Australia' Policy, is in contrast to official explanations, defending the policy as non-discriminatory given by Menzies as well as members of his Government in the face of criticism from Asia in the 1950s and 1960s.

138. AA, Cablegram, 27 March 1961, Crocker to DEA, Series A1838/2, Item 169/11/128 pt 1.

139. *India's Foreign Policy: Selected Speeches*, September 1946-April 1961, Ministry of Information & Broadcasting, Government of India, New Delhi, 1961, p 550.

140. Rajan, M.S., *India and the Commonwealth-Some Studies*, Konark Publishers, Delhi, 1990. p 118.

141. CNIA, Statement to the (H of R), by R.G. Menzies, on 11 April 1961, Vol. 32, 1961, p 30.

142. *Ibid.*

143. *Ibid.*

144. *Ibid.*, p 31.

145. Galbraith, J.K. *Ambassadors Journal*, Hamish Hamilton, London, 1969, p 86.

146. Manne, Robert 'Revisiting Menzies', *The Age*, 29 November 1999, p 15.

147. Prasad, Bimal 'Nehru and the New Commonwealth', *International Relations and Foreign Policy of India, Great Britain, Commonwealth*, Verinder Grover, (ed.), Deep & Deep Publications, New Delhi, 1992. p 257.

148. Gopal, S. 'The Commonwealth: An Indian View', *TRT*, No. 240, Diamond Jubilee Number, p 615.

149. Rajan, M.S., 'India and the Commonwealth: 1954-56', *International Relations and Foreign Policy of India, Great Britain, Commonwealth*, Verinder Grover, (ed.), Deep & Deep Publications, New Delhi, 1992, p 370.

150. *Ibid.*

151. 'The Commonwealth An Indian View: The Pioneer Republic', *TRT*, No. 200, September 1960, p 377. Also see, 'Commonwealth, South Asia and the Enlarged Community: The Continued Value of the Commonwealth Link', *TRT* No. 244, October 1971, pp 507-510.

152. F. Mills to Sir Alexander Cutterbuck, 24 May 1961, DO 161/161, Public Records Office, London in David Goldsworthy, ' Menzies Britain and the Commonwealth: The Old Order Changeth', *Menzies in War and Peace*, Frank Cain (ed.) Allen & Unwin, NSW, 1997, p 100.

153. 'India: The Sun also Sets', *TRT*, No. 190, March 1958, p 177.

154. See 'Canada-India Reactor Inaugurated', *The Hindu Weekly Review*, Bombay, 23 January 1961; 'The Kundah Project', *The Hindu Weekly*, Madras, 23 January 1961.

155. See Richard A. Preston, *Canada in World Affairs 1959-1961*, Oxford University Press, Toronto, 1965, pp 200-208.

156. Eayers, James, ' The Overhaul of the Commonwealth', *TRT*, No. 225, January 1967, p 48.

157. 'The Commonwealth An Indian View: the Pioneer Republic', *TRT*, No. 200, September 1960, p 373.

158. Lord Garner, 'Commonwealth Under Strain: problems of Expansion and Attrition', *TRT*, No. 258, April 1975, pp 210-211.

159. AA, Despatch No. 23, 6 December 1954, from W.R. Crocker to R.G. Casey, Series A1838/283, Item 169/10/1 part 2, p 3.

160. Gopal, S., 'The Commonwealth: An Indian View', *TRT*, No. 240, Diamond Jubilee Number, 1970, p 615. Lester Pearson, like Nehru, was critical of the Anglo-French action on Suez, and told the House of Commons in November 1956 that it, brought the Commonwealth, close to disintegration. See S.N. Misra, *India: the Cold War Years*, South Asian Publishers, New Delhi, 1994, pp 216-217.

161. *Ibid.*, p 614.

162. *Ibid.*

163. Kamath M.V. 'Commonwealth Overhauled at Ottawa', *Times of India*, 12 August 1973.

164. Bidwai, Praful and Nayer, Kuldip (former High Commissioner for India to the UK), 'Is there any Common Weal in the Commonwealth?' *The Sunday Times of India*, New Delhi, 2 November, 1997, p 20. Also see, *ibid.*, L.K. Sharma, 'Commonwealth: a New Survival Instinct', p 15.

165. 'British Interest in the Commonwealth', *TRT*, No. 234, April 1969, pp 170-171. Also see, S.C. Leslie, 'British Attitudes to the Commonwealth: Dream and Daylight' *TRT*, No. 251, July 1973, pp 363-375.

**4**

# Nehru and Menzies: Morality and Internationalism vs Self-Interest

Thus far, the discussion in Chapter 3 provides an insight into the early background of these two men as well as their attitudes to South Africa's racist policy and membership of the Commonwealth, including India's membership as a new Republic. However, in determining how they affected the bilateral relationship in the 1950s, it is necessary to focus also on the different ways in which the two men viewed practices such as colonialism, and the threat of Communism to the free world. These differences not only throw light on the ideological barrier that separated the two, but also on their responses to the contentious Cold War environment of the period, reflected in their policy actions on international conflicts of the time some of which are examined in this chapter.

## Colonialism

One obvious manifestation of their differences is the way that the two men viewed colonialism. For Nehru, the long struggle of the independence movement, during which he personally suffered the ignominy of being imprisoned[1] as well as being separated from his only child Indira, was a poignant and perhaps salutary experience. The exchange of letters between him (written from prison), and his daughter speaks of the anguish of this period in his life.[2] Consequently, the effects of colonialism with all its manifestations of exploitation and brutality [3] were a strong force in the shaping of Nehru's attitude to the outside world: anti-colonialism, racial equality and non-alignment combined to become the seed-bed of India's foreign policy[4] under its first Prime Minister. Not surprisingly, then, responsibility for Foreign Affairs was firmly in Nehru's hands. Brecher does not exaggerate when he writes about Nehru's hold on Foreign Affairs:

Nowhere does one man dominate foreign policy as does Nehru in India. Indeed, Nehru is the philosopher, the architect, the engineer and the voice of his country's policy towards the outside world.[5]

His eloquent defiance of colonialism was strong from the very outset of his entry into the political arena, as was his persistence with it throughout the 1950s, describing it as 'obsolete in the modern world.'[6] Frustrated by the lack of action by the UN Security Council on Indonesia's independence, Nehru convened a conference of eighteen nations, to demand swift action on the question by the international community.[7] Speaking at the Asia Relations Conference in March 1947, (attended by Australia as an observer, with a Labor Government in Canberra), on the subject of the emergence of Asia after centuries of imperial dominance, Nehru said: 'during the past two hundred years, we have seen the growth of Western imperialism and of the reduction of large parts of Asia to colonial or semi colonial status.'[8]

Menzies, on the other hand, driven by historical impulses and possessed by a British Empire-centred world view, played down the immorality of colonialism, in one instance pointing to an apparent double standard in the selective recognition and criticism of the practice:

> ... when the word 'colonialism' is used in the Asian or African countries, it connotes control of an Asian or African community by a Western or European power. So understood, the Soviet Union is innocent of colonialism; Australia is a colonial power in relation to East New Guinea and Papua; Indonesia with control of West New Guinea is not a colonial power at all![9]

Clearly, Menzies failed to recognise the history of military power of Western States which ultimately led to Western colonialism and dominance of the weaker states of Asia and Africa as Copland asserts here:

> The rapid growth of Western military power in the eighteenth century liberated the Europeans from the need to go cap-in-hand to Asian rulers for permission to trade ... Hesitantly at first, and then with increasing assurance and swagger, they moved from defence to offence -...'[10].

Furthermore, for Menzies, the emergent nationalism in Asia, accompanied by a surge in the granting of independence to former European-held Asian colonies in the aftermath of World War II posed a number of fears. Unlike Britain and European colonial powers, Australia, in the 1950s - itself a small colonial power because of Papua (New Guinea) - was, for Menzies, too close for comfort to turbulent and non-White Asia, Australia's 'near north', as he has described it. Lowe explains the dilemma:

> Decolonisation in Australia's region also challenged the tenets of faith; such as racial homogeneity, protection from Asia, and regional European influence, which had circulated in Australia from the time of federation.[11]

At a time when decolonisation was an important issue for Nehru and other European colonies demanding independence from their colonial rulers, Australia's record in the Menzies era on decolonisation debates was not a proud one:

> ... not only did the Australians oppose the anti-colonial demands ... they were the most rigid in their opposition. Only a handful of the colonial old-guard such as South Africa, Belgium and Portugal showed greater hostility to decolonisation.'[12]

In fact, Percy Spender, as Australia's Minister for External Affairs in (1949-1950) and later Ambassador to the US, was active in obstructing the UN from discussing questions of decolonisation.[13] Then, there were those in the Menzies government like Anderson, Liberal Party (MHR) for Hume, who would seriously question the belief that colonialism was detrimental to the lives of those subjected to it. In an address to Parliament, Anderson asks: '...but is it so bad? Most colonies were originally established to provide markets and to improve the standard of living of the people'.[14]

Anderson's grotesque view on the virtues of colonialism was certainly not shared in India, in fact quite the contrary. Nehru, in an address to Parliament, referred to the difficulties India faced stepping up to 'all the problems that had accumulated during the period of our arrested growth in the past ...'[15]. Downer, like Menzies and Anderson, failed to understand Asia's resentment of colonialism, seeing the attaining of nationhood by the constituents of the Empire as 'England's goal for the past 100 years, despite all the propaganda and all the misrepresentations about the alleged evils of colonialism.'[16] His address to Parliament, (when he made the above comments on colonialism) studded with criticisms of India' s opposition to NATO, the Baghdad Pact, (which later became

CENTO), SEATO and the Anglo-Australian attitude to the Suez issue, added to the acrimony that prevailed between the two countries in the Menzies era. Surprisingly, Casey too in 1957, was no less laudatory in his reference to Britain's record on decolonisation when he said:

> No country in the world's history has anything approaching Great Britain's record of statesmanship on the grand scale, by way of the development of one country after another to self-government and independence.[17]

Making a virtue of decolonisation after centuries of enforced rule was not Nehru's view of it. India, according to Nehru's assessment, underwent economic exploitation and deprivation of numerous human rights, before Britain consented to the granting of independence in the face of growing unrest within India, as well as the pressure of world opinion. Then again, Casey's own account[18] of British neglect of India,[19] gained at first hand as Governor of Bengal is hardly a flattering testimonial for colonialism. In contrast to Menzies, Spender, Downer and Anderson, there were Indian leaders who, shared Nehru's contempt for colonialism. For instance, Dr Kashar (Deputy Minister for External Affairs) described Indonesia winning freedom from the Dutch as 'the first victory of India's policy in eliminating Colonialism in all parts of the world. Some of the countries, he said, were angry with India because of her anti-colonial policy, but India had to follow the path of justice and righteousness.'[20] There is also the Krishna Menon perspective. In a wide ranging interview with Brecher, Menon, speculating on the future of India's Commonwealth links, mentions a number of determinants for its continuance, and includes his admonition that 'there is no conscious effort to deliberately liquidate colonialism and liberate yourselves (the white Commonwealth members) from colonial ideas.'[21] In another critique of the exploitative relationship between the coloniser and the colonised, Rajendra Prasad comments on the horrors of colonial practices:

> The British policy of colonialism in India and China was remarkably consistent in terms of ends accomplished ...Brute force, bribes, intrigues and subhuman instruments of subordination were common to experiences of both the societies.[22]

Nehru, a victim of the undemocratic laws of the colonial authorities (used regularly to suppress the right to freedom of speech and movement), was acutely sensitive to the thousands of his fellow countrymen who voluntarily sacrificed their lives[23] as co-participants with him in the civil disobedience movement against British rule, against colonialism. In Nehru's words, the British reaction to the non-violent quit-India campaign 'took the shape of fierce repression of the typical fascist kind, with suppression of civil liberties, of Press, ...'[24]. Speaking of the British presence in India and specifically the absence of civil liberties, Nehru, addressing the Indian National Congress in 1936, said:

> A Government (British) that has to rely on the Criminal Law Amendment Act ..., that suppresses the press and literature, that bans hundreds of organizations, that keeps people in prison without trial ..., is a government that has ceased to have even a shadow of a justification for its existence ... I find them (these conditions) intolerable.[25]

Nehru spoke of his friendship with the English that started from his time at Harrow and Cambridge, but stressed 'that friendship, I am afraid, does not extend to the British Government in England.'[26]

Consistent with his commendatory view of colonialism, Menzies never felt it necessary to lament the absence of justice and democratic rights in British India, while he lost no opportunity to speak, in glowing terms, about the virtues of British law, traditions and institutions. But not all in Australia shared Menzies' view of colonialism. The Labor Opposition led by Chifley and Evatt in the 1950s was opposed to the Menzies philosophy. There was also sympathy in Australia for India's anti-colonial struggles early in the century. In 1909, *The Worker* in Sydney published an article which took the view that 'India is tired of being the slave of a useless aristocracy trampling her under the feet of an alien contempt,' and, on Britain's attitude to freedom for India, the newspaper said that it was, 'regrettable that a nation should be decimated by rapacity and misrule ... and its reasonable appeals for the franchise, to a country boasting of its love of liberty, be answered by the methods of the Tsar.'[27]

## The UN: A Nehru-Menzies Coloseum

For all his and India's consistent criticism of racial discrimination, Nehru did not use the Commonwealth forum to raise his concerns about it because he saw it as 'an occasion and a body for seeking agreement and friendship rather than on pressing on differences.'[28] But, of course, when something as abnormal as Sharpeville occurred, then the notion of camaraderie within a harmonious Commonwealth family was tested to its limits and failed to endure South Africa's presence. A further reason for Nehru's accommodating attitude to Commonwealth conferences (before Sharpeville) was that Nehru 'had another view of the United Nations where he had no compunction in exciting racial controversy and attacking other countries...'[29]. Indeed, Menzies too saw the UN as the more appropriate place for the airing of differences. Ironically, it was the one point of convergence between Nehru and Menzies, but it also became the forum for their policy divergence and their most virulent encounter.

This neatly leads the discussion to two other issues of an international dimension that saw the two warring protagonists in action: the Five Power Resolution and the Suez Canal Crisis. Of the two, the encounter over the Five Power Resolution was quite easily the most gruelling. In the end, both men were criticised for their performance on it by their Parliaments as well as the Press; chronology dictates the conflict over Suez be examined first. There were other policy issues on which the two differed (Korean War and SEATO) but, the conflict was less direct: these are examined later in this chapter even though they took place earlier in the sequence of events.

## The Suez Canal Crisis

The international event which exemplifies the different approaches taken by Nehru and Menzies to international conflict resolution during the Cold War occurred in July 1956, when Egypt's President Nasser nationalised the Suez canal. It also strained the Commonwealth relationship to its limits and 'marked the first occasion when a major act of British policy (supported by Menzies) was actively opposed by the other members of the Commonwealth.'[30] In India, the major Opposition parties (the Praja Socialist Party, the Communist Party and the Hindu Mahasabha) asked for a re-evaluation during a Lok Sabha debate on the Commonwealth link.[31]

The canal, under Anglo-French control for over a century, was seen in the Third World countries as a symbol of imperialism.

Menzies was returning to Australia from London when Nasser's announcement reached him. He decided with the concurrence of the Australian government, which he sought, to return to London. Menzies viewed the action by Nasser as illegal, but found the Press in Britain and in America thought otherwise as did the Law Officers in London.[32] The twenty-two nation London conference that swiftly followed was not attended by Nasser or Nehru, the latter being represented by Krishna Menon, a fact not lost on Menzies who described Menon's attendance as 'unhappily' the case.[33] Menon, like Nehru, did not have Menzies' blessing. The conference ended with Menzies elected to chair a committee representing Western interests in resolving the crisis through a proposal which he was to carry to Nasser. In the event, Menzies' mission to Egypt failed resulting in an invasion of Egypt by Anglo-French troops, but preceded by Israel's attack on Egypt in October 1956.

Once again, Menzies' interest was in supporting the British position. In Parliament, he said 'an open canal is essential to British prosperity, ...a closed canal could mean mass unemployment in Great Britain, a financial collapse there, a grievous blow at the central power of our commonwealth, ...'[34]. Nehru responded to the crisis in an address to the Lok Sabha in September 1956, when he said 'at the conference held in London we pleaded ... for steps to be taken to bring about negotiations, and certain broad proposals were laid out by us, ...'[35]. India's proposal put by Krishna Menon was, according to Hudson, 'very close to Eisenhower's concept of a solution,' and the only uncomplicated alternative. It was rejected by Menzies who described it as 'pious talk about peace ... would give Nasser practically everything and which no self-respecting British government could accept.'[36] The US clearly did not agree. Given the explosive environment, Eisenhower sought Nehru's help (inviting him for talks in Washington) to avoid nuclear conflict in the wake of the Soviet invasion of Hungary and the British-French-Israeli attacks on Egypt.[37]

Failure of the British and French governments to obtain US support for the invasion was not well received in Australia. Casey described this as, 'the most grave rift between the UK and the US in living memory...'[38] and disagreed with Menzies' support for the use of force. Menzies, clearly unhappy with the US stand, in a message to Canberra argued that 'it is all very well for people to denounce the idea of force, but in a negotiation of this kind, it is good sense to keep the other man guessing.'[39] Like Menzies, who had little sympathy for Egypt's position, Britain's Prime Minister Eden was determined to demolish Nasser. In *No End of a Lesson: The Story of Suez*, Anthony Nutting (at the time working in the Foreign Office) states 'Eden reverted to his theme that compromise with Nasser would only serve to whet his appetite and that I must get it into my head that this man must be destroyed before he destroyed all of us.'[40] In the domestic sphere, Menzies got no support from the Labor Opposition; Labor's foreign policy demonstrating again that it not only contrasted with that of the Menzies' government, but was more in line with India's. Evatt, its leader, criticised Menzies for suggesting 'full-blooded economic sanctions; failing that, the use of force - that is war against Egypt; ... a gross breach of international law and no one will deny that.'[41] He described the Anglo-French invasion as, 'one of the greatest and most appalling events in history...'[42]. The crisis was eventually settled with the majority of UN members, including the US, voting for a withdrawal of the Anglo-French-Israeli forces from Egypt. Evatt told Parliament the reason for the UN's decision to have Britain, France and Israel leave Egypt was, 'because they had taken the law into their own hands ...'[43], not unlike Nehru's view of it.

Nehru's performance however, in the Suez crisis showed his sense of fairness. He condemned the Anglo-French plan and said, 'I cannot think of a grosser case of naked aggression than what England and France are attempting to do.'[44] Yet, despite his close association with Nasser, a fellow member of NAM and his bitterness about the former colonial powers, his approach to the settlement of the crisis was evenhanded. He told the Lok Sabha that a settlement reached should, 'not only guard the rights of nations or sovereignty of nations concerned, but also be fair to the interests of the international community.'[45] This was in the face of pressure within India to break its links with the Commonwealth, a demand made by the Opposition in the Lok Sabha.[46] Also, in contrast to Menzies, Nehru rejected the use of force. Gopal comments on Nehru's capacity for fairness:

> The Suez crisis had brought out the best in Nehru. He had at no time compromised on principles... but he had combined such firmness with a genuine desire to protect British interests and, as the crisis developed, to rescue Britain from the mistaken decisions of her Prime Minister.[47]

Confirmation of Gopal's view is seen in the fact that despite the British government's criticism of Nehru during the Suez crisis, Aneurin Bevin, (a prominent British politician of the 1940s and 1950s) in a later visit to Delhi, spoke with approval of India's attitude, and emphasised how greatly it had helped to bring the British government back to the right path.[48] Looking back on the crisis, Krishna Menon, spoke of the Menzies' Government's maverick position within the Commonwealth on Suez:

> British public opinion, Commonwealth public opinion, were almost entirely against the invasion. ... I say "almost" because Australian governmental opinion was an exception. The man who played the biggest foolish role in this was Robert Menzies, ...[49]

## The Five Power Resolution: A Gladiatorial Contest

The Five Power Resolution, sponsored by India, Ghana, Yugoslavia, Indonesia and the UAR, was intended to bring about a renewal of contact between the two major powers, the USA and the USSR, to ease the prevailing Cold War tensions. Nehru, explaining the reasons for limiting the meeting to the two major powers in the first instance (which became the grounds for Menzies' amendment), although agreeing that success will require the efforts of many nations, said 'we think that in the present situation of dangerous drift, even a small approach on behalf of the two great countries would make a difference and might mark a turn of the tide.'[50] Menzies was not happy with the meetings being limited to the two great powers. In Parliament, he proclaimed 'the resolution moved by Mr Nehru did not call for a summit meeting of the four; ... It did not call on the four great men, ... the four men who led atomic powers, to meet again; it called on two people out of the four.'[51] Menzies wanted to see Britain and France involved from the beginning.

The matter did not rest there; it was the start of parry and thrust between the two men. Nehru assumed the resolution would face no opposition because it was not, as he described it, directed, 'against any individual or this group or that group. But did represent a strong and passionate desire that things should get moving, and that this assembly should not sit paralysed'[52]. Menzies' amendment, therefore, caught Nehru by surprise, and led him to mount a fierce attack. Having first acknowledged his admiration for Menzies' ability, Nehru went on to ask in reference to the Menzies amendment, whether 'that keen mind and ability had not tried to cover-up, with a jumble of words, something which had no meaning at all - or the wrong meaning.'[53] Nehru was clearly annoyed at what he felt was an unnecessary intervention by Menzies. Commenting further he said, 'he has missed the point of the draft resolution and has considered, possibly, that there is some kind of a secret motive behind this,' and rejecting Menzies' suggestion that the sponsors of the resolution 'had fallen into some communist trap... ', Nehru, expressed regret 'that the Prime Minister of Australia has done very little justice to himself ...'[54].

Disturbed by the bad Press he was getting in Australia on the issue, Menzies, in a personal cable from New York to his deputy, John McEwen, wrote, 'I am very sorry to learn that I appear to have got the Government into trouble. As this mystifies me a great deal, I will set down in terms which I could hardly use publicly the story of what occurred.'[55] Menzies then proceeded to give McEwen a detailed explanation of what took place, but not without a stinging attack on Nehru in the process. He alludes to Nehru's response to his amendment, 'he bared his teeth; he sneered. It was really a nauseating exhibition, although it appears to have given great pleasure to the Australian newspaper reporters.'[56] He then refers to the annoyance that his own actions might have caused the Australian newspapers, but adds that it has 'greatly strengthened our relations with the United States and with the United Kingdom, ...'[57]. He ends the cable to McEwen with, 'I feel very sick about the position at home ... When you have discussed this letter with a few of our senior colleagues you might perhaps be good enough to shoot me off a cable about my own movements.'[58] Plainly, the issue was troubling Menzies.

In a separate personal letter to Justice Frankfurter, Menzies was just as derisive describing Nehru's attack as, 'the most intemperate kind. He did not revert to the Kashmir Brahmin. He seemed to me to revert almost to the branches of the trees.'[59] Also of some interest on understanding the Menzies-Nehru personality difference and prevailing hostility are Menzies' comments to Frankfurter when he speculates on the probable reasons for Nehru's involvement in the Five Power Resolution. He attributes it to an interpretation which he obtained 'in many quarters', and one that 'seems more probable ...'

that it was an idea developed by Tito and Nasser, who then felt it necessary to draft Nehru, 'the man of traditional detachment and of standing with the Western world.'[60] Consequently, Nehru was, Menzies proceeds to state, flattered into believing that his 'name would be the chief one associated with what would be regarded as the first constructive resolution of the Assembly.'[61]

But then Nehru's interest in world peace and efforts to lessen Cold War tensions were in evidence from the time of independence and non-alignment. For example, in the early 1950s, it was anticipated that Nehru and Churchill would work together for 'an all out attempt by the West to try and reach some sort of a new understanding with the Soviet Union.'[62] Reporting on imminent Commonwealth Prime Ministers' talks, *The Sunday Leader* referred to Churchill's dependence at the meeting on Nehru 'who is expected to press strongly for a high level international conference ... to relieve present world tensions.'[63] The Australian High Commission in New Delhi, DEA in Canberra and Menzies could not have been unaware of this newspaper headline in India and, it could be assumed, with Churchill's involvement it made news in Britain and Australia too. The 1953 newspaper report also stated that, 'the chief opposition among the Commonwealth leaders to such a move is expected to come from the Australian Prime Minister,...'[64]. In what was perhaps a foretaste of his response to the Five Power Resolution seven years later, Menzies' obstructionist attitude (anticipated by the Indian newspaper) to initiatives that had Nehru's participation, provides an insight into how India saw the Menzies' personality from an early stage. It also suggests that Menzies' dislike of Nehru was consistent and not related to any single policy difference.

Kevin Perkins provides another example of what was, it seems, a long-standing Nehru-Menzies rancour when he makes reference to an earlier undertaking by Menzies (at Churchill's request) to negotiate on Kashmir between Nehru and Liaquat Ali Khan. Before he set off on his mission, Menzies indicated to associates 'how he intended to drive Mr Nehru into a cul-de-sac from which he would not be able to escape.' Menzies was also warned, Perkins adds, that Nehru 'was one of the world's most elusive men and told: "if you succeed, you will be the man of the age." '[65]

Menzies' address to Parliament on his return defending his actions at the UN (on the Five Power Resolution) further reveals the depth of the bitterness that had prevailed between him and Nehru. In his speech, Menzies said, 'I understand that the first complaint is that I was being used by the United States and the United Kingdom ... our most powerful and devoted friends.'[66] To criticisms in the Australian Press that he had deferred to Eisenhower and Macmillan's views rather than please Australia's Asian neighbours in its own interests,[67] Menzies responded with, 'I have learnt to know who are our friends.'[68] Clearly, Menzies was embarrassed by the reaction at home on his performance as this statement during his speech explaining his actions suggests: 'many people have been eager beavers to say that my amendment was just ridiculous and that I had made a fool of my country. When I make a fool of this country I hope that you will expel me.'[69]

Menzies also came in for much criticism from the Labor Opposition. Calwell accused Menzies of having 'isolated Australia from the great majority of world powers and angered the Afro-Asian bloc ...' and added that criticism 'by some people' in Australia of Nehru, 'the well-loved leader of more than 400,000,000 Indians ...' had more to do with Nehru's policy of neutralism than with any enmity he had towards Australia.[70] Whitlam in his speech, accused the Prime Minister of having 'deliberately snubbed and thwarted the Prime Minister of India by his amendment ...'[71] and reminded Menzies that India, 'has, not by force but by prestige, the primacy in Asia and Africa among all the nations of those continents that belong to the United Nations.'[72] Concluding his speech to Parliament, Whitlam accused Menzies of having 'indulged his own personal vanity and itched to cut a great figure on the world stage. Suez was the other occasion. He has an atlas complex; ...'[73]. It is worthy of note that Whitlam's speech reflects not only the importance he attached to India regionally, as early as 1960 in this instance but also its consistency. This is referred to in Chapter Seven as one reason for the positive way in which India responded to Australia in the Indira Gandhi-Whitlam period in the early 1970s.

Nehru too was not spared criticism for his rejection of Menzies' amendment to the resolution calling it 'negative, untenable and verging on absurdity.'[74] Perkins cites a correspondent who described

Nehru's speech as having left Menzies' 'reputation as a world statesman ... in tatters on the floor of the assembly.'[75] Coming from a man who has consistently preached peaceful approaches to mediation of conflicts, some in India were disappointed by Nehru's uncharacteristic belligerence in this instance,[76] although he did admit later to regretting it. Nehru's Parliamentary Secretary, Sadath Ali Khan, told Crocker in New Delhi that 'Nehru suffered "pangs" over the offending phrases in his speech against the Australian Resolution; he was sorry he did it.'[77] Menzies, by contrast, did not regret his actions but continued to defend them including his argument that the Americans welcomed his stand at the UN because of their concerns about the non-aligned group.

## The Peacemaker

The Five Power Resolution and the Menzies counter attack had the appearance also of being the opportunity for each to ventilate long suppressed antipathy. While the gulf between the two men remained, any interest at other official levels had little opportunity to flow on to benefit the bilateral relationship. Yet, Nehru's world view and commitment to peace and non-violent approaches to international conflicts echoed the thoughts of numerous world leaders and men of eminence, both within and outside the political sphere. He was able to enjoin others to his vision of world peace. Among those whose praise Nehru enjoyed were Bertrand Russell, Aldous Huxley, Dwight Eisenhower, Marshall Tito, Gammar Abdul Nasser, Pearl Buck, Ludwig Erhard, Clement Atlee, Mahatma Gandhi, Albert Einstein, Winston Churchill, Dean Acheson, Malraux, Kwame Nkrumah, Lyndon B. Johnson, S. Radhakrishnan and J.K. Galbraith.[78] Menzies, a man of stature himself, not only failed to understand Nehru's ideology of non-alignment and distaste for such things as racialism, colonialism, war and military alliances, he also did not share this admiration others had for Nehru. This may be partly explained by Perkins' view that Menzies' had a tendency to be vindictive if persuasion failed to bring 'a strong person (who) was not inclined to follow his line of thinking, ...' and that '... he was not a forgiving man.'[79] This pre-disposition to bearing grudges is best demonstrated in Menzies' attempt, supposedly planned, to undermine Nehru during his planned visit to negotiate between Nehru and Ali Khan on the Kashmir impasse, referred to earlier. There is also the temptation to conclude that this antipathy towards Nehru was self serving, in that it enhanced Menzies' image in Washington and London where, for him, it mattered most. In contrast, the absence of spite in Nehru's personality is best seen in Churchill's testimony: 'this man has overcome two of the greatest failings in human nature; he knows neither fear nor hatred ...'[80]. This was high praise coming from a man who was at the time opposed to Nehru and India's independence.

## International Policy Divergence

The discussion on Suez and the Five Power Resolution, has focused on differences that have brought the two men into direct conflict. There were, however, international issues that involved third party countries in which India and Australia, as opposed to their two leaders, were involved as mediators or participants that also illustrate the Nehru-Menzies ideological gulf. It is sometimes forgotten that while, as strong personalities, Nehru and Menzies exercised dominance over foreign policy, there were others such as Krishna Menon in India, and Casey in Australia, along with senior bureaucrats and diplomats on both sides, who were very much involved in the negotiations and the implementation processes even if they were carrying out their Prime Minister's policies. Two conflicts that arose between the two countries involving third party international issues, examined here, demonstrate further the implacable commitment to ideology and the influence of the personality factor on foreign policy framing and in this case, the bilateral relationship.

Much of the Indian position on the two issues is presented here in terms of Nehru's attitude to them because of his dual portfolio (Prime Minister and Minister for External Affairs). It is important to the discussion to recognise that Nehru was dominant in India's foreign policy formulation. A directive issued to all foreign diplomats in India by the Ministry of External Affairs that in their communications with various Indian government departments they should comply with the following requirement, underscores this:

> ... every issue of substance, and of more than ephemeral interest, which it is desired to take up with or bring to the notice of the Government of India, should, *in the first instance, be referred to the Ministry of External Affairs.*[81] (Emphasis in original)

S.N. Misra, who has produced a major work on Indian diplomacy, believes 'Nehru was the principal author of India's foreign policy. His ideas have been one of the most important formative influences upon Indian foreign policy.'[82] Nehru, however, relied heavily on Krishna Menon, a pivotal figure in Indian Cold War politics upto 1962. Consequently, Menon's influence on the Indian stance on international issues was a strong factor, sometimes affecting the bilateral relationship because, it seems, his forthright and persistent manner was not always appreciated by the Australian side.

## Korean War

An international crisis that brought the two countries' foreign policy responses into conflict (and with it illustrates the impact of the personality factor), was the 1950 Korean War. Here, the divergence between Australia and India was marked not so much by ideology as by India's moral stance, as well as its incipient mediatory role in international disputes widely accepted as helpful to the achievement of a resolution in the Korean crisis: 'Indian mediation became a novel experiment in international diplomacy during the Nehru period.'[83] Nehru, symbolised India's ethos of non-violence and peaceful methods in his approach to the crisis. His letter to the Soviet Leader Stalin and the US Secretary of State, Dean Acheson, containing an initial proposal for the cessation of hostilities pending a final settlement is evident of India's evenhanded attitude to the crisis.[84] In an analysis of India's role during the Korean War, Steinberg also comes to the conclusion that India's conduct was impartial.[85]

The subsequent Indian resolution which broke the *impasse*, drew complimentary references from the UK and Canada. Mr Eden said 'the support which the resolution had received was a remarkable tribute to this Indian initiative.'[86] Canada's Mr St Laurent described India's initiative as 'an encouraging demonstration of the strength and solidarity of democratic feeling throughout the world.'[87] At the time, an editorial in *The Daily Mirror*, (London) - carried in *The Leader*, an Indian Daily - confirms this accolade:

> Today he (Mr Nehru) figures as the statesman who more than any other has shown shrewd understanding of the New Asia and India looms as the only power trusted by both sides in Korea. Within the Commonwealth as within the UN she speaks authoritatively for the New Asia.[88]

India's attitude to, and involvement in, the Korean crisis is conveyed by Krishna Menon who felt that the United Nations 'at that time was the United States.'[89] He asserted: ' I believe the whole of the Korean business was an understanding - I don't use any stronger word - between Trygue Lie (Secretary General of the United Nations 1946-1953) on the one hand and the Americans on the other.'[90] Perhaps, a trace of hyperbole here on Menon's part but, if a British Cabinet Meeting Minute is anything to go by, then they too had misgivings about the US and being kept fully informed on the unfolding military and political situation in Korea. The Minute states:

> The PM (Churchill) said that the UN had entrusted the conduct of the Korean campaign to the US; and we should be well-advised to avoid a position in which we share the responsibility without the means of making our influence effective.[91]

A good example of both, the gulf in foreign policy between India and Australia as well as India's view of Australia as a virtual satellite of the US under Menzies, is seen in the observations made by a member of the Indian delegation Govinddas (MP), to the Commonwealth Parliamentary Association meeting on the Korean War held in Wellington and Canberra. Govinddas' comments were that:

> At New Zealand, the Conference atmosphere permeated with a sense of equality amongst the delegations. But at Canberra, it was not so; a place of prominence over all others was given to the two representatives from the USA.[92]

The Indian Parliamentarian, who stressed India's 'opposition to war' and preference for 'settling all conflicts by arbitration', thought his speech 'served as a discordant note...'[93], because of its anti-war tone. He also observed that at the Conference, which was inaugurated by Menzies, ' all discussion ... centred round war and how soon it could be waged. ... If anybody did not show blind faith in American leadership, he was a disturber of world peace and a coward.'[94] This serves to identify another difference between Nehru and Menzies, namely, support for peaceful solutions and support for war respectively. Nehru, who was unequivocal in his condemnation of war as a method to resolving a conflict, said: 'the more I live and the more I grow in experience, the more convinced I am of the futility, of the wickedness of war as a means of solving a problem.'[95]

Menzies, on the other hand, preoccupied with Australia's security, was not averse to using force in achieving the West's objectives, exemplified by his support for the Anglo-French approach to the Suez crisis. David Lowe's observation that Menzies' 'concentrated efforts to gear Australia for readiness in a third world war,'[96] furthers this perception of the man.

Although India did not take sides in the war, Nehru's position on North Korea's guilt was unequivocal. In an address to the Lok Sabha, on 3 August 1950, he said 'aggression has taken place by North Korea over South Korea. That is a wrong that has to be condemned and resisted.'[97] He was however emphatic that the war should not spread outside Korea, other issues not be linked to the resolution of the war, and the country's future be decided by the Koreans themselves.[98]

In Australia's case, its policy on the Korean War was aligned with that of the United States with Menzies ensuring that nothing jeopardised the Australia-US alliance. Any policy divergence between India and the Americans on the crisis was, therefore, no less reflective of the differences which existed between India and Australia on their respective attitudes to the Korean issue. For instance, at the Commonwealth Prime Ministers Conference of 1951, when the discussion turned to a united Commonwealth policy on Korea, Nehru, who had difficulty with the lordly approach the Americans took at negotiations on the Korean issue, was in conflict with Menzies who stressed that 'any security calculations by the Commonwealth would be "unrealistic" if they contemplated serious differences with the United States.'[99]

Responsibility for India's involvement in the settlement was assigned to Krishna Menon, although he was number two to Vijayalakshmi Pandit who led the Indian delegation to the UN.[100] India's inventiveness that finally broke through the Korean impasse was the agreement proposed for the handling of the prisoners of war. Questioned by Brecher on this and India's search for a stratagem, this was Menon's response:

> ...I said, if we can bring it down to some formula on a basis which has a wide moral appeal it must be an international agreement in regard to the treatment of POWs. I said in my speech at the UN, in regard to the prisoners, it should neither be 'push nor pull'.[101]

Again, there was a moral underpinning to India's approach in line with Nehru's philosophy. There were others in India's Parliament for whom the moral dimension (in the Korean War) was an important consideration. During a debate in the Lok Sabha on the Korean situation, Alva Joachim, (MP), on 3 August 1950 drew attention to it:

> The moral aspect is the bright side of our foreign policy. That moral aspect is the treasure and the heritage given to us by Mahatma Gandhi ... This moral policy has stood the test of the clash of arms.[102]

## The Krishna Menon Personality

This discussion of the Korean War helps reinforce the thesis' central theme of the personality factor in the nature of bilateral relations. It is also indicative of another theme that Australia's identification with US policy contributed to the disaffection between India and Australia. Menon found that the Americans were not well disposed to India's successful proposal which was an alternative to the 21-power resolution they supported:

> I think the Americans found that I had broken the unity of the Western group. They said so. They thought I was a vicious Machiavellian person. I really think the main reason was that everybody was getting tired of the war. Secondly, the deadlock was a thing to be got over if there was to be an end to the Korean war.[103]

At this point, it helps to draw attention to Menon's unease with the Americans which was no less felt by India's Parliamentarians. Menon's antipathy is exemplified in this comment: 'until the US is able to give up the idea of running the world - and not use the words "racial and national superiority" or "world dominion" there is little hope for the world.'[104] The flow-on effect of this on India's view of Australia and its impact on the bilateral relationship should not be understated.

The relevance of India's success as a mediator and the Indian attitude to America is that it provides an insight into the policy maker's personality (his psychological and operational environment), and its impact. For example, Brecher suggests that Menon's denunciation of the United States role in world politics in contrast to his milder treatment of the Soviet Union's breaches of international conduct, reveals an anti-West bias. He explains its origins:

It is deep-rooted and pervasive, an extension of his political philosophy and his emotional propensities – bitterness towards 'the West', a compound of colonialism, imperialism, and racism....[105].

Then, again, there were those who saw Menon as an embodiment of justice and equality for the Third World: 'their eloquent advocate, their brave defender, their doughty champion. When he spoke, he gave vent to the mute feelings of half the world.'[106] It would be all too easy to ignore the effect of nationalism in this. Nationalism, of course, was the overriding power that drove India's campaign for independence. Krishna Menon was not devoid of this stirring force having lived under the hand of British colonialism. R. Venketaraman, India's one time President, saw the Menon phenomenon through Indian eyes, understandably, and not without a measure of pride with India's growing international stature as a peacemaker under Nehru and Menon:

> I had the privilege of being a member of the Indian delegation led by Krishna Menon over a number of years. ... Participating in the work... led by him was to share in the articulation of India's renascent ethos. After every address of Krishna Menon we on the delegation felt inches taller - as Indians, as Asians and as representatives of a whole generation of newly emerging nations.[107]

There was a tendency among Australian diplomats (and even Menzies) to ignore, if not play down, Menon's authority in pursuing Indian foreign policy. Here, Ramachandram's description of the Nehru-Menon team is important because it dispels any doubt about Menon's effectiveness at this point in Indian foreign affairs.

> ... the Nehru-Menon symbiosis, unique in many ways, helped India to mediate in global crises with great success. ... It is not an exaggeration to say that India's role of mediation and conciliation would not have become an effective instrument of international diplomacy without Krishna Menon. It is necessary for historians to give this credit to Menon.[108]

Brecher provides a valuable aid for the International Relations scholar's task of trying to understand foreign policy behaviour through the statements, actions and views of decision makers and their perceptions of the environment. He defines the environment as made up of three separate levels at which a state's foreign policy reciprocity takes place, 'global, subordinate, and bilateral.'[109] By applying this analytical paradigm to Menon, who occupied a position in the Indian political hierarchy only one removed from Nehru, the Prime Minister, Brecher arrives at the conclusion that: 'a structured analysis of Menon's View of the World then will also cast light on the View of the World held by the Indian foreign policy elite during that period.'[110] He is also of the view that the analysis in this case is facilitated by Menon's 'intellectual flare and agile mind, his carefully nurtured images of his environment, and his tendency to state these in a brilliant and often a passionate flow of words.'[111]

In spite of his impressive contribution to India's foreign policy formulation, Australian officials showed little regard for Menon, who accused them of frequent subservience to the US position.[112] Australia's External Affairs personnel were also piqued by his criticisms of them, which did little to facilitate better communications between the two countries.[113] J. Plimsoll Australia's High Commissioner to New Delhi, in a despatch to Hasluck, refers to Menon as the man responsible for, '... some of the more wayward features of foreign policy and was increasingly more pro-Soviet Union than uncommitted, ...'[114]. But, then, by its presence in the Western alliance and involvement in the Korean War on the American side, Australia was not excluded from Menon's antipathy towards the West.

Canada's Arnold Smith, (Commissioner, International Supervisory Commission for Cambodia), in a memorandum dated May 1956, to the Secretary of State, External Affairs Canada, entitled 'Indo-China Chessboard' and seen by the Department of External Affairs, Canberra, states, 'India is conscious and understandably so, of great powers, and many Indians, like Krishna Menon, have a smouldering resentment that their potential power is not yet actualised.'[115]

In contrast to India, Australia's stand on Korea was an early indication of its relentless commitment to the containment of Communism, if necessary by force. Apart from any disagreement between the two states related to the forthright Menon style, Australia was the first to support the Americans in the war with infantry, fighter squadrons and naval escorts.[116] Reflecting on Australia's support of the military intervention, Casey said:

> When war broke out we were second in time only to the United States in having forces in action. ... Australia has deep and continuing interest in Korea which can be regarded as the northern anchor to the defensive island chain of the eastern mainland of Asia.[117]

By way of further comparison, India did not provide military assistance to the UN force in Korea. In a report on India's attitude to military assistance to UN forces, Francis Stuart, Acting High Commissioner for Australia in India, states, 'remarks have been passed that India can no longer be regarded as a reserve of cannon fodder for foreign wars, as she was under British Rule.'[118]

Then, there was the question of the Australian Government's support for General MacArthur's plan to invade North Korea,[119] which brought the Chinese into the conflict. The *quid pro quo* for this support of US actions in Korea was 'an overwhelming ovation' from Congress in Washington for Menzies on his visit to the US and a significant loan for Australia.[120] Yet, the Indians saw MacArthur as one of the reasons for subsequent American set backs in the war.[121] In a cable to Vijayalakshmi Pandit at the UN, Nehru wrote:

> General MacArthur's recent statement which President Truman disapproved is just the kind of thinking which creates a bad impression here, more specially his reference to oriental psychology.[122]

India's D.N. Malik saw the Korean War as the ' biggest immediate factor behind the Republican extension of the US policy of "containment to containment plus," ... and pursuing diplomacy from the position of strength.'[123]

One of the factors that emerges in the book is that, on foreign policy, Australia's Labor leaders and Indian counterparts were closer than during Liberal Coalition governments; this is seen in the Korean conflict too. While Australia's Labor Opposition was supportive of the Menzies Government's decision to send troops to Korea at the UN's request, it was critical of the decision to go beyond the 38th parallel, which drew the Chinese into the war, with Chifley (like Menon)[124] lamenting the death and destruction caused by the UN's decision with over 1,000,000 casualties and 2,500,000 made homeless.[125] Chifley told Parliament that:

> ...it was great folly for the United Nations forces to move as far north as they went in Korea. ... I regret that the United Nations in making its move in Korea, which was completely justified, unfortunately produced in that country a complete shambles.[126]

For Korea, the North-South division, the post-War conflict between the two superpowers, the intervention of China, among other questions, brought war and destruction to the country. Carl Berger setting the war in a historical context argues 'The true tragedy of Korea was, so often, its destiny had been determined by others.'[127] Australia and India were participants and mediators, respectively, in the Korean war. But their very different roles, India as peacemaker and Australia aligned with the US in combat against the North Koreans, did little to close the wide gap that kept the two from a closer relationship. It is worth noting that when it ended, President Eisenhower wrote to Nehru in early 1953 thanking him for India's 'successful handling of the delicate operation.'[128]

India also played an influential role in bringing about a settlement of the Indo-China crisis. Anthony Eden (then British Foreign Secretary) told the Indian High Commissioner to London that he would like to see Nehru's proposals for a settlement of the Indo-China issue.[129] Both Nehru and Krishna Menon were involved through a six point proposal, and in subsequent negotiations. India's contribution was acknowledged by China's Prime Minister, Zhou En Lai, and Pierre Mendes France, the Prime Minister of France.[130] In Australia's case, Menzies, who had supported French actions in Indo-China, paid tribute to Eden and Casey for their roles, in his reactions to the Geneva Accords.[131] Discussion of the Korean and Indo-China settlements and India's roles in them serves also to confirm one of the hypotheses of the study that India with its wider interests (global peace) did not see Australia as important to its international objectives. It should be noted that there were differences between India and Australia over the Vietnam war, discussed in Chapter Seven.

## SEATO Pact

SEATO, the collective defence treaty, was another reason for deep divisions between India and Australia at the international level. With its preoccupation with Communism and its containment, the Western alliance, including Australia, felt the need for a South East Asian defence strategy. This was seen as urgent because, in their view, the Geneva Accords just concluded with a partitioned Vietnam 'appeared a very uncertain block to the advance of communism in Southeast Asia.'[132] The resultant strategy took the form of a collective defence pact, (SEATO) formally established in 1954 in Manila. Besides Australia, the pact included the United States, the United Kingdom, France, New Zealand, Thailand, Pakistan and the Philippines.

In an address to Parliament, Casey explained the *raison d'être* for SEATO's establishment:

> ... the problem of physical defence is clearly of the first importance. That is why we have joined with others in the creation of SEATO, under which important and promising defence machinery has been set up.[133]

Menzies' explanation of the alliance was no less reflective of Australia's security-driven foreign policy of the 1950s. Addressing Parliament he said:

> SEATO represents the overall predominant conception, ... Indeed in time of war, it is quite certain that SEATO will establish overall commands and that our forces, by suitable arrangements, will be under them.[134]

For India, the significance of SEATO went beyond its effect on increasing tensions in Asia, on account of Pakistan's membership of it and the potential thereby for its military enhancement, an aspect stressed in a Casey speech:

> It is important that the forces of every member of the SEATO organization should be developed to an adequate level of strength and effectiveness. ... Self defence must be both individual and collective.[135]

India's attitude to SEATO was evident from the start when Nehru showed his unease within a month of its formation. He expressed his fears in the Lok Sabha:

> It seems to me this particular Manila Treaty is looking dangerously in this direction of spheres of influence to be exercised by powerful countries. It is the big and powerful countries that will decide and not the two or three weak and small Asian countries that may be allied to them. ... this Manila Treaty is not only a wrong approach but a dangerous one from the point of view of any Asian country.[136]

As for Nehru's attitude to Australia's involvement in SEATO, he argued that, while Australia's security fears were understandable, the pact increased rather than reduced the tensions in South East Asia and, consequently, failed to make a contribution towards peace.[137] Besides, India, at the time a country gaining international recognition as a mediator in the settling of disputes through peaceful approaches (e.g. Indonesian independence, the Korean War and the Indo-China settlement), saw SEATO as an expression of force which brought the

Cold War closer to its own borders. R.G. Neale took a similar view of the thrust of SEATO: 'as a means to peace it has substituted the threat of force for the conference table and methods of violence for non-violence.'[138]

Obviously, Australia's membership of SEATO and its commitment *ipso facto* to any future military engagement by Pakistan, exacerbated the relationship with India. Quoting Article II of the SEATO Treaty, Menzies made this abundantly clear when he wrote: 'not one of us can avoid the Treaty obligations by making our performance dependent upon the action of any other Party.'[139] In New Delhi, *The Statesman* reported the SEATO plan as a strategy apparently made urgent by the Indo-China settlement and that 'Australia would be willing to provide troops under the agreement for mutual action to repel aggression in Asia ...'[140].

Nehru's warnings against SEATO was not ignored by some of the Asian leaders. For example, on a visit to Australia in 1959, Prime Minister Tunku Abdul Rahman, with whom Australia shared a common stand on Communist aggression, informed Australia that 'Malaya would not join SEATO, because popular opinion had been influenced by the opposition of India and Indonesia to the treaty organisation.'[141]

What of the attitude of Australia's alternative government, the Labor Opposition, to SEATO? Its leader, Calwell, described SEATO as 'a toothless wonder'[142]. R.W. Holt, (Labor, MHR) saw no virtue in it either when he addressed Parliament:

> ... this Government (Menzies') has sought consistently to clothe with flesh and blood the military skeleton of SEATO, ... which was facetiously described by Madam Pandit (India's permanent Envoy to the UN and later its President) with great truth as 'a South-East Asia alliance minus South-East Asia.'[143]

Yet again Whitlam was alive to Asian sensitivities, in this instance India's, when he addressed the House in 1956 on the implications of SEATO for the Australia-India relationship. Referring to a meeting of the SEATO Council, Whitlam said:

> The first business it dealt with was the question of Kashmir, and I shall quote from the *Washington Post* and *Manchester Guardian* to show what a deplorable effect was created thereby.[144]

Whitlam then referred the House to *The Washington Post* which commented that, 'Kashmir had no place on the agenda of the (SEATO) conference ...' and that it would 'stir up as much resentment as did Mr Dulles's ill-timed Goa statement.' Whitlam's quote from *The Manchester Guardian* criticised the use of SEATO for a purpose never intended when the organisation was established, namely to achieve a peace between India and Pakistan, concluding that 'SEATO's intervention makes it less likely, not more likely that it (a peace) will be reached.'[145]

The plethora of arguments on Kashmir[146] are complex with interpretations affected by the perceptions and interests of India, Pakistan, the Kashmir people themselves as well as political agendas of third party countries. Yet, for India, Kashmir was then, and still is, a very sensitive issue, something Australia could not have been wholly unaware of. Naturally, Nehru was quick to respond to the inclusion of Kashmir on the SEATO Council Agenda. Drawing attention to SEATO's stated objective of defence against outside aggression and internal subversion, he said :

> How the question of Kashmir could come within the scope of the SEATO Council is not clear to us. Its reference to Kashmir could only mean that a military alliance backing one country, namely Pakistan, in its dispute with India.[147]

Nehru went on to assert that such damaging behaviour from any organisation towards another which enjoys cordial relations with its members 'would at any time be considered an impropriety ...', adding that 'we have noted with regret that three other Commonwealth countries have associated themselves with the offending declaration.'[148] Australia was one of the three. Nehru's periodic statements of concern had no effect on the SEATO Council, for example when he argued that such pacts are 'dangerous things ... which add to hatred, fear and apprehension ...',[149] pointing also to the reality of the Cold War being brought to the borders of India.[150] The Council's disregard for India's concerns was clearly seen in the final communiqué of its third meeting which, in a none too subtle reference to India, states:

> Among the topics discussed by the Council was that of neutralism. It was observed with concern that some governments have in varying degrees adopted a line of active opposition to collective security arrangements such as SEATO ...[151].

By this time there was enough evidence of the nationalism sweeping through resurgent Asia to realise that the priority was not membership of military pacts but the ending of colonialism and economic development. For all the hard work and costs associated with Australia's involvement in SEATO, it did little else than add to distrust in parts of Asia. The SEATO question, from the perspective of the bilateral relationship, has also to be weighed in the context of the triangular Australia-India-Pakistan relationships considered in Chapter Six below. Greenwood makes the point well with this observation:

> Australian membership of SEATO was an affront to neutral and uncommitted opinion in Asia and the alliance contributed little or nothing to the security of either Australia or the non-Communist countries of South-East Asia.[152]

While Chapter Three, and Four have addressed several aspects of the bilateral relationship under Nehru and Menzies, two separate but closely related conclusions emerge: the first is that the personalities of the two men was a significant factor in shaping the psychological view of their contemporaneous world. The second is that this led to mutual exclusiveness in their operational world reflected in foreign policies they adopted as participants or mediators in several Cold War international issues. The analysis of the Nehru-Menzies period in particular, but also the bilateral relationship in general, is multi-dimensional. Therefore, without an appropriate weighting for the personality factor, any study of the India-Australia bilateral relationship in the Nehru-Menzies period would lack an important dimension.

In Nehru and Menzies, we have two men, both dominant in foreign policy decision making with their different views of the world, their particular scales of personal values, influencing choices which not only created a personal gulf, but also affected the bilateral relationship between the two nations. Obviously, the personalities of the two men had much to do with their dissonance. All political leaders have perceptions of the world they live in conditioned by their accumulated experiences. Nehru and Menzies, with their strong influence on foreign policy, were no exception to this rule. Ironically, England became a common reference point for both men. Nehru with his genuine English education was never consumed by it. It certainly influenced his thinking, but he discarded any status that may have attached to the English experience. Menzies, on the other hand, a self confessed Anglophile, received his education in Australia, but hankered after a more authentic English stamp. Yet, in an ironical sense, there was the cultural divide. The defining difference between the two men was the particular twist each gave to their relationship with England, their reference point, and its impact on foreign policy, although each reflected the broader political culture of their respective countries. Each had an idealised view of the world, yet were capable of pragmatic decisions in their country's as well as their own interest. For example, Menzies refusal to condemn Apartheid and the Sharpeville massacre was partly prompted by his awareness of Australia's vulnerability to criticism of its Aboriginal record and the 'White Australia' Policy. An ANZUS Treaty (without the Britain he loved) to secure Australia's protection, and opposition to decolonisation (e.g. Indonesia), because of Papua New Guinea, are other examples of Menzies' realism. Nehru's actions in Goa, albeit in the face of Portugal's intransigence (seventeen years of it according to Krishna Menon), as well as his acceptance of military aid from the West, and Australia, during the 1962 Indo-China border war, exemplify his willingness to compromise in the real world.

While both used their backgrounds, consciously or otherwise, as a framework of reference for their actions, fundamental divergence on world views and political ideology meant incompatibility from the start between these two men - Nehru, the internationalist seeking peace, and Menzies, the traditionalist, using international circumstances to his and ostensibly, Australia's, benefit. Ramachandram quotes Norman D. Palmer who said of Nehru that he 'belongs to the world for he was a true citizen of the world, a true internationalist.'[153] Menzies was not the internationalist Nehru was. His construction of the world was primarily in terms of the Cold War and how he viewed Australia's role in it, which was an enmeshment with the Anglo-US strategic goals; a *modus operandi* for protecting a 'White Australia' with a relatively high standard of living from a rapidly decolonising, resurgent Asia with a low standard of living.

Important also to a comparison of these two men, is the recognition of Menzies' anachronism. He clung to his views, while the world around him was changing rapidly. There was a sense of previousness about his views, a chronological mystery, which was made more conspicuous by the relative synchronism that characterised the immediately preceding period between 1947-1949, a brief but immensely cordial one under Chifley. About Menzies belonging to a different time is best captured by Judith Brett who refers to the perceptions held by those 'who were young in the 1950s and 1960s, and for whom Australian cultural life then seemed frozen by its smugness, fear and indifference and dominated by the values and assumptions of the bygone age'[154].

On independence, Nehru, his Congress colleagues and indeed the whole of India, understandably looked forward with eager anticipation to the eventual announcement that would return India to freedom and sovereignty after centuries of colonial subjugation. When the transfer of power came, it was not without many months of blood, sweat and tears; of hard, yet delicate, negotiations, often harrowing, between the principal figures.[155] Nehru's ecstatic reaction to the imminence of independence with his speech, made soon after the formation of an interim Government in September 1946, conveys the great pride that comes with being a free and sovereign nation, the restoration of India's self respect, long deprived. What he said is important for the comparison with Menzies:

> A new Government came into being in this ancient land, ... the stepping stone to the full independence of India. Many thousands of messages of greetings and good wishes came to us from all parts of the world. ... The freedom we had envisaged and for which we had laboured, through generations of trial and suffering, was for all the people of India, ... We are particularly interested in the emancipation of colonial and dependent countries and peoples, and the recognition in theory and practice of all equal opportunities for all races.[156]

Years later, when asked whether as a young student he had a vision, Nehru replied, 'of course, the dream of India's independence was always there.'[157]

The difference in attitude to independence and sovereignty between Nehru and Menzies was as wide as was the difference between Menzies and Chiefly in their enthusiasm for India's attaining freedom from Britain. Labor, in office at the time, reacted to Atlee's announcement of India's imminent independence, with genuine felicitations conveyed to Nehru.[158] Menzies' reaction at the time, in stark contrast, and in a foretaste of what might become of the relationship between the two countries under a future conservative government, can only be described as ungracious:

> It is a dubious thing to endeavour to compress into sixteen months ... a process which took Australian colonies, with all their community of race, religion and ideas, twenty five years. ... to abandon control of a people who have not yet shown a real and broad capacity for popular self government is to do a disservice to them. ... I have great fears about the fate of the institution of self government in a country which, quite obviously, has not yet reached a stage at which the majority of its people are, by education, outlook and training, fit for self government ...[159].

But then, years earlier, in contrast to India's persistent demand for self-rule, Menzies, with his commitment to the idea of dependence on Britain, criticised the whole process that culminated in the 1931 Statute of Westminister,[160] which had the effect of confirming the independence granted to the dominions in 1926. While Canada and South Africa, both dominions at the time, were enthusiastic about this British gesture, seeing it as the first step towards their goal of sovereign nationhood,[161] Australia refused to ratify the statute till 1942.[162] Against this, India's desire for independence stood in stark contrast. S. Sastri's speech at the Round Table Conference held in London in December 1931 is a good example of this difference:

> Prime Minister, what is wanting in our loyalty to the Commonwealth is not admiration of its greatness or of its material glory, but it is the lack of occasion for us to take pride in this Empire and to call it our own. The one thing wanting is that you should place us upon an equality with the self-governing parts of the Commonwealth.[163]

Menzies' lack of interest in independence may further explain his tactless response to India's freedom. But there were other instances when Menzies criticised the granting of independence to an Asian country under colonial rule, for example, his objection to the then Labor Government's support of Indonesia's claim to independence from the Dutch, seeing it as unhelpful to the British remaining in Malaya, and Australia's colonial presence in Papua and New Guinea.

The difference between Nehru and Menzies was also one of nationalism, reflected in Australia's inability under Menzies to understand what pride in the attaining of nationhood meant to a new country. In Nehru's case, years of hard work, personal sacrifice and humiliation experienced at the hands of the British authorities acted as a rallying point, symbolising the people's burning desire for freedom, a redefined nationalism. It left him feeling bitter as these words of his convey:

> The British Government in India has not only deprived the Indian people of their freedom but has based itself on the exploitation of the masses, and has ruined India economically, politically, culturally and spiritually.[164]

Thakur captures this nationalistic attribute in the Nehru of free India:

> ... Nehru's personality combined an intense nationalism with the pride and sensitivity of a young nation struggling to cope with the problems of modernisation under the heritage of an immediate colonial past.[165]

The contrast between Nehru and Menzies here, is not surprising considering the absence of a nationalistic fervour in Australia's political evolution; as Meaney observes, viewed from the standpoint that, here was a nation that arose from the coming together of immigrants for whom ' there has been no simple coincidence between the nation of idea and place, between the nation as a source of values and as a protector of interests.'[166] Bruce Grant comments that, 'nationalism, as an assertion of the value of being particularly and even peculiarly Australian, has had to force its way through international loyalties, connections and inclinations.'[167] While Australia's cultural influences have, in the main, been Britain (the Empire) and the USA, (the protector), it was, unlike India, hardly straining to break free from the embrace of the Empire.

Menzies also spoke of being a colonial, but his experience was different to Nehru's; it was circumscribed by a form of voluntary based settler colonialism, a colonialism of choice. Therein lies the difference between Nehru's nationalistic fervor, born of subjugation, and Menzies' lack of it, with his preference for British traditions and the monarchy which he revered. It was a case of Nehru trying to disconnect from the British past, Menzies clinging to it. As Meaney observes: 'Australians do not have a self-sufficient nationalism, that is, a nationalism that arises out of the consciousness of a commonly shared and unique past.'[168]

When contrasted with republican India, all of this hardly portrays the conditions for a stirring nationalism and a uniquely Australian identity under Menzies, who once described himself as 'British to the bootstraps' and earned the sobriquet, 'Queen's Man'. In June 1936, he wrote that, 'the Crown was, and I am happy to say, is, an essential ingredient in Australian Government life.'[169]

Then, there were the international conflicts throughout the 1950s and early in the 1960s that exemplified their policy divergence. Notable among them was the Suez crisis in 1956, and the Five Power UN Resolution which brought Menzies and Nehru on to centre stage. The other areas of strong conflict that militated against the development of a mutually beneficial bilateral relationship was the two countries' differences in their perception of South Africa's policy of Apartheid and the SEATO pact.

What can be concluded from the discussion on foreign policy divergence is that both Nehru and Menzies dominated their respective country's external policy with their strong personalities. While Menon and Casey were there to advise, neither were as strong as their leaders; Menon did enjoy the confidence of his Prime Minister but Casey's influence on Menzies was minimal. But, then, Nehru and Menzies were remarkably dominant personalities which gave them unchallenged power within their Cabinets and almost total command of policy. They virtually transferred their self image, their fears, their experiences, their biases, their prejudices, into their foreign policy actions. As Lowe would write, 'when Menzies thought of Asia he continued to see it in an imperial, global context and in relation to world war.'[170] For Nehru, ever fearful of war the protection of Asia from Cold War rivalry was paramount.

Unfortunately for the relationship, these individual characteristics and idiosyncrasies were disconsonant rather than consonant. To put it another way, the strategic and other interests of India and Australia in the Nehru-Menzies period, (1949-1964), compounded by their contrasting personalities, had nothing in common to help the bilateral relationship.

# Endnotes

1. Nehru spent about a decade in prison over nine separate terms, (one of three continuous years) between 1921 and 1945. Indira Gandhi too was arrested and jailed in 1942.

2. Gandhi, Sonia (ed.), *Freedom's Daughter: Letters Between Indira Gandhi and Jawaharlal Nehru 1922-1939*, Hodder & Stoughton, London, 1989.

3. See *Jawaharlal Nehru: An Autobiography*, John Lane The Bodley Head, London, 1936, pp 178-179, for Nehru's account of '... battering with lathi and long batons ...' he personally endured at the hands of the British Police.

4. See API Report of Nehru's Press conference in Pattabhi Sattaramaya, *History of the Indian National Congress*, Padua's Publications, Bombay, 1947, vol. 2 , pp CCXLV-CCLII.

5. Brecher, Michael, *Nehru: A Political Biography*, Abridged Edition, Oxford University Press, London, 1961, p 216.

6. Gopal, S. (ed.), *Jawaharlal Nehru: An Anthology*, Oxford University Press, New Delhi, 1980, p 64.

7. Rao, Amiya and Rao, B.G., *Six Thousand Days*, Sterling Publishers, New Delhi, 1974, p 245.

8. *Jawaharlal Nehru's Speeches*, September 1946-May 1949, Vol. I, Ministry of Information & Broadcasting, Government of India, New Delhi, 1949, p 299.

9. Menzies, R.G., *Afternoon Light*, Cassell, Melbourne, 1967, p 232.

10. Copland, Ian, *Europe's Great Game: Imperialism in Asia*, Melbourne University Press, Victoria, 1986, pp 43-44.

11. Lowe, David (ed.), *Australia and the end of Empires*, Deakin University Press, Victoria, 1996, p 5.

12. Lowe, David, 'Australia at the United Nations in the 1950s: The Paradox of Empire', *Australian Journal of International Affairs*, Vol. 51, No. 2, 1997, p 171.

13. *Ibid.*, pp 173, 175.

14. CPD, (H of R), Vol. 19, 1 May 1958, p 1377.

15. *Jawaharlal Nehru's Speeches*, September 1946-May 1949, Vol. 1, Ministry of Information & Broadcasting, Government of India, New Delhi, 1949, p 236.

16. CPD, (H of R), Vol. 14, 21 March 1957, p 158.

17. CPD, (H of R), Vol. 14, 2 April 1957, p 415.

18. Richard Casey to Lord Wavell, 1 March 1945, TOP, Vol. V, in W.J. Hudson, *Casey*, Oxford University Press, Melbourne, 1986, p 169.

19. Casey, R.G., *An Australian in India*, Hollis & Carter, London, 1947, pp 25-26.

20. AA, Transcript from New Delhi Radio, 6 December 1949, Series A1838/283, Item 382/4/1.

21. Brecher, M., *India and World Politics*, Oxford University Press, London, 1968, p 30.

22. Prasad, R., *Colonialism, Lumpenization, Revolution*, Vol. I, 1850-1914, Ajanta Books, Delhi, 1995, p 27

23. See P.N. Chopra, (ed.), *Whose Who of Indian Martyrs*, Vol. I (1969), Vol. II (1972), Ministry of Education & Youth Services, Government Of India, New Delhi. The history of British colonialism in India is replete with instances of many thousands of Indians who called themselves 'freedom fighters' and lost their lives at the hands of the police, were sentenced to death or died in prison. Also see, *India's Major Non-violent Movements 1919-1934: British Secret Reports on Indian Peoples' Peaceful struggle for Political Liberation*, P.N. Chopra, (ed.), Vision Books, Delhi, 1979, for an in depth assessment of British curbs and references to the whipping of

political prisoners and freedom fighters as well as correspondence about it between the Viceroy, the British Government and the Monarch.

24. Gopal, S. (ed.), *Jawaharlal Nehru: An Anthology*, Oxford University Press, New Delhi, 1980, p 343.

25. Mutukumaru, N. (ed.), *Thoughts of Jawaharlal Nehru*, Sri-Lanka-India Society, Sri-Lanka, 1994, p 37.

26. Pandey, B.N., *Nehru and India*, Macmillan, London, 1976, p 30.

27. Stargardt, A.W., *Australia's Asian Policies: The History of a Debate 1839-1972*, Institute of Asian Affairs, Hamburg, 1977, pp 308-309, (Document No. 6).

28. 'Commonwealth Relations: the Coronation Conference', *TRT*, No. XLIII, December 1952 - September 1953, p 363.

29. *Ibid*.

30. Lord, Garner, 'Commonwealth Under Strain: Problems of expansion and attrition', *TRT*, No. 258, April 1975, p 210.

31. Mansergh, Nicholas, *Documents and Speeches on Commonwealth Affairs: 1952-62*, Oxford University Press, London, 1963, pp 523-527.

32. See, Public Records Office, London, Law Officers Department, WC 2, reply dated 5 March 1957, to UK Cabinet on the legality of the Anglo French invasion, c (57) 55, p 54.

33. Menzies, *op. cit.*, p 150. Krishna Menon, a trenchant critic of the West, became Menzies' *bete noir*.

34. CPD, (H of R), Vol. 12, 25 September 1956, p 825.

35. Lok Sabha Debates, 13 September 1956, Col. 6964.

36. Hudson, W.J. *Blind Loyalty: Australia and the Suez Crisis 1956*, Melbourne University Press, Victoria, 1989, p 71.

37. Wolpert, Stanley *Nehru: A Tryst with Destiny*, Oxford University Press, New York, 1996, p 466.

38. CNIA, Statement by R.G. Casey, 1 December 1956, Vol. 27, 1956, p 829.

39. Menzies, *op. cit.*, pp 165-166. For an insightful analysis of the motives that lay behind the actions of Nasser, the British-French-Israeli governments and Eisenhower's refusal to support them, see 'Suez Crisis', Australian Broadcasting Corporation, Television programme, on 31 October, 1998, presented by Jeremy Bennett.

40. Nutting, A., *No End of a Lesson: The Story of Suez*, Constable, London, 1967, p 58. Also see, Thomas Barman, Book Review, (*No End of a Lesson: The Story of Suez*, 1967), *International Affairs, A Quarterly Review* Vol. 44, No. 1, January 1968, pp 84-85.

41. CPD, (H of R), Vol. 14, 2 April 1957, p 420.

42. *Ibid.*, p 419.

43. *Ibid.*, p 421.

44. Eayers, James, *The Commonwealth and Suez-A Documentary Survey*, London, 1964, p 250, in S.C. Gangul, *India and the Commonwealth*, Shiva Lal Agarwala, India, 1970, p 36.

45. Lok Sabha Debates, 25 March 1957, Part II, Col. 652.

46. Misra, S.N., *India: the Cold War Years*, South Asian Publishers, New Delhi, 1994, p 215.

47. Gopal, S., *Jawaharlal Nehru: A Biography*, 1947-1956, Vol. II, Jonathan Cape, London, 1979, p 290. For India's objectives in its role in the Suez Canal crisis see S.N. Misra, *India: the Cold War Years*, South Asian Publishers, New Delhi, 1994, pp 236-239.

48. 'The Commonwealth An Indian View: The Pioneer Republic', *TRT*, No. 200, September 1960, p 372.

49. Brecher, Michael, *India and World Politics*, Oxford University Press, London, 1968, p 71.

50. *Jawaharlal Nehru's Speeches*, September 1957-April 1963, Vol. IV, Ministry of Information and Broadcasting, Government of India, New Delhi, 1964, p 326.

51. CPD, (H of R), Vol. 29, 20 October, 1960, p 2265.

52. *Jawaharlal Nehru's Speeches*, September 1957-April 1963, Vol. IV, Ministry of Information and Broadcasting, Government of India, New Delhi, 1964, p 327.

53. *Ibid.*, p 328.

54. *Ibid.*, p 329.

55. NLA, Cable from Menzies to McEwen, dated 9 October 1960, MS4936, Series 8, Box 332, Folder 9, p 1.

56. *Ibid.* p 2.

57. *Ibid.* p 3.

58. *Ibid.*

59. NLA, Letter from Menzies to Justice Frankfurter dated 21 November 1960, MS 4936, Series I, Box 12, Folder 109, p 1.

60. *Ibid.*, pp 1-2.

61. *Ibid.*, p 2.

62. 'Nehru-Churchill All Out Bid for World Peace', *The Sunday Leader*, Allahabad, 31 May 1953, p 1. A Newspaper in London carried a report on 15 May 1953, on Nehru's support for 'Churchill's proposal for a high level conference ... to try to rid the world of the fear of war.' See AA, Series A1838/278, Item 169/7/1, Part 2.

63. *Ibid.*

64. *Ibid.*

65. Perkins, Kevin, *Last of the Queen's Men*, Rigby, Adelaide, 1968, p 250.

66. CPD, (H of R), Vol. 29, 20 October 1960, p 2267.

67. Joske, Percy, *Sir Robert Menzies 1894-1978: A New Informal Memoir*, Angus & Robertson, Sydney, 1978, p 308.

68. CPD, (H of R), Vol. 29, 20 October 1960, p 2268.

69. *Ibid.*, p 2270.

70. CPD, (H of R), Vol. 29, 6 December 1960, p 3578.

71. *Ibid.*

72. CPD, (H of R), Vol. 29, 25 October, 1960, p 2340.

73. *Ibid.*, p 2341.

74. Perkins, *op. cit.*, p 249.

75. *Ibid.*, p 249.

76. Joske, *op. cit.*, p 308.

77. AA, Record of conversation between Sadath Ali Khan and W.R. Crocker in New Delhi, 3 November 1960, Series A1838/2, Item 250/10/7/1, Part 5.

78. For complimentary comments about Nehru, in general, see G. Ramachandram, *Nehru and World Peace*, Radiant Publishers, New Delhi, 1990; Sheila Dikshit, *et.al.* (eds.), *Jawaharlal Nehru, Centenary Volume*, Oxford University Press, New Delhi, 1997; N. Mutukumaru, *Thoughts of Jawaharlal Nehru*, Sri Lanka -India Society, Colombo, 1994. The UNESCO in conjunction with the Government of India held

an international Round Table Conference on Jawaharlal Nehru. For former President S. Radhakrishna's inaugural address to the Round Table Conference, see MEA, *Foreign Affairs Record*, September 1966, Vol. XII, No. 9, Government of India, New Delhi, pp 233-234.

79. Perkins, *op. cit.*, p 185.

80. Chaudary, Ramanarayan (ed.), *Nehru in His Own Words*, Navajivan Publishing House, Ahmedabad, India, 1964, p 95.

81. AA, Note from Ministry of External Affairs, Government of India, dated 24 November 1961 to all Diplomatic Missions in India, Series A1838/1, Item 1602/47.

82. Misra, S.N., *India: The Cold War Years*, South Asian Publishers, New Delhi, 1994, p 27. Prem Bhatia, believed the Ministry of Foreign Affairs was essentially 'a department reflecting Nehru's views and methods.' See *The Statesman*, Calcutta, 7 December 1957, in Gordon Greenwood and Norman Harper, (eds.), *Australia in World Affairs 1956-1960*, F.W. Cheshire, Melbourne 1963, p 329.

83. Ramachandram, G., *Nehru and World Peace*, Radiant Publishers, 1990, New Delhi, p 3. Also see, NAI, File No. 1(66) EURII for Scandinavian Ministers expression of hope that India could settle the Korean War.

84. Misra, S.N., *India: the Cold War Years*, South Asian Publishers, 1994, New Delhi, p 124.

85. Steinberg, B., 'The Korean War: A Case Study in India's Neutralism', *ORBIS* VIII (Winter, 1965), p 953, in S.N. Misra, *India: The Cold War Years*, South Asian Publishers, New Delhi, 1994, p 83.

86. Public Records Office, London, United Kingdom Cabinet Meeting, Thursday, 4 December, 1952, Minutes cc(52) 102nd Conclusion, p 136.

87. *Ibid*.

88. *The Leader*, India, 'A Rosy Light in the East' 18 June 1953.

89. Brecher, Michael, *India in World Politics*, Oxford University Press, London, 1968, p 34. For India's policy on the Korean War, see AA, Cablegram 19 December 1950, from the Australian High Commissioner in New Delhi, Series A1838/278, Item 3123/7/13.

90. *Ibid*.

91. Public Records Office, London, United Kingdom Cabinet Meeting, Thursday 19 June, 1952, Minutes, cc (52) 61st conclusion, Foreign Affairs, p 171. Also see Cabinet Meeting Thursday 26 June, 1952, for PM Churchill's statement on, U.K. ought to have been consulted in advance on bombing attacks on Yalu River power station, cc 63 (52) item 1, p 185; '... there was disagreement between the British and American views regarding the stand on the Korean issue, and that the U.S.A. could not "go along" with Britain in support of the Indian resolution to resolve, the Korean deadlock'. See *The National Herald*, Lucknow, 24 November 1952, p 1.

92. Govinddas, *On Wings to the Anzacs*, Adarsh Publishing, India, 1954, pp 203-204.

93. *Ibid*.

94. *Ibid*.

95. Narasimha Char, K.T., *The Quintessence of Nehru*, George Allen and Unwin, London, 1961, p 72.

96. Lowe, David, Abstract of Seminar Paper 'Menzies, Memory and Britain: Australian Perspectives on International Affairs in the 1950s', Sir Robert Menzies Centre for Australia Studies, London.

97. AA, Nehru's speech to the Indian Parliament on 3rd August 1950, as reported in *The Statesman*, New Delhi, 4th August 1950, Series A1838/278, Item 3123/7/13.

98. See AA, Cablegram, June 1950, from the Australian High Commissioner's Office, London, to DEA, and Report 27 July 1950, from the Acting High Commissioner for Australia in India (Francis Stuart) for Nehru's early difficulties within India on Korean involvement, and subsequent mediatory role in the War, Series A1838/278, Item 3123/7/13; 'China Rejects Indian Formula on Korea', *National Herald*, Lucknow, 27 November 1951, p 1.

99. PMM (51) 2nd Meeting, 4 January 1951, CAB 133/90, PRO, in David Lowe, *Menzies and the 'Great World Struggle': Australia's Cold War 1948-1954*, University of NSW Press, Sydney, 1999. Also see, NAI, statement by prominent Indians on the Korean War, File No. F16/102-XPP/53(s).

100. Mrs Pandit was President of the UN General Assembly in 1953 and later, High Commissioner for India in the U.K.

101. Brecher, Michael, *India and World Politics*, Oxford University Press, London, 1968, p 37. India was also credited with the creation of the concomitant Neutral Nations Repatriation Commission (NNRC) with Menon's insistence that the composition of the body be made up of 'an equal number from both sides with a neutral chairman,' which position was assumed by India. See Michael Brecher, *India and World Politics*, Oxford University Press, London, 1968, p 39. The two Indian resolutions, one introduced into the UN and the other to the league of Red Cross Societies at Geneva in 1952 on the prisoners-of war issue, brought about the cease-fire. With all sides accepting the Indian initiatives, 'the log jam had finally broken.' See Carl Berger, *The Korea Knot*, Revised Edition, Greenwood Press, New York, 1986, pp 155-157. In *The Cairo Documents: Biography of Gamal Abdul Nasser*, an Egypt based author Heikal offers an illuminating insight into the crisis with correspondence between Nasser and Nehru and accolades for Menon for his part in helping to achieve a settlement.

102. Parliamentary Debates, (Lok Sabha) Vol. V, Part II, 1 July to 14 August, 1950, p 269.

103. Brecher, Michael, *India and World Politics*, Oxford University Press, London, 1968, p 38. In an interview on Korea, Owen Lattimore, an expert on Far Eastern affairs from the John Hopkins University, USA, was to suggest that ' a mistake was made in clapping down the Indian suggestion ...' in reference to the West's approach of military action followed by diplomacy, as opposed to India's formula of diplomacy together with military action. See 'An Act of Unusual Diplomacy', *The National Herald*, Lucknow, 15 December 1950, p 5. Also see, 'Nehru Deplores Failure of Peace Plan', *The National Herald*, Lucknow, 7 December 1952.

104. Brecher, Michael, *India And World Politics*, Oxford University Press, London, 1968, pp 180-181.

105. *Ibid.*, p 309.

106. 'Regional Cooperation and Security', *The Daily News*, Sri-Lanka, 9 January 1997, p 6. The Krishna Menon Memorial Centenary Lecture, delivered by L. Kadirgarmar, (Minister for Foreign Affairs, Sri-Lanka,) on 15 December 1996, Pune, India.

107. Venketaraman, R., 'Foreword', *Krishna Menon at the United Nations, India and the World*, E.S. Reddy & A.K. Damodaran (eds.) Sanchar Publishing House, New Delhi, 1994, p xii.

108. Ramachandram *op. cit.*, p 3.

109. Brecher, Michael, *India and World Politics*, Oxford University Press, London, 1968, p 299. Also see, Michael. Brecher 'Specific Sources in Indian Neutralism', *Studies in Indian Foreign Policy*, K.P. Misra (ed.), Vikas Publications, New Delhi, 1969, p 52.

110. Brecher, Michael, *India And World Politics*, Oxford University Press, London, 1968, p 299.

111. *Ibid.*

112. AA, Despatch 21 March 1955, from W.D. Forsyth to DEA, Series A1838/2 Item 169/10/1, Part 3.

113. NLA, Plimsoll to Heydon, 18 June 1957: Papers of Sir Peter Heydon, MS 3155, Box 15, in Meg Gurry, 'No will or No way? Australia's Relations with India 1947-1993' Ph.D. Thesis, Latrobe University, Victoria, 1993, p 159. Within India too, Menon was not without his critics, particularly in 1959, in the face of the Chinese border incursions and the resultant row between Menon and the Chief-of-Staff, General Thimayya, on strategy. A political analysis of India's seeming humiliation at the time concludes, that 'whatever else he (Menon) has done as Minister, he seems to have made a sad mess of human relations.' See, *The Times*, Ceylon, 15 September, 1959, p 10.

114. AA, Despatch No. 2/64, 2 June 1964, Series A1838/272, Item 169/1/3, Part 3, p 3. For Australia's poor opinion of Menon, see AA, letter 13 June 1956, from P.R. Heydon to DEA, Series A1838/183, Item 169/11/110, Part I.

115. AA, Memorandum May 1956, from Arnold Smith, Series A1838/283, Item 169/11/10 part 1. Menon's central role (if sometimes aggressively played) in the formulation and implementation of India's foreign policy under Nehru, ended with his political demise in 1962 consequent to the Chinese invasion for which India was ill-prepared, with Menon Defence Minister at the time.

116. Andrews, E.M. A *History of Australian Foreign Policy*, Longman Cheshire, Melbourne, 1979, p 127.

117. CPD, (H of R), Vol. 23, 23 April 1959, p 1520.

118. AA, Report 27 July 1950, from the Acting High Commissioner for Australia in India (Francis Stuart) Item 3. Series A1838/278 Item 3123/7/13.

119. Andrews *op. cit.*, p 127.

120. *Ibid*.

121. 'The recent defeat has been regarded as an American defeat and United States prestige had suffered throughout the continent. The personality of General MacArthur had contributed to this.' See AA, Cablegram 19 December 1950, from Australian High Commissioner in New Delhi - conversation with Bajpai, Series A1838/278 Item 3123/7/13.

122. *Selected Works of Jawaharlal Nehru*, 1 August-25 October 1950, Vol. 15, Part I, S. Gopal, (ed.) J. Nehru Memorial Fund, New Delhi, 1993, pp 388-389. MacArthur warned that oriental mentality looks to 'respect and to follow aggressive, resolute and dynamic leadership ...'.

123. Malik, D.N. *Post-War International Politics*, Veena Mandir, 1973, p 514, in S.N. Misra, India: *The Cold War Years*, South Asian Publishers, New Delhi, 1994, p 227.

124. Discussing the Korean War, Menon told Brecher, '...I was also ... moved by this sort of thing, killing people, killing people all the time.' See *India and World Politics*, Oxford University Press, London, 1968, p 37.

125. CPD, (H of R), Vol. 212, 7 March 1951, p 83.

126. *Ibid*.

127. Berger, Carl *The Korea Knot*, Revised Edition, Greenwood Press, New York, 1986, p 159.

128. *Ibid.*, p 176.

129. AA, Mr Anthony Eden to Sir H. Graves (Saigon), Conversation between the Secretary of State and the Indian High Commissioner on 10 March 1954. Series A1838/278, Item 169/7/1, Part 3. For UN request for Indian Draft on Peace and Security see, NAI File, No. 9(8)-UN II/52.

130. Varma, S.N., 'Trends in India's Foreign Policy, 1954-57', *Aspects of India's Foreign Relations*, Indian Council of World Affairs, New Delhi, 1964, pp 1-18.

131. Edwards Peter G. & Pemberton, Gregory, *Crises and Commitments*, Allen & Unwin, Sydney, 1992, p 146.

132. *Ibid.*, p 153.

133. CPD, (H of R), Vol. 9, 22 February, 1956, p 116.

134. CPD, (H of R), Vol. 16, 19 September 1957, pp 795-796.

135. CPD (H of R), Vol. 9, 22 February 1956, p 116.

136. Lok Sabha Debates, 29 September 1954, Col. 3680.

137. *Ibid.*, Col. 3677.

138. Neale, R.G., 'India', *Australia in World Affairs 1956-1960*, Gordon Greenwood and Norman Harper (eds.), F.W. Cheshire, Melbourne, 1963, p 342.

139. Menzies, R.G., *Afternoon Light*, Cassell, Melbourne, 1967, p 269.

140. *The Statesman*, Delhi, 'Australia to Attend Talks', 21 July 1954, p 1.

141. Edwards & Pemberton, *op. cit.*, p 190.

142. CPD, (H of R), Vol. 14, 2 April 1957, p 432.

143. *Ibid.*

144. CPD, (H of R), Vol. 9, 14 March 1956, pp 804-805.

145. *Ibid.* p 805. For a reference to the Western powers ignoring 'Asian feelings' in their military strategies see, 'India after SEATO', *The Eastern Economist*, 17 September 1954, p 457, in S.N. Varma, 'Trends in India's Foreign Policy, 1954-57' *Aspects of India's Foreign Relations*, Institute of Pacific Relations, Indian Council of World Affairs, New Delhi, 1964, pp 1-18.

146. The Kashmir imbroglio is steeped in a myriad issues which go back to the pre-independence negotiations between the Muslim League led by Mohammed Ali Jinnah and the Congress Party led by Gandhi and Nehru. Briefly stated, these questions include the following: the Instrument of Accession and the Theory of the State as it applies to the Indian States at the time of independence; India's secularism symbolised through Muslim majority Kashmir; Pakistan's internal politics and the legitimisation of military rule; India's stand possibly influenced by Nehru's personal attachment as a Kashmiri; India's security interests; and, support at the UN for Pakistan by important Western States and, likewise, for India from the Soviet Union. See, K. Subrata Mitra, 'Nehru's Policy Towards Kashmir: Bringing Politics Back In Again', *The Journal of Commonwealth and Comparative Politics*, Vol. XXXV July 1997, No. 2, pp 55-70. Also see Verinder Grover (ed.) *The story of Kashmir: Yesterday and Today*, Deep & Deep Publications Delhi, 1995.

147. Lok Sabha Debates, 20 March 1956, Part II, Col. 3042.

148. *Ibid.*

149. Lok Sabha Debates, 21 March 1957, Col. 240.

150. Lok Sabha Debates, 23 March 1957, Col. 4741.

151. CNIA, Communiqué of the Council of SEATO on 11 May 1957, Vol. 28, 1957, p 237.

152. Greenwood, Gordon, 'Australian Foreign Policy in action', *Australia in World Affairs 1956-1960*, Gordon Greenwood & Norman Harper, (eds.) F.W. Cheshire, Melbourne, 1963, p 97.

153. Ramachandram, G. *Nehru and World Peace*, Radiant Publisher, New Delhi, 1990, p 5.

154. Brett, Judith *Robert Menzies: Forgotten People*, Macmillan, Sydney, 1992, p 2.

155. Nehru Memorial Library, New Delhi, Manuscripts Section, Dennis Tuohy, An interview with Lord Mountbatten (undated), Accession No. 656, pp 1-14. For an useful insight into the stirring but eventful last days of British rule in India

see, L. Collins & D. Lapierre, *Mountbatten and the Partition of India, March 22-August 15, 1947*, Vikas Publishing, New Delhi, 1982.

156. *Jawaharlal Nehru's Speeches* Vol. 1, September 1946-May 1949, Ministry of Information & Broadcasting, Government of India, New Delhi, 1949, pp 1-2.

157. Chaudary, R. (ed.), *Nehru in His Own Words*, Navajivan Publishing House, Ahmedabad, 1964, p 18.

158. Hudson W.J. & Way, Wendy (eds.), *Documents on Australian Foreign Policy 1937-1949*, Vol. X, July-December 1946, DFAT, AGPS Canberra, p 178. Churchill, Menzies' erstwhile British colleague, a member of the Conservative Opposition at the time, opposed the British Government's plan to grant independence to India. See, Gilbert Martin, *Churchill*, Books for Pleasure, Sydney, 1979, p 112.

159. CPD, (H of R), Vol. 190, 19 March, 1947, p 855.

160. CPD, ( H of R), Vol. 154, pp 91-92, in E.M. Andrews, *A History of Australian Foreign Policy*, Longman Cheshire, Melbourne, 1979, pp 63-64.

161. Andrews, E.M., *A History of Australian Foreign Policy*, Longman Cheshire, Melbourne, 1979, p 53.

162. *Ibid.*

163. Sastri, S., Speech at the Round Table Conference , 1 December 1931, London, in *Famous Letters and Speeches*, L.F. Rushbrook Williams (ed.) The Times of India, Bombay & Associated Newspapers of Ceylon, (n.d.) p 569.

164. *Jawaharlal Nehru: An Autobiography*, John Lane The Bodley Head, London, 1936, p 601. See Appendix A.

165. Thakur R., *The Politics and Economics of India's Foreign Policy*, St Martin's Press, New York, 1994, p 26.

166. Meaney, Neville, *Australia And The World*, Longman Cheshire, Melbourne, 1985, p 28.

167. Grant, Bruce, *What Kind of Country?*, Penguin Books, Victoria, 1988, p 90.

168. Meaney, *op. cit.*, p 28.

169. Whitington, Don, 'The Liberal Party and the Monarchy', *Australia and the Monarchy: a Symposium*, G. Dutton (ed.), Sun Books, Melbourne, 1966, p 143.

170. Lowe, David, *Menzies and the 'Great World Struggle' Australia's Cold War 1948-1954*, University of NSW Press, Sydney, 1999, p 87.

**5**

# 'White Australia' and 'Non-alignment': Crucial and Conflicting Policies

India's policy of 'Non-alignment' and Australia's (exclusion of non-European) 'White Australia' Immigration Policy were central to each country's external response. Non-alignment with its multi-dimensional character was as crucial to independent India's future, as New Delhi saw it, as the 'White Australia' Policy was a major underpinning of Australia's response to its region. And, yet, both policies served to undermine the nature of the relationship, particularly in the Menzies era. Nehru, for instance, viewed all forms of racially based policies as abhorrent and Indians generally, whilst not particularly interested in migrating to Australia, were nevertheless resentful of its discriminatory immigration policy. Menzies' steadfast refusal to condemn Apartheid, and even providing tacit support for South Africa in its struggle to retain membership of the Commonwealth, compounded this resentment.

On the other hand, after World War II, the effect of non-alignment on the West was palpable; Menzies saw it as a weak policy and thought it helped the Communists. Both men, of course, defended their policies as serving the interests of their respective countries. This Chapter examines the history of the two policies, the reasons for their existence and how they affected the bilateral relationship. In a sense, it continues the theme of the Nehru-Menzies dissonance but focussing on two crucial policies which had an adverse effect on the bilateral relationship. The Chapter starts with an examination of the 'White Australia' Policy and then goes on to consider India's policy of 'non-alignment'.

## 'WHITE AUSTRALIA' POLICY

While independent India, and indeed many of Australia's Asian neighbours, struggled to overcome the humiliations of colonialism in the aftermath of World War II, the issue that perhaps more than any other sharpened the political divergence between India and Australia was the exclusion of non-European ('White Australia') Policy, the cornerstone of Australia's immigration policy. From India's perspective, its existence did more to undermine the relationship between the two countries than any other issue. Nothing attests to the truth of this better than Stewart Wigmore's (Australia's Publicity Officer in the High Commission, New Delhi) comments to DEA: 'I have been told by a highly placed Indian intellectual that ' "Australia is one of the most hated countries in India" primarily because of the White Australia policy.'[1] Its enforcement, offensive to Indians, was strenuously defended by leaders of both sides of the Australian political spectrum, conservative and Labor, till a gradual softening of its impact commenced with selective application of the policy from the mid 1960s. Its eventual abrogation took place in 1973 with the advent of the Whitlam Government.

## Background

The formula for placing restrictions on the source of Australia's post-federation migration, (referred to as the Immigration Restriction Act) came into legislative effect immediately after federation in 1901: 'it was simply a case of "ignominy thirsting for respect", and the infamous "White Australia" policy is born.'[2] Ironically, the spectre of immigrant labour and the emotion it stirred in the colonies before federation had much to do with Indian workers who, T.B. Millar observes, 'were the first to awaken the reaction in the Australian colonies that led to the White Australia policy.'[3] For a proper understanding, however, of the impact the 'White Australia' Policy had on Indian sensibilities, it helps to focus briefly on the history of this racially based immigration policy 'which was central to Australian national life.'[4] W.K. Hancock believed it became 'the indispensable condition of every other Australian policy,'[5] an integral component of foreign policy *ipso facto*. Sean Brawley, in his critique on the abolition of the 'White Australia' Policy, laments Australia's ignorance of the ubiquitous nature of the 'White Australia' Policy: 'this lack of firm historical knowledge is a gap in our understanding of Australian history and is certainly not good for the nation's collective memory.'[6]

The centrality of the policy, the initiatory milestone event in this chronologically sequenced narrative, was the original Parliamentary debate, unique for the unanimity of support for the Bill.[7] Two decades later, Prime Minister, W.M. Hughes' strong opposition to non-white immigration and Fowler's racial fears about India's surplus population, demonstrated Australia's persistent commitment to exclusion.[8] Australia's War time Labor Prime Minister, John Curtin, was another leader who felt comfortable with the retention of the 'White Australia' Policy, defending its discriminatory basis:

> We did not intend that to be and, it never was an affront to other races. It was devised for economic and sound humane reasons ... We intend to maintain that principle, because we know it to be desirable.[9]

After World War II, and despite the cordiality that characterised Australia's relationship with India with the Chifley/Evatt-Nehru camaraderie, the exclusion policy continued to be enforced to India's chagrin and, 'even resentment, which is implied, sometimes tacitly and sometimes explicitly, in the questions asked by Indians,' according to Iven Mackay, Australia's High Commissioner in New Delhi.[10]

## Diplomatic Advice Strong: Government Response Weak

While Australia's diplomats were at the coal face of criticism, they were also in the best position to make assessments of the host country's sensitivity to the 'White Australia' Policy, in conjunction with the high priority issues of trade and security. In a strongly argued case made to Evatt (Minister for External Affairs), a prescient Mackay stresses the importance for Australia of an intake of migrants from India, a country on the verge of independence, and, in his assessment, destined to become a major power among Australia's neighbours.[11] His argument begins with India's one-dimensional image of Australia.: 'the large majority of Indians today associate Australia, first and foremost, with the traditional "White Australia" policy.'[12] And despite India's understanding of Australia's exclusion of Indian labourers on the grounds of its adverse economic effects, Mackay made a case for consideration of Indian migrants with higher skills:

> ... the Indian view is that the exclusion of educated and Westernised Indians, such as qualified engineers, doctors, lawyers, journalists

> etc., can only be described as racial discrimination, especially ... in the present period of general economic expansion and development, Australia needs as many competent individuals as she can attract.[13]

In an interesting parallel, similar sentiments underlined India's resentful response to a request, purely utilitarian in nature, from Queensland for indentured Indian labour to work on the sugar cane and cotton plantations in the 1860s. Author S. Chandrasekhar captures India's reaction at the time with this argument:

> If educated and respectable Indians could not come to an Australian colony settled by British convicts, there was no point in asking for labourers to work in the midst of the Lily-White subjects from Great Britain.[14]

Clearly, Mackay was ahead of public opinion and prevailing attitudes in post-War Australia. In a letter to Evatt, he finally pleads his case for an Indian intake:

> ... as a gesture of goodwill to India as she enters upon her new national status. The present juncture in world affairs seems to be eminently suitable for a modification of the existing regulations with regard to Indians.'[15]

If High Commissioner Mackay's plea to Canberra, based on what he considered was on an objective analysis of the relevant issues for Australia, were ignored, then any failure of the bilateral relationship in the Chifley period (1947-1949) to achieve its full potential was not due to a lack of positive advice being available to the policy makers in Canberra. But rather Australia's reluctance to compromise on its commitment to a 'white Australia', described by Manning Clark as, 'one gigantic act of protection.'[16] Arthur Calwell, as Labor's Minister for Immigration, was unflinching in his determination to ensure the 'White Australia' Policy remained intact and, despite the warm relationship Chifley and Evatt had with Nehru, Labor's position on immigration was unequivocal, emphasised by this statement of Calwell's: 'so long as the Labor Party remains in power there will be no watering down of the White Australia policy.'[17] In Opposition too, Labor's defence against criticism of its stand on immigration, was just as resolute. For example, in Parliament, F.M. Daly referred the House to Calwell's article in *The Argus* of 24 October 1949, under the title 'I Stand by White Australia',[18] to reinforce Labor's commitment to the policy; in the process, he described Calwell as 'the greatest advocate of our immigration policy, as it affects Asian nations.'[19] Labor

Stalwarts, Evatt and Clyde Cameron were no less supportive of the policy urging the British character of the Australian community be preserved.[20]

## Defending the Indefensible

In its wish to minimise criticism of the policy, seen as discriminatory in India, Australia provided reasons which were often couched in sophistry and semantics. For example, the familiar language of Calwell and Menzies, who would preface their explanations of the policy with words such as 'underlying the White Australia policy there is no suggestion of racial superiority ... '[21] and that the policy 'is based not upon any foolish notion of racial superiority...'[22] respectively. In the face of media controversy over Australia's immigration policy, Holt, as Minister for Immigration, issued a statement to the press referring it to his address to the Third Australian Citizenship Convention in 1958:

> I stated that our policy of restriction was not based on any notion of racial superiority but on a frank and realistic recognition that there are important differences of race, culture and economic standards which make successful assimilation unlikely, ... I gave the Convention an assurance that we would maintain a general policy designed to preserve the homogeneity of the Australian nation. The present Government has not wavered in its support of this policy which has played so important a part in the building of the Australian nation.[23]

Casey, unlike Menzies, saw no difference in the capability of other races: 'I personally could never accept the myth of racial superiority.'[24] Yet, Casey was to object to any reference being made to it as the 'White Australia' Policy, another example of Australia's untenable reasoning in defending the policy:

> Our immigration policy is not called a White Australia Policy. I should like that to be emphasised. That offensive expression has never been used officially ... and I protest against its use in this chamber.[25]

From India's perspective, it was the practical effect of the policy that offended, and mere substitution of words that did nothing to remove the discriminatory quality of the policy was of academic interest. Sir Bertram Stevens, returning from a visit to India, offered this advice on softening the impact on sensibilities through appropriate language:

When during the war a Minister of the Australian Government declared that one of the reasons why Australia was participating in the war and making heavy sacrifices was 'to keep Australia white', there were headlines in the Indian press and expressions of indignation were heard on every hand. It becomes a matter of utmost importance to re-examine the principles underlying the White Australia policy and to attempt their restatement in terms less offensive to the national pride of Australia's Asiatic neighbours.[26]

Given these subtle attempts by the policy makers in Canberra to mask the true intent of the policy, some of Australia's diplomats, faced with criticism of the policy in Asia, were not reluctant to question Canberra on its uncompromising application. Again, it was Mackay, with his forthright comments to Evatt from his New Delhi post in pre-independent India, who exemplified this spirit:

> The official defence of our 'White Australia' policy is that it is based on economic and social grounds, and not on racial grounds. Nevertheless, it has to be admitted that Australia's immigration policy, as it stands at present, is also racial and not merely economic and social.[27]

Not long after the war, High Commissioner Massey, writing from Singapore, expressed similar concerns to Canberra:

> So long as our immigration policy remains what it is (and we know there is no thought of changing it) we will always have to face the general bitterness towards it which I have found lies under the surface and which has been recently shown here in such a crystallised form.[28]

Then there was diplomat Crocker (in Bruce Grant's view was more a radical conservative)[29] who, as High Commissioner to India in the 1950s, in a Despatch to Casey wrote:

> ... in the case of the politically conscious Indian, Australia was likely to conjure up two thoughts: one, which was favourable, the line taken by Australia for the independence of Indonesia; the other, which was unfavourable, the Australian Immigration Policy. The latter tended (and still tends) to be a more frequent or more enduring thought than the former.[30]

Crocker went further and suggested a parliamentary group should visit India to help improve understanding, but cautioned that 'they should be briefed to deal with questions about our empty spaces and about immigration policy.'[31] Discussion of immigration and related issues in the Australian Parliament too drew attention to the discriminatory policy. In one instance, Alexander Downer cautioned Members of Parliament about changing the existing policy which, at the time, required a person to have 15 years of residence, among other conditions, to qualify.[32] Then there was the case of the Indian High Commissioner to Australia, General Cariappa, who was criticised in the press and accused of 'intruding in Australia's domestic affairs' when he suggested a migrant quota be used by Australia and New Zealand.[33] The Indian Government took the opportunity to stress that 'even if Australia asked for Indian immigrants, the Government of India would have to consider whether Indians could live in that country with dignity and honour, as full citizens...'[34].

India was not alone in its resentment of the policy. In the 1950s and 1960s, criticism came from others in the region. A newspaper in Malaya expressed its distaste of Australia's policy in these words: 'there is an evil jinn inside one of the secret files of the Australian immigration department which sees that the department never, but never, does the right thing.'[35]

In a stinging attack on Calwell's efforts to rationalise the discriminatory immigration policy, an editorial in the *Daily News*, Ceylon (Sri Lanka) argued:

> Ironically, the Australians have preferred white aliens to Commonwealth citizens. Against that record, Mr Calwell's sanctimony only adds insult to injury. ... The quotas, the visual tests, the preference for certain blood ratios all these are erected on the basis of economic theory. No colour bar. Only massive humbug.[36]

## Selection Criteria, not Admission the Root Cause

Gaining admission to Australia for permanent settlement was not an important goal for Indians, for whom ultimately the humiliation caused by the 'White Australia' Policy lay as much in its disguised (and transparent) connotations as in its application. Self respect and sensitivity to any inference of inferiority,[37] rather than the question of actual admission, were the real concerns for India. The sophistry and semantics failed to hide the message, palpably clear: an unequivocal, and unpalatable, refusal to accept non-white immigration. Academic L. Jayasuriya explains the xenophobia implicit in the policy:

It was partly a matter of economic competition, a threat to white living standards, and the practices and Institutions of the dominant groups in society; but it was also to some extent conceived as a reaction to threatened racial purity ... and above all, it was linked with colour.[38]

Settler arrivals[39] (shown in Table 1 below) from India before and after the complete abrogation of the 'White Australia' Policy by the Whitlam Government in 1973 appear to vindicate High Commissioner Mackay's prediction (made in 1946) that removal of the barrier would not result in any significant increase in migrants from India, his argument at the time being that 'India's pride resents any bar which she thinks is exclusively directed against her nationals. ... What they would like to feel, however, is that there is no bar against their entry.'[40]

### Table 1

### *Settler Arrivals from India pre and post Whitlam*

|                        | 1965-70 | 1970-75 | 1975-80 | 1980-85 | 1985-90 |
| ---------------------- | ------- | ------- | ------- | ------- | ------- |
| Arrivals (From India)  | 12,310  | 13,330, | 4,580   | 7,700   | 13,850  |

Expressed as a percentage of total migrants from all the countries of Asia, these figures represent a significant drop in the Indian component of migrants.

|                        | 1965-70 | 1970-75 | 1975-80 | 1980-85 | 1985-90 |
| ---------------------- | ------- | ------- | ------- | ------- | ------- |
| Arrivals (From India)  | 22.38%  | 16.32%  | 4.01%   | 4.97%   | 5.37%   |

*Source*: Australian Bureau of Statistics, *From India to Australia*, S. Chandrasekhar (ed.) Population Review Books, California, 1992, p 123.

## The Menzies View: Maintain the *Status Quo*

The 'White Australia' refrain continued to be voiced under Menzies into the 1960s. His defence of the policy was premised on the argument that preserving social harmony is best achieved through racial homogeneity, essentially, a European population:

> ... while I believe that our immigration policy is both wise and just, is based not upon any foolish notion of racial superiority, but upon a proper desire to preserve a homogeneous population and so avert the troubles that have bedevilled some other countries, it is a domestic policy.[41]

Menzies defence of the 'White Australia' Policy extended to the argument that it was a matter that came within Australia's domestic jurisdiction, not unlike the position he took when in Opposition against independence for the Netherlands East Indies from the Dutch; citing Article 2, Clause 7 of the United Nations Charter, Menzies had argued against the Chifley Government's position which was more in line with Nehru's support of Indonesia's independence. Menzies' statement in Parliament on the Immigration Policy was that:

> Australia, of all countries, has a keen interest in preserving its authority over matters which are within its own domestic jurisdiction, because, to be perfectly plain, that clause was designed to safeguard Australia's right to maintain the White Australia policy.[42]

*The National Herald* in Lucknow asserted: 'to talk of the need for protecting Australia's homogeneous European civilization is to speak the language of Dr Malan (the South African Leader).'[43] This use of legal means 'to justify Australia's negative policies on anti-racist and anti-colonial initiatives in the United Nations ...'[44] was characteristic of Australia's conservative diplomacy in the 1950s.

While actual cases of the maltreatment of non-white visitors to Australia in this period were not often reported, reference to a couple of instances will help understanding of the prevailing climate and India's perceptions of this racially discriminatory policy. The first of these concerns the treatment experienced by two Indians, Mr K.V. Krishnamoorthy and Mr Sukhla while visiting Australia.[45] The second incident, a more celebrated one, involved a Fijian, who, in 1961, as a transit passenger *en route* to India, had the contents of his suitcase tipped out by a customs officer at Sydney airport. The then minor government official (of a British-ruled Fiji) Kamisese Mara went on to become Prime Minister of independent Fiji.[46] A decade later, at the conclusion of the Seven Nation Pacific Forum held in Sydney in April 1972, (at which discussion of Australia's immigration policy was an item on the agenda), Sir Kamisese, recalling the embarrassing incident at a news conference, said 'I never pass through Australia if I can avoid it.'[47]

It is noteworthy that Prime Minister William McMahon and Immigration Minister A.J. Forbes, representing Australia at the Sydney forum, advised it that the Australian Government 'had no intention of "radically" altering its policy of limiting non white immigration to persons who had the needed skills as well as an ability to get along socially in an overwhelmingly white community.'[48] To place the McMahon Government's stance on immigration in context, it was stated just eight months before the Whitlam Government took office in December 1972 and removed the 'White Australia' Policy from the Statute Books, ensuring white and non-white migrants competed on an equal footing to settle in Australia. Thus, the widely held view that the 'White Australia' Policy had effectively been rescinded by the mid-1960s is not entirely accurate. It continued to be selectively applied to non-white migrants till the Whitlam Government's decisive action. Indians were not unaware of this. A year earlier, Prime Minister John Gorton, addressing a gathering in Singapore, also made clear the Government's intention to maintain the prevailing policy.

## 'White Australia': A Fundamental Identification

Nehru's resentment of racial inequality was no less felt by ordinary Indians whose knowledge of Australia was limited to the existence of the 'White Australia' Policy as the following example illustrates. Returning from a visit to India, Labor's K.E. Beazley, (MHR for Freemantle) in a wide ranging speech in Parliament in 1955, delivered a message on Asia's aspirations of freedom and equality, reflective of the repugnance Indians felt about racial inequality:

> It has been well said that Asia wants freedom from the white man's colonial control, freedom from the white man's economic control, but above all freedom from the white man's contempt ... as far as I could see in Malaya, Burma and India, if the people thought of the white man's contempt, they thought of the White Australia policy.[49]

Unquestionably, the continued application of the 'White Australia' Policy triggered early stirrings of doubt with regard to Australia's interest in a genuine and independent regional role. These doubts were shared by many of Australia's newly independent neighbours of Asia, and Africa too, in the wake of the nationalism sweeping through these regions. Again, their sense of outrage was experienced at first hand by Beazley, who was clearly surprised at the kind of questions raised at an invitation to address Indian trade unionists. His address to Parliament on this experience is another example of advice resulting from knowledge gleaned at first hand, in this case by a Member of Parliament, unheeded by the policy makers to the detriment of the bilateral relationship:

> The questions that my audience asked me were almost all concerned with the White Australia policy, and with race relations in South Africa. ... That is sensitivity to discrimination and what they regard as injustice.[50]

In 1957, Kenneth Rivett, (Writer/Academic, who spent six months in India), in his informative article 'From White Australia to the Present', makes the point that very few Indian villagers at the time were aware of Australia, but those who were 'would know only two things about it - that we had nearly exterminated our Aborigines ... and that we maintain a White Australia policy.'[51] Even the announcement of the tactful and well liked Casey to the Governorship of Bengal in pre-independent was at first received with derision, because, as Hudson describes the Indian reaction, 'to be governed by a Briton was for many bad enough, ... to be governed by a colonial Briton from a country well and unfavourably known for a publicly proclaimed restrictive immigration policy based on race and colour was insulting.'[52] Casey of course was free of prejudice and proved to be one Australian who was well regarded by Indians in the Menzies period.

## South Africa and the Unavoidable Association

While the earlier discussion in Chapter Three on the issues that brought Nehru and Menzies into direct conflict within the Commonwealth included South Africa's expulsion from the association because of its Apartheid policies, it is examined in this chapter from a different and important perspective: its links to Menzies' political support for South Africa being related to his strong defence of the 'White Australia' policy and the Western alliance.

Menzies support of South Africa to the bitter end affected the Indian view of Australian foreign policy and of course the bilateral relationship. The strong emotion attached to the racial discrimination issue in India did not differentiate between Apartheid and Australia's immigration policy. This is evident from a conversation L.H. Border of the Australian High Commission in New Delhi had with India's Frank Moraes, the well known, one time editor of *The Times of India* and author of *Nehru: Sunlight and Shadow: A Critical Assessment*. Border's conclusion was that:

> Moraes could see no difference in the policies of the two countries:
> (Australia and South Africa) he ... fulminated for some time against
> the 'White Australia Policy'. ... a European might migrate to
> Australia: an Indian, a fellow member of the Commonwealth, could
> not ...[53].

While South Africa's Apartheid policy was a third party issue as
far as India-Australia relations were concerned, during the period of
heightened sensitivity in India's post-colonial attitude to the West
(which included Australia), Australia's reluctance to condemn
Apartheid at the official level, exacerbated the resentment Indians
already felt towards it on account of the 'White Australia' Policy;
and, understandably from India's standpoint, their view of Australia
as racially biased continued. Nehru was relentless in his
condemnation of Apartheid grasping every opportunity, within India
as well as at international forums, to speak out on it. His contention
was that 'it is the greatest immorality, international immorality for
a nation to carry on this way...'[54]. Lamenting the fact that, while
Canada's Prime Minister Diefenbaker spoke out strongly against the
policy, other democracies had failed to do so, Nehru added:

> ... it has been a matter of some distress for me that from others
> who stand for the democratic tradition, who stand for the dignity
> of the individual, ... not a voice can be heard ...[55].

Of course, Menzies' voice was indeed heard, but on the side of
South Africa rather than in condemnation of its discriminatory policy.
In *Afternoon Light*, Menzies speaks of his distress when Nehru rejected
the draft communiqué at the conclusion of the 1961 Commonwealth
Prime Ministers' Conference which led to South Africa's termination
of its Commonwealth membership:

> My pleasure was short-lived. No sooner had Verwoerd said that he
> would accept the draft, then Nehru was heard to say that *he* would
> not; ... not only at Prime Ministers' meetings but at every opportunity
> that presented itself, he would urge war on *apartheid* and the country
> which practised it.[56] (emphasis in original)

South Africa's Apartheid policy was doubly hurtful to Nehru
because, besides Africans, his fellow Indians too were victims of it.
Consequently, the treatment of Indians in South Africa[57] was a matter
of concern to the Indian Government. When the issue came up before
the UN, Nehru raised the subject in the Indian Parliament as an issue
of international importance: 'it has once again raised issues that are

vital not only for us but for the whole world. If I may say so, it is the issue of racialism that is of paramount importance.'[58]

Australia's record on the Apartheid question in the Menzies era was poor. For instance, when the question of including the treatment of Indians in South Africa on the agenda of the UN General Assembly came up before the Steering Committee (and was passed by ten votes to one), Australia voted against it.[59] Menzies' own performance on Apartheid at the Commonwealth Prime Ministers' Conferences weakened Australia's persistent but unconvincing arguments, (aimed at deflecting Asian criticism), that its own 'White Australia' immigration policy was other than racially based. Charles Price makes the point well:

> The relics of racial discrimination, plus the apparent reluctance of the Government to introduce the changes it eventually did introduce, together with its habit of sometimes supporting South Africa, fostered overseas the notion that Australians were a "racist" people almost as bad as the South African Nationalists...[60].

In contrast to Menzies' support for South Africa, Nehru advised the Lok Sabha of his early refusal to agree to South African Prime Minister Smuts' request that India restores its severance of trade relations and diplomatic representation before any discussion of the treatment of Indians in South Africa could commence.[61] He told the House, 'we shall not falter ... in our resolve to secure justice for Indians in South Africa ...'[62]. J.S. Bain in his book, *India's International Disputes:A Legal Study*, writes that South Africa 'ever since 1946, ... have questioned the legality of accepting the Indian complaint on the agenda and have charged it as a "violation of the charter,"...'[63]. This was not unlike Menzies' use of the 'domestic jurisdiction' argument to fend off the Nehru led push for South Africa's expulsion from the Commonwealth. Clearly, Australia and South Africa were at one on the approach to handling the issue of colour and racial-based discrimination.

The unavoidable inference is that the convergence of interests between Australia and South Africa, was all too strong for Menzies to adopt a harder line on South Africa. Then, again, Menzies' reluctance to condemn South Africa's racially based policy could also be attributed to Australia's obligations to the Western alliance, apart from the need to defend its own 'White Australia' Policy. For example, the West's economic interests in South Africa, through its investments, had helped the country to resist changes to Apartheid. A UN report suggested that 'Foreign investment in South Africa bears ascribable responsibility for *apartheid*.'[64] While Australia's share of this investment may have been negligible, Menzies' commitment to the Western alliance was not. Bandyopadhyaya, who argues the existence of a global racial dichotomy in his challenging critique, *North Over South*, speaks to the pertinence of this Western alliance acting as a connecting medium:

> Racial phenomena, like most other contemporary international phenomena, are characterized by strong global linkages, making racial schisms in the USA, South Africa, ... or the discriminatory immigration policies of the USA, UK and Australia, inseparable from the global racial dichotomy across the colour line.[65]

With specific reference to South Africa, he claims that the country has 'become the symbol of international white racism and its structural links with national white racism.'[66] By implication, Menzies' demonstrably strenuous defence of South Africa, albeit for selfish national interest, gives credence to arguments about the existence of historically based racist linkages within the Western alliance, its origins rooted in colonialism and imperialism. There was also South Africa's importance in terms of its support of the West's ideologically based strategic global objectives, for example, the Simonstown naval base. One writer refers to this with the following observation:

> One constant and repeatedly emphasised theme in the formulation of South Africa's foreign policy of the 1960s has been the assertion of the vital contribution its government and people are making to the defence of Western interests with the global struggle to contain the spread of communism.[67]

Eventually, Australia withdrew its support for South Africa's Apartheid policy in the early 1960s, although it was contingent on the UN guaranteeing that any action taken against South Africa will not be used against Australia.[68] For the bilateral relationship, however, it was too late. *The Dominion* in Wellington reported India's Deputy Minister for External Affairs telling India's Upper House of Parliament that, 'the Indian Government is considering the imposition of reciprocal restrictions on Australian nationals visiting India ...'.[69] South Africa's departure from the Commonwealth and subsequent *pariah* status progressively conferred on the country with its ex-communication by the international community, 'brought White Australia into even more graphic international relief.'[70] A few months after South Africa's departure, a contributor to *The Round Table* wrote that Australia could be the next in line:

> Indeed, the argument has already been heard that the self-exclusion of South Africa in consequence of the condemnation of *Apartheid* leads to the logical consequence that the Commonwealth ought to intervene against the 'White Australia' Policy.[71]

As a consequence of the subtle deception practised by Menzies with his arguments on the South African question India was less convinced about many of Australia's views on international issues in the Menzies era. In *The Administration of the White Australia Policy*, Palfreeman refers to the international scrutiny the 'White Australia' Policy receives on account of some of Australia's foreign policies being greeted with scepticism by the international community. [72]

## The Minimalist Approach to Reform: Push and Pull

Given the failure of Australia's High Commissioners and Members of Parliament to move the policy makers in Canberra, early success for the Immigration policy Reform Group[73] (established in the late 1950s) was certainly not assured. The official doors to a 'White Australia' remained impregnable. But men like Peter Heydon, Head of the Department of Immigration (and at one time High Commissioner to India), did much to introduce reforms to the immigration policy. Yet, these initial efforts were limited. There were detractors and opponents to reform, including Menzies who in 1961 commented that those who criticised Australia's immigration policy consists mainly of 'a few itinerant Australians and a few gentlemen in Australia.[74] Kenneth Rivett draws attention to a number of factors which helped bring the Reform Group's efforts to fruition in 1966;[75] the timing of the measure of success eventually achieved was not without its irony: 'The turning point came in March 1966, following with indecent haste on the retirement of Sir Robert Menzies as Prime Minister.'[76]

Despite the welcome watering down of the 'White Australia' Policy in 1966, its application continued to be seen by some Asian countries as discriminatory even in 1970. For example, reporting on the Commonwealth Parliamentary Conference being held in Canberra, *The Observer*, Ceylon, (Sri Lanka), while describing the meeting as symbolising 'the mutually binding ideals of the various nations of the Commonwealth',[77] drew attention to the country's representative, the Speaker of the House, Stanley Tillekeratne's 'polite if incisive censure of Canberra's lingering "White Australia" Policies ...'.[78] The Speaker's remonstrance is hardly surprising considering Australia's delayed reaction to Asian sensibilities and then the minimalist approach Australian Governments took to modifying the policy.

Then there was the occasion of the Commonwealth Heads of Government Conference of January 1971 hosted by Singapore and attended by the Prime Ministers of Australia and India among others. At a dinner given for the Australian Prime Minister, John Gorton, and attended by a prominent gathering of Singaporeans, Ong Tek Joong (ex-Australian Universities Singaporean Alumni President) speaking on Australia's ostensibly liberalised immigration policies said, 'we feel it our duty to focus attention on the need to find a more rational and equitable criterion ...' and added that relations between the two countries 'were "somewhat superficial"... Australians and Asians must look at each other as human beings and friends on an equal footing ...'.[79] Gorton responded to criticism of the 'White Australia' Immigration Policy 'with a firm declaration that he had no intention of abandoning it.'[80] The message could not have escaped the attention of India's Prime Minister, Mrs Indira Gandhi.

Looking back at the Holt Government's easing of the policy in the aftermath of Menzies, *The Age* newspaper's Michael Gawenda refers to Cabinet papers to argue that the action was not motivated by a nation's troubled conscience, but rather 'because of increasing criticism of it in Asia and from the rest of the world.'[81] The truth of Australia's unblushing response is apparent from the then Immigration Minister Sir Hubert Opperman's submission to Cabinet which, in his words, ensured 'the fundamental soundness of a policy directed to social homogeneity ...'.[82]

For Indians, the continued absence of any logical basis to the balance between the European and Asian migrant intake conveyed a clear message that the discrimination continued. Camilleri observed that, 'there had been no fundamental conversion in Australian attitudes, but simply a diplomatic readjustment.'[83] This perception was made all the more credible in the light of Australia's support of the European countries at the UN 'on the most sensitive issues of decolonization and racial discrimination ...'[84], issues that for India, were of paramount importance. Charles Price in his insightful critique 'Beyond White Australia' in reference to Australia's often stated 'social harmony' argument states that:

> No amount of talk about the dangers of racial tensions and conflict if the doors opened wide to Asian immigration, ... could satisfy the hostility sometimes shown by the press and politicians of newly independent Africa and Asia.[85]

The Whitlam Government, with its undisguised reformist immigration policy, dealt the *coup de grace*, the decisive dismantling of the 'White Australia' Policy from the Statute in 1973, making its legal force null and void. Chandrasekhar compared this historic Whitlam initiative to President Lyndon Johnson's 1965 Immigration Act, which allowed in immigrants from all countries of the world.[86] Whitlam's positive impact on India because of his often stated abhorrence of racial discrimination, among other reasons, is examined in Chapter Seven.

## INDIA'S NON-ALIGNMENT IN THE COLD WAR: A MULTI-FACETED WEAPON

Any study of India-Australia relations between 1947 and 1975 has to include an examination of the impact of India's non-aligned stance taken soon after the country's independence in 1947. It was no less central to India's foreign policy than the 'White Australia' Policy was to Australia for nearly seven decades after federation. The birth and reasons behind this policy are therefore essential to an understanding of what it meant for the bilateral relationship. That such examination is helpful is seen in J.W. Burton's observation that, 'no theory of International Relations is complete without an explanation of the development, and theory of, non-alignment.'[87] Much has been made of India's decision to adopt this philosophy, the cornerstone of the country's international strategy, in a post-War bipolar world drifting inexorably towards two ideologically distinguished and hostile blocs.

## Background

In the Cold War environment of the 1950s and 1960s the newly independent countries of Asia and Africa found themselves facing a decision about alignment with one or the other of the two camps, a process vigorously encouraged by each of the superpowers and their allies, including Australia. Non-alignment provided an alternative, an instrument for non-involvement:

> The concept of non-alignment as envisaged by the founders - Nehru, Nasser and Tito - was to serve the purpose of a safety valve for the smaller nations against pressures from the big powers and as a profilaxis against being drawn into the politics of cold war.[88]

Indeed for India, and a majority of the Afro-Asian nations emerging from years of colonialism, the idea of remaining outside the influence of the two superpowers through non-alignment was seen as the best option: a message from the Third World of their wish to remain free and immune from superpower Cold War rivalry. Australian diplomat, Francis Stuart's despatch to DEA from New Delhi on India's attitude to the Korean War, illustrates India's satisfaction with its neutralist international stance:

> ... the Indian Parliament's mood as a whole, ... remains one of refusal to face the logical conclusions of even an impeccable foreign policy, when these seem to run counter to pacifist neutrality.[89]

But it held more than that for Nehru for whom 'non-alignment was not conceived merely as a response to the military blocs or the cold war, but as a global egalitarian movement to restructure the existing inequitable world order in all its aspects; political, social and economic ...'[90]. There were other reasons, too, as the narrative will show, but for India, a co-founder of the Non-aligned Movement (NAM), the choice of non-alignment in the wake of freedom was an obvious one, even an unavoidable one. The two men most responsible for India's external relations, Nehru and Krishna Menon, moulded the doctrine into a global weapon to protect itself and others against past injustice and inequitable practices. Ramachandram defines the multi-dimensional thrust of their policy fulcrum:

> Nehru and Krishna Menon together turned non-alignment into an effective world movement against colonialism, imperialism, racialism and the growing menace of military alliances.[91]

On the last of these, namely military pacts, which Nehru often criticised, Richard Park, in a reference to the complementary measures India adopted to support its non-alignment objectives, states that:

> What was (and is) less well known is that India, in order to help create "conditions of peace," would exercise its influence to lessen the effectiveness and the range of membership in ... mutual defence arrangements, particularly those which, like SEATO and CENTO, impinge on the region of southern Asia.[92]

For the India-Australia bilateral relationship, India's decision, which did not find favour in Australia, particularly with the policy makers in Canberra, was another factor that contributed to the indifference that characterised the relationship in the 1949 to 1972 period. But India's non-alignment *per se* could hardly have constituted a serious obstacle to Australia's forging better bilateral relations with it, given Australia's willingness, indeed strong interest, in pursuing good relations with its northern neighbour, Indonesia, itself an enthusiastic member of NAM in the 1950s. Obviously, the geo-political imperatives associated with its nearest neighbour outweighed any discomfiture Australia felt with Indonesia's non-aligned status. In India's case, apart from being a democracy, there was little else, such as trade or security, at the time, to commend it to Canberra. For a proper understanding, however, of how India's philosophy affected the bilateral relationship, a brief look at the genesis and character of NAM is a necessary pre-requisite. It enables an understanding of the breadth of the doctrine, an Indian view of its place in the world. Besides, it had to be understood at several levels; Australia's understanding of it in the Menzies era was guided at a different, limited level, one that assessed bilateral choices in terms of security, trade and how the country stacked up in the context of the Empire and the Western alliance. Non-alignment by itself was a poor qualification against such criteria as far as Australia was concerned.

## Policies, Terms and Meanings

As useful to a better understanding of India's policy, pivotal to its external relations, the use of the terms 'neutralism' and 'neutrality' to mean the same thing as 'non-alignment,' demands clarification, because, from India's perspective, the difference in meaning between neutralism and non-alignment is an important one. Besides, Australia and its Western allies often used the word neutral to mean non-aligned. While the concept of India's non-alignment may have defied a precise interpretation, neutrality it certainly was not. Nehru, for one, was at pains to correct the misunderstanding in the West that India's foreign policy was synonymous with neutrality. He explains the distinction with this interpretation of neutrality:

> ... it means a person who sits on the fence and who cannot decide between right and wrong. India is certainly not neutral ... She believes in non-alignment because she feels that the only way to achieve peace is to extend the climate of peace and to prevent the Cold War spreading into other parts of the world.[93]

Author R. Thakur extends the Nehru metaphor with his comment that, 'they saw themselves not so much as fence-sitters as believers in the need to uproot the fence.'[94] Obviously, non-alignment was more than a mere moral compass, it was an active foreign policy that involved India in international conflict resolution and the attainment of peace. It was a multi-faceted foreign policy instrument which gave India freedom to choose when, where and how it would involve itself in international questions while also protecting its own security.

During the debate in the Lok Sabha on Korea, Nehru referred to neutrality:

> ... when you say you are neutral that is a policy of not doing anything... The whole essence of our policy is independence of action, that is to say that at any moment we decide for ourselves what is best in our interests and in the interest of world peace ...[95].

## Bandung: A Third World Voice

NAM, which effectively represents the Third World giving it an Afro-Asian character, can be traced to the 1955 Bandung Conference which brought together leaders from Asia and Africa representing twenty-five countries; prominent among them were Nehru of India, Chou En Lai of China, Tito of Yugoslavia, Nasser of Egypt, Sukarno of Indonesia, and U Nu of Burma. Given the heterogeneous nature of the Bandung grouping, finding a single unifying criterion for determining membership of NAM, on which to formulate objectives, was no mean task. One writer describes this dilemma for the Bandung Conference organizers, (an informal group comprising

India, Pakistan, Indonesia, Sri-Lanka and Burma, referred to as the Colombo Powers): 'Ideologies and military alliances have now so cut across frontiers of geography and skin that even to agree on Agenda was no easy undertaking.'[96]

The relevance of non-alignment to India's relationship with Australia in the 1950s, a country seen by India as obsessed with the containment of Communism, and as a consequence, actively involved in drawing Asia's newly independent states to support the strategic goals of the Western camp, becomes more apparent when the aims of the Bandung conference are examined:

> To promote goodwill and cooperation among the nations of Asia and Africa ... to consider social, economic, and cultural problems. ... to consider problems of special interest ...(such as) racialism, and colonialism ... to view the position of Asia and Africa and their peoples in the world today and the contribution they can make to the promotion of world peace and cooperation.[97]

Juxtaposed with Australia's Cold War strategy, the divergence becomes apparent.

The Bandung Conference crystallised Nehru's plea for political and economic equity to generate a Third World voice. It created an awareness in the Third World of their entitlement to a greater say in, and a fairer share of, the world system, 'an augur of a future protest against the subordinate status of the developing countries in the international system.'[98] Indian writer C.S. Jha saw the Bandung declaration as having affected global interaction, providing the newly independent countries with a model to guide their post-colonial futures. He describes the historic Bandung affirmation as having 'powerfully influenced the subsequent course of international relations and became the code of the nations that emerged from colonial domination after 1955.'[99]

NAM did not excite much attention in Australia, which, under Menzies, was more concerned with supporting Australia's Western allies in their strategic goals and, when required, through involvement in war (Korea and Vietnam), ensuring the protection of a white population and a high standard of living from 'Asia's hordes'. While the Colombo powers did not extend an invitation to Australia to attend the Bandung Conference, the Menzies Government was uninterested in the international conference anyway; it ignored

Opposition Leader Evatt's appeals to the Government for Australia to be represented and 'looked upon these meetings with the disdain and suspicion it had always reserved for "Peace" conferences, and would have nothing to do with it.'[100]

For India, it was as exciting as 1947 and independence. The stature of Prime Minister Nehru,[101] who played an initiatory role in bringing the non-aligned philosophy to fruition, rose in the Third World in the aftermath of this preliminary gathering of Afro-Asian states. Nehru's modest post-conference assessment of the Bandung gathering was that 'it may develop into something which holds together.'[102] In the Lok Sabha, however, he was more expansive:

> While the achievements and the significance of the meeting at Bandung have been great and epoch making, it would be a misreading of history to regard Bandung as though it was an isolated occurrence and not part of a great movement of human history.[103]

According to Braillard and Djalili, Professor Senghor (former President of Senegal ) saw Bandung 'as the most important historical event since the Renaissance.'[104] Recognition of Nehru's place in the non-aligned world is important not least because of how his world view contrasted with that of Menzies', a common thread through much of this study. It helps demonstrate Nehru's unflinching commitment to world peace, the process of decolonisation, racial equality and fairer global economic equity, none of which figured strongly in Australia's security-driven, alliance diplomacy under Menzies. This also helps to explain Australia's failure to persuade many of the newly independent countries, (which sought refuge in NAM after the rigours of colonialism), to align themselves with the Western camp. In fact, inspired by the spirit of Bandung, non-alignment became a potent symbol of unity and went on to find expression in new forms such as The Afro-Asian Peoples Solidarity Organisation. Yet, NAM was not without its share of internal disagreements,[105] which, some would argue, makes its achievements of unity and growth through the 1950s and 1960s commendable.

## Policy Underpinnings: Economic, Geo-political and World Peace

Free India's policy of non-alignment was seen as one of its more controversial decisions by other states, besides Australia. In understanding, however, the rationale for the decision, it is useful to note that India's independence was not the result of British benevolence, but rather something Britain was forced to consider as unavoidable after World War II with the growing intensity of the Indian campaign for freedom led by Gandhi, Nehru, *et al.* Left with meagre resources at the termination of colonial rule under the British - whose primary interests were concerned more with the enrichment of Britain,[106] and consolidation of the Empire than with a free India's future economy - the options for India were not exactly abundant. India's geography too was a particularly worrying factor for its leaders. As if the ever present threat from China to its north was not difficult enough, it had to contend also with Pakistan, and Middle East instability to its west. Then, there was the potentially dangerous situation in the Indian Ocean to her south, with both the US and the USSR increasing their naval presence there. In the circumstances, with expenditure for expansion of its military capacity restricted by modest economic circumstances, India had little choice but to pre-empt and prevent potential aggression against her by resorting to friendly regional and international diplomacy; hence non-alignment, a natural policy choice.

Mabbett describes India's non-aligned pragmatism simply as 'not taking sides in the cold war, the tension between the West and the Communist powers. It meant trying to have good relations with as many countries as possible on both sides, and indeed getting help from both sides.'[107] In fact, Nehru said as much when he addressed the constituent assembly on India's foreign policies:

> We want the help of other countries; we are going to have it and we are going to get it too in a large measure. ... Even in accepting economic help, or in getting political help, it is not a wise policy to put all our eggs in one basket.[108]

Nehru's interests went beyond political and economic equity for the Third World to embrace world peace, more urgently needed in the aftermath of the destruction of World War II, and the inevitable Cold War race by both sides to gain nuclear weapons superiority. He saw the advocacy of world peace as a responsibility for India, and once told the Lok Sabha that Bertrand Russell had 'called upon India especially to point to the world the horrors of war.'[109] Nothing illustrates the depth and reach of India's non-alignment better than

Nehru's early foreign policy statement issued in 1946 as head of India's interim Government pending finalisation of full independence.[110]

## Australia's Response: Strategic Interests and Misperceptions

Non-alignment as a concept was accorded little interest by the Australian media. Under Menzies, Australia was critical of India's non-alignment as the narrative will show. Like the USA, Australia's view of non-alignment has tended to be premised on whose interests were served by the nonaligned country concerned, Australia's or those of the Communists, exemplified in its willingness to ignore non-alignment in the case of Indonesia. This approach is also evident in Australia's relationship with other countries of the region in the post-war period, where mutual economic or strategic interests as well as ideological sympathy with the West, rather than adopting non-alignment, or, the type of government, (democratic, authoritarian, military rule) dictated the tone of the relationship. Good examples of such relationships pursued by Australia are those it had with Japan, Indonesia, Thailand, the Philippines, South Vietnam, South Korea, Pakistan, Burma and Malaya; and, in the case of the last named, despite its refusal to join SEATO.[111] Democratic India, on the other hand, was not only seen by Australia to be less than unequivocal in its censure of the Soviet Union for breaches of international conduct, but also as persistent in its espousal of China's admission to the UN, a proposition consistently opposed by Australia.

Australia's major partner, America, was also critical of India's non-aligned policy and, because of Australia's identification with US policy in Indian eyes, its reaction to Australia was compounded by the American attitude to non-alignment. An example was Krishna Menon's comments in relation to the Bandung Conference that 'the Americans were against the idea; they tried to kill it - until it emerged and succeeded. Then they simulated enthusiasm about it. They sort of "came to scoff and remained to pray-..." '[112]. Then there was President Kennedy who said, 'we find some who call themselves neutrals, who are our friends and sympathetic to us, and others who call themselves neutralist, who are unremittingly hostile to us.'[113] Nixon went further to accuse the advocates of moral neutralism of using US economic aid, but then proceeding to oppose the US in the diplomatic sphere.[114] Nixon, who categorised neutralism by military, economic and moral groupings, was also critical of those leaders who used different criteria for the measurement of Western and Communist international behaviour.[115] Australia's principal ally's negative attitude to India's policy was not restricted to Presidents and the Administration in Washington. For example, the Americans for Democratic Action, an influential organisation, wrote to Nehru that India's foreign policy was not neutralist and was cause for concern:

> We find it tragic indeed that a great people such as yours, having fought for generations and fought successfully for its own freedom, should now, having attained it, seem blind to the grave threat to freedom in other parts of the world.[116]

Nehru's reply to the American Group exemplifies India's insistence that both ends and means must be worthy, and reflects his aversion to military approaches to the achieving of political objectives including the protection of peoples' freedom:

> Our policy is not neutralist but one of active endeavour to prepare and if possible establish peace on a firm foundation. ...On fundamental issues such as liberty of the individual and the rule of law, there is no difference between India and other like minded countries. It is only as regards the methods to be employed to achieve the purpose that you have felicitiously described as 'the survival of freedom with peace' that differences exists ...[117].

Author C.V. Crabb observes that the West's perception of non-alignment is that 'countries dedicated to this ideology either had become or were becoming *de facto* members of the Communist bloc.'[118] Consorting with the enemy is the inference. Yet, the evidence suggests that India had shown a firm resolve to protect its political independence ensuring that the aid accepted from the West, or the Communist bloc, did not compromise its freedom to make independent judgments in the conduct of international diplomacy, free of any obligations of loyalty that may be expected by the donor country. In fact, Nehru made this very clear in an address to the Lok Sabha.[119] On the other hand, Menzies with his strong commitment to SEATO and military alliances, was clearly uncomfortable with the notion of neutralism which he described as 'one of those rather rotund words which does not readily admit of definition,'[120] but then proceeded to qualify the remark with, 'What he (Nehru) has consistently made clear is that he stands for non-alignment, in the sense that he will not engage in any special military or quasi-military alliance. My own country does not subscribe to this view ...'[121]. Menzies' limited understanding of Nehru's definition of non-alignment illustrates the futility of the efforts made by Australia's High Commissioners and Federal MPs for an improvement in the bilateral relationship. Labor's Calwell in a speech in Parliament condemning Menzies' treatment of Nehru at the UN, argued that Nehru was criticised in Australia because of his policy of non-alignment and questions the grounds for such criticism: 'in the weakness of his country, what other policy could he adopt?'[122] Again, unlike Menzies, Casey, understood well Nehru's wider reasons for his choice of non-alignment which included its capacity for influencing world peace, as this observation suggests:

> Mr Nehru has explained the policy of non-involvement or non-alignment by maintaining that by not adding to the countries publicly lined up with the West against Communism, India is helping to maintain the peace of the world; ... and that if the world situation ever came to crisis, she would have more influence for peace by throwing her weight against war than if she had been merely one of the countries formally and publicly committed in advance to the West.[123]

## The Soviet Connection: Indian Tilt or Clever Diplomacy

While not everyone denies India took a softer line when forced to be critical of the Soviet Union, for instance, Nehru's delayed condemnation of the Soviet invasion of Hungary, Bandyopadhyaya explains this partiality of the non-aligned towards the Soviet Union by pointing to the Soviet's support for independence movements and its abstention from establishing 'hegemonistic military alliances involving the new states of Asia and Africa,' in contrast to the West's continuing post-War involvement in these regions through CENTO, SEATO, etc. As well, he draws attention to the Soviet Union voting at the UN against 'racist policies and practices'[124]. Furthermore, with non-involvement in military pacts being at the core of non-alignment, SEATO - because of Pakistan's membership - compounded India's disenchantment with the West; and, of course, this attitude to the West included Australia under Menzies, a strong advocate of SEATO.

Casey alone as Minister for External Affairs understood the Indian ethos. He told Parliament:

> ...in some countries nationalist emotion manifests itself in a philosophy of neutralism or non-involvement in the affairs of the principal power blocs ... . Extreme expressions of nationalism are fostered by feelings of opposition to colonialism - or even, it might be said the memories of colonialism.'[125]

Unfortunately, for the bilateral relationship, Casey's discerning judgement was denied expression by the negative attitude of Menzies and most of his Cabinet colleagues to India's philosophy. While Australia along with others in the Western alliance saw India's non-alignment as pandering to the Moscow-Peking interests, a writer to *The Round Table* observed that 'it would be mistaken of Americans to continue to see Mr Nehru's Government as a collection of sitters on the fence whose allegiance to the "free world" was tempered by the desire to flirt with Moscow and Peking.'[126] On the perception of partiality, the Indians were quick to point out that 'non-alignment did not mean equidistance, it meant reciprocity,'[127] implying that if the Russians showed a more friendly attitude to India than the Americans did, 'then naturally Indians would reciprocate ...'[128]. When Krishna Menon described India's reasons for adopting non-alignment, he stressed that India was not interested in identifying itself with the Soviet Union either:

> In 1945, immediately before India got her independence, it was all 'one world;' but by 1947 it was 'two worlds,' and we, for the first time had to make up our minds on the issue, ... We would not go back to the West with its colonialism; and there was no question of our going the Soviet way; we did not even know them much. ... we desired not to get involved in foreign entanglements.[129]

For newly independent India, however, where a majority of people were poor, the Soviet system of economic planning was preferred over the West's free market approach; a preference for the Soviets was also influenced by the Soviet Union's criticism of British colonialism and its early support for India's nationalistic aspirations.[130] The country's embryonic development demanded an agricultural and heavy industrial emphasis rather than consumer products oriented manufacturing.[131] B.H. Farmer, in his informative analysis of South Asia, refers to 'the influence of Nehru and his fellow western-style socialists, impressed by the Soviet-model and whole-heartedly in favour of central planning of the economy, ...'[132]. Casey, recognised the immensity of the problems India faced and saw fit to praise India's socialist approach to economic development. In an address to Parliament, he said: 'an inspiring example to the whole of Asia, and indeed to other countries as well, has been given by the Government of India with its imaginative and courageous second Five-Year Plan.[133]

It was Casey, also, who pointed out to an American audience in 1958 that many Asian countries opted for a socialist approach, because, in his view, 'it is useless to expect private enterprise to do the job, if the wherewithal of private enterprise - private savings on an appreciable scale - does not exist.'[134] For India, the inadequacy of private savings was unquestionably a limiting factor. But not everyone in the Menzies Government shared Casey's discerning objectivity about Asia, and certainly not his grasp of post-colonial India with all its aspirations amid complex and competing demands. This is not to say that India, made familiar with liberal Western democracy under the British, rejected the West to embrace socialism or help the Communist cause. Rather, the country chose for itself, 'the perpetuation of a mixed form of government in an independent India.'[135]

It would also be reasonable to ask whether the Soviet Union's support for India was purely altruistic, and it was going to let an opportunity slip during its Cold War rivalry with the West to advance its own strategic interests and political influence in South Asia. Post-colonial Asia, in relative turmoil in the 1950s, was vulnerable to all forms of influence. A telegram from the Secretary of State for Commonwealth Relations to Canberra sent in December 1955, with reference to the Soviet Leaders' visit to India, is a good example of this:

> They won applause by their demagogic speeches in support of resurgent Asia and 'colonial' peoples struggling for independence by domineering military blocs and praising India as a 'Truly peace-loving' nation. Their unabashed flattery fell on all ears more receptive because the West is supposed to be unsympathetic towards Indian neutralism.[136]

John Darwin, in his analysis of the 'Colonial World Order' and its post-war disintegration, discusses a militarily and technologically powerful Soviet Union, with its new status as a global power able 'to fashion a remarkably skillful ideological appeal to political movements in colonial and emergent countries, encouraging neutralism, offering clientele without tears and promising economic and military sponsorship to liberate them from former masters in the West.'[137] But, for all that, Nehru was nobody's fool and not easily impressed by blandishments whether it came from the Soviet leaders or those of the West. Nehru's objections to the Soviet leaders' criticism of the West during their tour of India, reported in *The Canberra Times* in December 1955 under the title 'Nehru Objects to Twists by Soviet Leaders on Tour ...'[138], is evidence of his capacity for impartial judgement. Nehru's willingness to criticise both sides when justified is borne out by an Australian High Commissioner in New Delhi who wrote that, in the pursuit of peace and democracy, India 'did not mind incurring the displeasure of either of the blocs.'[139] What emerges is that while India may have sought aid from the West and the Soviets (as well receiving the latter's support on Kashmir), its early decision to remain independent of both was not anticipated by either of the two great powers, as P. Nayer posits here:

> The West naively anticipated that the historical links between India and the West would naturally keep India within their orbit. Soviet analyses until about the middle of the fifties held that the so-called independence of India represented only a deal between the Indian bourgeoisie and British imperialism and that the struggle for the real independence of India was still continuing. They also, therefore, took it for granted that India would naturally gravitate into an alliance with the West.[140]

The problem for the India-Australia relationship was that Australia was aligned with the USA whose strategies in Asia were military in nature while the Soviets were more subtle with their approach. But this did not worry Menzies whose commitment to the US leadership was overriding. For example, during his Five Power Resolution battle with Nehru in the UN, Menzies in a letter to McEwen, not only attacked Nehru (a leader of the non-aligned group of countries) for his part in the resolution but added that the 'Americans in particular are desperately worried about the growth in the Neutralist block. ... Because of this, they welcomed both of my speeches and also my amendment.'[141] John Burton in 1954 observed 'Australian policy is now follow America.'[142] Menzies was also never really convinced of India's commitment to democracy, because in his mind, non-alignment hindered the cause of the 'democratic' West's strategic objectives, even though Nehru himself was unambiguous on India's commitment to it: 'democracy ... is the best of all the various methods available to us for the governance of human beings.'[143] He also made it clear that, 'democracy means tolerance of not merely of those who agree with us, but of those who do not agree with us.'[144] Even the US Secretary of State Dulles was in no doubt about India's commitment to democracy when, on a visit to India in 1953, he said that he was 'thoroughly convinced that India is acting according to its best judgment to promote democracy in the world and prevent the spread of totalitarianism.'[145] This was genuine praise indeed from a man who frequently criticised India's policy of non-alignment.

## 1962 and Brutal Cold War Realism: the Ultimate Test

Ironically, the Cold War rigidified international politics, challenging India's non-aligned stance which some saw as an idealistic approach. Given that non-alignment helped India avoid becoming a client state under the influence of either the US or the Soviet Union, enabling it to focus on economic priorities, the country's security was vulnerable by virtue of its geography and its military weakness. In the event, India's idealism was tested as it faced the bitter reality of external aggression with the 1962 border confrontation with China, resulting in a deep sense of outrage and betrayal being felt throughout India. Questioned on the idealism of the non-aligned state, and specifically the arguments in defence of this policy *vis à vis* the Chinese confrontation, Krishna Menon offered this argument.

> In my opinion, apart from the national excitement, disappointment and anger in India, the China clash, if anything, only reinforces non-alignment. Where would we be today supposing we were aligned with America.[146]

When it was suggested to him by Brecher that India might have been better off at the time had the country been aligned to America, Krishna Menon responded that India might have been atom bombed because the Americans would have said, 'well, go and bomb China.'[147] For those who saw Menon as less critical of China over the years, it is noteworthy that Menon thought China saw India as being sympathetic to the West: 'the Chinese like to malign us and fault us, calling us imperialists and a satellite of the US.'[148]

In the event, it was the US, Britain[149] and Australia which came to India's aid with military supplies. In Australia's case, while the Government's support and sympathy for India was unequivocal, the public was critical of the Government's belated response to India,[150] a Commonwealth partner. Stargardt takes the view that Australia's changed attitude to India in respect of its War with China 'was symptomatic, and like much else, it fitted the view that foreign policy was primarily an instrument of domestic politics.'[151] However, the Chinese border intrusion led to an exchange of letters between Nehru and Menzies on what Nehru described in his letter as 'a very serious situation ... The consequences of this ... are not only serious for India, but also for the rest of the world.'[152]

While the reality of the China-India border war had brought these two protagonists to find some common ground, the shattering experience failed to force India (under Nehru) to soften, if not abandon, its rigid adherence to non-alignment. *The Hindu Weekly Review*, reported a speech Nehru made in Calcutta in which he said 'if we give up non-alignment then we shall have to discard our peaceful pursuits, friendship with all countries and make the nation weak.'[153] In a statement to the Lok Sabha, while acknowledging that India had since developed more friendly ties with those who helped the country in its hour of need, Nehru made the future position on non-alignment clear which was no significant diminution of the doctrine:

> It is true that because of the Chinese aggression we have developed closer bonds with some countries who helped us. That was natural, but that does not mean that we have weakened in our desire to adhere to non-alignment ...[154].

This attitude of Nehru's to adhere to the policy irrespective of circumstances was not new. In 1952 he stressed that despite India's trade being predominantly with the UK and USA as well as accepting their help, India had 'not deviated from our policy of not aligning with any particular group.'[155] Fred Greene, an International Relations specialist argues that while India began to weigh 'the tenets of neutralism against the realities of aggression ... they remained uncommitted to the Cold War ...' a position that gave them military support from the Soviets and kept them (the Soviets) away from the Chinese.[156]

Australia's 'White Australia' Policy and India's decision to remain 'non-aligned' were, for different reasons, pivotal to each country's response to its external environment and, in both cases, came into effect from the birth of the nation, 1901 and 1947 respectively. And, yet, in their practical effect in relation to each other, the two policies stood as obstacles to better bilateral engagement. Once again, they demonstrate the influence of personal philosophy and public opinion on bilateral relations.

The protection of Australia from an influx of non-European immigrants was carefully nurtured during nearly seven decades after federation and enactment of the Immigration Restriction Act. In the meantime, the mutual indifference that characterised the bilateral relationship between Australia and India, some of it ascribable to the 'White Australia' Policy, continued. This was particularly true of the Menzies period in office. Menzies not only defended the 'White Australia' Policy from criticism abroad, but once told Opperman that he thought the existing policy held 'the right sort of discrimination.'[157] Furthermore, Menzies' gratuitous support for South Africa, in the face of repeated condemnation by Nehru of that country's Apartheid policies and the treatment of Indians there, led to an early rift between the two men (played out at Commonwealth Conferences), that had damaging consequences for the bilateral relationship. The two countries' voting records on racial issues at the UN were also evidence of this conflict. Then, whilst Menzies was impervious to colonialism, as seen in Chapter Three above, Nehru was acutely sensitive to its existence in other parts of the world.

From the Indian perspective, what can be concluded is that the whole question of racism with all its repugnant manifestations, represented an issue that went beyond Australia's restrictive immigration policy. It challenged the wider question of racial equality (which ostensibly ceased with the ending of colonialism) and, also, the contempt of the colonial power for its subjects, with the associated denial of political and economic freedom. For Nehru, it was also a moral issue that challenged the international conscience, a recurrent theme of this examination. For the India-Australia bilateral relationship, the resentment in India continued until the arrival of the Whitlam Government in 1972, and with it, finally, an unequivocal policy on Asian immigration, representing a turning point. With its potential for altering Australia's image in India (for long, synonymous with 'White Australia', as testified to by Mackay, Crocker, Beazley, Border, Rivett and others), the climate for improvement in the bilateral relationship between the two countries changed for the mutual good.

India's choice of non-alignment, the mainspring of its foreign policy, operated on different planes fulfilling a number of needs, international and domestic: among them, strategic, economic and social cohesion were key objectives. For Nehru, its adoption had a global purpose: it was 'a part of the broader policy of working for world peace and cooperation. ...any other policy may lead to world disaster.'[158] Former Pro-Vice Chancellor of Delhi University, V.P. Dutt, describes the backdrop to India's strategy in the ideological polarisation:

> The world in which Nehru evolved India's foreign policy was a world in deep trouble and anguish, divided and increasingly drawn into the whirlpool of a ferocious Cold War. Two powers were arising on the international horizon ... They demanded absolute loyalty and blind obedience.[159]

Noted philosopher Bertrand Russell recognised the global dimension to India's non-aligned policy and India's capacity, as a result of its independence, to mediate successfully at the international level. Referring to India's choice of non-alignment he said:

> This decision was responsible for the possibility of a third force of neutral and non-aligned nations, and as such may be a decisive factor in the survival of humanity. Had India foregone non-alignment it is seriously doubtful that other nations could have maintained it, and areas of conflict would be many more and the sources of mediation non existent.[160]

Undoubtedly, the policy helped India play an important and successful role as a mediator in international conflicts during the 1950s. Thus, India's non-aligned stance, on occasion, earned for the country accolades from the international community[161], but also criticism from the US and Australia which of course hurt. One writer commented on India's sensitivity to outside criticism of its non-aligned status, a consequence of its success as an impartial international mediator with this observation:

> New Delhi will learn some badly needed lessons in international affairs ... Indians have been shown that the mere conviction of self-righteousness and moral superiority does not protect a nation from criticism when it actively intervenes in matters of world importance.[162]

Non-alignment was also a reflection of India's early determination to develop its own foreign policy positions on international questions free of outside influence in contrast to Australia whose policies under Menzies were firmly aligned to those of the West, dependent rather than independent. But, then, Menzies disapproved of such independence in foreign policy being exercised by former colonies, with his observation that:

> In these modern days we are all a little disposed to think and speak so much of our own characteristics: our own independence, our own variations from others, that we quite easily tend to think that independence in law is independence in fact; that we can live to ourselves, that we can, so to speak, let the rest of the world go by ... the more turbulent the world, the more we all need friends.[163]

This was, clearly, another misreading by Menzies of India's reasons for preferring independence, and Nehru's consistent appeals to all sides for peace through friendly relations sans alignments. Addressing the Lok Sabha on India's policy of non-alignment, Nehru stressed that 'a deliberate policy of friendship with other countries goes further in gaining security than almost anything else.'[164] But there was an important rider to this: according to Casey, Nehru was also careful to stress that, 'if you are over friendly with certain countries you are expected to be unfriendly with or hostile to their potential enemies, which increases the divisions in the world, a menace to peace.'[165] While Nehru did not offer examples of such friendships, Australia's close friendship with, and dependence on, the US is probably a good example of this.

Unfortunately, for the bilateral relationship, Casey's sensitivity to India and its policy of non-alignment, while genuinely held, was not enough to materially influence the bilateral relationship. His authority to use his responsibility for External Affairs to influence the bilateral relationship was all too contingent on Menzies' support. From a leader who failed to understand the widely acknowledged wisdom of Nehru's reasons for non-alignment and independence in foreign policy, such support for his Minister for External Affairs was anything but forthcoming.

While India's lack of sympathy for Australia's views on its non-aligned stance was often conveyed in diplomatic despatches to DEA, India's attitude was also coloured by its palpable displeasure with the American response to its pivotal policy. Unfortunately, for the bilateral relationship, this displeasure spilled over to its attitude to Australia whose views were identified closely with those of America. Badyopadhyaya in his analysis of the motivation behind NAM concludes that the West:

> ... have failed to understand and evaluate the broad historical forces which have gone into the making of non-alignment as a foreign policy strategy, and erroneously regarded it entirely as a stance of professed neutrality in the contemporary bipolarity of international politics.[166]

Mediansky, in his analysis of Australia's foreign policy under conservative governments, points to their leaders' dislike of neutralism, which they viewed as 'centrifugal, and therefore an undesirable process in international affairs.'[167] Then, again, the less than harmonious relationship between Nehru and Menzies (examined in Chapters Three and Four), combined with other foreign policy differences to prevent any genuine progress being made in the bilateral relationship during the 1950s and 1960s.

The arrival of the Whitlam Government in 1972 with greater independence in foreign policy and Whitlam's broader ideology capable of greater sensitivity to India's non-aligned policy saw the beginning of a relationship based on mutual respect and accommodation. In India, while the policy of non-alignment continued to be upheld under Indira Gandhi as being at the core of its foreign policy, (proclaimed by her as no less pivotal), it was less rigidly applied possibly because of the uncertainty of the future with an unpredictable China and also some easing of the Cold War tensions from the early 1970s. It may also be argued that the new generation of India's leaders at the political and administrative level had not experienced the struggles and humiliation of their predecessors under British colonialism which contributed to the newly independent India's resolve to opt for non-alignment. Consequently, for the leaders of the 1970s, as an ideology, it was probably not as crucial.

# Endnotes

1. Wigmore to External Affairs, 4 April 1945, AA, A10661/1, p 145/47 in Sean Brawley, *The White Peril*, University of NSW Press, Sydney, 1995, p 243.

2. Chandrasekhar, S., 'A Chronology of Australian History with Special Reference to Asian Immigration' *From India to Australia*, S Chandrasekhar (ed.), Population Review Books, California, 1992, p 130.

3. Millar, T.B., *Australia's Foreign Policy*, Angus & Robertson, Sydney, 1968, p 102. Also see, A.T. Yarwood, *Attitudes to Non-European Immigration*, Cassell, NSW, 1968.

4. Rae, Lindsay, 'Arthur Calwell: resentful ageing,' *Political Lives*, Judith Brett, (ed.) Allen & Unwin, NSW, 1997, p 85.

5. Hancock, W.K., *Australia*, E. Benn, London, 1930, p 66, in Neville Meaney, 'The End of "White Australia" and Australia's Changing Perceptions of Asia, 1945-1990', *The Australian Journal of International Affairs*, Vol. 49, No. 2, November 1995, pp 174-175.

6. Brawley, Sean, 'Slaying the White Australia Dragon: Some Factors In The Abolition of The White Australia Policy,' *The Abolition of The White Australia Policy: The Immigration Reform Movement Revisited*, Nancy Viviani, (ed.) Australia-Asia Paper No. 65, Centre for the study of Australia-Asia Relations, Griffith University, Qld., 1992, p 1.

7. The Labor Party's first leader, J.C. Watson endorsement was:'the objection I have to the mixing of these coloured people with the white people ... lies in the main in the possibility and probability of racial contamination.' See Neville Meaney, 'The End of "White Australia" and Australia's Changing Perceptions of Asia, 1945-1990' *The Australian Journal of International Affairs*, Vol. 49, No. 2, November, 1995, p 174. Prime Minister Edmund Barton was equally strong when he said that he did not believe, '...the doctrine of the equality of man was really ever intended to include racial equality.' *ibid*, p 175. Also see, H.I. London, *Non-White Immigration and the White 'Australia Policy'*, Sydney University Press, Sydney, 1970; Myra Willard, *History of the 'White Australia' Policy to 1920*, Melbourne University Press, 1967.

8. Hughes, in his address to Parliament, conveyed his support, 'remember this is the only country in the Empire, if not, indeed, in the world where there is so little admixture of race ... we are more British than the people of Great Britain, and we hold firmly to the great principle of the White Australia...'. See CPD (H of R), Vol. 89, 10 September, 1919, p 12167-12179, in E.M. Andrews, *History of Australian Foreign Policy*, Longman Cheshire, Melbourne, 1979, p 58. Fowler's rhetorical question concerned India's surplus population and where they might be settled ,'A very grave danger to our White Australia policy is to be apprehended from this source, ... All may be well for us, but certainly not... for our children unless we seize upon the one thing that is vital to the continuance of a White Australia, ... the introduction of immigrants of our own race.' See CPD, (H of R), Vol. 99, 13 July, 1922, p 429.

9. Chandrasekhar, S., 'A brief History of Australia's Immigration Policy with Special Reference to India's Nationals,' *From India to Australia*, S. Chandrasekhar, (ed.) Population Review Books, California, 1992, p 23.

10. Hudson, W.J. & Way, Wendy (eds.), *Documents on Australian Foreign Policy 1937-1949*, Vol. X, July- December 1946, DFAT, AGPS, Canberra, 1995, p 534.

11. *Ibid*. p 535.

12. *Ibid*.

13. *Ibid*.

14. Chandrasekhar, S., 'A brief History of Australia's Immigration Policy with Special Reference to India's Nationals,' *From India to Australia*, S. Chandrasekhar, (ed.) Population Review Books, California, 1992, p 18. The pre-federation Queensland request, was not without its opponents who even petitioned the Queen on it,

their argument being 'that the presence of Coolies amongst us in great numbers would entail woes which no money can compensate.' See, A.W. Stargardt, *Australia's Asian Policies: The History of a Debate 1839-1972*, The Institute of Asian Affairs, Hamburg, 1977, p 291.

15. Hudson, & Way, *op. cit.*, p 535.

16. Clark, C.M.H., *A Short History of Australia*, Heinemann, London, 1964, p 195.

17. *The Sydney Morning Herald*, 24 March 1949, in Neville Meaney, 'The End of "White Australia" and Australia's Changing Perceptions of Asia, 1945-1990', *The Australian Journal of International Affairs*, Vol. 49, No. 2, November, 1995, p 177. Also See, Cable from Frank Ford and Evatt to Chiefly, dated 18 May 1945, DAFP, p 169, for Evatt's efforts to prevent the UN from having authority to intervene in a country's control of its Immigration policy, in Neville Meaney, 'The End of "White Australia" and Australia's Changing Perceptions of Asia, 1945-1990' *The Australian Journal of International Affairs*, Vol. 49, No. 2, November, 1995, p 177.

18. CPD (H of R), Vol. 14, 4 April 1957, p 537.

19. *Ibid*. In an assessment of Calwell the politician, Lindsay Rae observes, 'more than any other individual his name has come to be associated with the retention of the racist immigration policy ...'. See 'Arthur Calwell: resentful ageing' *Political Lives*, J. Brett, (ed.), Allen & Unwin, NSW, 1997, p 85. Also see, A.T. Yarwood, *Asian Migration to Australia: The Background to Exclusion, 1896-1923*, Melbourne University Press, Victoria, 1964.

20. CPD, (H of R), Vol. 18, 27 February 1958 p 115; CPD, (H of R), Vol. 21, 16 September 1958, pp 1256-1257, in Neville Meaney, 'End of "White Australia" and Australia's Changing Perceptions of Asia, 1945-1990, *The Australian Journal of International Affairs*, Vol. 49, No. 2, November 1995, p 178.

21. CPD, (H of R), Vol. 14, 4 April 1957, p 537.

22. CNIA, Vol. 32, 1961, p 32. Statement in the House of Representatives by Prime Minister Menzies, 11 April 1961.

23. AA, Statement by H.E. Holt, 7 July 1954, Series A1838/278, Item 169/10/7 Part 1.

24. Casey, Lord (R.G.) *Personal Experiences 1939-1946*, Constable & Company, London, 1962, p 180.

25. CPD, (H of R), Vol. 14, 4 April 1957, p 537.

26. Stevens, *New India*, p 34, in S. Brawley, *The White Peril*, University of NSW Press, Sydney 1995, p 244.

27. Hudson, W.J. & Way, Wendy (eds.), *Documents on Australian Foreign Policy 1937-1949*, Vol. X, July- December 1946, DFAT, AGPS, Canberra, 1995, p 534.

28. Hudson, W.J. and Way, Wendy (eds.), *Documents on Australian Foreign Policy 1937-49*, Vol. XII, DFAT, AGPS, Canberra, 1995, p 810.

29. Interview with Bruce Grant, 19, May 1999, Domain Street, South Yarra, Melbourne.

30. AA, Despatch No. 23, 6 December 1954, from Crocker to Casey, Series A1838/283, Item 160/10/1, Part 2, pp 1-2.

31. *Ibid*. p 4.

32. CPD, (H of R), Vol. 32, 5 September 1961, p 791.

33. Brawley, S., *The White Peril*, University of NSW Press, Sydney 1995, p 299.

34. Rajan M.S., *India in World Affairs: 1954-56*, Asian Publishing House, New Delhi, 1964, p 404.

35. Nihal Singh, 'Projecting a new Image of Australia', *The Statesman*, Delhi, 30 October 1962, p 6. (citing a Malayan Newspaper)

36. 'No colour bar, Digger!' (Editorial), *The Daily News*, Ceylon, 21, December, 1969, p 12.

37. For a summary of a range of issues related to Australia's immigration and travel restrictions imposed on Indians, see AA, File on Immigration-Migration from India, Series A1838/275, Item 1531/99, Part 1.

38. Jayasuriya, L. 'The Australian-Asian Connection: Retrospect and Prospect,' Revised Edition, of paper first presented to University of Third Age, Perth, p 23. Also see, 'Prejudice and Xenophobia', *Racism: The Australian Experience*, Vol. 1, C.F. Stevens & E.P. Wolfers (eds.) Australia and New Zealand Book Co., Sydney, 1974.

39. Australian Bureau of Statistics, *From India to Australia*, S. Chandrasekhar (ed.), Population Review Books, California, 1992, p 123 , (extracted from Table 4,) If the arrivals from Africa were to be added to those from Asia, then the Indian percentage drops even further.

40. Hudson, W.J. & Way, Wendy (eds.), *Documents on Australian Foreign Policy 1937-1949*, Vol. X, July- December 1946, DFAT, AGPS, Canberra, 1995, p 536. Also see, R.G. Neale, 'Australia's Changing Relations with India', *India, Japan, Australia, Partners in Asia?* J.D.B. Millar (ed.), ANU, Canberra, 1968, p 77.

41. CNIA, Statement in the House of Representatives by the Prime Minister, R.G. Menzies, 11 April 1961, Vol. 32, 1961, p 32.

42. CPD, (H of R), Vol. 193, 24 September, 1947, p 176.

43. *The National Herald*, India, 15 July 1948, in S. Brawley, *The White Peril*, University of NSW Press, Sydney, 1995, p 247. Malan was associated with the establishment of Apartheid.

44. Mediansky F.A., 'The Conservative Style in Australian Foreign Policy' Australian Outlook, Vol. 28, No. 1, April 1974, p 55.

45. NAI, 'Treatment of Indians' - File No. 1012/IANZ, 1949.

46. 'No Radical Alterations of Immigration Policy', *The Sun*, Ceylon, 18 April, 1972, p 4.

47. *Ibid.*

48. *Ibid.* Also see, Marie de Lepervanche, 'Sikh Turbans in Resistance and Response: Some Comments on Immigrant Reactions in Australia and Britain', *From India to Australia*, S. Chandrasekhar (ed.), Population Review Books, California 1992, pp 105-106 for evidence of Australian discrimination against Sikh Indians.

49. CPD, (H of R), Vol. 6, 28 April 1955, p 305.

50. *Ibid.*

51. Rivett Kenneth, 'From White Australia to the Present', *From India to Australia*, S. Chandrasekhar, (ed.) Population Review Books, California, 1992, p 58.

52. Hudson, W.J., *'Casey'*, Oxford University Press, Melbourne, 1986, p 160.

53. AA, 'India-Relations with the Commonwealth.' Confidential Memorandum 14 May 1954, from W.R. Crocker, New Delhi, to DEA, Series A1838/2, Item 169/11/1, Part 3.

54. Lok Sabha Debate, 9 December, 1958, Col. 3966.

55. *Ibid.* Also see AA, Savingram 18 July 1953, from Australian High Commission, New Delhi to DEA, Series A4534/1, Item 44/6/2, referring to Nehru's fears of an upheaval in Africa brought on by racial discrimination. 'No Asian country can tolerate this. We do not want to fight anybody but there can be no compromise on this issue and India will exert full pressure to remove this discrimination ...'.

56. Menzies, R.G., *Afternoon Light*, Cassell, Melbourne, 1967, p 214.

57. NAI, 'Treatment of Indians in South Africa-Publicity Overseas,' File No. 14(2)-AFRI-1950.

58. *Jawaharlal Nehru's Speeches*, August 1949-February 1953, Vol. II, Publications Division, Ministry of Information & Broadcasting, Government of India, New Delhi, 1954, p 248.

59. *Selected Works of Jawaharlal Nehru*, Second Series, Vol. 15, Part I, S. Gopal, (ed.), Jawaharlal Nehru Memorial Fund, New Delhi, 1993, p 408. Also see, NAI, 'Treatment of Indians in South Africa-UN Agenda', File No. (25)UN11-1951.

60. Price, Charles, 'Beyond White Australia,' *TRT*, Vol. 258, April 1975, p 371.

61. 'India Won't Falter to Secure Justice in South Africa', *The Tribune*, Simla, 13 December, 1947.

62. *Ibid.*

63. Bain, J.S. *India's International Disputes: A Legal Study*, Asia Publishing House, Bombay, 1962, p 9.

64. Friedman, Julian R., *Basic Facts on the Republic of South Africa and the Policy of Apartheid*, United Nations Centre Against Apartheid, New York, 1977, p 71, in J. Bandyopadhyaya, *North over South*, South Asian Publishers, New Delhi, 1982, p 64.

65. Bandyopadhyaya, J., *North over South*, South Asian Publishers, New Delhi, 1982, pp 75-76.

66. *Ibid.*, p 65. John Darwin in his examination of the 'Colonial World Order', and the links that bound the essentially European club together, argues that the '... Colonial World Order was powerfully buttressed by a set of dominant cultural assumptions and by a demographic regime.' A dichotomy of a north providing capital to compliment the material producing region, led to an economically successful formal empire's dominance over the informal empire to keep alive the 'cultural triumphalism.' The ensuing cultural glory, 'drew strength from the demographic order and licensed the racial exclusion on which it had come to depend.' See 'Decolonisation and world politics', *Australia and the End of Empires*, David Lowe, (ed.) Deakin University Press, Victoria. 1996, pp 8-9.

67. 'South Africa and The Defence of The West: Liability or Asset to the Free World' *TRT*, No. 241, January 1971, p 15.

68. Brawley, Sean 'Slaying The White Australia Dragon: Some Factors in the Abolition of the White Australia Policy', *The Abolition of the White Australia Policy: The Immigration Reform Movement Revisited*, Nancy Viviani (ed.), Australia-Asia Paper No. 65, Centre for the Study of Australia-Asia Relations, Griffith University, Qld., 1992, p3.

69. AA, 'India May Restrict Australians', *The Dominion*, Wellington, New Zealand, 25 August, 1961, Series A1838/275, Item 1531/99, Part 1.

70. Brawley, Sean, 'Slaying The White Australia Dragon: Some Factors in the Abolition of the White Australia Policy', *The Abolition of the White Australia Policy: The Immigration Reform Movement Revisited*, Nancy Viviani (ed.), Australia-Asia Paper No. 65, Centre for the Study of Australia-Asia Relations, Griffith University, Qld., 1992, p3.

71. 'A Leaf Falls: South Africa Outside the Commonwealth', *TRT*, No. 203, June 1961, p 222.

72. '... it has been pointed out that since Australia's policy is stamped with a degree of racialism (whatever its true motives) certain of Australia's foreign policies generally have become tainted and suspect. The rest of the world, in scrutinizing Australia's attitudes to South Africa and the Portuguese colonies, or its policies in New Guinea and its motives in South-east Asia, does not conveniently pigeon-hole away Australia's immigration policy as an untouchable domestic issue. On the contrary, it is used to complete the picture.' See A.C. Palfreeman, *The Administration of the White Australia Policy*, Melbourne University Press, Victoria, 1967, p 133.

73. The beginning of any substantial attempt at reform of Australia's restrictive immigration policies came with the forming of the Reform Group with Kenneth Rivett, Jamie Mackie and other prominent Australians as its members in early 1959, although there were efforts made earlier by the church (Dr Daniel Mannix), the Communist party and others seeking change. See 'Kenneth Rivett

'From White Australia to the Present' *From India to Australia*, S. Chandrasekhar, (ed.) Population Review Books, California, 1992, pp 58-59. The 1901 Immigration Restriction Act was superseded by the 1958 Migration Act, which merely replaced the method of non-European exclusion from the "dictation test," to "Ministerial discretion". See S. Chandrasekhar, 'A Chronology of Australian History with Special Reference to Asian Immigration', *From India to Australia*, S. Chandrasekhar, (ed.), Population Review Books, California, 1992, p 135.

74. Melbourne *Age*, 1 April 1961, in A.C. Palfreeman, *The Administration of the White Australia Policy*, Melbourne University Press, Victoria, 1967, p 130. Jamie Mackie notes that the opponents to reform were numerous and included Labor under Calwell, unremitting in his opposition to change, and sir John Latham, a retired Chief Justice and former leader of the United Australia Party who saw the reform group as, 'simply threatening to create a problem for Australia's happily homogeneous society where none currently existed.' See 'The Immigration Reform Group: Some Recollections,' *The Abolition of the White Australia Policy: The Immigration Reform Movement Revisited*, N. Viviani (ed.) Australia-Asia Paper No. 65, Centre for the study of Australia-Asia Relations, Griffith University, Qld., 1992, p 29.

75. For an analysis of the 'White Australia' Policy and the Reform Groups progressive achievements, see Kenneth Rivett, 'From White Australia to the Present', *From India to Australia*, S. Chandrasekhar (ed.), Population Review Books, California, 1992, pp 58-74.

76. Rivett, Kenneth, 'From White Australia to the Present', *From India to Australia*, S. Chandrasekhar (ed.), Population Review Books, California, 1992, p 60.

77. 'Colour of Prejudice', *The Observer*, Ceylon, 6 October, 1970, p 1.

78. *Ibid.*

79. 'Gorton: We will not Abandon White Australia policy,' *The Daily News*, Ceylon, 20 January 1971, p 5.

80. *Ibid.*

81. Gawenda, M., 'Proponents of homogeneity missed the boat,' *The Age*, 6 January 1997, p A11.

82. *Ibid.*

83. Camilleri, J.A., *An Introduction to Australian Foreign policy*, 4th Edition, The Jacaranda Press, Qld., 1979, p 25.

84. *Ibid.*

85. Price, Charles *TRT*, 'Beyond White Australia', No. 258, April 1975, p 371.

86. Chandrasekhar S., 'A Brief History of Australia's Immigration Policy with Special Reference to India's Nationals,' *From India to Australia*, S. Chandrasekhar (ed.) Population Review Books, California, 1992, p 28. Changes to the 'White Australia' Policy were inevitable, in line with both domestic and external realities confronting Australia. Brawley explains the shift as being forced by societal changes generated by the growth in a post war educated middle class, as well as the censurable and constraining influences the discriminatory immigration policy had on Australia's foreign policy and external relations. See Sean Brawley, 'Slaying The White Australia Dragon: Some Factors'. *The Abolition of the White Australia Policy: The Immigration Reform Movement Revisited*, Nancy Viviani (ed.), Australia Asia Paper No. 65, Centre for the study of Australia-Asia Relations, Griffith University, Qld., 1992, pp 2-3 .The early 1970s also saw a culmination of these liberalised trends. Don Dunstan, a pioneer in social and political reform as Premier of the State of South Australia, predicted changes to the immigration policy under a future federal Labor Government. Speaking on an Australian Broadcasting Commission's television programme, Dunstan said, ' "a homogeneous Australia is nonsense. ... I think there's great virtue in diversity." ' See 'Labour will change Aussie policy on immigrants', *The Observer*, Ceylon, 14 July, 1971, p 7. Dunstan's reference to ' "racial bigots in the corridors of power" and a stance of "ethnic superiority" ' were strenuously denied by the then Minister for

Immigration, James Forbes. See 'Immigration policy not based on racialism', *The Daily News*, Ceylon, 23, July 1971, p 7.

87. Burton, J.W., *International Relations: A General Theory*, Cambridge University Press, Cambridge, 1967, p 163.

88. *The Hindustan Times*, India, 'The Dilemma of the non-aligned,' 11 September 1973, in Sri Ram Sharma, *Indian Foreign Policy Annual Survey: 1973*, Sterling Publishers, New Delhi, 1977, p 130.

89. AA, Report on the Korean War, 10 August 1950, from Francis Stuart, New Delhi to DEA, Series A1838/278, Item 3123/7/13.

90. Kashyap, Subash (ed.), *Jawaharlal Nehru his Life Work and Legacy*, Indian Parliamentary Group, Lok Sabha Secretariat, New Delhi, 1990, pp 52-53.

91. Ramachandram, G., *Nehru and World Peace*, Radiant Publishers, New Delhi, 1990, p 149. Also see, *ibid.*, Eisenhower's letter to Nehru, p123.

92. Park, Richard L., 'India's Foreign Policy' *Foreign Policy in World Politics*, Roy C. Macridis (Ed.), 5th Edition, Prentice Hall, New Jersey, 1976, p 327.

93. Crabb C.V., *The Elephants and the Grass*, Frederick A. Praeger, 1965, New York, p 7. According to Geir Lundestad, 'Non-alignment was to be active and positive, whereas neutrality had been passive and negative.' See *East, West, North, South, Major Developments in International Politics since 1945*, Fourth Edition, Oxford University Press, New York, 1999, p 297.

94. Thakur, R. *The Politics and Economics of India's Foreign Policy* St Martin's Press, New York, 1994, p 26.

95. Lok Sabha Debates, 4 August 1950, Col. 382.

96. 'India: Bandung Balance Sheet' *TRT*, No. 179, June 1955, p 278. Crocker, refers to a move by Nasser and Tito for a 'neutral' summit, endorsed also by *The Hindustan Times*, the rationale being that the Bandung meeting 'had the defect of being or seeming racial' and a neutral summit would allow countries of Europe and Latin America to be included. See AA, Cablegram 10 May 1961, from Crocker to DEA, Series A1838/2, Item 169/7/1, Part 8.

97. Kahin, George Mc Turnan, *The Asian-African Connection*, Ithaca, Cornell University Press, New York, 1956, p 3, in Robert A. Mortimer, *The Third World Coalition in International Relations*, 2nd Edition, Westview Press, Colorado 1984, p 7. Also see Jasjit Singh (ed.) *India-China and Panchsheel*, Sanchar Publishing House, New Delhi, 1996, p 5, for a reference to the five principles of Panchsheel which springs from the Buddhist moral tenet of Pansil and primarily concerns international diplomacy, co-existence and non-interference. It was first established between India and China in their Panchsheel Agreement of 1949. Bandung was a precursor to NAM (1961) followed by the Group of Seventy Seven.

98. Mortimer, R.A., *The Third World Coalition in International Relations*, 2nd Edition, Westview Press, Colorado, 1984, p 9. While there were many reasons for the motivation behind the meeting, Djordje Jerkovic of Yugoslavia thought Nehru's principal aim in initiating the conference, was: '... to speed up the process of the awakening and emancipation of the peoples of Asia and Africa, to bring the people and the countries of the two continents closer and to make them active in the struggle for peace, progress and co-existence.' See G. Ramachandram, *Nehru and World Peace*, Radiant Publishers, New Delhi, 1990, p 29.

99. Jha, C.S., *From Bandung to Tashkent*, Sangam Books, Madras, 1983, p 69.

100. Martin, A.W., *Robert Menzies a Life*, Vol. 2, 1944-1978, Melbourne University Press, Victoria. 1999, p 302.

101. See, Michael Brecher, *India and World Politics*, Oxford University Press, London, 1968, p 57. Krishna Menon told Brecher, when asked about Nehru's role at Bandung, 'Nehru was the spirit of the Bandung conference - ... He was a kind of elder statesman ... At that time he held that position in the eyes of most individuals who came to Bandung, ...'.

102. Brecher, Michael, *The New States of Asia*, Oxford University Press, London, 1963, p 210.

103. Lok Sabha Debates, Vol. IV, Part II, 30 April 1955, Col. 6973. Also see, Leopold Sedar Senghor on Bandung in Phillipe Braillard, and Mohammad Reza Djalili, *The Third World and International Relations*, Lynn Rienner Publishers, Colorado, 1986, pp 57-59.

104. Braillard, Philippe and Djalili, Mohammad Reza *The Third World and International Relations*, Lynne Rienner Publishers, Colorado, 1986, p 59. Sedor Senghor pursued the concept of 'Negritude' or African Culture.

105. According to Phillipe Braillard and Mohammad Reza Djalili who cite R. Vukadinovic, conflict within the non-aligned had much to do with, 'a complex combination of different agents and factors affecting international relations ...' and includes 'the historical legacy of colonialism, ...'. *The Third World and International Relations*, Lynne Rienner Publishers, Colorado, 1986, p 147. There were other disagreements: Libya's Gadaffi and Egypt's Sadat's proposal for a permanent Secretariat with authority for NAM, was opposed by Tito and others. See the "The Dilemma of the non-aligned', *Hindustan Times*, India, 11 September 1973 in Shri Ram Sharma, *India's Foreign Policy Annual Survey: 1973*, Sterling Publishers, New Delhi, 1977, p 128. Also see J.D. Singh, 'Areas of Accord and Discord at Algiers', *Times of India*, 11 September 1973 in Shri Ram Sharma, *India's Foreign Policy Survey: 1973*, Sterling Publishers, New Delhi, 1977, p 128.

106. For example, the benefits from more than a doubling of India's trade during the latter stages of World War II went to Britain whose arrangements ensured that 'the surplus dollars should be credited to the Empire dollar pool.' See Misra, S.N. *India: The Cold War Years*, South Asian Publishers, New Delhi, 1994, p 101.

107. Mabbett, I.W., *A Short History of India*, Cassell, North Melbourne, 1968, p 235.

108. *Jawaharlal Nehru's speeches*, September 1946-May 1949, Vol. 1, Ministry of Information & Broadcasting, Government of India, New Delhi, 1949, p 219.

109. Lok Sabha Debates, Vol. II, Part II, 6-25 March, 1954, Col. 2801. Former pro-Vice Chancellor of the University of Delhi, V.P. Dutt, in his article, 'India's Foreign Policy: How Nehru Shaped it', states Einstein once described J. Nehru as the Prime Minister of tomorrow ...'. See *The Tribune*, Lucknow, 14 November 1997, p 10.

110. Statement issued by Jawaharlal Nehru on Foreign Policy on 26 September 1946, *Indian Information*, Government Of India, Information Bureau, New Delhi, 15 October 1946.

111. Greenwood, Gordon, 'Australian Foreign Policy in Action', *Australia in World Affairs 1956-1960*, Gordon Greenwood and Norman Harper, (eds.), F.W. Cheshire Melbourne, 1963, p 95.

112. Brecher, Michael, *India and World Politics*, Oxford University Press, London, 1968, p 302.

113. Crabb C.V., The *Elephants and the Grass*, Frederick A. Praeger, New York, 1965. p 14.

114. *Documents on American Foreign Relations: 1956*, Harper Brothers, New York, 1957, p 394; 'Moral Neutralism? Bunk!' *The New York Herald Tribune*, 16, November 1961, in C.V. Crabb *The Elephants and the Grass*, Frederick A. Praeger, New York, 1965, p 15.

115. Crabb, *op. cit.* pp 14-15.

116. 'India's Policy is not Neutralist', *National Herald*, Lucknow, Vol. X, No. 291, 4 November, 1951, p 1.

117. *Jawaharlal Nehru's speeches*, Vol. 1, September 1946-May 1949, Ministry of Information & Broadcasting, Government of India, New Delhi, 1949, p 219.

118. Crabb *op. cit.*, p x, (Introduction)

119. *Jawaharlal Nehru's speeches*, September 1946-May 1949, Vol. 1, Ministry of Information & Broadcasting, Government of India, 1949, New Delhi, p 219.

120. CPD (H of R), Vol. 29, 20 October 1960, p 2272.

121. *Ibid*. Also See, NLA, Canberra, Menzies' Papers, Overseas Diaries' for Menzies' poor opinion of nonalignment, MS 4936, Series 8; Subrata Roy Choudary, *Military Alliances and Neutrality in War and Peace*, Orient Longman, New Delhi, 1966, for an insightful legalistic analysis of Military Alliances vis-a-vis the UN Charter facilitating further understanding of the doctrine of nonalignment.

122. CPD, (H of R), Vol. 29, 6 December 1960, p 3578.

123. Casey, R.G., *The Future of the Commonwealth*, Frederick Muller, London, 1963, p 66.

124. Bandyopadhyaya, J., *North Over South*, South Asian Publishers, New Delhi, 1982, p 202.

125. CPD (H of R) Vol. 18, 15 April 1958, p 867. In 1947 Casey also spoke of India's 'three choices of friends for the future: the British, the Americans and the Russians.' And if forced to choose, he said, 'they would undoubtedly (although with some misgivings) choose the British as being the devil they know.' See, R.G. Casey, *An Australian in India*, Hollis & Carter, London, 1947, p 107. Australia does not appear on Casey's list of India's potential friends for the future.

126. 'India: Aid From America', *TRT*, Vol. XLIII, December 1952-September 1953, p 170.

127. Sharma, Shri Ram (ed.), *India's Foreign Policy Annual Survey: 1973*, Sterling Publishers, New Delhi, 1977. p 364.

128. *Ibid*.

129. Brecher, Michael, *India and World Politics*, Oxford University Press, London, 1968, p 3.

130. Park, Richard L., 'India's Foreign Policy', *Foreign Policy in World Politics*, 5th Edition, Roy C. Macridis (ed.) Prentice Hall, New Jersey, 1976, p 320.

131. Ahluwalia, I.J., 'New Economic Policies: Reform of Public Sector Enterprises and Privatisation in India', *India's Policy Problems: Economics and Political Challenges*, Volume I, V.A. Pai Panandiker, (ed.), Centre for Policy Research, Konark Publishers, New Delhi, 1996, p 17. Also see, AA, Report entitled 'Australia's Trade Relations with India', for a summary of India's economic problems and priorities for the first Five Year Plan, 1951-56, Series CP554/1, Item 2/174/B/1.

132. Farmer, B.H., *An Introduction to South Asia*, Methuen, London, 1983, p 168.

133. CPD (H of R), Vol. 18, 15 April 1958, p 869.

134. CNIA, 'Foreign Policy of Australia', Address by Minister for External Affairs R.G. Casey, Michigan State University, 6 October 1958, Vol. 29, 1958, p 661.

135. Park, R.L., 'India's Foreign Policy', *Foreign Policy in World Politics*, 5th Edition, Roy C. Macridis (ed.) Prentice Hall, New Jersey, 1976, p 320. For an account of the constitutional and institutional structure of Indian democracy, see Ramesh Thakur, *The Government and Politics of India*, Macmillan, London, 1995.

136. AA, Telegram, 28 December 1955, from the Secretary of State for Commonwealth Relations, Series A1838/283, Item 169/11/52, Part 3.

137. Kulski, W.W., *The Soviet Union in World Affairs: A Documented Analysis 1964-1972*, Syracuse University, 1973, pp 152-171; Braghoorn, F.C., *The Soviet Cultural Offensive*, Princeton University, 1960, Chapter 7, in John Darwin, 'Decolonisation and world politics', *Australia and the End of Empires*, David Lowe, (ed.), Deakin University Press, Victoria, 1996, p 18.

138. AA, Report in *The Canberra Times* of 24 December 1955, Series A1838/283, Item 169/11/52 Part 3. Also see, Memorandum from Arnold Smith, (Canadian Commissioner, International Supervisory Commission for Cambodia) to Secretary

of State for External Affairs, Canada, dated 23 May 1956, analysing India's foreign policy motives relative to both the US and the Soviet Union in respect of Indo-China in the mid 1950s, AA, A1838/283, Item 169/11/110, Part 1.

139. AA, Cablegram 9 September 1950, from the Australian High Commissioner in New Delhi, Series A1838/278, Item 3123/7/13. For an interesting analysis of the Soviet Union's political strategies in South Asia in the early 1970s, see Vijay Sen Budhraj, 'The South Asia policy of the Soviet Union', *Australian Outlook* Vol. 30, No. 1, April 1976, pp 101-119.

140. Nayer Parameswaran, 'Nationalism as a factor in India's Foreign Policy', *India Year Book of International Affairs*, Delhi, 1962, Vol. XI, p 439.

141. NLA, Letter from Menzies to McEwen dated 9 October 1960, MS 4936, Series 8, Box 332, Folder 9.

142. Burton, John, *The Alternative: A Dynamic Approach to our relations with Asia*, Morgan Publications, Sydney, 1954, p 93.

143. Alhuwalia, Shashi, *Nehru: 100 Years*, Manas Publications, Delhi, 1988, pp 174-175.

144. *Ibid.*

145. Bowles, Chester, *Ambassador's Report*, Victor Gollancz, London, 1955, p 258.

146. Brecher, Michael , *India and World Politics*, Oxford University Press, London, 1968, p 14.

147. *Ibid.*

148. *Ibid.*, p 146.

149. In Britain's case, Prime Minister Macmillan unhappy at the news of India's decision to buy MIG Fighter planes from the Soviet Union, as well as with India's policy of non-alignment, yet told the House of Commons that: 'If some of us doubt whether the Indian point of view has been sufficiently realist in the past; if, carrying as we are the heavy burden of defence we are sometimes impatient with what is called neutralism or non-alignment, we must in fairness remember how deeply based in Indian philosophy are some of these concepts...'. See H. Macmillan, *At the End of the Day*, 1973, p 228, in G. Zacharial, 'Britain and the Sino-Indian Border War of 1962', unpublished thesis, University of Oxford, 1994, pp 23-24.

150. FO371/164925/1061/331 in G. Zacharial, 'Britain and the Sino-Indian Border War of 1962' unpublished thesis, University of Oxford, 1994, p 60.

151. Stargardt, A.W., *Australia's Asian Policies: The History of a Debate 1839-1972*, Institute of Asian Affairs, Hamburg, 1977, p 228. Australia was probably unaware of the secret border talks between China and Pakistan which started in October 1962. See FO371/164928/1062/22 in G. Zacharial, 'Britain and the Sino-Indian Border War of 1962' unpublished thesis, Oxford University, p 20.

152. CNIA, Mr Nehru's letter of 27 October to Mr Menzies, Vol. 34, 1963, p 48.

153. *Hindu Weekly Review*, Madras, 8 July 1963.

154. *Jawaharlal Nehru's Speeches*, March 1963- May 1964, Vol. IV, Ministry of Information & Broadcasting, Government of India, New Delhi, 1968, p 199.

155. *The National Herald*, Lucknow, 13 June 1952, p 4.

156. Greene, Fred, *Dynamics of International Relations: Power, Security and Order*, Holt, Rinehart and Winston, New York, 1964.

157. Brawley Sean, *The White Peril*, University of NSW Press, Sydney, 1995, p 307.

158. *Jawaharlal. Nehru's Speeches*, March 1963-May 1964, Vol. IV, Ministry of Information & Broadcasting, Government of India, New Delhi, 1968, p 199.

159. 'India's Foreign Policy- How Nehru Shaped it' *The Tribune*, India, 14 November 1997, p 10.

160. Singh, Natwar (ed.) *The Legacy of Nehru*, Har Anand Publishers, India 1996, pp 82-83.

161. One example of this is when Canada's High Commissioner to India said, 'it was Mr Nehru's voice ... that pleaded ... for a ceasefire in Indo China. It was Mr Nehru again who later put forward six suggestions for a peaceful settlement.' See 'Nehru Opens Delhi Talks on Indo-China', *The Statesman*, Delhi, 2 August 1954, p 1. Others include India's mediatory roles in Korea and Suez.

162. 'India: Lessons for a Neutral', *TRT*, 173, December 1953, p 79.

163. Mediansky, F.A., 'The Conservative Style in Australian Foreign Policy', *Australian Outlook*, Vol. 28, No. 1, April 1974, pp 54-55.

164. Lok Sabha Debates, 12 December 1958, Col. 3959.

165. Casey, R.G., *The Future of the Commonwealth*, Frederick Muller, London, 1963, p 113.

166. Bandyopadhyaya, J. *North over South*, South Asian Publishers, New Delhi, 1982, p 204.

167. Mediansky F.A., 'The Conservative Style in Australian Foreign Policy' *Australian Outlook*, Vol. 28, No. 1, April 1974, p 54.

**6**

# A Case of Bias

If, as argued in Chapters Three and Four, the Nehru-Menzies dissonance acted as a substantial barrier to a better India-Australia bilateral relationship, then the juxtaposition of Pakistan in the relationship emerges as another impediment. Thus, the theme of policy conflict between the two countries continues, although the focus in this Chapter is on Australia's political partiality towards Pakistan, which sharpens further the understanding of the Indian view of the bilateral relationship.

The effectiveness of the Colombo Plan as a genuine aid programme, and its level of success in relation to India, is also examined in the second part of the Chapter. With Australian aid too, there is evidence of greater generosity shown to Pakistan in the early years of the Cold War!

## INDIA-AUSTRALIA-PAKISTAN: A TRILATERAL CONUNDRUM

The conventional view is that Australia's relationships in the 1950s and 1960s with India and Pakistan, both members of the Commonwealth Association, have been more in the nature of a trilateral balancing act than a bilateral one with each. While at first glance this is the impression gained, the research shows that Australia was not impeccably evenhanded in its handling of sensitive issues, such as the Kashmir question, that found India and Pakistan deeply divided. On the contrary, its tilt to Pakistan, particularly in the Menzies era, was clearly unhelpful, and there were concerns in India of Australian propaganda against it on Kashmir.[1] As essential to a better understanding of the India-Australia relationship in the context of the Pakistan factor, this Chapter examines those issues on which India and Pakistan have had fundamental differences confronting some of the assumptions and conclusions reached by Australia's policy makers and diplomats in handling the India relationship. While the documents examined and authorities quoted, are numerous, for the student, or reader, interpretation can be subjective; there are no absolute truths with some things. This is possibly true with conclusions drawn from the Australian, Indian and Pakistani policy responses discussed in this chapter.

## Partition, Preferences and Management of Ethnicity

Much of the reasons for Australia's preference for Pakistan may be traced to British India. In saying this, however, several questions have to be examined. The difference in the kind of relationship that the leaders of India and Pakistan had with the British Raj, throws light on the hypothesis that Australia with its own British heritage preferred loyal Pakistan to rebel India in its bilateral diplomacy in the subcontinent. To understand this, however, it helps to start by considering a few examples of Britain's use of Hindu-Muslim differences to manage pre-partitioned India. The introduction of separate electorates in British India by the then Viceroy, Lord Minto, was seen as, 'a device adopted ..., to win over the Muslims and set them against the Congress movement.'[2] An entry about this change in Lady Minto's diary on October 1, 1906, records that the strategy was praised by British officialdom who described it as 'nothing less than the pulling back of 62 millions of people from joining the ranks of seditious opposition.'[3] Then there was Ramsay Macdonald, British Prime Minister (1920s and 1930s), who observed that, 'the Mohamedan leaders are inspired by certain Anglo-Indian officials, and these officials have pulled wires at Simla and in London, and ... sowed discord between Hindu and Mohamedan communities by showing special favour to the Muslims.'[4] According to Indian Scholar and diplomat, K.M. Panikkar, the British preferred Muslims as recruits to the army rather than Hindus to ensure it 'did not get infected by political ideas...' adding that the chosen people were made to feel 'that they were the special favourites of the empire.'[5] Indian scholar Ravinder Kumar refers to the devious tactics Britain employed with its 1935 Constitution, 'whig' rather than 'Liberal' in design, facilitating domination over India:

> Through a carefully contrived balancing of different constituencies
> within Indian society, the British thus hoped to draw South Asia, on
> a durable basis, into a relationship of political, economic and
> strategic subordination to Great Britain.[6]

Ian Copland in *The princes of India in the endgame of empire, 1917-1947*, provides further valuable insights into the arcane political forces at work, as they applied to the relationship between the Raj and the Princes, in pre-independent India.[7]

There is evidence to suggest that Pakistan was more comfortable dealing with Australia than India was in the Menzies period. But, then, their respective attitudes to partition are also reflective of their predisposition to relations with Britain and Australia as these examples show: Casey, three years before the history making division of India, as British Governor of Bengal said, 'the great majority of educated Indians dislike us and want us out ...'[8]. According to Mountbatten's account of those last momentous days of the Raj, 'Mr Jinnah would be quite happy to carry on under the British the whole time ... Congress wanted the British to go but absolutely not at the price of the partition of India.'[9] A saddened Nehru, reflecting on partition, told Heikal 'Jinnah told us that he would not sign the document, demanding the exit of the British from India, unless he knew first the borderlines we would leave for Pakistan. It was a tragedy, I felt partition was a knife cutting into the living flesh of India.'[10] In Bradnoch's view, partition 'disrupted many of the economic, social and political ties which had until that point been vital features of the political geography of the subcontinent.'[11] *The Washington Post* on 19 August 1951 reported Vijayalakshmi Pandit, India's Ambassador to the USA at the time, as saying, 'We Indians have never accepted the two-nations theory. We agreed to partition because failure to do so would have perpetuated foreign rule. The British, not ourselves, are the ones who kept Hindu-Moslem antipathy alive.'[12] Ravinder Kumar writes that the liberation of India from colonial rule 'ranks among the three or four seminal events which transformed the world in the twentieth century...' but, also sees the partition of India as 'the single most important failure of the nationalist movement.'[13]

Given that an insight into colonial relationships in the subcontinent is considered essential to a better understanding of the India-Australia bilateral relationship, then, *ipso facto* understanding of the Indo-Pakistan post-partition problems require some insight into the role of the British in the subcontinent during its colonial administration. Chopra argues that, 'during the Indian freedom struggle, some parts remained out of the Indian mainstream, not out of the desire of the people of those regions but because of the designs of the British.'[14] Stanley Wolpert, examines the linguistic, religious, social and other imperatives rooted in the subcontinent's history [15] which are of some relevance to this question. In trying to understand the extent to which these complex factors influenced Mountbatten's daunting task of transferring power to India in 1947, and in the light of subsequent events, the influence they had on British-Australian attitudes to the two new nations on the Kashmir conflict, is not entirely irrelevant. Therefore, the maelstrom of what was essentially Hindu-Muslim incompatibility on the question of political power and the carving up of India, the environment in which Britain negotiated independence, is valuable background to better understanding the nature of the post-partition India-Pakistan-Australia trilateral relationship. H.V. Hodson's description of the competing interests and conflicting forces at the time conveys accurately the enormity of the problem:

> ... -the mounting communal violence, the cat-and-dog enmity of the Congress and Muslim League factions of the Interim Government, the weakened authority and morale of the police and civil services, the threat of a communal rift in the Indian Army, the total incompatibility of Hindu demands for democratic independence of a single India and the (Muslim) League's insistence upon the creation of Pakistan and on the other side the terms of British Government policy announced with his (Mountbatten's) appointment.[16]

Another important dimension that was a part of this imbroglio was the requirement to resolve the question of integrating the princely states with the provinces of India during the negotiations with specific instructions on it from Atlee to Mountbatten.[17]

Casey, with his experience as Britain's Governor of Bengal, described the irreconcilable political aims of the two main parties, the Indian National Congress Party and the Muslim League, as: 'quite the most intractable major problem of its kind that any Government has ever had to face.'[18] He even thought the 'idea of Pakistan impracticable ...'[19] Yet, as Australia's Minister for External Affairs, Casey too was more kindly disposed to dealing with Pakistan than with India despite his affinity with the Indian people as the narrative will show.

## Australia's English View

A factor that helps understanding why Australia was more disposed to dealing with Pakistan than with India is traceable to the difficulties the British Raj had in coming to terms with Hindu India. In fact, Chopra argues that without an understanding of the role played by imperialism in British India, 'no objective study of Indo-Pak relations is complete.'[20] While this may not be the place for a detailed analysis of that question, nor is it necessary, the critique of V. Subramaniam may have some relevance: one of his arguments, based on Mughal influence, states, 'this Muslim overlay over the Hindu cultural core completely blinded them (the British) to the real basis of Indian unity, namely, the varied but still unifying Hindu culture...', and importantly adds that this 'British misunderstanding of the historical factor in India's integration has continued to colour their judgement and through them that of other Western observers as well.'[21] Of course, it is useful here to point out that after independence from Britain, Nehru's commitment to a secular state was passionately felt and continued by those who came after him during the period of this analysis, (1947-1975).

Undoubtedly, Australia, with its English heritage and Anglophillic view, particularly in the Menzies era, was no less influenced by the British perceptions, although Casey alone, with his experience of India which was more than the others of his time, was able to concede the West had difficulty in understanding India in all its complexities. A good example of this is Casey's admission about Gandhi whom he had met many times and yet, admits 'I don't pretend to understand him at all fully. He is of the East and I am not.'[22] While India's population contained a large Muslim component, some of the difficulty the British had in understanding India is related to the complexities of Hinduism and the relationship between the ruler (the British) and the Brahmin (the keeper of the moral order).[23] This separation of the secular and the spiritual authority kept the British rulers uncertain of their acceptance by the devout Hindu Indian.[24]

Britain's administration of its former colony was also characterised by its master-servant relationship and even in the post-independent era according to Lipton and Firn 'many Britons ... view the ex-colonies with a somewhat possessive paternalism.'[25] Probably, some of Australia's policy makers in the 1950s, infused with a colonial British sense of racial superiority, used this (vicariously derived) imperial orientation in dealing with their Indian counterparts at a time when the notion of Empire remained steadfast, at least in Menzies' mind; and unquestionably, Menzies was the arbiter of foreign policy choices in the conduct of external affairs. Perhaps, foremost among those who were adept at using an imitative English manner was Menzies himself and this is borne out by his attitude to Nehru. A number of Australia's diplomats in the Menzies era, moulded in British traditions, including their education, may have also taken a British approach to dealing with the subcontinent. The effect on Indian sensitivities of this colonial attitude is exemplified by Krishna Menon's comments to Brecher although it is in relation to Menzies' failed mission to Cairo during the Suez crisis:

> ... You can imagine the pigheadedness of imperialism. ... Imagine sending Menzies to the Egyptians! ... Menzies went to lay down the law to them; they asked him to go away. ... Menzies was the worst man to have selected.[26]

In understanding Australia's bilateral relations with India, not enough has been made of this aspect of Australia's colonial inheritance, namely the flow-on effect of its English view of India.

## The Kashmir Impasse and an Australian Tilt

The Kashmir question is relevant to the student of the India-Australia relationship only because it illustrates further Australia's partiality. But, first, it is useful to provide some essential background to show why India was sensitive to Australia's policy positions on the issue. For the period examined in this book, (1947-1975), the real bone of contention between India and Pakistan has been Kashmir, arguably the most celebrated international conundrum of the 20th century.[27] Some insights into how political, religious and racial dynamics have combined to stand in the way of a settlement of the issue reveal an Australian interest biased in favour of Pakistan at the time.

The vexed question of the state of Jammu and Kashmir (hereafter referred to as Kashmir) and where it belongs, in India or Pakistan, has its genesis in that historic 1947 division of British India creating the independent nations of India and Pakistan, an anomalous colonial legacy. Consequently, from a geo-political standpoint, the Pakistan factor constituted an integral component of India's foreign policy, affecting its relationship with not only Pakistan but at various times and in different ways since partition, with Australia, China, the USA, Britain and the USSR. In Bandyopadhyaya's view,

> the partition of the subcontinent removed the very foundations of the politico-military edifice that the British had built on it. A compact defence area provided with the best natural barriers of the world became divided within itself with consequent systemic disintegration, locking up of the armed forces of the area in hostile confrontation and dissipation of resources in general.[28]

Rajendra Sareen makes a valuable contribution to understanding the Indo-Pakistan conundrum through his analysis of the factors of geo-politics and great power rivalry in South Asia while also examining the subsequent views expressed by Prime Ministers Indira Gandhi and Ali Bhutto on Kashmir and bilateral questions.[29]

The strategic importance of Kashmir to India - Kashmir shared boundaries with India and Pakistan in the south and the USSR and China in the north - may not have been fully appreciated by Australia. The importance of the geo-political dimension, particularly in relation to the presence of the two Communist giants, may be gauged by a conversation India's Minister for Economic and Defence Coordination, T.T. Krishnamachari, had with Australia's High Commissioner Plimsoll in New Delhi, about his meeting with President Kennedy, during which Krishnamachari told Kennedy: 'you are right not to let Pakistan go. If you do, it will swing right across to the other side like a pendulum.'[30] For India, despite its preoccupation with Pakistan over Kashmir and its consistent criticism of US aid to its nemesis, the overriding concern it appears from the above conversation was its two giant Communist neighbours. A Pakistan in the Sino-Soviet camp was not a prospect it wished to contemplate at the time.

Indo-Pakistan clashes over Kashmir and Australia's response to the two protagonists fit with a degree of importance into this study of the India-Australia bilateral relationship. Here, then, is the starting point to understanding the impact of Australia's Pakistan connection on the Australia-India relationship. Like most other countries, Australia would have been aware of the violence in Kashmir only months after partition which triggered the first of three wars between the two subcontinent nations and, of course, the continuing impasse.[31] Not long after, Australia found itself playing a part in the dispute, when it sought a mediatory role as this memorandum reveals: 'there was much to be said for pushing the appointment of an Australian mediator. Australia would largely reap the benefit of a successful settlement.'[32]

In the event, Australia's Justice Owen Dixon was assigned the task of mediating by the UN's Security Council, a choice that Nehru thought could not have been better.'[33] Dixon's mission, however, failed with both sides rejecting a number of compromise proposals he put to them.[34]

In the politically charged environment, any mediatory efforts demanded the most sensitive diplomacy but, Australia's sympathies on the Kashmir question seemed not with India, as a number of official documents tend to suggest. For example, in a despatch to Casey from New Delhi on the stability of the Nehru Government, Crocker says, 'his Government acts ... not unlike Talleyrand over Kashmir.'[35] A Brief prepared for Prime Minister Menzies in May 1952, (specifically in relation to UN representative Dr Graham's negotiations with the two countries on the demilitarisation of Kashmir, and the holding of a plebiscite), reveals further where Australia's sympathies lay on the Kashmir question. The document states that, 'as the party in possession of the larger and the more desirable part of Kashmir, India has had more to gain than Pakistan by the postponement of a formal settlement.'[36] No mention is made of the Security Council's two resolutions on Kashmir (passed in August 1948 and January 1949) or Nehru's consistent position that Pakistan forces continue to occupy Kashmir territory in defiance of the UN resolutions. Yet, there were appeals to India from Australia and the West to settle its differences with Pakistan, to which Nehru replied:

> While that (Pakistan's occupation) continues we are asked repeatedly by some Western powers to make it up with Pakistan, to agree to what Pakistan says, or to agree to a plebiscite.[37]

A further comment in the same brief prepared for Menzies refers to a Casey proposal that, should Dr Graham's efforts fail, 'the matter should "in effect but not formally" be taken out of the hands of the United Nations and taken up by the United States, United Kingdom, Canada, Australia and New Zealand,....'[38]. According to the document, the proposal found favour with the Pakistan Premier, Mr Nazimuddin, who had informed Casey that, 'he would greatly welcome a Commonwealth and if possible United States initiative if Graham's report does not advance matters.'[39] With regard to India's reaction to the idea, the Australian document states, 'the Indian authorities have not been sounded (out)'.[40] The probably more important issue here is the conspicuous absence of an Asian or African country in Australia's alternative proposal, especially, given Nehru's noted lack of enthusiasm for Western initiatives in the settling of disputes.

Further evidence of a tilt to the Pakistan position is seen in a communication sent by Australia's High Commissioner in New Delhi to External Affairs, Canberra. The High Commissioner laments the absence in Graham's correspondence of any wish on India's part to seek a formula 'on which, Pakistan could reasonably be asked to come to terms', and then adds, 'my doubt is reinforced whether the Indian Government has ever had a Kashmir policy other than the one preventing a plebiscite from taking place until it is certain that this would be in India's favour.'[41] And, yet, an earlier memorandum from the Australian High Commission in Pakistan to DEA appears to contradict this expression of doubt: when asked to give an assurance that partition of Kashmir will not be agreed to in settling the Kashmir issue as proof of his commitment to the interest of Kashmiris, the above memorandum refers to Nehru's statement that, 'ultimately it is the people of Kashmir and not my categorical assurances that will decide the matter.'[42]

Furthermore, there is no recognition in these Australian communications of the fact that it was Nehru who referred the Kashmir dispute to the Security Council at the very outset. Missing also was any reference to Nehru's specific attitude to a plebiscite, supportive at the time, but conditional on it excluding Indian or Pakistani involvement, because he said, 'we wanted to avoid this plebiscite being uitilised for communal purposes and communal propaganda and communal rioting.'[43] Given the communal violence following partition, and in Kashmir soon after, Nehru's caution was understandable. Nehru also rejected the notion of a UN supervised plebiscite under a neutral government in Kashmir on the grounds that it carried echoes of colonialism.[44]

Absent also from these Australian diplomatic communications between the Australian High Commission in New Delhi and DEA was any reference to the legality of the accession of Kashmir to India, which was legally never in question, the matter having been finalised when the Maharaja of Kashmir wrote to Mountbatten in October 1947 of his wish to integrate with India, followed by Mountbatten's official acceptance in the same month.[45] Also, with his commitment to democratic processes and support for the UN, Nehru felt obliged to make the accession contingent upon it being the preferred choice of the people of Kashmir,[46] a gesture of goodwill, rather than a requirement under previously agreed procedures for the negotiation of India's independence. Yet, that early demonstration of benignity by India (again not mentioned by Australia's diplomats) proved to be a costly mistake for India, one that continued to undermine the sustainability of its arguments later for rejecting a plebiscite on Kashmir. Then there was India's initial military response, seen by some as restrained, while it referred the dispute to the United Nations Security Council, resulting in the establishment in February 1948 of the UN Commission for India and Pakistan (UNCIP). A writer to *The Round Table* thought these actions were, 'to the Indians, acts of goodness and good world citizenship.'[47] Another thought that, if public opinion on Kashmir was tested, ' it would be found that the majority of Indians consider Mr Nehru's policy towards Pakistan far too soft, far too idealistic and far too dreamy.'[48]

The conclusion that may be drawn from these observations is that Australian diplomats, aware of the differences between India and Pakistan, took a more condemnatory view of India in their despatches to DEA. There were more examples of this. In a Memorandum from New Delhi to DEA, the Australian High Commissioner states 'India fudges the issue by talking about violations of the rules of procedure of the Security Council or referring to the legal validity of the accession of Kashmir to India.'[49] The Memorandum also refers to conversations the High Commission had with an Arab Ambassador, and a Report prepared by officers of the American Embassy, both of which point to 'no sense of feeling for India at all' among the Kashmiris.[50] According to a Public Servant interviewed in New Delhi during research in 1997,[51] these third party views conveyed by the Australian High Commissioner would have carried little conviction in India at that time (1954), given the relatively better relationship the Arabs and the Americans had with Pakistan.

Based on Australian diplomatic communications, the discussion to this stage would suggest that India, was given relatively less recognition by Australia's diplomats in their on-the-ground assessments of the Kashmir question.

## The Menzies-Casey View

Further up the Australian political hierarchy, the partiality was no less apparent. Menzies' strange statement in the House of Representatives in March 1951, when, he spoke, of the dangers Kashmir held for Australia, and consequently the importance of a virtually British Pakistan is but one example:

> Pakistan is a British country. It has ties of ancient friendship with the whole British world. Its troops have fought alongside other British troops in two Great Wars.[52]

Menzies' failure to recognise that this history of Pakistan that he alludes to was about a period when Pakistan was a part of British India and, therefore, would apply equally to independent India, is probably reflective of a tilt to Pakistan, as well as his Anglophilia. There were separate mediatory efforts on Kashmir made by Menzies and Casey in 1951, with each of them meeting Nehru and Liaquat Ali Khan. Unlike Menzies, Casey had a better appreciation of the Indian psyche. Yet, like Menzies, he was more comfortable dealing with Pakistan than India. Hudson explains this Casey affinity with Pakistan:

> Because he knew some Pakistani leaders from his Bengal days, and because initially Pakistan took a place in the Western camp, he liked visiting Pakistan and felt at ease with Pakistanis ... Whereas Casey had a comradely liking for Pakistanis, ... he was ambivalent about Indians.[53]

A conversation Casey had with an Indian illustrates this truth: the Indian told Casey that the British had a difficult problem choosing between Congress, representing the majority, and the Muslim League, representing a minority. The problem, he told Casey, was, 'that the difficult majority want the right thing, (a united India) the loyal minority want the wrong thing. (a divided India).'[54]

Menzies' efforts at mediation on Kashmir, through meetings with Nehru and Khan, failed to make an impression, although his meeting with Nehru, their first, was held in an atmosphere of relative affability. In a broadcast from New Delhi, Menzies spoke of those things that bound India and Australia, such as legal institutions and membership of the Commonwealth, (of which, predictably, he pointed out that the King was the Head), adding, 'yet in racial structure, popular tradition, religion, we are, broadly speaking, singularly different.'[55] Nehru, responding to Menzies on that occasion said 'whether we agree or differ in regard to various matters, we look with friendship towards Australia ...'[56]. While this early amicability should have augured well for the future of the bilateral relationship, it failed to lead to closer ties. Once back in Australia from New Delhi, Menzies' attitude to the Kashmir question was different, and more forthright in its interest in Pakistan, as reflected in this *Hindustan Times* report of his speech in the Australian Parliament in which Menzies warned that:

> ... so long as that dispute remains unsettled it will be provocative and dangerous full of the gravest menace for ourselves ... because of its direct and immediate effect upon the security of our position in the Middle East. ... the capacity of Pakistan to participate in the defence of the Middle East is a problem of major importance.[57]

Questioned on Menzies' fears, Nehru replied: 'I would say that Mr Menzies was slightly exaggerating. Shall we go on to the next subject?'[58] Menzies continued with his efforts to achieve a settlement with a proposal for the use of Commonwealth or UN troops for the maintenance of order in Kashmir,[59] but Nehru was unequivocally opposed to the idea of foreign troops because of its connotations of colonialism.[60]

## Choice between War and Peace

Australia, understandably, had to be concerned about a recurrence of war between India and Pakistan, yet the letters exchanged between Nehru and Liaquat Ali Khan in November 1950, press copies of which were sighted by External Affairs, Canberra, would have left little doubt as to where the Australian Government needed to apply its diplomacy, Karachi or Delhi. For example, in a letter to his Pakistan counterpart, Nehru said: 'I stated unequivocally that India would not attack Pakistan unless she attacked first. I asked you to make a similar declaration on behalf of Pakistan, but to this you did not respond.'[61] Replying to this, Liaquat Ali Khan states: 'I am sincerely sorry that I have failed to convince you that a mere 'declaration' of good intentions on our part unsubstantiated by concrete acts would carry conviction to nobody.'[62]

If the Menzies Government's handling of India-Pakistan differences over Kashmir was not particularly noted for its impartiality, it deserved praise for its persistence. In 1951, Menzies sent messages to the Prime Ministers of India and Pakistan offering to help resolve the dispute but, again, he met with no more success than his personal meetings with them had the previous year. A 1951 Paper, entitled 'The Kashmir Situation', conveys Nehru's response to Menzies' fresh attempt:

> Mr Nehru stressed that India had no aggressive intention towards Pakistan, ... thanked Mr Menzies for his offer of good offices, but added that in view of their peaceful intentions 'there is nothing really that need to be done as far as India is concerned.'[63].

Nehru was never in favour of going to war on the question of Kashmir exemplified by his outright rejection of 'Abdullah's suggestion that an ultimatum be given to Pakistan and war declared at the end of it, ...'[64]. Nehru also rejected calls from the Hindu Mahasabha in India for a tougher policy towards Pakistan describing them as 'crooked suggestions' emanating from 'crooked minds,...'[65]. On the Indo-Pakistan relationship, he said, 'our approach is a friendly one and we should take advantage of every opportunity to move towards a peaceful settlement of our problems.'[66] For Australia, there was to be further evidence of the relative attitudes of the two nations to war; for instance, General Ayub Khan when asked whether he would go to war, replied 'certainly if necessary,'[67] a response Nehru described as, 'not a very wise statement to make for the leader of a nation at any time much less a military leader who has just assumed power.'[68] Nehru also wrote to Ayub Khan assuring him that, 'the idea of any conflict with Pakistan is one which is repugnant to us, and we ... will never initiate it, ...'[69].

Menzies visited Karachi and Delhi again in 1959, but not without a little subtle advice on this occasion. A personal letter to him from Casey prior to the visit suggests some discretion from Menzies on Kashmir was being sought:

> You will have received suggestions from Cutler and Crocker about matters to be discussed in Karachi and Delhi. ... You will be lucky if you can avoid some contact with the press at the airports. I expect you will avoid saying anything about Kashmir in either place.[70]

## Australia's Strategic Alliances: An Anglo-American Image

Another pertinent focus to unravelling the India-Australia-Pakistan trilateral conundrum and through it gaining a better understanding of India-Australia relations, involves the US-Australia alliance. With its Cold War phobias and faced with strategic changes taking place in its region, Australia offered its fullest endorsement of Anglo-US global initiatives. As a consequence, the problem for the India-Australia bilateral relationship was that Australia's image in India was not always distinguishable from that of its Anglo-American allies. To use Camilleri's assessment to explain this perception, the Australia-US linkage reflected 'the growing interconnection between the interests of the American and Australian power elites and the near complete domination which the former came to exercise over the latter.'[71] For the bilateral relationship with India, this deepened the mutual indifference.

The formation of SEATO and the Menzies Government's active support for it made Australia's task of appearing evenhanded in its approach to the Kashmir question difficult. While the implications of SEATO for the India-Australia relationship from the standpoint of foreign policy divergence was examined in Chapter Four, it is of relevance to any discussion of Australia's tilt to Pakistan, to focus briefly on Pakistan's membership of the organisation. As far as Menzies was concerned, SEATO and the Australia-US alliance were inextricably linked and pivotal to Australia's defence. He told Parliament, 'we stand in good company in SEATO, in ANZUS, in ANZAM.'[72] He was more specific on the question of Australia's collaboration with the US in situations of war with his statement, 'we will be fighting side by side with the United States', and, on military equipment, he said, 'fit ourselves for close cooperation with the United States in the South-East Asian area.'[73]

For India, the SEATO component of the Australia-US symbiosis, led to grave fears. Nehru was never in doubt about the effects of

Pakistan's membership of the Pact and the US linkage. At a press conference on Kashmir, this is how he described it:

> In the name, perhaps, of fighting communism, Pakistan has got enormous aid from the U.S.A.; and it may be getting from the Baghdad Pact or SEATO. ... I should like our friends concerned to realize how by some of their policies of military alliances and military aid they have added, to the burdens of India a feeling of insecurity.[74]

Nehru's none too subtle allusion to 'our friends' here is primarily directed at the US, but obviously included Australia, a member of SEATO. But, then, Australia was not unaware of India's displeasure with the US. In one Memorandum from New Delhi, Australia's High Commissioner wrote:

> Despite denials from Washington, Nehru and his entourage are convinced that a deal is being worked out between Pakistan and the United States of America and that it includes provision for the United States base in Pakistan, modernising the Pakistan Army and other military commitments ... An increase in anti-American feeling is already noticeable in the press.[75]

Pakistan's involvement in essentially military agreements with the US was extensive[76] prompting Rajpal Budania to describe Pakistan as the United State's 'most allied ally'[77] by the mid-1960s. There were other examples of US attitudes to the Kashmir question being resented in India. For instance, *The Leader*, in an editorial commenting on Adlai Stevenson's visit to India and Pakistan, criticized what he said in each country because, it said his 'Kashmir statement is not wholly consistent with the New Delhi statement and will be resented by Indian opinion.'[78]

According to Stanley Wolpert, Nehru considered every American shipment of military equipment to Pakistan 'as at least potentially aimed at India's "head" in Kashmir, if not at its heart in New Delhi.'[79] Nehru's fears were not entirely unfounded. In 1965, 'Pakistan launched a Patton-tank attack against Indian outposts in the Rann of Kutch and a few months later rolled into Kashmir.'[80] The shipment of American military arms was the subject of debate in India's Lok Sabha too over a long period. Bhagwat Jha Azad (MP) in 1971 criticising Nixon, recalled that:

> ... when the then US Vice President Nixon returned after a tour of India and Pakistan, he publicly urged the President that aid must be given to Pakistan ... He (Nixon) said 'to withold American aid

because of the protest of neutralist India would be discouraging to those nations willing to stand up and be counted on the side of the free world.'[81]

India, which always thought of itself as being free with its non-aligned status, had difficulty with Nixon's view of the 'free world'. Questioning America's assumption that only they and their allies, but not India, were part of the 'free world',[82] Azad went on to refer to America's secretive diplomacy:

> What pains us most is that the American Government did not think it fit to tell our Foreign Minister while being given lunch and sweet talk that their ships have already left their harbours.[83]

There were more questions raised and accusations made about the US in the Lok Sabha, throughout the Cold War. For example, on American aid to Pakistan, Raghuramaiah (MP), said, 'I am afraid time will prove that it has been let loose in a zone of delusion comparable only to the zone of delusion fostered in Chiang-Kai Shek's China ...'[84]. Another MP, S.D. Sharma, said he hoped 'Mr Nixon ... may take a more realistic approach and give up his predilections in favour of Pakistan ...'[85]. Then there was Indrajit Gupta (MP) who accused the US of attempting to 'scuttle the bilateral relations which we were trying to build up between India and Pakistan for the first time arising out of the Simla agreement ...', implying that the US aim was to hold on to Pakistan with military and other assistance.[86]

On America's interest in Pakistan, and military aid given to it, Menon took this view: 'to be charitable, we may interpret it as part of American giantism. The Americans make themselves believe that the Pakistani's will help them against the USSR - with Sherman tanks they are going to fight Russia! No, they will use these tanks against us ...'[87]. Nehru too did not hold back on what he thought was the disruptive effect of America's support of Pakistan. In an address to the Lok Sabha on Kashmir, Nehru said:

> We were discussing various ways of settling the question with the Prime Minister of Pakistan when a new development took place. This was the promise of military aid from the U.S.A. to Pakistan, a promise which was subsequently fulfilled. This created not only a new military situation but a new political situation; ...[88]

Anupurna Nautiyal argued that the US preferred Pakistan to India because its geographic location suited US strategic aims in Asia, while

India 'with its rich democratic traditions did not fit into the US scheme of things.'[89] In other words, strategic interests outweighed democratic traditions. John Foster Dulles, US Secretary of State (1953-1959), described Pakistan's potential value in these words:

> Pakistan would be a cooperative member of any defence schemes that may emerge in the Middle East. We need not wait for the formal defence arrangements as a condition to provide military assistance to Pakistan because Pakistan is a potential strong point for the US.[90]

Nehru's concerns about SEATO from the beginning is reflected in Camilleri's interpretation of what the pact meant to the Americans with his contention that it is 'not far-fetched to argue that SEATO's underlying rationale was to provide a legal basis for direct American intervention in South-east Asia, and facilitate United States control of the strategic gateways between the Pacific and the Indian Oceans.'[91]

The point of these references to India's displeasure with America (Australia's most important ally) is to show that, because of Australia's closeness to Pakistan, through SEATO directly and indirectly through its security linkages with America, Australia's view of 'democratic' India's stand on Kashmir, and SEATO, was not entirely defensible against perceptions of bias.

The reality of SEATO also led to India increasing its ties with the USSR, and yet Menzies had difficulty understanding why India's foreign policy positions were more sympathetic to those of the Soviet Union. Australia's High Commissioner Plimsoll writing to DEA from New Delhi stated, 'one factor which has strengthened the USSR in India has been its support for India over Kashmir, in contrast with the American and particularly the British position, which was generally regarded here as pro-Pakistan.'[92] Plimsoll, whose assessments of Nehru and India were mostly discerning and objective, fails to mention Australia's own tilt to Pakistan directly or through the Western alliance although he does refer to India's perception of Australia's bias as the narrative shows.

In contrast to the US, Australia's other major partner of the Western Alliance, Britain, appears more evenhanded on the question of its own supply of arms to its former colonies, India and Pakistan, although its preference too for Pakistan over India was no less than Australia's. This was particularly the case at the UN when, in conjunction with Australia it tended to vote against India. Several British Cabinet meeting memoranda of the early 1950s, provide insights into the attitude of Britain on the issue of the supply of arms[93] to the warring protagonists. In one, it refers to the Pakistan Prime Minister's lament in 1952 that his country 'derived no advantage over India by reason of her (Pakistan's) continued allegiance to the Crown: ...'[94].

The Indians, however, had misgivings about Britain's attitude to the supply of arms to India and Pakistan. For example, when Britain's then Secretary of State, Anthony Eden, met with the Indian High Commissioner in 1954, the latter referred to American aid to Pakistan and told Eden that Britain's 'reserved attitude on this matter had not been very welcome to Delhi.'[95] Then, as Prime Minister a year later Eden, in an explanatory message to Nehru, stressed that, while Britain had sold to Pakistan whatever it had requested by way of military equipment, the supply to India had been comparatively more; and yet, in the same note, Eden also admits to Britain being aware of US military supplies going to Pakistan, but claims to have no detailed knowledge of it.[96] Of course, in reality Pakistan had been able to obtain 'far more, per head in aid from the West than has India, and far more, in absolute terms, in military aid.'[97]

In the political sphere, Britain's support for Pakistan was more palpable. In 1957, the British sponsored a UN resolution - backed by Australia - which supported Pakistan's request for a plebiscite in Kashmir. S.C. Gangul refers to the pro-Pakistan nature of this (and another resolution, also sponsored by Britain and Australia among others), with the observation that the resolution: '... had been finalized and circulated even before the Indian delegate V.K. Krishna Menon, had completed his speech in the Security Council.'[98] This conduct on Britain's part, supported by Australia, was serious enough to make Nehru - a strong supporter of the Commonwealth - tell the Lok Sabha that India's Commonwealth links may require 'further consideration.'[99] Relations between India and its former ruler were also strained after the 1956 Suez crisis where India took a critical, but evenhanded, attitude to Britain's role while Menzies worked strenuously on the Anglo-French side. Whether this stiffened Anglo-Australian criticism of India on Kashmir is an imponderable question. Krishna Menon referred to this 'unfortunate phenomenon' in an address to the Security Council in November 1957.[100] There was also 'the bad manners' of the British in India being a reason for the poor Indo-British relations according to Churchill.[101]

What all this suggests is that like Australia, Britain's sympathies on Kashmir were more with Pakistan than India, and the reasons have their roots in the subcontinent's history as well as in being a part of the West's strategic alliance with links to Pakistan through SEATO. As R.G. Neale observes, 'Britain was obviously partisan towards Pakistan before independence and after it, over Kashmir.'[102] However, apart from Australia's British links in the Western alliance (SEATO) in the scheme of things, this was less of a factor in India's displeasure with Australia than its (Australia's) strong American enmeshment.

There were some Australian diplomats who adopted an evenhanded approach to the subcontinent with a discerning and more realistic understanding of the complexities involved. J. Plimsoll (High Commissioner to New Delhi) was one of them. In an informed and mostly balanced analysis of Nehru's impact on India sent to Paul Hasluck, Minister for External Affairs, Plimsoll includes the comment that 'he (Nehru) probably felt that our support for Pakistan over Kashmir had been too uncompromising.'[103] Whilst this by itself does not amount to an admission of Australian bias, it suggests that Indian doubts about Australia's impartiality did exist although it was not referred to in earlier Australian diplomatic communications with Canberra. Then again, Pakistan too, understandably, did its best to make good use of Australia's perceived predilection, exemplified by this letter from P.R. Heydon (Australia's High Commissioner in New Delhi) to DEA, Canberra, on the Indo-Pakistan conflict:

> I am not alarmed at the Pakistan anxiety to get the matter before the Security Council while Australia is chairman - in fact I think it might be better for us in some ways to have the neutral position which the chairmanship will give us on some issues. But I do hope we can suppress the fact that the Pakistanis want it raised during our chairmanship because there is already a quite misleading impression that Australia identifies herself with Pakistan on almost all issues.[104]

One of the hypotheses of this book is that the bilateral relationship was sensitive to the Australian political party in office; this becomes evident in the policy differences between Labor and Liberal Coalition parties on SEATO and Kashmir. Take, for example, R.W. Holt's (Labor Opposition) address to Parliament lamenting Australia's lack of support for India:

> When Kashmir voted in favour of going with India, sufficient recognition was not paid to the decision of a Moslem state to go in with India. I believe that the Government has been afraid of alienating Pakistan and complicating that country's membership of the Baghdad Pact.[105]

Then, there was E.G. Whitlam who, quite early in his political career, alive to India's sensitivities, drew Parliament's attention to the implications of SEATO and the detrimental effects its policy statements on Kashmir had on the India-Australia relationship [106] referred to in Chapter Four.

## COLOMBO PLAN: THE POLITICS OF AID

Another area of relevance to discussion of India-Australia relations is the Colombo Plan Aid programme. In the aftermath of the Second World War with parts of Europe and Asia physically and economically destroyed, economic aid became an important strategic tool for both the US and the Soviet Union.[107] Aid was also used by the bigger powers and their allies in their wish to draw the countries of Asia, emerging from colonial rule, into their respective, ideologically divided, camps. A number of these newly independent countries, following India's lead in 1949 (as a Republic), sought membership of the Commonwealth in the 1950s. The Colombo Plan, a programme for the richer nations to provide economic assistance to the poorer members of the Commonwealth, (later extended to non-member countries also), was established at a Commonwealth Foreign Ministers meeting, held in Colombo, Ceylon, (Sri Lanka), in January 1950. Australia's representative was Percy Spender, Minister for External Affairs (1949-1950), in the Menzies Government elected to office in December 1949. Opinions, however, on the plan's effectiveness in influencing the bilateral relationship differ.

### Background

Consistent with Australia's preoccupation with security, Spender, early in his role as Minister for External Affairs, emphasised the threat to Australia from Communism: 'the rising and the menacing tide of communism in the East presents a definite threat - and not a remote threat either - to our national existence.'[108]

Consequently, Spender argued that it was in Australia's interest to help ensure the political stability of the region through aid observing that, 'the Colombo Plan marks the commencement of the special relationship between Australia and Asia.'[109] While a number of men contributed to the creation of the Colombo Plan, the initiative came primarily from Spender. In the view of author/diplomat Alan Renouf, 'pride of authorship of the Colombo Plan was claimed by several Australians in 1950, but it was Spender who saw that the idea, no matter who produced it, bore fruit. The Colombo Plan was truly Spender's creation.'[110] Casey, who replaced Spender as Minister for External Affairs, was no less enthusiastic about the Colombo Plan. At a press conference in New Delhi, Casey said:

> Australia is especially conscious of the importance which Governments of Asia attach to the improvement of the living standards of their people — an objective which Australia herself has always regarded as an essential accompaniment of her own political freedoms.[111]

This emphasis given to raising of living standards is important to the discussion of the Colombo Plan because the case for Australian aid under it was ostensibly about the alleviation of poverty, the Spender-Casey argument being that the poor countries of Asia, with their dire post-colonial economic circumstances, were vulnerable to Communist influences. Spender's position was that countries such as Australia,

> which have had the greater opportunities in the past, can help the countries of South East Asia to develop their own democratic institutions and their own economies and thus protect them against those opportunists and subversive elements which take advantage of changing political situations and low living standards.[112]

While Spender's Colombo Plan intentions and the high expectations from it were sincerely held, in pursuing the Plan's objectives Australia was not as successful as it had hoped. In making this observation a number of questions have to be faced: first, Australia's interests were aligned to those of the US (ANZUS and SEATO), and India was never comfortable with military alliances and their implications; secondly, the amount of aid, in monetary value, given by Australia,[113] was inadequate to counter that provided by the opposing camp, in India's case, Soviet aid. Then there was the Australian media's lukewarm support of the Plan's aid-to-Asia objective. *The Sydney Morning Herald* for instance, thought the initiative was valuable but argued that 'we are a European people who look to Europe for our origins and our culture. Our religious faith, our national philosophy, and our whole way of life are alien to Asia.'[114]

## Australian Aid: Genuine Succour or Strategic Tool?

From India's perspective, the aims of the Colombo Plan were commendable. Nehru, addressing the Prime Ministers' Conference in London in October 1948, argued that fighting Communism required political reform and improved living standards for the ordinary people.[115] But while the aid Australia gave India[116] - technical, educational and monetary - was of undoubted benefit to the country, it somehow failed to reach the hearts of the Indians. There was a ring of a public relations exercise about it, with the real motive seen as strategic rather than a well intentioned facilitation of India's economic development. *The Sydney Morning Herald*, of March 21st, 1952 under the title 'Second Front Against Communism', referred to the link between the future of South East Asia and Australia's security and stated that, 'in order to avoid offending the susceptibilities of some Asian participants, there has been painstaking care to disassociate the (Colombo) plan from any political considerations.'[117] Nehru's note to the Secretary General, India's Ministry of External Affairs, with advice for the Indian delegation about to attend the Sydney conference of May 1950, reflects India's guarded attitude to Australian aid:

> It is true that the urge to do something in South East Asia, in so far as Australia is concerned, arises chiefly from fear of communism spreading. Nevertheless, to talk about raising economic standards in order to counter communism is a wrong approach. The grace of the act goes and the people who might be benefited feel that this is incidental to some other and more opportunist purpose. Also, it puts the question of economic help to South East Asia in the sphere of political controversy and conflict.[118]

Australia's Labor Opposition in 1955 saw the Colombo Plan aid programme as having limited success in converting the minds of the peoples of Asia, whose real interests, it argued, had more to do with being treated equally and with respect. In an address to Parliament Labor's Beazley expressed these views: 'I think the people of Asia know how to interpret goodwill. I am not deriding the Colombo plan, but I should say that they are interested basically in our motives.'[119] Questioning Australia's motives for using South East Asia (led by Australian diplomatic initiatives) as a bulwark against Communist power, Beazley argued, 'We may regard that as supremely necessary, but Asia regards such a motive with the gravest suspicion.'[120] This perception is also exemplified in Millar's reference to Percy Spender's active role in the Colombo Plan initiative, and his contribution to preparing the ground for a regional security arrangement, (ANZUS), in the 1950s:

> Spender campaigned, pressed and negotiated until the (ANZUS Pact) possibility was a reality. ... Spender was active both in initiating the plan (Colombo) and in making it quickly effective. He thus managed to involve Australia in Asia and to get Australia protection from Asia.[121]

Another example of Australia's Colombo Plan aid not being totally altruistic in its aims is seen in the then Minister for Immigration, Alexander Downer's assertion that the Government's efforts to reduce the chasm between Australia's 'friendship with Asia foreign policy and our domestic "White Australia" Policy, was relying very largely on the Colombo Plan, and the influx of Asian students.'[122] The undoubted benefits to India and other countries from students attending Australian educational institutions under the Colombo Plan was used by Australia as evidence of the Plan's success. For example, a member of the Menzies Government told Parliament:

> If we in Australia want to remain in this Pacific area as a predominantly European race ... , then I believe that we will get great assistance from the students who come here under the Colombo Plan.[123]

The MP's argument was that, during their period of study in Australia, the students were treated 'as equals with the Australian people' and returned to their homelands as 'the finest ambassadors for Australia ...'[124]. This assessment seems to contradict Crocker's view of it gained at first hand: he wrote to Casey years earlier to say that 'the goodwill to Australia generated by the Colombo Plan had dried up.'[125] Author and former diplomat Stephen Fitzgerald observes that 'even under the great 1950s and 1960s Colombo Plan, Asians could come to study but could not stay.'[126] Understandably, the reality of the immigration barrier was never far from Indian thoughts, although it was primarily a concern with its basis of discrimination rather than the limiting of immigration opportunities.

## A Two-Edged Sword

India, of course, had other reasons to doubt Australia's motives. Australia in the 1950s was seen in India as a British outpost with Menzies determined to protect its European origins with its rigid application of the 'White Australia' Policy. The Indians were also resentful of Menzies' argument against decolonisation and had not forgotten his initial disapproval of India's independence in 1947. Menzies support of South Africa and his initial objections to India's continued membership of the Commonwealth as a republic were also acknowledged as being expressions of an unfriendly Australian attitude. Menzies, of course, was not alone in his negative attitude to Asian independence; his colleague, K.M. Anderson was of a similar mind, lamenting in an address to Parliament the premature granting of independence to the colonies.[127]

What men like Menzies and Anderson, failed to realise was that colonialism 'gave rise to its nemesis, nationalism', which, if anything, tended to work against Australia's political overtures in the Asian region to protect the newly independent states from Communist influences.[128] In the aftermath of independence, nationalism became an even more powerful force in India and influenced government thinking in formulating foreign policy, which it could be assumed included decisions on the question of accepting aid. Nehru, for instance, speaking of the pre-eminent place that nationalism occupied in India's character, observed that, 'nationalism was and is inevitable in the India of my day; ... For any subject country, national freedom must be the first and dominant urge; for India with her ... past heritage, it was doubly so.'[129] In this regard, Fred Greene makes the pertinent observation that, 'often Western aid programs must actually buck the nationalist tide that makes some states oppose any connection with the West.'[130]

But, then, concern about Western aid among the newly independent nations emerging from their bitter experience of colonialism was not unexpected. India was wary of anything that could compromise its non-aligned status. Nehru in a speech in the Lok Sabha stressed that accepting aid would not compromise India's independence in foreign policy determination or force loyalty to the donor.[131] While Colombo Plan aid often took the form of a bilateral transfer, financial or other, there were those who preferred aid *via* multilateral channels such as UN programmes because it appeared to be less compromising. Concerns about military pacts and the granting of bases, also had a bearing on the effectiveness of aid as a genuine instrument for helping to improve living standards in Asia, (which was Australia's stated objective) particularly with the Americans joining the list of Colombo Plan donor countries. It also did not go unnoticed in India that Australia gave aid to SEATO members, Pakistan, Philippines and Thailand.

## Tight Fisted and Equivocal Interest

While money alone may not have had the desired effect (because of the question of motives), it did count. The amount of Australian aid to India was unimpressive, for example, when compared to Canada's contribution.[132] There was a lack of genuine interest in aid during the Menzies period. While the Minister for External Affairs Casey was convinced of the importance of aid to Australia's anti-Communist campaign in Asia, he was unhappy with the lack of support he was getting from his Cabinet colleagues on funding. Referring to his difficulties with the Colombo Plan Budget Appropriation, Casey said, 'many people are hostile to the UN, hostile to the Colombo Plan, and unsympathetic with Asia. It is fairly generally believed that we can live to ourselves alone.'[133] Clearly, Casey's enlightened interest in Asia was not a shared one in the Australian Government of the Menzies period. As Hudson observes, 'at Government level he was almost alone. Few ministers had any interest in Asia and Menzies seems to have had none at all.'[134] An entry in Nehru's diary made at the Commonwealth Prime Ministers conference in May 1960, refers to a Menzies comment which appears to exemplify this equivocal attitude:

Menzies

World trade growing rapidly between highly industrialised countries but not with & among under-developed countries.[135]

(The telling Diary comment, made by Nehru which appears immediately below the above words attributed to Menzies, seems to convey his frustration at the West's policy contradictions:)

Colombo Plan on one side & barriers to trade ...[136].

Labor Opposition Member, R.W. Holt drew the Menzies Government's attention to its less than substantial monetary support for the Colombo Plan with this comment in Parliament:

> By emphasizing the cultural assistance rendered under the Colombo plan, which, in itself, is a good thing, this Government has tended to mistake the shadow for the substance. It has failed to appreciate that the true problem of Asia is not political but economic. [137]

Given the earlier discussion in this Chapter on Australia's tilt to Pakistan in the trilateral relationship, of some relevance to that perception is the disparity in the aid given to Pakistan and India. With a fraction of India's population, Pakistan received more aid from Australia (as at 1957) under the Colombo Plan than India did. Casey informed Parliament in April 1957, that Colombo Plan aid to India amounted to 6,700,000 with a further 4,160,000 pledged. For Pakistan, the comparable figures he tabled were 6,800,000 and 5,000,000 pledged,[138] a difference in Pakistan's favour of nearly 1,000,000. (all figures are in Australian Pounds, the currency at the time)

## The Winning Formula: Trade not Aid

Australia's diplomats worked hard to convince the new nations of Asia of the Western democratic way of life being the better option. At a press conference in New Delhi, Casey told the Indians that it was the democracies and not the Communists who have shown a determination to protect the freedom of the under developed countries and help them with improving their welfare.[139] Yet, for all Casey's good intentions, the facts failed to support this view, at least in India's case. The Soviet Union with its massive aid to newly independent India, helping the country with its high priority economic and social programmes, was far more successful in its aid objectives than Australia was with its Colombo Plan aid. Unlike the limited nature of the Australian aid, the Indians were able to establish trade agreements with the Russians involving the supply of aircraft, heavy industrial equipment, oil, tourism, as well as the exchange of students. In a memo to DEA from the Australian High Commission in New Delhi, W.K. Flanagan, commenting on the 1955 Kruschev-Bulganin visit to India, observed that:

> Generally speaking, the press appears to have accepted the Soviet Mission to India ... as part of a vast new Soviet offensive designed to win Asia and the Middle East to the Communist side. The main weapon ... will be, ... economic, with the Soviet aiming at assuming responsibility for the industrialisation of their economies which is 'craved' by all the countries concerned ...[140].

With reference to the Soviets proposal to give 'exceptionally easy and long term credit conditions ...'[141], Flanagan makes the important observation that 'the unhappy stigma of dependence associated with straight-out aid grants would be avoided by this technique.[142] At the time, the Australian High Commission in Wellington too drew DEA's attention to the press releases on the high level Russian visit to India, but in a different context; it pointed to the response of *The New Zealand Herald* which stated 'that ever since the days of the Tzars, the Russians have looked with covetous eyes on the riches of India ... Consequently, it is thought that Communist domination of India may well be a Russian long-term aim.'[143] In contrast, *The Manchester Guardian,* in an article entitled 'Russians achieve their aims in India', captures this failure of the West to understand India and its sensitivities. Taya Zinkin, commenting on the Russian visit, states one of its key objectives was to generate Western opinion against Nehru which, in turn would provoke hostile reactions from Nehru towards the West. She adds that 'the Western press has swallowed the bait hook, line and sinker, and has aroused in turn the Indian press ... The "Herald" (Mr Nehru's own paper) - "The reaction of the Western Press is an amusing exhibition of pettiness and petulance, and the press resents India's refusal to recognise Western democracy's assumption of moral superiority to the Soviets." '[144]

The relevance of all this is that it points to Australian aid to India under the Colombo Plan being of marginal consequence in its impact. J. Oldham, Special Advisor on Commonwealth Relations, in a memo to the Secretary, DEA, not long after the high-powered Russian visit to India, asserted:

> ... it would seem that our propaganda services in India should be increased and that more use be made of the fact that we are helping India, not by words, but by personal sacrifice of our material goods,

so that we can in every way, bring home to the people of that country that we are intimately and personally interested in their future.[145]

As stated above, with the exemption of Casey, such advice had little impact on the Menzies Government and its alliance based diplomacy. Then, again, just how important was India to Australia's policy makers of the 1950s and 1960s? The answer is very little, when measured against Australia's criteria of Cold War imperatives of security, preservation of its European population and trade.

Granted, some of the factors discussed in this chapter such as Indo-US and Indo-British relations were third party issues; yet, because of Australia's alliance with the US and inherited British attitudes to India, these issues did impinge on the India-Australia relationship. Britain's complex colonial relationship with India and Pakistan, its cultural links with Australia, including their close association as members of the old Commonwealth club, SEATO and the Western alliance had implications for the tripartite India-Australia-Pakistan wrangle particularly in the context of the Kashmir dispute. Nehru's note to India's UN Ambassador, illustrates why this was so: 'I must say that I just can't understand the attitude of U.K. and U.S.A. about Kashmir ... there appears to be an almost invincible prejudice against India.'[146] Krishna Menon in an interview with Brecher on the Kashmir question said as much: 'Britain, ably assisted by the United States, is and always has been the villain of the piece.'[147] The flow-on effect of this on India's perception of Australia was negative.

That said, the lack of genuine interest shown by Menzies' Australia in the world's largest democracy with preference for its neighbour Pakistan, whose record of democracy has not been nearly as impressive or continuous, was no accident. On the two countries record of democracy and political stability, Hugh Tinker observes that, 'if Nehru could return to India 20 years after his death he would still be able to recognise its politics and society. Jinnah would find nothing of the country he sought to create and inspire in the present-day truncated Pakistan.' [148] For Australia, non-aligned India contrasted sharply with Pakistan, a member of SEATO unambiguously aligned with Australia and the West. Besides, in the context of the Middle East being of importance to Australia under enzies, and Pakistan's geographic and cultural location *vis-à-vis* the Middle East, it is not surprising India was less favoured by Australia in its relations with the two states of the subcontinent.

As stated in Chapter One, bilateral relationships do not exist alone but are a part of a multilateral complex of relationships. In the India-Australia relationship, India's relations with Pakistan and China, and Australia's with the US and Pakistan, are important considerations affecting it. Underlying these multilateral networks is the common theme of mutual fear and distrust. While this obviously applies to India-Pakistan and India-China relations, the US-Australia-Pakistan network as well as those between India and the USSR were no less about great power strategic interests in Asia and, therefore, primarily fear-oriented. Eliot Cohen makes the point well: 'in any part of the world, regional politics and, hence, regional warfare will have as their pivots the mutual hostility of two states, about which all else will revolve.'[149]

There is also the question of Australia's lingering view of India, a legacy of its British heritage. Neale's critique of 'Australia's Changing Relations with India' and his specific reference to the paucity of Indian knowledge in Parliamentary debates and the press in Australia of the 1920s and 1930s is pertinent to Australia's colonial attitude to India:

> ...they reveal also an ingrained habit of thinking about India first from the point of view of a nineteenth-century imperialism based upon British and white dominance and secondly from the point of view of the use India might be to Australia.[150]

The adoption of an English attitude to India by some in the Menzies administration compounded India's resentment of its perception of partiality shown to Pakistan. Did Australia really understand the Indo-Pakistan complexities in all their manifestations, both before and in the aftermath of partition, and were not just responding to the changing geo-political imperatives affecting its own security? If it did, was its handling of the bilateral relationship with India subordinated to the larger interests of its Western alliance-dependent objectives in which Pakistan was a factor through SEATO? The evidence suggests that Australia may not have understood the deeper historical forces informing the Hindu-Muslim conflict, and even if it did, would it have lessened its tilt to Pakistan?

The India experienced Casey, speaking about the problem, says: 'Indian mentality, Indian logic, Indian ideas, the way the Indians have their cards stacked, are all quite different from ours. Their's are not necessarily wrong on that account.'[151]

The fact of India's commitment to democracy (difficult though it was for a country where millions lived in poverty) at a time when many Afro/Asian nations surrendered it not long after independence opting instead for military dictatorship, or alternative authoritarian forms of government, made no impression on Australia. This uninterest in India being a democracy, in some ways a paradox, stems primarily from the vagaries of Cold War compulsions and for Australia the associated isolationist, fear-driven, alliance-based approach to bilateral interests and diplomatic relations. That said, on the Kashmir issue Australia rightly felt that any settlement must ultimately have the acquiescence of the people of Kashmir themselves. In Ifthikar Malik's view too, 'the larger interests of the Kashmiris must receive priority. For a long time, rather than being the focal point, they were simply regarded as a side issue.'[152]

There was also the question of a choice between an economically and politically more settled India with its democratic traditions and commitment to secularism, and Pakistan whose experience of democratic civilian government since 1947 has unfortunately been interrupted by military regimes. In communications between Australia's diplomats and DEA in the 1950s, there is a conspicuous lack of any discussion of the importance of a country's democratic structures to the whole question of Kashmir and where it belongs; even though India's Ambassador, M. Chagla, told the UN Security Council in May 1964, that, while Pakistan demands democracy in Kashmir, 'she does not permit even a vestige of democracy in her own territory, ...'[153].

On the other hand there were some doubts in diplomatic circles as to India's commitment to secularism and equal treatment of its large minority Muslim population. Nehru's attitude to it was inviolable from the beginning and King Saud of Saudi Arabia in 1955 testified to its sincerity with this observation:

> I desire now, at the conclusion of my visit to India, to say to my Moslem brethren all over the world that the fate of Indian Moslems is in safe hands ... I desire to express my gratitude and that of my

Moslem brethren to Mr Nehru and all those through whom he executes this policy of equality and equity ...[154].

What emerges from the discussion of the Colombo Plan is that apart from military pacts involving some states in Asia, economic aid played a role in Australia's diplomacy in the region. In India too aid has played an important part, both as a recipient of aid as well as a donor. Not so widely known is the fact that India provided aid to over a hundred countries in the southern hemisphere. The practice continued as a part of the country's economic diplomacy, post-1962. It gave 30 billion rupees in aid for development work in Third World countries.[155]

As a measure of the effectiveness of the bilateral relationship, Australia's aid under the Colombo Plan, for all its undoubted value to India's development needs of gigantic proportions, failed to transcend the other issues of importance to India such as racial equality, economic equity through a fairer share of the world's economy, de-colonisation, non-alignment, and, being free of military alliances perceived as threatening to India. Furthermore, Australia's Colombo Plan contributions to India were not considered significant in the context of India's overall needs of economic aid. Consequently, the perception was that it served Australia's interests as an underpinning of its strategic aims in South East Asia rather than representing a genuine aid programme for the alleviation of India's poverty and the raising of living standards. Like others, India preferred greater opportunities for trading with Australia and the West. Mrs Gandhi's visit to Australia in 1968 prompted this pertinent editorial comment in *The Age* newspaper.

> Australian Government leaders are often free with self-congratulations on the role which Australian aid and trade have played in the development of Asian economies. ... now might be the appropriate time to consider ways in which the pattern of trade between the two countries could begin to work productively in India's favour.[156]

But, then, the Menzies Government, apart from Casey, showed little interest in aid and without the genuine support of the government, Australia's Colombo Plan aid to India remained largely inconsequential for the betterment of the bilateral relationship.

# Endnotes

1. See, NAI, Document 'Anti-Indian Propaganda (Kashmir) - Canberra', File No. 23/1/10-XPP. Also see, NAI, Comments from Indian Information Officer, Australia, on publicity offensive by Pakistan against India, File No. 260 IANZ.

2. Minto and Morley, *India*, p 20, in T.J.S. George, *India at Fifty*, Express Publications Limited, Chennai, India, 1997, p 27.

3. *Ibid*. Lord Morley, a noted Liberal Statesman, 'supported the ingenious device of "separate electorate" and "weightage" which was virtually a stab in the back of Indian Nationalism.'

4. *Ibid*.

5. Panikkar, K.M., *Asia and Western Dominance*, Collier Books, New York, 1969, p 113.

6. Kumar, Ravinder, 'Democracy: from Consolidation to Fluidity', *Fifty Years of Indian Independence*, Hiramay Karlekar, (ed.), Oxford University Press, New Delhi, 1998, p 8.

7. Copland, Ian, *The princes of India in the endgame of empire, 1917-1947*, Cambridge University Press, Cambridge, 1997.

8. Richard Casey to Lord Wavell, November 1944, TOP, Vol. V, pp 179-184, in W.J. Hudson, *Casey*, Oxford University Press, Melbourne, 1986, p 167.

9. Collins, Larry and Lapierre, Dominique, *Mountbatten and the Partition of India: March 22-August 15, 1947*, Vikas Publishing, New Delhi, 1982. Jinnah as Leader of the Muslim League, was spokesman for the Muslim population of India before partitioning.

10. Nehru Memorial Library, Manuscripts Section, New Delhi, M.H. Heikal Interview, 'A Dialogue with Nehru', at the Embassy of India, Cairo, Information Service of India, Accession No. 1097, p 27. For a valuable view of the conflicting proposals between the Congress Party and the Muslim League leading up to partition, see, Hugh Tinker, *Experiment with Freedom*, Oxford University Press, London, 1967.

11. Bradnoch, Robert W., *India's Foreign Policy since 1971*, Royal Institute of International Affairs, Great Britain, 1990, p 4.

12. AA, Report from the *Washington Post* of 19 August 1951, Series A1838/278, Item 169/11/148, part 4. Krishna Menon's view was that Partition was 'largely a reflex action against British imperialism, ...an out-of-date obscurantist doctrine ... we do not accept it.' See Michael Brecher, *India and World Politics*, Oxford University Press, London, 1968, p 196.

13. Kumar, Ravinder, 'Democracy: From Consolidation to Fluidity', *Fifty Years of Indian Independence*, H. Karlekar, (ed.), Oxford University Press, New Delhi, 1998, p 7.

14. Chopra, V.D., 'National Security and Terrorism in Kashmir' *Genesis of Regional Conflicts*, V.D. Chopra and M. Rasgotre, (eds.) Gyan Publishing House, New Delhi, 1995. p 47.

15. Wolpert, Stanley, *India*, Prentice Hall, New Jersey, 1965. Also see, Jawaharlal Nehru *An Autobiography*, John Lane The Bodley Head, London, 1936, p 460, for Nehru's ascribing of responsibility for communalism on British policy, 'preventing the Hindu and Muslim from acting together'; James Lawrence, *Raj: The Making and Unmaking of British India*, Abacus, London, 1998; Ayesha Jalal, *The Sole Spokesman: Jinnah, the Muslim League and the Demand for Partition*, Cambridge University Press, Cambridge, 1985.

16. Hodson, H.V., 'Earl Mountbatten's Role in the Partition of India', *TRT*, No. 277, January 1980, pp 102-103. For an informative examination of the India-Pakistan conflict over Kashmir since partition including interviews with politicians, diplomats, the military and the public on both sides, see 'Sunday' TV programme, screened on 27 March 2000 at 9 a.m. on Channel Nine, Melbourne.

17. Copland, *op. cit.*, pp 246-247.

18. Casey, R.G. *An Australian in India*, Hollis & Carter, London, 1947, p 56.

19. Hudson, W.J., *Casey*, Oxford University Press, Melbourne, 1986, p 167.

20. Chopra, V.D., 'Indo-Pak Relations: A Historical Perspective', Paper presented at a seminar - Studies in Indo-Pak Relations, April 1984, India Centre for Regional Affairs, New Delhi, 1984, p 259.

21. Subramaniam, V., 'Unity and Diversity in India: The Strength of the Indian Union', *TRT*, No. 248, October 1972, p 510.

22. Casey, R.G., *An Australian in India*, Hollis & Carter, London, 1947, p 62.

23. Heesterman, J.C., *The Inner Conflict of Tradition: Essays in Indian Ritual Kingship and Society*, University of Chicago Press, Chicago, 1985, pp 10-25. Also see, Mysore Hiriyanna, *Essentials of Indian Philosophy*, George Allen & Unwin, London, 1985.

24. *Ibid.*, pp 10-25. For an interesting account of the dichotomy between the West's materialistic priorities for the individual and Hinduism's selflessness, see Percival Spear, *India, Pakistan and the West*, 4th Edition, Oxford University Press, London, 1967. Also see, Shashi Tharoor, *India: From Midnight to Millennium*, Arcade Publishing, New York, 1997.

25. Lipton, Michael and Firn, John, *The Erosion of a Relationship*, Oxford University Press, London, 1975, p 6.

26. Brecher, Michael, *India and World Politics*, Oxford University Press, London, 1968, pp 71-72.

27. Subrata K. Mitra, captures the essence of the Kashmir question in 'Nehru's Policy Towards Kashmir: Bringing Politics Back in Again', *The Journal of Commonwealth and Comparative Politics*, Vol. 35, No. 2, July 1997, p 55, when he says 'the puzzle of Kashmir politics ... has deep roots in the partition of the sub-continent and the policies of Nehru and his successors.' In India, Kashmir was more recently declared as belonging to India, removing it 'from India's domestic political agenda.' In Pakistan, Mitra continues, where 'Kashmir was never to become an issue of domestic political contention ...' it was 'projected as history's (and Pakistan's) unfinished business.' He concludes that the two countries 'could never come to an agreement on basic parameters of how to talk about ... Kashmir as a part of their normal bilateral relations.'

28. Bandyopadhyaya, J., *The Making of India's Foreign Policy*, Allied Publishers, Delhi, 1980, pp 113-114. For references to Mountbatten's conversation with Jinnah during which he was advised by Mountbatten that West and East Pakistan, separated by distance (900 miles), linguistic and racial differences was not a sustainable proposition and unlikely to last more than a generation, see Dennis Tuohy, Interview with Lord Mountbatten, Nehru Memorial Library, New Delhi, Manuscripts Section, Accession No. 656.

29. Sareen, Rajendra, 'South Asia: Indo-Pak Relations-a Case Study', *South Asia: The Changing Environment*, C. Chanana (ed.) MERB Bookshelf, New Delhi, 1979. pp 103-109.

30. AA, Record of conversation with T.T. Krishnamachari from J. Plimsoll, dated 20 June 1963 to DEA, Series A1838/2, Item 169/10/1, part 6.

31. *Sunday Tribune*, Simla, 21 December 1947, Vol. LXVII, No. 309. 'the raiders consisted of tribesmen and men from West Punjab (estimated at over 10,000 men in the same report), some of whom described themselves as deserters from Pakistan Army and others from soldiers.' Also see, NAI, 'Pakistan Border Raids', File No. PIII/52/19350/1.

32. AA, Memorandum 27 March 1950, to the Secretary entitled 'Kashmir-Australian Mediator', (writer unknown), Series A1838/283, Item 169/11/148/6. The Australian Government was also approached later by the UN Secretary General for provision of transport services for the UN 'Military Observers group in India and Pakistan', see letter 29 December 1953, from Australian Mission UN, to DEA, AA, Series A1838/283, Item 169/11/148/12, Pt 2.

33. Wolpert, Stanley, *Nehru: A Tryst with Destiny*, Oxford University Press, New York, 1996, p 460.

34. For a precis of Justice Dixon's report to the Security Council and several memoranda from Australian diplomats in New Delhi and Pakistan to DEA, on the Pakistan-India intransigence on Kashmir, see AA, Series A1838/283, Item 169/11/148/6.

35. AA, Despatch 23 December 1954, from W.R. Crocker, Australian High Commissioner, New Delhi, to R.G. Casey, Series A 4534/1, Item 44/6/2. Talleyrand (1754-1838) was a French politician and diplomat.

36. AA, Document entitled 'Kashmir: Dr. Graham's Negotiations', (writer unknown), prepared for Prime Minister's brief, May 1952, Series A1838/283, Item 169/11/148/12, part 2, p 2.

37. *India's Foreign Policy, Selected Speeches Sept. 1946-April 1961*, Ministry of Information and Broadcasting, Government of India, New Delhi, 1961, p 488.

38. AA, Document entitled 'Kashmir: Dr. Graham's Negotiations', (writer unknown), prepared for Prime Minister's brief, May 1952, Series A1838/283, Item 169/11/148/12, part 2, p 3.

39. *Ibid.*

40. *Ibid.*

41. AA, Cablegram 27 December 1952, from Australian High Commissioner, New Delhi to DEA, Series A1838/2, Item 169/11/148/10, Part 1.

42. AA, Memo 26 May 1950, from the Australian High Commission, Karachchi, to DEA, Series A1838/283, Item 169/11/148/6

43. *Selected Works of Jawaharlal Nehru*, 1 August-25 Oct. 1950, Second Series, Vol. 15, Part I, S. Gopal, (ed.) J. Nehru Memorial Fund, New Delhi, 1993, p 228.

44. Mitra, Subrata K., 'Nehru's Policy Towards Kashmir: Bringing Politics Back in Again', *The Journal of Commonwealth and Comparative Politics*, Vol. 35, No. 2, July 1997, p 58.

45. See letter of 26 October 1947, from Maharajah Sir Hari Singh to Lord Mountbatten in C.B. Birdwood, *Two Nations and Kashmir* Robert Hale, London, 1956, Appendix 5, pp 213-214 and reply of 27 October 1947, from Lord Mountbatten to Maharajah Hari Singh, *ibid.* p 214. India's case on Kashmir was argued by Krishna Menon before the Security Council in 1957. See J.S. Bain, *India's International Disputes: a Legal Study*, Asia Publishing House, Bombay, 1962, p 209.

46. Nehru stated that the Government of India, ' had always proceeded on the basis that Kashmiris must decide their own future' see 'India Ready for Non-aggression Pact with Pakistan', *National Herald*, Vol. X, No. 291, Lucknow: Sunday 4 November, 1951.

47. 'India: Retreat from the West', *TRT*, No. 177, December 1974, p 71.

48. 'India and Her Neighbours: Hostility on Right and Left', *TRT*, No. 184, September 1956, p 337. For UN Security Council Resolutions on Kashmir, correspondence between India and Pakistan and Prime Ministerial Statements, numerous Declarations and Agreements etc., on the Kashmir question, see A. Appadorai, *Select Documents on India's Foreign Policy and Relations, 1947-1972*, Vol. 1, Oxford University Press, Delhi, 1982.

49. AA, Savingram, 20 March 1954, from J. Plimsoll, to DEA, Series A1838/2, Item 169/11/148, part 15. For further examples of criticism of India also see AA, Despatch 30 May 1951, from the Australian High Commissioner, New Delhi to DEA, Series A1838/2, Item 169/11/148/10, Part 1.

50. *Ibid.*

51. Interviews with V.K. Jain, Director, Library & Information, MEA, 10 October 1997, at MEA Offices, New Delhi.

52. *The Hindustan Times*, New Delhi, 10 March 1951, p 5.

53. Hudson, W.J. *Casey*, Oxford University Press, Melbourne, 1986, p 35. Casey, writing to Anthony Bolger, on 27 July 1970, about his days in Bengal, said, 'I have had many opportunities in life - but I think the time in Bengal ... was probably the most interesting and useful,' in W.J. Hudson, *Casey*, Oxford University Press, Melbourne, 1986, p 179.

54. Casey, R.G., *An Australian in India*, Hollis & Carter, London, 1947, p 58.

55. AA, Text of Menzies' Broadcast in a Cablegram 20 December 1950, from the Australian High Commission, New Delhi to DEA, Series A1838/2, Item 169/10/11/3 part 1.

56. AA, Press Report from *The Sydney Morning Herald*, 28 December 1950. Series A1838/2, Item 169/10/11/3 Part 1.

57. 'Menzies view on Kashmir Issue', *The Hindustan Times*, New Delhi, 10 March 1951, p 5.

58. *Selected Works of Jawaharlal Nehru*, Second Series, Vol. 16, Part II, S Gopal, (ed.), J. Nehru Memorial Fund, New Delhi, 1994, p 366.

59. AA, Document entitled 'Kashmir, Dr Graham's Negotiations', (writer unknown), prepared for Prime Ministers brief, May 1952, Series A1838/283, Item 169/11/148/12, Part 2, pp 2-3.

60. *Ibid.*, p 3. Sheik Abdullah too, an important player in the triangular imbroglio, was dismissive of Commonwealth involvement an action he described as 'imperial control by the back door...'. See C.B. Birdwood, *Two Nations and Kashmir*, Robert Hale, London, 1956, p 135.

61. *India's Foreign Policy, Selected Speeches September 1946-April 1961*, Ministry of Information and Broadcasting, Government of India, New Delhi, 1961. p 494.

62. *Ibid*. Reply from Khan to Nehru, dated 27 November 1950. Nehru wrote to S. Radhakrishnan, in May 1950, about his concerns on Kashmir a day before the arrival of Owen Dixon: 'Liaquat Ali Khan's speeches in America have not been good. There has been plenty of insidious propaganda in them and he has not, if I might say so, played the game...' see *Selected Works of Jawaharlal Nehru*, Second Series, Vol. 14, Part II, S. Gopal, (ed.) Jawaharlal Nehru Memorial Fund, 1993, p 439. Also see, 'Nehru-Liaquat Ali Correspondence', NAI, File No. PIII/52/55669/2.

63. AA, Paper entitled 'The Kashmir Situation', (Writer unknown) dated 25 July 1951. Series A1838/2, Item 169/11/148/10, Pt. 1.

64. Mitra, Subrata K., 'Nehru's Policy Towards Kashmir: Bringing Politics Back In Again', *The Journal of Commonwealth Studies*, Vol. 35, No. 2, July 1997, p 62.

65. Neeraj, *Nehru and Democracy in India*, Metropolitan Book Company, Delhi, 1972, p 158.

66. 'India Ready for Non-Aggression Pact with Pakistan', *The National Herald*, Lucknow, , Vol. X, No. 291, 4 November, 1951.

67. *India's Foreign Policy: Selected Speeches September 1946-April 1961*, Ministry of Information & Broadcasting, Government of India, New Delhi, 1961, p 494. Also see, Chanchal Sarkar, 'Background to the Indo-Pak Dispute', *The Times*, Ceylon, 12 September, 1958, p 6.

68. *Ibid*.

69. Lok Sabha Debates, 7 May 1963, Col. 14195.

70. NLA, Canberra, Letter from R. Casey to R.G. Menzies dated 22 June 1959. MS 4936, Series 8, Box 329.

71. Camilleri, J. A., *Australian-American Relations: The Web of Dependence*, Macmillan, South Melbourne, 1980, p 1.

72. CPD, Vol. 14 , 4 April 1957, p 572. Liberal MHR, Anderson condemning the opposition for its criticism of SEATO, said, "Seato was originally formed for the defence of Australia.' See CPD, (H of R), Vol. 19, 11 May 1958, p 1378.

73. *Ibid.*, p 573. An year later, Casey told Parliament that he would, 'make available to the Asian members of SEATO a further Pounds Sterling 1,000,000 for purposes generally related to SEATO defence.' CPD, Vol. 18, 15 April 1958, p 868.

74. *India's Foreign Policy: Selected Speeches September 1946-April 1961*, Ministry of Information and Broadcasting, Government of India, New Delhi, 1961, pp 487-488. Also see, Sardar Swaran Singh's (Minister for External Affairs) speech to Rajya Sabha, on 9 August 1966 on the resumption of US military supplies to Pakistan in MEA, *Foreign Affairs Record*, Vol. XII, August 1966, No. 8, Government of India, New Delhi, pp 213-214.

75. AA, Cablegram from Australian High Commission, New Delhi, to DEA, dated 15 November. 1953, Series A45341/1, Item 44/6/2. Nehru wrote to Vijayalakshmi Pandit at the UN that his attendance at a meeting in the US to discuss the Korean War would be pointless because ' I shall merely get entangled in interminable arguments. I can hardly function in the United States in any other capacity.' See *Selected Works of Jawaharlal Nehru*, Second Series, Vol. 15, Part I, S. Gopal (ed.) J. Nehru Memorial Fund, New Delhi, 1993, pp 388-389.

76. Pakistan and the USA first signed a Mutual Defence Assistance Agreement in May, 1954, with Pakistan becoming a member of SEATO in the same year. Pakistan also joined the Baghdad Pact in 1955, resumed CENTO cooperation with the US in 1959. Also see, NAI, Press cuttings on Pakistan-US Military Pact, File No. 16/2-XPP/53(Part I & II) (S).

77. Budania, Rajpal, 'The United States and South Asia', *Indian Journal of Asian Affairs*, Vol. 8-9, No. 1-2, 1995-1996, p 56. For Mohammed Ayub Khan's Analysis of the Pakistan-American linkage in relation to India and Kashmir, see, 'The Pakistan-American Alliance: Stresses and Strains', *Foreign Affairs*, Vol. 24, 1964, pp 195-209.

78. 'USA and Kashmir', Editorial, *The Leader*, India, 19 May 1953, p 4.

79. Wolpert, Stanley, *Nehru: A Tryst with Destiny*, Oxford University Press, 1996, New York, p 466. For Nehru's assertion that US military aid to Pakistan increases its intransigence, see Lok Sabha Debates, 17 March 1959, Cols. 6687-6688.

80. *Ibid.*

81. Lok Sabha Debates, June 28 1971, Col. 108, Motion re: Statement by the Minister for External Affairs on shipment of American arms to Pakistan.

82. *Ibid*. Col. 110.

83. *Ibid.*

84. Lok Sabha Debates, Vol. II, Part II, 1954, 6-25 March, Col. 2823.

85. Lok Sabha Debates, Fifth Series, Vol. VII, July 31- August 12, 1971, Col. 241.

86. Lok Sabha Debates, 15 March 1973, Cols. 167-168. Also See, NAI, US anti-India pamphlet on Kashmir, File No. PIII/52/99147/2.

87. Brecher, Michael, *India and World Politics*, Oxford University Press, London, 1968, p 209.

88. *India's Foreign Policy, Selected Speeches September 1946-April 1961*, Ministry of Information and Broadcasting, Government of India, New Delhi, 1961, p 484.

89. Nautiyal, Anupurna 'India, Pakistan and the United States in the Post-Cold War Era', *Asian Studies*, Vol. XV, No. 1, January-June 1997, p 3.

90. *Ibid.*, p 4. Also see, C.B. Birdwood, *Two Nations and Kashmir*, Robert Hale, London, 1956, pp 134-156.

91. Camilleri, J. A, *Australian American Relations: the Web of Dependence*, Macmillan, South Melbourne, 1980, p 11.

92. AA, Despatch 2/64, 2 June 1964, from Plimsoll to DEA, Series A1838/272, Item 169/1/3, p 4.

93. Public Records Office, London, Note by the Prime Minister and Minister of Defence to Permanent Secretary, Ministry of Defence, dated 20 February 1952, c (52) 50, Copy No. 74.

94. Public Records Office, London, Record of UK Cabinet Meeting dated 8 December 1952, cc(52), Item 3, p 142.

95. AA, Record of conversation between the Secretary of State and the Indian High Commissioner on 10 March 1954, Series A1838/278, Item 169/7/1, part 3.

96. Public Records Office, London, Outward telegram No. 2731, from Commonwealth Relations Office, to UK High Commission in India dated 9 December 1955.

97. Millar, T.B., *Australia's Foreign Policy*, Angus & Robertson, Sydney, 1968, p 105.

98. SCOR (Security Council Official Records) yr. 12, Mtg. 765, 24 January 1957, p 4, in S.C. Gangul, *India and the Commonwealth*, Shiva Lal Agarwala, India, 1970, p 37.

99. Lok Sabha Debates (1957) Vol. I, (Part II), p 670, in S.C. Gangul, *India and the Commonwealth*, Shiva Lal Agarwala, India, 1970, p 38.

100. *The Hindu*, 20 November 1957, in S.C. Gangul, *India and the Commonwealth*, Shiva Lal Agarwala, 1970, India, p 37.

101. Crocker speaks of a conversation with Vijayalakshmi Pandit during which she said that Churchill had told her, 'the main reason for the tragic misunderstandings between the Indian people and the British in the past had been due to the bad manners of too many of the British in India.' Whether the comment meant both Hindu and Muslim Indians were affected by the British truculence is not clear. See AA, Record of conversation between W.R. Crocker and Mrs Pandit, 24 April 1954, Series A1838/2, Item 169/10/10/4.

102. 'Mr Wilson's Partisan Neutrality', *Indian and Foreign Review*, Vol. 3, No. 7, 15 January 1966, pp 21-23, in R.G. Neale, 'Australia's Changing Relations with India', *India, Japan, Australia, Partners in Asia?* J.D.B. Miller (ed.), ANU, Canberra, 1968, p 8.

103. AA, Despatch No. 2/64, 2 June 1964, from J. Plimsoll to Paul Hasluck, Canberra, Series A1838/272, Item 169/1/3, Part. 3, p 6.

104. NLA, Letter dated 24 April 1956 from P.R. Heydon to J. Plimsoll, MS 3155, Box 15.

105. CPD, (H of R), Vol. 14, 2 April 1957, p 432.

106. CPD, (H of R), Vol. 9, 14 March 1956, pp 804-805. For a range of documents on Kashmir in the post-Nehru period including letters exchanged between Prime Minister Shastri and the Secretary General of the UN, see MEA, Foreign Affairs Record, vol. XI, September 1965, No. 9, Government of India, New Delhi, pp 185-254.

107. A good example of economic aid on a massive scale, was that provided by the Marshall Plan for Europe's recovery after the war.

108. Spender, Percy, *Exercises in Diplomacy: The ANZUS Treaty and the Colombo Plan*, Sydney University Press, Sydney, 1969, p 195.

109. *Ibid*.

110. Renouf, Allan, *The Champagne Trail: Experiences of a Diplomat*, Sun Books, Melbourne, 1980, p 44.

111. AA, Statement by R.G. Casey, at a press conference, New Delhi, 26 October 1951, Series A1838/278, Item 169/10/1, Part 1. Also see, 'Australia and the Colombo Plan', *TRT*, No. 190, March 1958, pp 203-204.

112. *The Sun*, Sydney, 3 January 1950, in Percy Spender, *Exercises in Diplomacy: The ANZUS Treaty and the Colombo Plan*, Sydney University Press, Sydney, 1969, p 196. For Spender's Colombo Plan speech, see Gordon Greenwood *Approaches to Asia: Australian Post-War Policies and attitudes*, McGraw-Hill, Sydney, 1974, p 41.

113. In 1953-54, Australia gave A$ 0.80 cents per capita, New Zealand A$ 1.40, Canada A$ 1.80 and the USA A$ 1.90. See T.B. Millar (ed.), *Australian Foreign Minister: The Diaries of R.G. Casey*, Collins, London, 1972, p 173.

114. *Sydney Morning Herald*, 22 January, 1950, p 2, in David Lowe, 'The Colombo Plan', *Australia and the End of Empires*, David Lowe (ed.) Deakin University Press, Victoria, 1997 p 108.

115. Public Records Office, London, Minutes of 4th Meeting of Prime Ministers Conference, London, 12 October 1948, PMD File 57/5826, CRS A462, AA, p 57.

116. See, AA, Series CP 554/1/1, Item 2/174/B/1, for a statement of goods requested by India under the Colombo Plan Economic Development Programme.

117. *The Sydney Morning Herald*, 21 March 1952.

118. Note to Secretary General, Ministry of External Affairs, dated 6 May 1950, File No. 330-CJK/50, *Selected Works of Jawaharlal Nehru*, Second Series, Vol. 14, Part II, S. Gopal (ed.) J. Nehru Memorial Fund, New Delhi, 1993, p 438.

119. CPD, (H of R), Vol. 6, 28 April, 1955, p 306. Also see, Stephen Fitzgerald, *Is Australia an Asian Country?*, Allen & Unwin, NSW, 1997, p 2, for his comments on Australia's lack of '... understanding of the elemental forces at work within Asian societies.'

120. CPD, (H of R), 28 April, 1955, Vol. 6, AGPS, Canberra, p 306. The late Professor MacMahon Ball, once argued that Australia's security and prosperity depended on working friendships with Asia and not on a Western military presence to keep Asia away. Ball's view was that Australia knew little about how Asians felt about Asia and a lot about how America and Britain felt about Asia, seen in the incongruity of Australia's expenditure of $ 1100 million in 1967/68 on defence from Asia and a mere $ 50 million on aid to Asia. See, W.M. Ball, 'Australia's role in Asia' - 18th Roy Milne Memorial Lecture, 1 November 1967, at the Australian Institute of International Affairs, Melbourne.

121. T.B. Millar (ed.) *Australian Foreign Minister: The Diaries of R.G. Casey 1951-1960* Collins, London, 1972, p 16.

122. Palfreeman, A.C., *Administration of the White Australia Policy*, Melbourne University Press, Victoria, 1967, p 129.

123. CPD, (H of R), Vol. 24, 2 September 1959, p 852.

124. *Ibid.*

125. AA, Crocker to Casey, Despatch 1/54, 5 January 1954, A4231/1, New Delhi, 1954, in Shawn Brawley *The White Peril*, University of NSW Press, Sydney, 1995. p 256.

126. Fitzgerald, Stephen, *Is Australia An Asian Country?* Allen & Unwin, NSW, 1997, p 3.

127. See CPD (H of R), Vol. 19, 1 May 1958, p 1377. Labor's Clyde Cameron in his speech to Parliament which followed Anderson's reveals India as being the example to which Anderson alluded. *ibid.* p 1381.

128. Nayar, Baldev Raj, 'India as a Limited Challenge', T.V. Paul and John A. Hall, (Eds.), *International Order and the Future of World Politics*, Cambridge University Press, Cambridge, 1999, p 215.

129. Nehru, Jawaharlal, *Discovery of India*, The John Day Company, New York, 1946, pp 40-41.

130. Greene, Fred, *Dynamics of International Relations*, Holt, Rinehart & Winston, New York, 1964, p 494.

131. *Jawaharlal Nehru's Speeches*, September 1946-May 1949, Vol. I, Ministry of Information & Broadcasting, Government of India, New Delhi, 1949, p 220.

132. Lal, Sham (ed.) *The Times of India Directory and Year Book 1978*, The Times of India Press, Bombay, 1978, p 291, . Also see, Colombo Plan - Australian Contribution to India to 31 December 1954, AA, CP Series 554/1, Item 2/174/B/1.

133. Millar, T.B. (ed.), *Australian Foreign Minister: The Diaries of R.G. Casey*, 1951-1960, Collins, London, 1972, p 173.

134. Hudson, W.J. *Casey*, Oxford University Press, Melbourne, 1986, p 287.

135. Nehru Memorial Library, New Delhi, Manuscripts Section, Diary of J. Nehru, Commonwealth Prime Ministers Conference, May 1960, Accession No. 1423, p 33.

136. *Ibid.*

137. CPD, (H of R), Vol. 14, 2 April 1957, p 433.

138. *Ibid.* p 417.

139. AA, Statement 26 October 1951, by R.G. Casey, at a press conference, Constitution House, New Delhi, Series A1838/278, Item 169/10/1, Part 1, p 2.

140. AA, Memorandum 25 November 1955, from W.K. Flanagan, Australian High Commission, New Delhi to DEA, dated 25 November 1955, Series A1838/283, Item 169/11/52, Part 3. For an assessment of Soviet aid to developing countries as a part of its policy see A. Krassowski, Book Review, (Marshall I. Goldman, *Soviet Foreign Aid*, Praeger, 1967), *International Affairs, Quarterly Review*, Vol. 44, No. 1, January 1968, pp 107-108.

141. *Ibid.*

142. *Ibid.*

143. AA, Savingram, 2 December 1955, from Australian High Commission, Wellington to DEA, Series A2838/283, Item 169/11/52, Part 3.

144. AA, Press Report from *The Manchester Guardian*, 3 December 1955, Series A1838/283, Item 169/11/52, Part 3.

145. AA, Memorandum 12 December 1955, from J. Oldham to DEA, Series A1838/283, Item 169/11/52, Part 3.

146. Wolpert, Stanley, *Nehru: A Tryst with Destiny*, Oxford University Press, New York, 1996, p 460.

147. Brecher, Michael, *India and World Politics*, Oxford University Press, London, 1968, p 195.

148. Nehru Memorial Library, New Delhi, Manuscript Section, Hugh Tinker Book Review (Stanley Wolpert *Jinnah of Pakistan*, Oxford University Press, New York, 1984, and S. Gopal, *Jawaharlal Nehru: A Biography*, Vol. 3, Jonathan Cape, London, 1984) Accession No. 952, pp 248-249.

149. Cohen, Eliot A., 'Distant Battle: Modern War in the Third World', *International Security*, 10, 4, 1988, p 146, in R.H. Bruce, 'A Framework of Expectations for the Impact of India's Growing Military Capabilities on Australia', (paper presented at a Seminar, 14-16 January 1991), *Prospects for Peace: Changes in the Indian Ocean Region*, Robert H. Bruce (ed.), Indian Ocean Centre for Peace Studies, Perth, 1992, p 199.

150. Neale, R.G., 'Australia's Changing Relations with India', *India, Japan, Australia, Partners in Asia?* J.D.B. Miller (ed.), ANU, Canberra, 1968, p 78.

151. Casey R.G., *An Australian in India*, Hollis & Carter, London, 1947, p 103.

152. Malik, Ifthikar H., 'The Continuing Conflict in Kashmir: Regional Detente in Jeopardy', Conflict Studies No. 259, Published by the Research Institute for the Study of Conflict and Terrorism, (risct), March 1993, p 18.

153. Wolpert, Stanley, *India*, Prentice Hall, New Jersey, 1965, p 27.

154. Khilnari, N.M., *Socio Political Dimensions of Modern India*, MD Publications, New Delhi, 1993, p 10.

155. Jaisingh, Hari *India and the Non Aligned World: Search for a New Order*, Vikas Publishing, New Delhi, 1983, pp 85-87.

156. *The Age*, Melbourne, 21 May 1968, Editorial.

**7**

# The Whitlam-Indira Gandhi Demarche, 1972-1975: A New Beginning

The arrival of the Whitlam Government in 1972 on the Australian political scene drew more interest in post-independent India than any previous government in Canberra. The interest was mutual. While it is true to say that the international climate had changed since the Menzies era, so had the leadership of the two countries. In Mrs Gandhi and Whitlam the two countries had leaders who were undoubtedly strong-minded and capable of making policy decisions independent of big power influnces.

Whitlam's interest took him to India early in his first year of office for talks with Mrs Gandhi, who was clearly impressed by the honour accorded to India by the Whitlam visit, unprecedented for its timing, the first Australian Prime Minister to do so in his first year in office; it was also the first visit in fourteen years. Whitlam's broader ideology and departure from the protectionist policies of the past were able to transcend India's non-alignment policy and its less than enthusiastic response to the West's Cold War strategies which, by association, extended to Australia under Menzies and his successors. With his regional focus, Whitlam saw India as important to his vision of Australia's future role as an equal partner in Asia. This comment by author Ross Garnaut is an appropriate beginning for this chapter which examines the Whitlam impact on the bilateral relationship:

> For the first seven decades of the Federation a fearful, defensive Australia built walls to protect itself against the challenge of the outside world and found that it had protected itself against the recognition and utilisation of opportunity.[1]

The mutual recognition and affinity that emerged between India and Australia in the Indira Gandhi-Whitlam period in contrast to what existed before is the central theme. Also important to understanding the Whitlam impact on the India-Australia relationship, and considered here for the first time, is the identification of the closeness of views on a range of issues held between Whitlam (1953 and 1975) and Nehru (1946-1964).[2] Together it became the harbinger of a new relationship. But, first, some broad insights into the political circumstances that prevailed in Australia and India in the post-Menzies pre-Whitlam period of the relationship are seen as essential background to the two themes of this Chapter. Of equal importance is recognition that Cold War tensions had lessened by the 1970s and new friendships and alignments were being developed.

## Australia 1966-1972: Holt, Gorton, McMahon

From the Indian perspective, the departure of Menzies from Australian politics in 1966, and the ascendancy of Indira Gandhi to the Prime Ministership of India in the same year, did nothing to alter the mutual indifference that had characterised the bilateral relationship during the previous seventeen years of conservative rule in Australia. Menzies' chosen heir was Harold Holt (1966-1967) whose death in tragic circumstances found John Gorton elevated to the position of Prime Minister. Faced with questions of Australia's future defence in an environment of British-US military contraction, with the aim of eventual withdrawal of military forces in Asia[3] Gorton had little interest in trying to breathe new life into the post-Menzies bilateral relationship with India. With the Liberal-Country Party's (as in coalition) majority in Parliament reduced from forty to seven seats under his leadership at the 1969 General Election, the position of Prime Minister passed on to William McMahon in 1971.

Australia's involvement in Vietnam, a Menzies' legacy,[4] was another issue on which the Holt, Gorton and McMahon Governments faced criticism from Asian countries and India was no exception. The tone and content, particularly in relation to Vietnam, of the speeches of Prime Minister Holt and India's Minister for External Affairs Sardar Swaran Singh, at the Commonwealth Heads of Government Meeting in September, 1966 are good illustrations of how deeply divided the two countries were on policy.[5] At home, the Labor Leader of the Opposition in 1967, Arthur Calwell, stated that Australia's actions in Vietnam were 'sowing a harvest of hatred in Asia '[6], while

Dr J.F. Cairns (MHR) argued that Australia by ' "taking sides in history" ... would incur the severe disapproval of the people of Asia for generations to come.'[7] Whitlam himself in 1968 argued that the lessons to be learned from Vietnam (a war he later described as 'the war of the great lie')[8] was 'the futility of reliance on military means alone to resolve or even to approach the problems of our region.'[9] Blaming the 'easy acceptance of the idea that the mightiest military nation in the world must automatically prevail against so backward and weak a power as North Vietnam, ...' Whitlam criticised Australia for 'clinging pathetically to the coat tails of a military machine, ' with all its consequent errors. He went on to tell Parliament that, 'our real task, and America's real task, is, therefore, to see, not just that she will never be involved in another Vietnam, but that there will not again be a Vietnam anywhere in Asia.'[10] As with many of the other views Whitlam had expressed in the 1950s and 1960s, this endeared him to the policy makers in New Delhi. Mrs Gandhi, for example, was critical of the military approach to resolution of the Vietnam conflict. Condemning the bombing of Vietnam, she urged withdrawal of all outside forces 'to insulate that unhappy country from every foreign interference so that the people of Vietnam determine their own future ...'[11] . Asked about Australia's policy on Vietnam, she told reporters in Sydney that India's position was 'that war would not provide a solution.'[12] Questioned by Kuldip Nayer, Editor, *The Statesman*, about America's 'Domino theory' which envisaged that should Vietnam fall, Laos, Cambodia and the rest of South East Asia would follow, she stated:

> I think the Americans themselves do not believe in the Domino theory anymore. We have never believed in foreign presence anywhere because we feel that this is an invitation to tension ... it produces a reaction.[13]

Clearly, the governments of Holt, Gorton and McMahon that followed Menzies continued with Australia's traditional foreign policy thrust: support for those countries of the region which were anti-Communist; alignment with US strategic objectives in Asia including slavish reliance on the logic of its actions in Vietnam; and, showing no more genuine interest in the demands of poorer nations of Asia and Africa for greater political, economic and racial equity in international affairs than was the case under Menzies. As Stargardt observes, 'Australian conservatives tended to look on Asia as an arena for action, rather than on Asians as actors.'[14] More evidence of this is seen in the Minister for External Affairs, Paul Hasluck's statement to a Conference of South East Asian and South West Pacific Nations and Organisations in Canberra in April 1967 that 'a withdrawal from Asia ... is isolation in its most foolish form.'[15] On Vietnam, Hasluck's statement below, contrasting sharply with Whitlam's, was a good example of why India with its constant appeal to those outside the region to not involve themselves in Asia, had difficulty in engaging any more constructively with the post-Menzies Australia:

> Australia is part of this struggle because we cannot allow it to be lost by default. ... We are in it by our own choice and our own decision because the result is a matter of crucial importance to us, to all the people of Australia.[16]

Contrary to Hasluck's view of the dire consequences of failure in Vietnam, academics Robert Hunter (who also worked in the White House on the President's staff), and Phillip Windsor in a critical analysis of US-Vietnam policy and its implications for Asia, observed in 1968 that, 'the arguments in favour of US involvement in Vietnam are based upon hypotheses which, although they *may* be true, have little basis in experience of Asian conflicts and do not permit calculations that can be made with a reasonable degree of probability.'[17] (emphasis in original)

While India was not impressed by Australia's support of US policy in Vietnam (and in Korea in the early 1950s), a part of its forward defence philosophy,[18] it was Australia's discriminatory immigration policy that was seen as one of its worst features, the unkindest cut of all. While some easing of the 'White Australia' Policy between 1966 and 1972 did take place, it did not completely remove the colour-based nature of the discrimination. For example, preferential treatment for Europeans with assistance on passage costs to Australia and, on residential requirements for naturalisation, continued. A British subject required an year's residence to gain citizenship; for non-British persons it was five years.[19] In July 1969, just three-and-a-half years before Whitlam came into office, Australia's Minister for Immigration, Billy Snedden, stated that: 'we must have a single culture. If migration implies multiculture activities within Australian society, then it is not the type of culture Australia wants.'[20]

Relaxation of the policy beyond the concessions made beginning in 1964, with allowing the entry of part Europeans, was ruled out by Prime Minister McMahon as late as 1971 when he said that in conditions of *'over full employment* (my emphasis) then special consideration will be given to non-Europeans being integrated into Australia ...'[21]. Thus, a degree of discrimination continued till the abrogation of the policy by Whitlam along with a number of related Whitlam initiatives to remove discrimination in the treatment of non-Europeans.[22] These had a significant impact on the way Australia was perceived in India as the narrative reveals.

## India 1966-1972: Indira Gandhi

This leads neatly to Mrs Gandhi, who became Prime Minister in 1966, and her operational and psychological view of the world seen as important because it was Mrs Gandhi with whom Whitlam dealt on bilateral issues during his Prime Ministership. India too, like Australia, faced a very different world by the early 1970s. While the Cold War tensions of the 1950s and 1960s had substantially eased, and Nehru, the architect of modern India had gone, the country's foreign policy, in Narayanan's view, 'approximates more closely to the world-view of Jawaharlal Nehru and the non-aligned than to that of the protagonists of Cold War alignment.'[23] R.L. Park, in an analysis of India's external policy, makes the observation that 'one measure of Mr Nehru's lasting influence on foreign policy has been the pledge made by his successors, ... Shastri and ... Mrs Gandhi, to continue the policies he shaped.'[24] Like her father, Mrs Gandhi was determined to rid the world of colonialism. She told the Lok Sabha:

> We have been subjected to foreign domination and we, at least my generation, cannot forget the arrogance - or the humiliation - of the domination. Therefore it is natural for us to speak out when we see similar things happening to other people.[25]

In the new environment, Mrs Gandhi was no less committed to non-alignment as India's basic foreign policy position and even told Parliament that, 'all countries were becoming non-aligned today though they might not call themselves so.'[26] At the NAM summit of 1973 in Algiers, she said, 'non-alignment was born as an assertion of our will to be sovereign and not a mere object of imperial history. ... It was a principled contribution to peace. Non-alignment has not lost any of its relevance even though the rigid attributes of the Cold War have softened.'[27] James Plimsoll, who was Australia's High Commissioner to India in the mid-1960s, had this view of the policy when he wrote to Canberra about the neutralism of the post-Nehru India: 'India's policy of non-alignment acquired a new slant, born out of a desire to keep the Soviet Union from combining with China against India.'[28] Whilst this reason has also been used to explain why India did everything it possibly could to ensure the Soviet Union kept to its deliveries of arms to India during the 1962 Border War with China, non-alignment nevertheless remained an important moral premise for India under Mrs Gandhi. For instance, rejecting the view that the 1962 War had made non-alignment unsustainable, she told reporters in Sydney that 'Chinese aggression had in fact made non-alignment all the more valuable ...'[29]. Nehru too affirmed India's continuing adherence to non-alignment notwithstanding the 1962 Chinese aggression and the support India received from many Western countries including Australia: 'but that does not mean we have weakened in our desire to adhere to non-alignment policy.'[30] Krishna Menon offered a similar explanation when questioned on it by Michael Brecher referred to in Chapter Five.

However, the 1971 Bangladesh War and the Sino-American support for Pakistan led Mrs Gandhi closer to the Soviet Union resulting in questions being raised about India's claim to being non-aligned. She said, 'it was against this background of dangerous Pakistan-Sino-US collusion that I signed the Treaty of Peace, Friendship and Cooperation with the Soviet Union on August 9 1971.'[31] She has also commented that, 'detractors have made strenuous efforts to misinterpret the purpose and contents of the treaty, but the last two years have proved that these allegations and insinuations are without foundation ...'[32] . In an obvious reference to US support for Pakistan in the conflict, Mrs Gandhi referred to the US sending 'the warship *Enterprise* to support a ruthless military dictatorship and to intimidate a democracy, and the extraordinary similarity of the attitudes adopted by the United States and China.'[33] According to an editorial in *The Round Table*, in the aftermath of the India-Pakistan War over East Pakistan in 1971, the US saw rapprochement with China as a part of its wider interest, and Pakistan's geographic value to China provided Nixon with a ready link to Peking through its SEATO partner.[34] V.P. Dutt, in his critique on Sino-US policies in the Sub-Continent, argues that at the time of the East Pakistan crisis 'the United States was preoccupied with the development of detente with Peking and the contours of the Washington-Peking-Islamabad equation were already visible.'[35] It is not surprising then that Mrs Gandhi in her speech welcoming Whitlam on his visit to New Delhi in 1973, stated that, 'the relaxation of cold war postures have exposed the hollowness of military alliances but old concepts of balance of power still overshadow us.'[36]

It is important to note that on Bangladesh too the Whitlam Government's view expressed by the Minister for Foreign Affairs, Lionel Bowen, in Australia months before Whitlam's meeting with Mrs Gandhi, were more understanding than India could have expected from someone like Menzies. The Minister told Parliament:

> In looking at the new situation, we acknowledge too that the power balance has changed. Instead of two states, not so dissimilar in capacity, we now have three, of which India is largely the pre-eminent in terms of population, economic strength and military capability. This is not necessarily a disrupting factor. It may in fact lead to a more settled situation; but it is an important change.[37]

As a part of this background leading up to the Gandhi-Whitlam 1972-1975 period of the bilateral relationship, it is also useful to see how Mrs Gandhi saw the two super powers in her foreign policy sweep, in contrast to the Holt-Gorton-McMahon view. On her relations with the Soviet Union she said:

> The Soviet Union shares the Indian view on the maintenance of peace and the elimination of racialism and colonialism. On these issues it has supported the Afro-Asian stand in the United Nations and elsewhere. When matters vitally concerning our national security and integrity, such as Goa, Kashmir and more lately Bangladesh, became subjects of international controversy, the Soviet assessment of the merits of the case coincided largely with our own.[38]

In explaining Indo-US relations, she referred to the divisions generated by bloc politics and India's resolve to remain independent of it:

> A newly freed people, jealous of their independence, could not resign themselves to this position, nor could we isolate ourselves from what was happening around us. Successive US administrations have

ignored the fact that India must see her problems and her relationships in a different perspective. ... India was regarded with disapproval and resentment because of her independent policy. ... Despite fluctuations of mood, our relationship as a whole has been uneasy over a long period.[39]

The supply of arms to Pakistan and its membership of SEATO were also issues that Mrs Gandhi saw as impediments to better relations with the US,[40] Australia's principal ally. But more than her father, Nehru, Mrs Gandhi was a realist, aware not only of where the power lay in relation to regional security but also the dynamics of changing alignments. She once told the press that India wished to be friendly with all, 'but let us not be too exercised where we stand with Russia, China and America. What is important is that we stand for ourselves.'[41]

## The Maiden Indian Prime Ministerial Visit

Mrs Gandhi visited Australia in May 1968 (the first by an Indian Prime Minister) in a bid to narrow the wide gulf that separated the interests of the two democracies under the previous Nehru-Menzies governments. *The Age* Newspaper in an editorial comment on the visit stated:

Australia's adoption of an alliance strategy and India's pursuit of the permissive principles of non-alignment have pointed them along separate paths in many of the major international crises of the post-war years.'[42]

Referring to a 'new imperial' China and Britain's 'east of Suez' withdrawal policy - which the editorial argued were reasons for closer convergence between the two countries - it added that Mrs Gandhi's visit symbolised 'the growing identity of interest between her country and ours.'[43] In India, Dilip Mukherjee reporting the visit in *The Statesman*, observed that the talks between Mrs Gandhi and Prime Minister Gorton were 'seen as a first step towards a common approach to problems of troubled South East Asia ...' particularly in the circumstances of Britain's planned withdrawal; he said Mrs Gandhi saw the talks as 'the beginning of a new relationship between the two countries.'[44] Gorton's response at a meeting with the visiting Indian reporters was that 'it had been useful to both to get to know and understand the thinking underlying their respective attitudes to problems of mutual concern.'[45] Whitlam, then Leader of the

Opposition, had a separate meeting with Mrs Gandhi and also 'urged greater Australian help both by way of aid for Indian agricultural programmes and through greater access to Australian markets for India's manufacturers.'[46]

In spite of Australian media expectations at the time that 'Mrs Gandhi's visit will provoke a re-examination of Australia's own role in Asia and, in particular, our policy towards India itself ...'[47], there was little to mark the bilateral relationship during the Gorton-McMahon period by way of an improvement on the indifference that characterised it in the Menzies years.

## The Whitlam Impact

Arriving in a new environment, the Whitlam Government took a positive view of the impact of the new US policy of withdrawal from Asia, seeing it as reducing international bipolar rivalry and helping regional stability. But, of course, there were other significant international changes that had altered the political environment. Whitlam himself acknowledged this when he told Parliament, 'the change in the Australian Government came at a time of very great changes in international relations, particularly affecting our region.'[48] Camilleri has stated that these changes 'had greatly altered Australia's domestic as well as external environment ...' observing that the Whitlam Government, when it gained office, 'was acutely aware of the need to question many of the assumptions which had for so long limited Australia's diplomatic freedom of action.'[49] R.A Woolcott, Deputy Secretary Department of Foreign Affairs, in an address to the Australian-Asian Association in May 1974, argued with much truth that 'all Governments must be responsive to changes in their external surroundings otherwise their policies become outmoded and anachronistic.'[50] Continuing the theme of external change and the need to react appropriately, Woolcott reasoned:

> By 1972 we needed a new China policy, a different and more mature relationship with the United States, a new approach to our historic links with the United Kingdom, a fresh and more genuine approach to the international issues of race and continuing colonialism and a new emphasis on our involvement with the neighbouring South East Asian region.[51]

It must be remembered, however, that Whitlam's interest in Asia was consistently in evidence from the time he entered Parliament in

1953, exemplified further with his announcement within months of gaining office that 'a second Asia Division would be established within the Department of foreign Affairs.'[52] Not surprisingly, educated Indians were aware of this different Australian politician with many of his political views similar to India's. As far as they were concerned, -and this included Mrs Gandhi as the narrative shows - the Australian political landscape changed with the Whitlam arrival. His decisive action to remove the residual effects of the 'White Australia' Policy and determination to remove racism at the international level were some of the reasons for the change in the way India saw Australia. Any lingering resentment from the Menzies era was removed by Whitlam's actions and policy declarations.

Then, again, international interest in the Indian-Australian regional context, had also started to change by the end of the 1960s. The Cold War preoccupation of the Menzies era with Communism and the fear of China, given expression through dependence on the Western alliance, was no longer of the same significance to Australia. President Nixon's policy of easing US involvement in Asia[53] perceived in Australia as less military, and psychological support, redefined foreign policy perspectives and choices for Australia. Yet, the conservative governments of Gorton and McMahon had difficulty coming to terms with these changes, seeing them as increasing Australia's exposure to the traditional enemy, the Communists. There was Whitlam's historic visit to China in mid-1971 which was frowned upon by the Australian Government with Prime Minister McMahon accusing Whitlam of "an impertinence to the leader of the United States ... and it is not likely to be forgotten by the American administration."[54] But, then, only to find President Nixon had sent Kissinger to China on a similar diplomatic mission to prepare the way for his own visit, without even informing McMahon.[55] Australia's then Minister for External Affairs, Leslie Bury's comments on the proposed Nixon visit to meet with Chou En Lai illustrate the Liberal Coalition Government's reaction to the shift in America's attitude to China:

> The setting aside of so much knowledge and experience and the substitution of amateurs impelled by democratic political motives is in my view fraught with danger. I hate to see the far reaching interests of Australia and our friends and allies to the near north dragged by the chariot wheels of American political processes. ... It

is deplorable when foreign policy which runs to the very root of national security, is allowed to become the plaything of party politics.[56]

Bury also warned the Australia-Malaysia-Singapore Association in an address in Sydney that the US had 'given notice that Australia and other Asian nations must be more self-reliant in defence.'[57]

For the hypothesis that Whitlam's arrival had a positive impact on the India-Australia relationship, it is necessary to contrast the pre-Whitlam policies and concerns with those of the Whitlam Government's. Unlike his predecessor McMahon, Whitlam responded to the external changes through a number of foreign policy initiatives, but only some of these are of relevance and interest to this Chapter on the Whitlam impact on India relations. Among them, the decisive repudiation by Whitlam of the 'White Australia' Immigration Policy, which the Indians found offensive, ranks high. Naturally then, in the chronology of India-Australia relations, the election of the Whitlam Government in December 1972 is an important event and relative to the Menzies period, a second peak, as opposed to the preceding trough, measured in terms of mutual bilateral interest.

Coupled with Whitlam's decisive removal of the remnants of the 'White Australia' Policy, the new direction he gave to Australia's foreign policy laid a catalytic foundation for improved bilateral relations between India and Australia with real gains taking place in subsequent decades. Whitlam's departure from the established approach to Australian foreign policy caught the attention of the Indians. Addressing Parliament not long after his election to office Whitlam stated:

> The change of government provides a new opportunity for us to reassess the whole range of Australian foreign policies and attitudes. ... Our thinking is towards a more independent Australian stance in international affairs, and towards an Australia which will be less militarily oriented and not open to suggestions of racism; an Australia which will enjoy a growing standing as a distinctive, tolerant, co-operative and well regarded nation not only in the Asian and Pacific region, but in the world at large.[58]

Whitlam's independence in foreign policy is even attested to by Marshall Green, the US Ambassador to Australia, who, speaking on the changes in Australian-American relations, told an international audience in New York that Australia was 'determined to do its own thing', and that, 'they don't want to be in lock-step with American policy.'[59] This was indeed independence in policy considering the years of loyalty to American policy famously endorsed by Prime Minister Harold Holt's 'all the way with LBJ'[60] commitment to US policy in Vietnam, loyalty that India, had assumed as being central to Australia's foreign policy determination. Nehru thought Australia was 'a stooge of the United States and was convinced that we could have no opinion of our own on the great international issues, or freedom to express it.'[61] Viviani captures the momentous Whitlam impact with this observation:

> ... the years of post-war reconstruction and the Menzies era are a kind of black hole in our minds. For many of our students, and their parents history starts with the Whitlam Government, and with respect to the White Australia Policy, that Government is seen in an unquestioning way as responsible for its abolition.[62]

For the Indians, there was also Whitlam's speech to the UN General Assembly in 1974 which encapsulated his world view[63] and stood in contrast to that of Menzies' and those who followed him between 1966 and 1972. Like Nehru who started to stamp his personality on Indian and international politics twenty-five years earlier when from 1947 he adopted an independent stand free of great power dictates, Whitlam too sought to assert Australia's independence in foreign policy. Fitzgerald's description of the new and courageous Australia, has echoes of India's post-independence response to the outside world under Nehru:

> There was also the discovery which is that of the child when it suddenly finds there is something in its environment it can control, and thereby grows in personality and self-confidence. We had gone against the United States and the sky had not fallen. We went on to go against it in Vietnam and still the sky remained suspended. We could do Australian things, as we had done with China, and then with other neighbours. We could define ourselves as we wanted to and in relation to our Asian neighbours, who were our new points of reference.[64]

## Colour-Blind Immigration: The Test of Good Faith

A recurrent theme of this book has been India's deep sensitivity to racial discrimination. Although Nehru was no longer there, his abhorrence of colour-based discrimination was no less felt by Mrs.

Gandhi's Government.[65] In 1973 the Minister for External Affairs at the time, Swaran Singh, addressing the UN General Assembly in October, 'laid particular stress on the twin phenomena of colonial domination and racial bigotry in Africa, as the greatest burden on the conscience of the world.'[66] He also assured the UN of India's support for outlawing Apartheid in South Africa.[67]

A mark of Whitlam's character, and evident from the time he entered politics, was his disdain for racial discrimination. Before he became Prime Minister, in an article entitled 'Australia and Her Region', Whitlam wrote, 'the taint of racism which tarnishes our reputation through our attitudes to South Africa, New Guinea and our own Aborigines must be removed if we are to be a good neighbour in our region.'[68] During research for this study it was found that some of the public servants interviewed in India were also familiar with Whitlam's consistent stand against racism.[69]

Because of India's consistent condemnation of racial policies, the 'White Australia' Policy is of singular importance to any discussion of the bilateral relationship. It therefore warranted the specific examination carried out in Chapter Five. However, a few of Whitlam's policy actions to exemplify his government's enlightened attitude to immigration and other questions are useful in explaining why India saw him as a leader aware of Australia's geography, with its cultural and economic diversity, and not just obsessed with protecting its European history. The restrictive situation that existed on immigration under previous governments (Menzies to McMahon, 1949-1972) conveyed in Whitlam's words best illustrates the contrasting environments seen through Indian eyes:

> Until the end of 1972 residents of Asia and Africa who wished to come to Australia, even if they were British-protected persons, had to come to the nearest Australian post to be visually assessed. The resentments over the racist deportations and exclusions from White Australia in 1949 and 1964 were not expunged in our region and especially in India, the Philippines and Fiji until Grassby introduced the comprehensive, rational and humane Australian Citizenship Bill in April 1973 and I visited India in June 1973 ... My Government not only jettisoned the White Australia practices but introduced equal opportunities for Australians of all ethnic, religious and cultural backgrounds.[70]

S. Chandrasekhar states Prime Minister Gough Whitlam deserves 'all credit for this definitive declaration of a progressive policy ...'[71].

Kenneth Rivett captures the depth of the change and incredulity with which news of the Whitlam Government's decisive abandonment of the 'White Australia' Policy in 1973 was received in 'diplomatic and perhaps other political circles in Asia ...'[72] with this question, 'but can it be believed, when any account of earlier policies towards actual, and would be migrants from India makes such depressing reading?'[73]

There were a number of related initiatives, apart from the removal of immigration restrictions based on colour, that India warmed to. In February 1975 Whitlam introduced a Bill in Parliament to ensure Australia conformed with the International Convention on the Elimination of All Forms of Racial Discrimination. The Whitlam Government rejoined the UN Committee of Twenty Four on Decolonisation and also supported, with greater vigour, Australia's stand at the UN against Apartheid and the white minority regimes in South Africa and Rhodesia. It terminated trade with Rhodesia and closed the Rhodesian Information Centre in Sydney. In the Lok Sabha, Mrs Gandhi herself observed that, 'the festering of Rhodesian sore is poisoning the Commonwealth relations ...'[74].

In another first for Australia, the Whitlam Government contributed to a UN fund for assisting 'the educational development and other aspirations of the people of Southern Africa.'[75] Whitlam once spoke of the value of removing racist governments in Africa, and in a television interview with Lord Chalfont in London, in December 1973, described the leaders of South Africa as being 'as bad as Hitler ...'[76]. He even went further than Nehru, a trenchant critic of the racist South African regime, to suggest that, 'violence would be justified in the South African context, ...'[77] a comment that drew a rebuke from South Africa's Prime Minister Vorster.[78] In 1972, Whitlam enforced a policy of disallowing entry into Australia, even in a transit capacity, of sports teams that were selected on a racial basis, and wrote later that, 'the African nations had no doubts about my consistent and persistent attitude.'[79] Charles Price, in an analysis of the Whitlam Government's immigration record says, 'on every point this Government has done far more than modify the work of its Liberal predecessors: ...'[80].

The effect of all this on India (1972-1975), a nation that consistently showed its contempt for racialism through Nehru, Menon and others in the Congress Party from the inception of nationhood, (and even in the days of the Raj), was obviously very favourable and cannot be overstated in understanding the Whitlam period of the bilateral relationship.

## Colonialism and Vestigial Links

There were other policy areas of concern to India where Whitlam's strong stand earned him a lot of respect in India. One of these was his abhorrence of colonialism. As early as 1957, in a speech to Parliament on Indonesia's claim to Dutch-held West New Guinea, Whitlam spoke of the principle that people of a territory have the right to determine their own government, and observed that the Dutch colonial arguments were 'comparable to what would have been the position if Britain had retained Kashmir ...'[81] . The stand he took was all the more remarkable because the 'support for continued Netherlands control in West New Guinea (WNG) was part of the Evatt-Burton (Labor) legacy.'[82] An expression of the anti-colonial sentiment sweeping through nationalistic Asia, Australia's stand on WNG under Menzies was hardly in consonance with India's unrelenting attitude to colonialism. In his argument supporting Indonesia's claim, Whitlam drew Parliament's attention to the voting at the UN to stress that a majority of Commonwealth Nations, as well as most members of SEATO, did not vote with Australia and the Dutch:

> What is it that brings about this catastrophic lack of support for Australia amongst all the members of the Commonwealth and particularly amongst the people in our own Area? ... I believe it is that we have constantly put forward wrong points of view or support wrong points of view.[83]

Arguing that the days when the United States could muster a majority of votes in the UN were long past, and that Russia had an even smaller bloc, Whitlam said it was an Australian obligation to make the West understood in Asia and *vice versa,* and 'in the countries around the Indian Ocean in particular' lamenting the missed opportunity of the previous ten years, he said, 'we should at least learn that during the 1960s we must work and work hard to understand the aspirations of those countries.'[84]

Again in 1960 speaking in Parliament on the Five Power Resolution (which saw a bitter clash between Nehru and Menzies at the UN), Whitlam reminded Menzies that India, 'has, not by force but by prestige, the primacy in Asia and Africa ...'[85]. In the same speech, Whitlam also referred to the 1950s, throughout which Menzies, Nehru and Sukarno had led their respective countries; yet, he said, Menzies had failed to make any attempt to improve relations with them:

> There was an unexampled opportunity for the leader of Australia to establish cordial and understanding relations with the leaders of the other two great powers in the Indian Ocean. The opportunity was lost.[86]

Barely six months in office, Whitlam informed Parliament in May 1973 that Australia had attended an international meeting of 'experts for the support of victims of colonialism and apartheid ...' the aim of which was to develop a 'programme of peaceful action to facilitate and hasten the process of decolonisation and the elimination of apartheid.'[87] And, at the UN in September 1974, Whitlam made his attitude to colonialism clear to India and all the other nations of the world assembled there:

> Of all the changes which have occurred in the international community since World War II none has more profoundly altered the face of the world than the accession to independence by those peoples and states formerly under colonial rule. The process is not yet complete, but we look to a time in the near future when no territory will be controlled against its choice by a metropolitan power with whom it has no geographical, social, racial or cultural affinity.[88]

When Whitlam made this statement, his government, nearly an year earlier, had made Papua New Guinea self governing, (made effective after PNG's own Parliament formalised it in 1975), a process he described as, 'ending a false, demeaning, unworthy power over others.'[89] Whitlam's prompt action on Papua New Guinea's independence contrasts with the Menzies' Government's protracted colonisation of it. In 1962, India's High Commissioner to Australia Samar Sen, told J.G. Bowden, Secretary, External Affairs, that, 'Australia would get more sympathy in respect of New Guinea if it publicized its undoubted good work there particularly if it declared a target date for independence.' Bowden responded by saying that, 'we consider political target dates bogus.'[90] The reference in Chapter One to Minister Howson's Diary entry questioning the value of spending money on New Guinea's defence if Australia was to give it independence, illustrates Australia's previous attitudes to decolonisation.[91]

For India, the issue of decolonisation was inseparable from its abhorrence of racial discrimination and was no less important as a precondition to progress and world peace. Nehru, himself, when he spoke of the evils of colonialism, which he often did, used the argument of self-determination as a fundamental right of subject peoples. For example, reporting to the Lok Sabha on the 1955 Bandung Conference of Afro-Asian nations, Nehru said: 'In the condemnation of colonialism in the well understood sense, namely, the rule of one people by another, with its attendant evils, the conference was at one.'[92]

Other areas of Whitlam affinities with India's view of the world included those related to India's attitude to constitutional links with its former colonial master, Britain; not the least of this was the concern India had with the role of the Monarchy in the affairs of the newly independent nation in 1947. There were other Whitlam reforms that India found were in accord with her own views: Australia's abolition of the British honours system; replacement of the British national anthem 'God Save the Queen' with a distinctive Australian one; replacement of Britain's Privy Council with Australia's High Court as the highest Court for hearing of Australian appeals; Whitlam's rejection of membership of the Privy Council, the first Australian Prime Minister to do so; and, the removal from Australian passports of the words 'British Subject'. While these changes did not have any material effect on the India-Australia relationship, in the view of several Indian public servants and diplomats interviewed during research in India and Sri-Lanka,[93] they were, nevertheless, actions that had echoes of India's own nationalistic pride and enthusiasm for independence from the British Raj. As Nehru strove to free India for the Indians, Whitlam sought to create an Australian environment. As Stephen Fitzgerald states, he 'Australianised it.'[94]

## Regionalism, Common Causes and Consistency

Among the many Whitlam foreign policy positions which found favour in New Delhi, his stand on the Indian Ocean as a Zone of Peace was particularly well received. He told Parliament: 'we do our best to see that in the Indian Ocean the present installations and bases are not expanded and that their numbers are not increased.' [95] On another occasion, he said, 'no country in the Indian Ocean region wishes the two super powers to promote their rivalry in the Indian Ocean.'[96] India's stand on keeping the Indian Ocean as a Zone of Peace, articulated at the UN, the Commonwealth Conferences and the Non-Aligned Summits, stemmed from its deep concern as well as those of the region, over great power rivalry there, and the US decision to expand its facilities in the island of Diego Garcia in the Indian Ocean.

Making reference to Whitlam's visit to India in 1973, India's then Minister for External Affairs, Swaran Singh, expressed India's pleasure at Whitlam's support for, and sharing of, India's view that, 'the Indian Ocean should be kept as an area of peace ... free from naval rivalry.' Describing it as a 'distinct improvement in the situation', the Minister added that 'the powerful voice of Australia is also on this side and that is a positive factor.'[97] The Minister's pleasure was shared by India's southern neighbour, Sri Lanka, whose Prime Minister (Mrs Sirimavo Bandaranaike) introduced the original proposal. Describing the election of the Whitlam Government as a 'pleasing change' after many decades during which the foreign policies of Australia (and New Zealand) 'were an unhappily blunt expression of their cloistered conservatism ...'[98], an editorial of a major newspaper in Sri-Lanka observed that:

> Even more heartening to us in Sri-Lanka is the immediate change in Australia's attitude to Mrs. Bandaranaike's proposal for the Indian Ocean peace zone. With Mr. Whitlam's election Australia has now decided to support our resolution.[99]

From the perspective of India's judgment of Australian leaders and their particular view of the world, it is important to note that their appreciation of Whitlam's foreign policy stance in relation to Asia did not start only after Whitlam came to office. From the time he entered the Australian Parliament in 1953, he articulated his stand on a number of foreign policy areas. In most, if not all, he disapproved of the policy positions taken by Menzies and the Liberal Coalitions Governments that followed. The Indians naturally identified with Whitlam's basic view of the world manifested in his discerning pronouncements made throughout his political career. For instance, in 1967 Whitlam told the House that the 'conservatives have too long fostered the delusion that Australia's security depends on Western forces being on the mainland of Asia.'[100] In the same speech he argued that, 'the passion of countries in this region is not ideology but nationalism and economic advance. Vietnam and anti-Communism blur the real issues as our neighbours see them.'[101]

India, no less, had consistently deprecated the argument that its own security depended on the West's or the Communists involvement in the region. Nehru, in fact, articulated the case for regional strategic and economic cooperation, repudiating military alliances such as SEATO as endangering regional harmony. He also saw Australia's participation in a regional approach as important because it shared common problems with the others, particularly in South East Asia and the Pacific. On this too, Whitlam's view mirrored Nehru's. In an address to Parliament, he spoke out on Australia's case for regionalism:

> In the long run Australia cannot rely on guarantees from outside its region. We must seek an accommodation within the region as the only basis for a lasting and secure peace. Our continuing relations with Indonesia, ... Japan, ... and with India which is the largest democracy of all, are more important to us than any temporary alignment with the United States in Vietnam or with Britain in Malaysia and Singapore.[102]

Mrs Gandhi too had argued the case for India's policy of regional cooperation with emphasis on inclusion of all countries irrespective of their particular 'economic, political or social system ...', stressing that 'it would be sad if regional cooperation was to intensify the Cold War atmosphere instead of promoting understanding within the region.'[103]

Again, in 1967, on the question of not doing the bidding of bigger powers, Whitlam's advocacy was analogous to Nehru's consistent defence of India's non-aligned position, unwilling to be pushed around by either of the super powers. Whitlam stated: 'we should not regard ourselves as subsidiaries of world powers, formerly Britain and now the United States of America.'[104] And, then, on becoming Prime Minister, during his visit to India he said, 'Australia would no longer wait for "clearance" from Britain or the US as their interests might not always coincide with Australia's.'[105]

Whitlam also told the 1973 Ottawa Commonwealth Prime Ministers Conference that 'the 18 years that Australia spent in dutifully following the Dulles' doctrine were a waste.'[106] As early as 1954, Whitlam advised against Australian involvement with the US in the latter's actions in Indo-China, the first Australian politician to do so, preferring that any involvement had the prior approval of the UN,[107] an approach Nehru often stressed. Then there were the international questions like SEATO, the Suez Crisis, the Five Power Resolution and Vietnam. In each, Whitlam argued a policy position not unlike that taken by India, or was unsparing in his criticism of the Menzies Government's policy. For example, on the Suez issue, Whitlam described Menzies' involvement as 'the first diplomatic disaster he brought on Australia by his personal interventions. He humiliated us over the Suez canal incident.'[108] At the time India's Krishna Menon too thought Menzies' mission to Cairo was ill advised as described in Chapter Four. On the Five Power Resolution at the UN and Menzies' lodgement of a counter resolution against Nehru, Whitlam observed that it was ' a move which proved disastrous' and felt Menzies was probably influenced by Sir Owen Dixon's failed bid on Kashmir and 'continuing antipathy to Nehru.'[109] It must be said, however, that when the name of Owen Dixon as arbitrator on Kashmir was suggested by the Security Council, Nehru's response was 'no other choice was likely to be better ...'[110]. Whitlam, never an admirer of Menzies' pronouncements on Asia, said, 'the noises he makes about the importance of Asia to Australia are designed to maintain British and American commitments on the land in Asia.'[111] In 1967 he told Parliament that:

> ...there is deep suspicion of policies which are engineered from outside the region. Thinking and ideas must spring from within a region. There must be Asian solutions for Asian problems.[112]

Mediansky refers to a senior member of the DEA (in the 1950s) who observed that, 'some of our difficulties with India would be the less, in my opinion, if we chose to be less uniformly committed on United States foreign policy and methods.'[113]

## Mrs Gandhi and Whitlam: Personalities, Affinities and Fresh Prospects

Once again the influence of personal philosophy on policy and relationships is seen in the Whitlam-Gandhi affinity. The Whitlam personality with its broader view of the world was capable of accommodating India's policy of non-alignment, as well as rising above Australia's previously held critical view of India's preference for the Soviet Union over America during the Cold War. It is not difficult to understand why an experienced politician like Mrs Gandhi, subjected to colonialism and its attendant racism from childhood, including a period of ten months in prison in 1942 at an age of 25, was able to overcome her allegedly strong dislike of Europeans[114] (according to Howson) and find more things in common with Whitlam's political philosophy than with that of any previous Australian Prime Minister.

While the Whitlam personality has been referred to in Chapter Two, at this point it would help to also consider briefly the Gandhi persóna. From a very early age Mrs Gandhi was guided by Nehru. His influence in shaping her character was made even stronger by their separation, forced by his imprisonment at the hands of the British. Much of this influence was effected through the letters they exchanged while he was in prison: for Nehru, 'letters became the major medium of communicating with his daughter as also of educating her.'[115] And, yet, she had a mind of her own on international politics, and despite Nehru's strong influence, Mrs Gandhi sometimes disagreed with him and wrote to him about it.[116] Educated in Switzerland and Oxford (where her studies were ended prematurely by illness), Mrs Gandhi had her first major political break when she was elected as President of the Congress Party in 1959. Peter Lyons probably best captures Mrs Gandhi's personality with this analysis:

> the political style of Mrs Gandhi may be said to combine the modernising ideas of her father, Jawaharlal Nehru, but without his Hamlet-like hesitancy. Her decisiveness in practice, her skills in crisis management, is more reminiscent of Sardar Patel - tough, realistic, not given to gratuitous explanations and justifications though without his touch of Hindu Chauvinism.[117]

According to Sonia Gandhi, 'one of her distinguishing attributes was a special concern for the very poor.'[118] Writer M.S. Rajan refers to an Asian delegate who once observed that Mrs Gandhi, ' "reintroduced the spirit of India" into the United Nations after many years' with her formidable speech as Prime Minister of India, to the General Assembly on 14 October 1968.[119] While Mrs Gandhi's rule has been compared with that of her father's, Christopher Candland, in a recent critique of the Congress Party's dwindling fortunes, believes that while Nehru 'handled regional demands well' there were a number of challenges of great magnitude between 1966 and 1975 that the Party had to contend with under Mrs Gandhi's leadership.[120]

Addressing a central hypothesis of this analysis that personalities and policies influence bilateral relations, it helps to focus on a few more dimensions of Mrs Gandhi's persona. Ralph Bultjens described her as 'a great leader' which requires in his view, 'a sense of guile and manipulative genius ...'[121] . He also thought that, 'in her strengths and her weaknesses, in her contradictions ... Indira Gandhi more than any other leader - refracted the Indian psyche.'[122] Her undoubted sense of nationalism did not inhibit her internationalism.[123] Another of her attributes (which she shared with Whitlam) was her 'wide interests and great intellectual curiosity, she was comfortable in many cultures...'[124] . If there was a troubling factor during 1975, it was Mrs Gandhi's imposition of emergency rule in June 1975 (which continued to March 1977) seen as a set back for India's democracy with basic rights and press freedom arbitrarily withdrawn.

## The Whitlam Visit: A Turning Point

In Chapter Two reference was made to Whitlam's significant visit to India, another milestone event that affected the bilateral relationship favourably. Whitlam himself underscores the unprecedented nature of the visit describing it as, 'the only visit which an Australian Prime Minister has made specifically to India as distinct from a visit for an international gathering there or a visit *en route* to points west of Suez.'[125] Just before the Whitlam visit, Mrs Gandhi was questioned by the Australian Broadcasting Commission in New Delhi as to India's view of 'some significant changes in foreign policy' resulting from the change of Government in Australia, to which she replied, 'we think they are good changes especially in so far as India is concerned.'[126] In a speech welcoming Whitlam, Indira Gandhi said: 'Prime Minister, we are indeed pleased that you have come to India within months of assuming the reins of office.'[127] Referring to the two countries as an old India and a young Australia, she said:

Old or young, nations have constantly to renew themselves. And, under you, Australia is undergoing such a renewal. Your views on racial discrimination and your ideas on brotherhood and cooperation between nations have made a considerable impact on the attention and on the conscience of the world.[128]

Prime Minister Whitlam's speech in reply was no less reflective of his consistent commitment to India, which he referred to as the 'greatest democracy in the world.'[129] It reveals also his admiration for Nehru:

> We gratefully acknowledge the moral leadership India has so often given in the cause of world peace. In that continuing quest we can never forget or overestimate the pioneering role played by your father.[130]

For Mrs Gandhi, this praise would have been particularly pleasing. Lamenting the fact that fourteen years had lapsed since an Australian Prime Minister had come to New Delhi, Whitlam told Mrs Gandhi:

> I cannot help but feel that there has been something missing in recent years between our two countries ... relations with India have not been given the attention they should have. If this has been so, I intend to amend it and amend it wholeheartedly.[131]

While Whitlam's intentions to correct the anomalous nature of the relationship in the brief period his government was in office may not have been significant when judged in terms of solid achievements (although the import-export trade between the two countries rose sharply after 1972 as shown below), the Whitlam contribution was an important legacy because of its impact on Australia's image in India; it enlivened the dormancy that characterised the relationship in the Menzies era, (and between that and 1972) and, consequently, it set the ground for more constructive bilateral engagements to take place. India's Minister of State for External Affairs, in reply to a question on the outcome of the Indira Gandhi-Whitlam talks in New Delhi, told the Lok Sabha that:

> ...both Prime Ministers emphasised the importance of greater collaboration in economic matters, particularly the desirability of securing greater diversification of economic relations and the possibility of joint ventures. Specific proposals are under consideration of the two Governments.[132]

In his speech, the Minister also referred to the similarity of views between Whitlam and Mrs Gandhi on the Paris agreement on Vietnam and Laos, a free Indian Ocean, racial discrimination, nuclear weapons testing, the economic gulf between the developing and developed countries etc. Whitlam himself drew Mrs Gandhi's attention to the parallelism of his Government's policies with those of India:

> It is significant I think that all the departures from the previous pattern of voting have brought us in line with India. It has not been, of course, a question of our just following India: but it is an indication of the closeness of our views on a great range of issues facing the world - on race discrimination, on de-colonisation, on Southern Africa, on human rights, on the need to keep this region free of great power rivalries.[133]

Within months of the Whitlam-Indira Gandhi meeting, India's Deputy Minister for Commerce, A.L. George, advised the Lok Sabha that the Whitlam Government's new import scheme (effective from July 1974), would apply to Indian exports to Australia of 'manufactures, semi-manufactures and substantially processed primary products ... either duty free or at reduced rates ...'[134]. The economic benefits of this to India on an annualised basis were expected to be substantial and represented a positive start to a restoration of the relationship. This Whitlam initiative was in contrast to the situation on tariffs in the 1960s which India's Minister for Commerce at the time described as a ' "very serious question" ...a practice which is against all international policies of trade ...'[135]. This was not the first occasion on which Whitlam showed his interest in trade and preferential treatment for Commonwealth countries. At the 1973 Ottawa Commonwealth Heads Conference, Whitlam and India's Swaran Singh 'initiated discussion of inter-Commonwealth trade, Commonwealth preference system and other monetary matters.'[136]

While no major bilateral programmes were established during Whitlam's visit to New Delhi, the impact did not go unnoticed in the media in both countries. In India particularly the accolades were unreserved. The *Statesman* in Delhi reporting on the first day of Whitlam's visit stated, 'Australia's first Labour (sic) Government in more than 23 years has gained more friends and greater world attention than at any time during the placid years of Conservative rule. The man behind the new image is Prime Minister Gough Whitlam.'[137] In Australia, *The Age* in an editorial on the Whitlam visit to India commented that, 'as an exercise in international bridge-building the Prime Minister's visit to New Delhi has all the marks of success ... By demonstrating its friendship with India it is letting both Moscow and Peking know that there is an active and independent country in the South Pacific.'[138] Ian Clark makes this reference to the response of the media to the Whitlam visit:

> ... the press was unanimous in its assessment that a qualitative change had occurred in the Australia-India dialogue and a new identity in views created by Australia's proclaimed reorientation towards the region.[139]

Woolcott's assessment at the time was that, 'our relations with India have been reinvigorated as a result of the Prime Minister's visit in June 1973 - and of the increasing official contacts and discussions between the two countries.'[140] It must be said, however, that some bilateral activity did occur between the two countries in the Whitlam period flowing over to the year after he lost office. There was a sharp increase in import-export trade between the two countries during this period. It included a number of visits by government ministers, trade and cultural delegations to each others countries.[141]

Professor Marika Vicziany in an introduction to *Australia-India: Economic Links, Past, Present and Future*, states:

> After 1972 a more positive attitude emerged on the Australia side with various Prime Ministers suggesting that we should no longer ignore India. However, their positive statements appear to have had little to sustain them. Bilateral relations are built on real needs rather than wishes or preferences.[142]

This is a valid observation. While in the post-Whitlam years, the Asia-centredness of Australia's foreign policy has seen a gradual interest in India too, it must be acknowledged that trade and economic interests are the stuff of sound, sustainable bilateral relations, but, without the political will, all else is academic. In the period 1949-1972, there was little interest at the political level. Whitlam provided this interest and introduced a more sophisticated level of diplomacy capable of greater insights when dealing with the labrynthine complexities of a democracy such as India. The 1994 DFAT report, *India's Economy at the Midnight Hour: Australia's India*

*Strategy*, states, 'There have been waves of "rediscovery" - in the early 1970s, and again in the mid-1980s - when attempts were made to establish more solid ties.'[143] It is also worthy of attention that in the brief Whitlam period of the relationship,(1972-1975) the import-export trade between India and Australia rose sharply after a flat performance in the preceding twelve years as shown by the graph in Figure 3 below.

## Figure 3

*Total Import from and Exports to India 1963/67-1989-90*

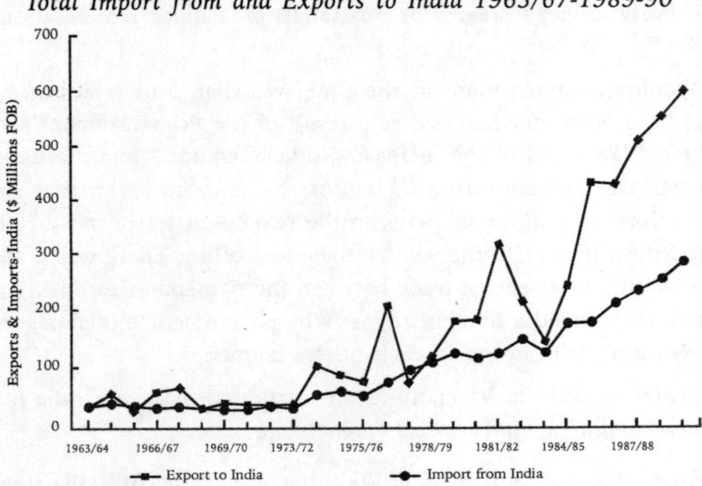


*Source*:    Marika Vicziany, 'Australian Companies in India: the Ingredients for Successful Entry into the Indian Market', Australia-India, Economic Links Past, Present and future, Marika Vicziancy (Ed.) Indian Ocean Centre for Peace Studies, Nedlands, Western Australia p61, Graph 2.

## Whitlam and Nehru: Different Times, Kindred Spirits, Common Aspirations

It is also important to draw attention to the effect that the closeness of views between Whitlam and Nehru had on the 1972-1975 period of the bilateral relationship (and, as a catalyst, beyond that) something not previously examined, and easily missed when the bilateral relationship is analysed from an Australian perspective. While this omission in previous writings is understandable, it is pertinent to the argument that Whitlam's position on many international issues from the 1950s fitted into India's moral framework which underpinned its own policies. And, unquestionably, the Nehruvian image endured in the imagination of Indians. It was the standard used for measuring the foreigner, the West's diplomats and politicians and their standing in relation to India's interests. While India's international stature as well as its view of the world had changed after Nehru, the shift was hardly paradigmatic. If there was a change, it was that Mrs Gandhi was less trusting of the Chinese and the Soviet Union than her father had been, (particularly after 1962 in the case of China), but, then, she was equally cautious in her dealings with the West from the outset. At a news conference on her return from an unofficial visit to Moscow, Mrs Gandhi (at the time India's Minister for Information and Broadcasting) was questioned on continued Soviet military aid to India in the light of Chinese support for Pakistan and Sino-Soviet rapprochement in the air, her response was that 'India must be alert to changes in both the West and the Soviet Union,' adding that 'an 18th century British statesman had once remarked, Britain has no permanent policy. It only has permanent interests.'[144]

Given then that Nehru's broader philosophy continued to be reflected in the Indira Gandhi period, more importantly for this analysis was that the basic Whitlam philosophy resembled that of Nehru's, two libertarian voices. Examination of Whitlam's Parliamentary speeches and other comments made during his political career (1953-1978), some of which have already been quoted above, would point to a similarity of views between him and Nehru in a number of areas: both men were social democrats but were not affected by dogma nor preoccupied by the anti-Communist fervour of the Menzies period; they had a breadth of vision that their political contemporaries of any political persuasion lacked; the two strove to influence regional and domestic issues without losing interest in international questions. One of Nehru's consistent pleas was concerned with the alleviation of world poverty through better sharing of the world's resources. Whitlam shared this concern when he addressed the National Press Club in Wellington in 1975 identifying, ' "the real problems of the world" to be "poverty overpopulation and mal-distribution of the world's wealth." '[145] In a reference to Nehru's commitment to a more just society and his own endorsement of it, Whitlam observed:

> His conviction that the roots of war lay in the inequitable
> distribution of the fruits of labour led him to recognise that society
> is weakened by one group bettering itself at the expense of another.
> ... His view that the whole society has a duty to ensure the quality
> of life of all its members strikes a resonant chord in me, ...[146].

While Whitlam's interest in the world outside was not shared by
his countrymen with the same enthusiasm, it was unquestionably
strong and evident in his foreign policy. Nehru's wish to see Indians
extending their interests to the outside world, was an early interest,
attested to by this observation by Frank Moraes:

> If Gandhi made India aware of herself, Nehru made Indians aware
> of others. He set about enlarging his countrymen's political vision.
> Along side a hitherto introvert nationalism he helped India to
> develop an objective outlook and to be conscious of the neighbours
> around her and of the problems of more distant lands and peoples.[147]

Nehru's cabinet colleague Maulana Azad observed that Nehru
'could never erase from his mind what was happening in the world
beyond India.'[148] Nehru himself spoke of the need to serve not only
his people of India 'but also to serve all others beyond India ...'[149].
Whitlam's commitment to achieve greater equality everywhere is
seen in the Roy Milne Memorial Lecture he delivered as Prime
Minister in 1973 on the theme of Australia's 'Foreign Policy: New
Directions, New Definitions':

> An internationalist party, a socialist party like ours cannot on
> principle, remain indifferent to the conditions of its neighbours,
> particularly when its neighbourhood is the most deprived part of the
> globe. A party which promotes equality at home cannot be content
> with a world where the gap between the rich and poor nations
> widens yearly.[150]

Like Nehru, who refused to accept that there was a role for the
monarchy in republic India, Whitlam had a distaste for British
traditions and the symbols that reminded the nation of its colonial
past, including its links with the monarchy. Both men were
nationalistic, independent and did not take kindly to great power
dictates and intervention in regional affairs.

Both were critical of SEATO from the time of its formation,
Whitlam condemning strongly its discussion of Kashmir at its 1954
Council Meeting,[151] referred to in Chapter Four. Once in office, he
wanted it restructured because, he said, 'conceived as an instrument

for the containment of China in the cold war era, SEATO must be modified if it is not to become completely moribund.'[152] In the event, 'by the latter part of 1973, all SEATO members including the US, acceded to the organisation's reconstruction along Australia's preferred, largely non-military guidelines.'[153] Similarly, Nehru who condemned its formation observed, in reference to South East Asia, that the treaty 'converts it almost into an area of potential war.'[154] In the Lok Sabha, Nehru criticised Australia's (with UK and New Zealand) references to Kashmir at the SEATO Council Meeting in Karachi in March 1956 and (at the Baghdad Pact in April 1956).[155]

At various times both men rejected war as a means of settling disputes, arguing that the UN was the proper body to determine the basis for settling of international disputes and not by super powers acting independently. During the Korean War, Nehru told Parliament that, 'in the ultimate analysis no problem is solved by the bomb and the bayonet and tanks.'[156] Whitlam's abhorrence of war was made explicit in Parliament, for example, when he spoke on Vietnam.[157] Speaking about the UN in New Delhi, Nehru said, 'it is desirable and necessary that we should remind ourselves of the UN, the ideals it stands for, its fine charter. ... Most of us criticise the UN. I have criticised it, too, but it is difficult to imagine what the world would have been without the UN.'[158] Whitlam, like Nehru, thought the UN 'despite its imperfections, still represents for us our best hope of producing ... a more peaceful and secure world ...'[159].

Nehru regarded the Commonwealth as an important organisation even though he had occasionally criticised it. His effective use of, and contribution to, the Commonwealth is discussed in Chapter Three. Whitlam too regarded the institution as important to Australia because, as he told the Ottawa Conference, 'more than half the members of the Commonwealth are in the South Pacific or in or around the Indian Ocean ...'; it was, he said, 'the most natural and significant association to which Australia can belong and with which it can have regular, current, significant dealings.'[160] He told Parliament on his return from the Ottawa Conference that 'there is no other body or organisation in which it is possible to learn so intimately ... the views of responsible political persons ...'[161]. Writing about the then imminent Commonwealth Conference in Ottawa in 1973, Derek Ingram stated that Whitlam, unlike Holt, Gorton and

McMahon, 'has a feeling for the Commonwealth.' The former Prime Ministers who were in Menzies' Cabinet 'were influenced by his (Menzies') jaundiced view of the modern Commonwealth - that it had taken a wrong turning in becoming multi-racial ...'[162]. India's admission to it as a republic, welcomed at the time by Chifley and Evatt, was the turning point in the transformation of the Commonwealth which Menzies lamented.

Nehru and Whitlam also put great store on the parliamentary process seeing it as an instrument for change in the interest of the people. Nehru strove not only to influence world peace but also to bring about radical social and economic change within India through Parliament. Similarly, Whitlam's reforming zeal was never in question and was recognised in the Western world too, seen in this tribute:

> The London *Times* described Whitlam as 'a man who in stature, intellect and vision towered above his parliamentary colleagues, a man before his time. This Fabian reformer - a giant among pygmies - was one of the few modern political leaders who dreamed of using government, not to maintain the status quo, but to bring opportunities and services to people who would otherwise be deprived of them. He assailed the apathetic community with a blueprint for change that rectified many of the imbalances created by 23 years of inaction.'[163]

Nehru and Whitlam also shared a strong interest in equal educational opportunities for the young. The similarity in their thinking on this is seen in the words they used to describe their concern about student facilities. Speaking at a conference on Education, Nehru said:

> ... you come across the poor student not having any place even to sit, and practically no home surroundings. How can you expect him to study hard without a place where he can do some work properly.[164]

In Whitlam's case, when he was questioned by a reporter as to what he meant by equality, Whitlam replied, 'I want every kid to have a desk, with a lamp, and his own room to study.'[165]

Another recurrent theme in Nehru's speeches was a plea for racial equality. Both at home and abroad he sought equality of economic opportunity as well as in the treatment of people within political systems:

> There is another problem which we in Asia regard as a vital problem. ... that is the question of racial equality, which is something that is laid down in the provisions of the United Nations Charter ... Obviously there are large regions of the world which have suffered from this question of racial inequality. We also feel that there is no part of the world where it can be tolerated in the future ... to tolerate it is obviously to sow the seeds of conflict.[166]

For Whitlam too, the idea of the equality of people was fundamental to his philosophy and once observed that, 'equality with freedom is, I apprehend, the basic ideal and aspiration of democratic socialism.'[167] Freudenberg attests to Whitlam's commitment to the principle with this view:

> As a man, a party man or as a politician, Whitlam cannot be understood except on the basis of his commitment to the concept of equality. Anyone who cares to follow the development of his thinking over twenty years will find that equality is the consistent theme .[168]

Nehru often articulated the similarity in expectations of the future (including economic freedom) that bound India and others like it emerging from colonialism. No one doubts that Whitlam, 'saw a similarity of aspiration between his kind of Australia and the Asian neighbours.'[169] Then there was Whitlam's regional emphasis in foreign policy, notable for its departure from the views of those who preceded him. In this too he and Nehru were of like mind. Whitlam's address to the International Seminar held under the auspices of UNESCO celebrating the 100th anniversary of Nehru's birth reveals this shared interest:

> Nehru understood the intimate and inevitable place of Australia in the Asia-Pacific region perhaps earlier and better than many Australians themselves did. It was he who insisted on the presence of Australia and New Zealand at the Asian Conference of 1947, ... Nehru's perception of Australia as a partner in the region was typical of his foresight and his leadership.[170]

Not only does this identification of common views held by Whitlam and Nehru draw attention to the closeness of their ideology, their views on freedom and equality of opportunity, it helps to explain further why the Indians saw Australia through new eyes with the advent of the Whitlam Government in 1972. True, Whitlam and Nehru led two vastly different countries at different times with vastly different problems. Yet their vision, their nationalism, their resolve to bring equality for their respective people through Parliament, as well as for those outside their own countries through the Commonwealth and the UN, showed a remarkable similarity. This parallelism of views and commitment to causes, influenced India's response to Whitlam in Mrs Gandhi's period because of the lingering influence of the Nehruvian philosophy and Mrs Gandhi's commitment to many of the moral issues which both Nehru and Whitlam espoused. This, of course, includes Whitlam's Parliamentary speeches both in the Menzies era and after, when he spoke favourably about Nehru and India in a number of international policy debates.

However, there was one dark cloud in the Indira Gandhi-Whitlam period: India's testing of a nuclear device on 18 May 1974. While Whitlam was disturbed by it,[171] there was no strong protest made to New Delhi by the Australian Government apart from the sending of a senior scientific official to New Delhi for discussions.[172]

While there were no changes of a major magnitude affecting bilateral relations during the 1972-1975 period, India was clearly more impressed by the Whitlam Government than any previous one. This was because of Whitlam's progressive foreign policies in Government as well as his views in Opposition (between 1954 and 1972),which were more in line with Nehru's stand on many an international issue. The extraordinary closeness of their views on many questions undoubtedly placed Whitlam in Indian eyes on a level above any previous Australian Leader except perhaps Evatt whose vision, one Indian thought, it took Whitlam to finish. There may be a temptation to judge the moral basis of their world views, their basic humanity as self serving in terms of their domestic and international images. Close scrutiny, however, of their principled attitudes to a range of issues consistently articulated suggests they were men with deeply held convictions. In Whitlam's case, this one example of a statement he made helps illustrate this: 'if history were to obliterate the whole of my public career, save my contribution to the independence of a democratic Papua New Guinea, I shall rest content.'[173]

In Whitlam, India saw someone prepared to defy Australia's past and re-define its present and future direction in line with its geography. Whitlam's assertion of a new independent policy direction explains why India saw him differently:

> The obsessive concerns of former years, such as fear of China and dependence on the United States, have vanished like the phantoms they were, and Australians can breathe more easily for having come to terms with national and international realities and for accepting that they are now more than ever before masters of their own destiny.[174]

While the examination here has focused on the extent to which the Whitlam arrival affected the India-Australia bilateral relationship between 1972 and 1975, equally relevant was its impact as a catalyst for the future development of the bilateral relationship. He gave it a future. That said, any judgment must first take into account India's deep sensitivity to all forms of racial discrimination, another theme that runs through this book. The sharp contrast between Whitlam's policies and actions on the racial question (manifested in his Government's Immigration Policy, as well as at the international level on Apartheid) and the previous twenty-five years of the Australian record distinguished the Whitlam era in Indian eyes. Whitlam once told Parliament that, 'our relations, ... are too often inhibited by fear and exclusiveness, particularly on a racial basis.'[175] This is particularly relevant because of the plethora of differences that existed in the previous predominantly Menzies era of the relationship between 1949 and 1972 which included Indian perceptions of Australia's racial superiority and colonial English attitudes. Also, from India's perspective with its memories of centuries of British colonialism and the associated racially based subordinate treatment, Whitlam's declarations such as his stand on decolonisation and the illegality of the South African and Rhodesian regimes, backed by UN voting and other actions like Papua New Guinea's independence, meant a lot more to India than the previous rhetoric emanating from Australia and its partners in the Western alliance.

Furthermore, Whitlam's impact on Australia freeing it of some of the last vestiges of the colonial link, when viewed as a final phase of Australia's decolonisation, was not unlike the Nehru-led Indian Congress Party's own final phase (1946-1947) of *Swaraj* (self-rule). Whitlam's impact on the India-Australia relationship has been under-represented in Australian writings, largely because the criteria used have been predominantly Australian. Datta Ray, in his analysis of how Indians think of Australia, refers to the 'stirrings of serious interest when Gough Whitlam became Prime Minister' and in regard to radical policy shifts in Australia's foreign policy in relation to the Third World, he adds that, 'Mrs Gandhi's Government inspired the expectations.'[176] But there is no denying the Indian view, including that held by Mrs Gandhi, that Whitlam was a kindred spirit.

The Whitlam period also saw Australian diplomats free of preoccupations with the fear of Asia and Chinese Communism, capable of transcending the earlier rigid ideology in dealing with India. Whitlam's choice of Bruce Grant as Australia's High Commissioner to India is a good example of the sophistication that was needed to understand the complexities of Asia and, in particular, India. Datta Ray thought Bruce Grant embodied the essential attributes for dealing with India: 'Sufficiently Anglo-Saxon to evoke confidence without being too stand-offish, Bruce Grant went down well with the New Delhi establishment.'[177] With the decline of Cold War pressures, India's diplomacy too was less characterised by its previous caution in its dealings with the West. High Commissioner Plimsoll in a letter to Hasluck refers to the post-Nehru era to state that 'India will less and less be governed by an elite of politicians and civil servants who grew up under British influences ...'[178]. This was equally true of Australia of the Whitlam era.

Perhaps, *The Statesman* and *The Times of India* in New Delhi in their editorials on the Whitlam visit to India, provide a fitting end to this Chapter which argues that Whitlam's impact on the India-Australia bilateral relationship was two fold: firstly, it created a new image of Australia in Indian eyes shaking off the former one of an isolated Euro-centric Australia; secondly it acted as a catalyst to facilitate future engagement between the two countries. The *Statesman* wrote that:

> During the last 23 years of the Liberal and Country Party coalition Government, Australia had become closely identified with the West. None of Sir Robert Menzies successors was able to shake off the legacy though not altogether unaware of the absurdity of Australia's "Western" pretensions. ... in reaching out to India Mr Whitlam has certain advantages. His Liberal socialist image and now foreign policy with an Asian emphasis have a certain appeal for New Delhi. ... His mission to New Delhi is perhaps a part of his overall plan to find a place for Australia in the Asian sun.[179]

*The Times of India* in its editorial spoke of Whitlam's 'deep conviction that its (Australia's) salvation lies not in continuing its role as a Western outpost in the Far East but in actively associating itself with the endeavours of the Asian countries for a new order in the region.'[180]

In terms of effectiveness, the Whitlam-Indira Gandhi impact on the bilateral relationship in the three years 1972-1975 was palpable if transitional. It tells the story: an Indian reaction of excitement to the bilateral relationship after more than two decades of frigidity. They gave it a new life.

## Endnotes

1. Garnaut, Ross, *Australia and the North East Asian Ascendancy*, AGPS, Canberra, 1989, p 1.

2. Although India gained independence in 1947, Nehru as Head of an interim Government, developed and promulgated India's foreign policy in 1946. E.G. Whitlam was elected to Australia's House of Representatives in November 1952, was Prime Minister between December 1972 and November 1975. He resigned from Parliament in July 1978.

3. In January 1968, Britain's Prime Minister Harold Wilson announced that it would complete its military withdrawal from South-East Asia (East of Suez Policy) by the end of 1971. President Johnson in March 1969 made it clear that his intention was to end the war in Vietnam. See UK House of Commons, Parliamentary Debates, Vol. 756 (1967-1968) Col. 1608 in B. Vivekanandan, 'Naval Power in the Indian Ocean: A Problem In Indo-British Relations', TRT No. 257, January 1975, p 61.

4. When sending troops to South Vietnam in 1965, Menzies, justified it by stating that 'the takeover of South Vietnam would be a direct military threat to Australia and to all the countries of South and South East Asia.' See T.B. Millar, *Australia's Foreign Policy*, Angus & Robertson, Sydney, 1968, Appendix A, p 309.

5. Commonwealth Secretariat, London, Minutes of Meetings and Memoranda at the Commonwealth Prime Minister's Meeting, London, 6-15 September 1966, Copy No. 220, pp 137-138, 189.

6. Hughes, T.E.F., 'Australia in Free Asia: Both Economic and Military Efforts', *TRT*, No. 226, April 1967, p 183.

7. *Ibid*.

8. Meaney, Neville, *Australia and the World* Longman Cheshire, Melbourne, 1985, p 721.

9. CPD, (H of R), Vol. 61, 5 November 1968, p 2429.

10. *Ibid*.

11. Josh, Haricharan Singh (ed.), *India's Foreign Policy: Nehru to Rao*, Indian Council of World Affairs, Surjeet Publications, New Delhi, 1994, p 52. Also see, MEA, External Affairs Minister, Sardar Swaran Singh's statement in New Delhi, lamenting the bombing of North Vietnam on 29 June 1966, *Foreign Affairs Record*, Vol. XII, No. 6, Government of India, New Delhi, p 156.

12. Mukherjee, Dilip, *The Statesman*, Delhi, 22 May 1968, p 1.

13. Kumar, Satish (ed.), *Documents on India's Foreign Policy 1972*, Macmillan, Delhi, 1976, pp 27-28. In condemning the Vietnam War, Mrs Gandhi took the opportunity at the non-aligned summit at Lusaka to refer to the destruction of plant life and

food through chemical contamination in the Vietnam war and said that, 'the only way to have a clean war is not to have a war at all.' See *Aspects of our Foreign Policy: From Speeches and Writings of Indira Gandhi*, All India Congress Committee, Delhi, 1973, p 34.

14. Stargardt, A.W., *Australia's Asian Policies: The History of a Debate 1839-1972*, Institute of Asian Affairs, Hamburg, 1977, p 228.

15. CNIA, Statement by the Minister for External Affairs, Vol. 38, April 1967, p 163. A February 1970 report from, retiring Australian Ambassador to the US, Sir Keith Waller, warned of Washington's intention to down grade military and economic ties with the Asia-Pacific region. See *Inside Canberra*, 26 February 1970, in Neville Meaney, *Australia and the World*, Longman Cheshire, Melbourne, 1985, p 714.

16. CPD, (H of R), Vol. 50, 10 March 1966, p 177.

17. See R.E. Hunter and P. Windsor, 'Vietnam and United States Policy in Asia', *International Affairs, A Quarterly Review*, Vol. 44, No. 2, April 1968, p 212.

18. 'Australia's Military Commitment to Vietnam', Paper prepared from Department of Foreign Affairs Files and tabled in the House of Representatives, Department of Foreign Affairs, 13 May 1975, pp 11, 13-17, in Neville Meaney, *Australia and the World*, Longman Cheshire, Melbourne, 1985, pp 670-673.

19. T.B. Millar, 'The Australia-Britain Relationship: Where Has It Come To?' *TRT* No. 266, April 1977, p 199.

20. Whitlam, Gough, *Abiding Interests*, University of Queensland Press, Qld., 1997, p 86.

21. *The Daily News*, Ceylon, 29 January 1971, p 5.

22. See, Gough Whitlam, *The Whitlam Government: 1972-1975*, Viking, Victoria, 1985, pp 501-502, for details of the changes.

23. Narayanan, K.R., 'New Perspectives in Indian Foreign Policy', *TRT*, No. 248, October 1972, p 453.

24. Park, Richard L., 'India's Foreign Policy', *Foreign Policy in World Politics*, Roy C. Macridis (ed.) 5th Edition, Prentice Hall, New Jersey, 1976, pp 321-322.

25. MEA, *Foreign Affairs Record*, Vol. XIII, No. 7, July 1967, Division, Government of India, New Delhi, pp 98-101.

26. *Ibid.*

27. Dhar, A.N., 'Renewing a Faith', *Indian Express*, 17 September 1973, in Shri Ram Sharma, *Indian Foreign Policy Annual Survey: 1973*, Sterling Publishers, New Delhi, 1977, p 116. For a number of views presented at a symposium held in May 1980 in New Delhi, on how the policy of nonalignment may be made valid in a changing world environment, see K.P. Misra and K.R. Narayanan, *Non-Alignment in Contemporary International Relations*, Vikas Publications, New Delhi, 1981.

28. AA, Despatch No. 2/64, 2 June 1964 from J. Plimsoll, Australian High Commissioner in New Delhi, to DEA, Series A1838/272, Item 169/1/3, Part 3.

29. Mukherjee, Dilip, *The Statesman*, Delhi, 22 May 1968, p 1.

30. *Jawaharlal Nehru's Speeches*: March 1963 - May 1964, Vol. V, Ministry of Broadcasting & Information, Government of India, New Delhi, 1968, pp 199-200.

31. Bhatia, Vinod, *Indira Gandhi and Indo-Soviet Relations*, Panchsheel Publishers, New Delhi, 1987, p 46.

32. Sharma, Shri Ram, *Indian Foreign Policy Annual Survey: 1973*, Sterling Publishers, New Delhi, 1977, p 184.

33. *Aspects of our Foreign Policy from Speeches and Writings of Indira Gandhi*, All India Congress Committee, New Delhi, 1973, p 12.

34. 'The Reconstruction of the Sub-Continent', *TRT*, No. 247, July 1972, p 275.

35. Dutt, V.P., 'US and Chinese Policies in the Subcontinent', *South Asia, The Changing Environment*, Chandrajit Channa (ed.) MERB Bookshelf, New Delhi, 1979, p 82.

36. MEA, *Foreign Affairs Record*, Vol. XIX, No. 1, 1973, Government of India, New Delhi, 1973, p 215.

37. CNIA, May 1972, in Claire Clark, (ed.), *Australia's Foreign Policy: Towards A Reassessment*, Cassell, North Melbourne, 1973, pp 185-186. For Whitlam's view of the East Pakistan crisis of 1971, see A.W. Stargardt, *Australia's Asian Policies, A History of a Debate 1839-1972*, Institute of Asian Affairs, Hamburg, 1977, pp 270-271; *AFAR*, August 1973, Vol. 44, No. 8, DFAT, AGPS, Canberra, pp 554-555.

38. *Aspects of our Foreign Policy from Speeches and Writings of Indira Gandhi*, All India Congress Committee, New Delhi, 1973, p 10.

39. *Ibid.*, pp 11-12

40. *Ibid.*, p 12.

41. Narayanan, K.R., 'New Perspectives in Indian Foreign Policy', *TRT*, No. 248, October 1972, p 459.

42. *The Age*, Melbourne, 21 May 1968, The Editorial.

43. *Ibid.*

44. Mukherjee, Dilip, *The Statesman*, Delhi, 23 May 1968, p 1.

45. *Ibid.*

46. *Ibid.*, p 14.

47. *The Age*, Melbourne, 21 May 1968, (The Editorial).

48. CPD, (H of R), Vol. 84, 24 May 1973, p 2643.

49. Camilleri, J.A., *From Whitlam to Fraser*, Allan Patience & Brian Head (eds.), Oxford University Press, Melbourne, 1979, p 252. 'The election of Labour governments in both Australia and New Zealand during 1972 portended a readjustment of those countries' forward defence postures, and subsequent efforts by Whitlam and Kirk-Rowling governments to construct patterns of political and economic regional influence more independent of the American defence deterrent and of ANZUS. These policy realignments included increased diplomatic and economic contacts with both the Soviet Union and China.' See William T. Tow, 'Western Defence in the Asian Pacific-Region', *TRT*, No. 270, April 1978, p 159.

50. *AFAR*, 'Australia and Asia in the Seventies', May 1974, Vol. 45, No. 5, DFAT, AGPS, Canberra, p 316.

51. *Ibid.* p 317.

52. *AFAR*, March 1973, Vol. 44, No. 3, DFAT, AGPS, Canberra, p 201.

53. For President Nixon's speech at Guam on 25 July 1969 on US retreat from Asia (The Nixon Doctrine) see Neville Meaney, *Australia and the World*, Longman Cheshire, Melbourne, 1985, p 707.

54. Macleod, Alexander 'The New Foreign Policy in Australia and New Zealand', *TRT*, No. 255, July 1974, p 288. Also see, William McMahon's Speech to a Young Liberals Rally in Melbourne, on 12 July 1971, *The Australian*, 13 July 1971, in Neville Meaney, *Australia and the World*, Longman Cheshire, Melbourne, 1985, p 728; J.R. McLelland, 'The Australian Political Scene', *TRT*, No. 246, April 1972, p 256.

55. Peter Howson, a Minister in the McMahon government of 1971-1972, notes in his Diary that the Government's criticism of Whitlam for his statements made in China 'were made fatuous when it was learned that President Nixon was going to China also.' See *The Howson Diaries: The Life of Politics*, Don Aitkin (ed.), Viking, Victoria, 1984, p 684.

56. 'Nixon's Trip Condemned', *The Daily News*, Ceylon, 3 August 1971, p 5.

57. 'Defence: Asia must be more self-reliant', *The Observer*, Ceylon, 15 May 1971, p 3.

58. CPD, (H of R), Vol. 84, 24 May 1973, p 2643. Also see, E.G. Whitlam's address to the National Press Club, Washington, on 30 July 1973, *AFAR*, August 1973, Vol. 44. DFAT, AGPS, Canberra, pp 527-530.

59. Meaney, Neville, 'The United States', *Australia in World Affairs 1971-1975*, W.J. Hudson, (ed.), George Allen & Unwin, Sydney, 1980, p 205.

60. For Prime Minister Holt's Speech on 30 June 1966 at the White House and reported in *The Sydney Morning Herald*, see Neville Meaney *Australia and the World*, Longman Cheshire, Melbourne, 1985, pp 696-697.

61. Crocker, W.R., *Australian Ambassador: International Relations at First Hand*, Melbourne University Press, Victoria, 1971, p 200.

62. Viviani, N., 'Intellectuals and the abolition of the White Australia Policy', *The Abolition of the White Australia Policy: The Immigration Reform Movement Revisited*, Nancy Viviani, (ed.), Australia-Asia paper No. 65, Centre for the Study of Australia-Asia Relations, Griffith University, Qld., 1992, p 33. Also see, W.D. Borrie, 'Changes in Immigration Patterns since 1972', *The Australian People: An Encyclopedia of the Nation, Its People and their Origins*, James Jupp, (ed.) Angus & Robertson, NSW, 1988, p 111.

63. See Prime Minister E.G. Whitlam's Speech to the General Assembly UN, 30 September 1974, *AFAR*, Vol. 45, No. 9, September 1974, DFAT, AGPS, Canberra, pp 576-583.

64. Fitzgerald, Stephen, *Is Australia an Asian Country?*, Allen & Unwin, NSW, 1997, pp 24-25.

65. See B.R. Bhagat's (Minister of State for External Affairs) address to the UN on racial discrimination August 1968 in MEA, *Foreign Affairs Record*, Vol. XIV, NO. 8, August 1968, Government of India, New Delhi, pp 187-188; M.N. Naghnoor's (MP, representative of India) Statement in Special Committee UN, on Apartheid, 31 October 1968, in MEA, *Foreign Affairs Record*, Vol. XIV, No. 10, October 1968, Government of India, New Delhi, pp 257-259.

66. UN General Assembly Meeting 2136/2, October 1973, in Shri Ram Sharma, *Indian Foreign Policy Annual Survey: 1973*, Sterling Publishers International, New Delhi, 1977, p 176.

67. *Ibid*.

68. Whitlam, Gough, 'Australia and Her Region', *Towards a New Australia: Under a Labor Government*, John McLaren, (ed.), Cheshire, Melbourne, 1972, p 19.

69. Interview with V.K. Jain, Director, Library & Information, MEA, Government of India, 27 January 1999, at MEA Office, New Delhi.

70. Whitlam, E.G., *Abiding Interests*, University of Queensland. Press, Qld., Australia, 1997, p 87.

71. Chandrasekhar, S., 'A Brief History of Australia's Immigration Policy, with Special Reference to India's Nationals', *From India to Australia*, S. Chandrasekhar (ed.) Population Review Books, California, 1992, p 28.

72. Rivett, K., 'From White Australia to the Present', *From India to Australia*, S. Chandrasekhar (ed.) Population Review Books, California, 1992, p 58.

73. *Ibid*.

74. MEA, *Foreign Affairs Record*, Vol. XIV, No. 4, April 1968, Government of India, New Delhi, p 92.

75. CPD, (H of R), Vol. 84, 24 May 1973, p 2649. Also see, E.G. Whitlam's address to the UN General Assembly, on 30 September 1974 in *AFAR*, Vol. 45, September 1974, No. 9, DFAT, AGPS, Canberra, pp 580-583.

76. Albinski, Henry S., 'The Role of Foreign Policy in Australian Electoral Politics: Some Explanations and Speculations', *Australian Outlook*, Vol. 28, No. 2, August 1974, p 123.

77. Clark, Ian, 'The Indian Ocean', *Australia in World Affairs 1971-75*, W.J. Hudson, (ed.), George Allen & Unwin, Sydney, 1980, p 317.

78. *Ibid.*

79. Whitlam, E.G., *Abiding Interests*, University of Queensland Press, Qld., 1997, p 205.

80. Price, Charles 'Beyond White Australia: The Whitlam Government's Immigration Record', *TRT*, No. 258, April 1975, p 377.

81. CPD, (H of R), Vol. 17, 5 December 1957, p 2955.

82. Chauvel, Richard, 'Up the Creek Without a Paddle: Australia, West New Guinea and the "Great and Powerful Friends" ', *Menzies in War and Peace*, Frank Cain, (ed.) Allen & Unwin, Sydney, 1997, p 55. Evatt's view on WNG was that 'the sovereignty of Netherlands in Western New Guinea is undoubted.' See Amry & Mary Belle Vandenbosch *Australia Faces Southeast Asia*, University of Kentucky Press, Lexington, 1967, p 43.

83. CPD, (H of R), Vol. 17, 5 December 1957, p 2955. In his call for an understanding of the Indonesian claim, Whitlam also reminded the House that the Dutch caused more Indonesian deaths in the late 1940s than the Japanese inflicted in the early 1940s. *ibid.* p 2956.

84. CPD, (H of R), Vol. 29, 25 October 1960, p 2342.

85. *Ibid.*, p 2340.

86. *Ibid.*, p 2341.

87. CPD, (H of R), Vol. 84, 24 May 1973, p 2649.

88. Whitlam, E.G., *Abiding Interests*, University of Queensland Press, Qld, Australia, 1997, p 73.

89. *Ibid.*, p 74. Whitlam went to Papua New Guinea in September 1974 to celebrate its independence after its House of Assembly had ratified independence.

90. AA, Record of conversation between I.G. Bowden and Samar Sen dated 10 January 1962, Series A1838/2, Item 169/10/1, Part 5.

91. Howson, Peter *The Howson Diaries: the Life of Politics*, Don Aitkin, (ed.) Viking, Victoria, 1984, p 176.

92. Lok Sabha Debates, Part II, 30 April 1955.

93. Interview with Sibrabata Tripathi, Deputy High Commissioner for India in Sri Lanka, 10 February 1999, at the Indian High Commission Office, Colombo.

94. Fitzgerald, *op cit.*, p 23.

95. CPD, (H of R), Vol. 88, 3 April 1974, p 905. Also see, *The Australian*, 30 March 1974 for its report on Whitlam's attitude to US and Soviet aims in Diego Garcia and US Ambassador Marshall Green's American-interest oriented view of it, in Neville Meaney, *Australia and the World*, Longman Cheshire, Melbourne, 1985, pp 760-761.

96. CPD, (H of R), Vol. 97, 7 October 1975, p 1739.

97. Lok Sabha Debates, November 12, 1973, Col. 253.

98. 'Australia's 1956', (Editorial), *The Daily News*, Sri-Lanka, 14 December 1972. The Editorial title (Australia's 1956) draws a comparison of the Whitlam impact with the election of S.W.R.D. Bandaranaike, a democratic socialist committed to reform, as prime Minister of Sri-Lanka in 1956.

99. *Ibid.*

100. CPD, (H of R), Vol. 56, 17 August 1967, p 219.

101. *Ibid.*, p 220.

102. *Ibid.*, p 219.

103. 'Mrs Gandhi Calls for Regional Cooperation', *The Statesman*, Delhi, 20 May 1968, p 1.

104. CPD, (H of R), Vol. 56, 17 August 1967, p 219.

105. 'Participation in Algiers Talks', *The Times of India*, 6 June 1973, p 11.

106. Kamath, M.V., 'Commonwealth Overhauled at Ottawa', *The Times of India*, 12 August 1973, in Shri Ram Sharma, *Indian Foreign Policy Annual Survey: 1973*, Sterling Publishers, New Delhi, 1977, p 147.

107. Freudenberg, Graham, *A Certain Grandeur: Gough Whitlam in Politics*, Sun Books, South Melbourne, 1978, pp 56-57.

108. CPD, (H of R), Vol. 29, 25 October 1960, p 2340.

109. Whitlam, E.G., *Abiding Interests*, University of Queensland Press, Qld., 1997, p 20.

110. Wolpert, Stanley, *Nehru: A Tryst with Destiny*, Oxford University Press, New York, 1996, p 460.

111. CPD, (H of R), Vol. 56, 17 August 1967, p 220.

112. *Ibid.*, p 219.

113. Mediansky, F.A., 'The Conservative Style in Australian Foreign Policy', *Australian Outlook*, Vol. 28, No. 1, April 1974, p 50.

114. Howson, *op. cit.*, p 202.

115. Nanda, B.R., 'Father and Daughter', *New India Digest*, No. 42, September-October 1994, p 19. Also see, *Freedom's Daughter: Letters between Indira Gandhi and Jawaharlal Nehru 1922-39*, Sonia Gandhi (ed.) Hodder & Stoughton, London, 1989.

116. Gandhi, Sonia (ed.), *Freedom's Daughter: Letters between Indira Gandhi and Jawaharlal Nehru 1922-39*, Hodder & Stoughton, London, 1989, pp 8-9.

117. Lyons, Peter, 'The Indian Bomb: Nuclear Tests for "Peaceful Purposes" ?' *TRT* No. 256, October 1974, pp 403-410. Sardar Patel was a Congress Party stalwart and Cabinet member who was highly regarded for his efficiency and organisational skills by men like Nehru and Mountbatten. See Jagmohan (MP and former Governor of Jammu and Kashmir)'A Thought for the Great Sardar', *The Indian Express*, 30 October 1997.

118. Gandhi, *op. cit.*, p 1.

119. Rajan, M.S., *Studies on India's Foreign Policy*, ABC Publishing House, New Delhi, 1993, p 156. For her speech to the UN, see, MEA, Foreign Affairs Record, Vol. XIV, No. 10, October 1968, Government of India, pp 230-234. Also see, 'Indira Gandhi: A Dynamic Decade of Progress', A symposium held in 1976 at Punjab University, India.

120. Candland, Christopher, 'Congress Decline and Party Pluralism in India', *Journal of International Affairs*, Vol. 51, No. 1, Summer 1997. p 27.

121. Bultjens, Ralph, 'Image and Reality', *New India Digest*, No. 42, September-October 1994, p 9.

122. *Ibid.* Mrs Gandhi's numerous speeches on a wide range of issues made in India and in many other countries offer an insight into her personal philosophy and attitude on many issues: For some of these, see, *The Years of Endeavour: Selected Speeches of Indira Gandhi, August 1969-August 1972*, Ministry of Information & Broadcasting, Government of India, New Delhi, 1975.

123. *Ibid.*, p 8.

124. *Ibid*. Also see Norman D. Palmer, 'Some Personal Impressions', *New India Digest*, No. 24, September-October 1994, pp 13-26.

125. Whitlam, Gough, *The Whitlam Government 1972-1975*, Viking, Victoria, 1985, p 123.

126. Kumar, Satish, (ed.), *Documents on India's Foreign Policy: 1972*, Macmillan, New Delhi, 1976, p 217.

127. MEA, *Foreign Affairs Record*, Vol. XIX 1973, No. 1, Government of India, New Delhi, p 215.

128. *Ibid*.

129. *Ibid*., p 217.

130. *Ibid*., p 216.

131. *Ibid*.

132. Lok Sabha Debates 2 August 1973, Col. 1776.

133. *AFAR*, June 1973, Vol. 44, No. 6, DFAT, AGPS, Canberra, p 394.

134. Lok Sabha Debates, 29 March 1974, Col. 83. For details of numerous areas of agreement between Mrs Gandhi and Whitlam, see India-Australia Joint Communiqué dated 6 June 1973, *Asian Recorder*, Vol. 19, 1973, Government of India, New Delhi, pp 11492-11494.

135. *Hindustan Times*, 14 May 1965 in S.C. Gangul, *India and the Commonwealth*, Shiva Lal Agarwala, India, 1970, p 57.

136. Sharma, Shri Ram (ed.), *Indian Foreign Affairs Annual Survey: 1973*, Sterling Publishers, New Delhi, 1977, p 145.

137. Nair, V.M., 'Mr Whitlam's Australia: The Search for Friendships nearer Home', *The Statesman*, Delhi, 4 June 1973, p 6.

138. *The Age*, 6 June 1973, (Editorial).

139. Clark, Ian, 'Indian Ocean' *Australia in World Affairs 1971-75*, W.J. Hudson (ed.) George Allen & Unwin, Sydney, 1980, p 316. Clark cites the *Australian Financial Review*, 5 June 1973; *The Times*, 7 June 1973; *Hindustan Times*, 14 June 1973.

140. AFAR, 'Australia and Asia in the Seventies', May 1974, Vol. 45, No. 5, DFAT, AGPS, Canberra, p 320.

141. MEA, Government of India, New Delhi, *Foreign Affairs Record, Report 1973/1974*, pp 35-36, *Report 1974/1975*, pp 33-34, *Report 1975/1976*, pp 23, 109, 127.

142. Vicziany, M, *Australia-India: Economic Links Past, Present and Future*, Indian Ocean Centre for Peace Studies, University of Western Australia, Perth, 1993, p 3 (Introduction).

143. East Asia Analytical Unit, *India's Economy at the Midnight Hour: Australia's India Strategy*, DFAT, AGPS, Canberra, 1994, p 3.

144. AA, UPI News Report dated 2 November 1964, Series A1838/2, Item 169/11/52, Part 7.

145. Whitlam E.G., Address to the National Press Club, Wellington, 8 May 1975, Department of Foreign Affairs, *A Selection of Extracts from Statements on Foreign Affairs*, p 6, in David Lee and Christopher Walters, (eds.) *Evatt to Evans: Labor Tradition in Australian Foreign Policy*, Allen & Unwin, NSW, 1997, p 186.

146. Whitlam, E.G., 'Nehru Champion of Freedom', Address to an International Seminar- Nehru the Man and His Vision, UNESCO House, Sydney, 27-29 September, 1989.

147. Moraes, Frank, *Jawaharlal Nehru*, Macmillan, New York, 1956, pp 11-12 in G. Ramachandram, *Nehru and World Peace*, Radiant Publishers, New Delhi, 1990, p 13.

148. Seton, Marie, *Panditji: A Portrait of Nehru*, Dennis Dobson, London, 1967, p 149.

149. Nehru, Jawaharlal, 'Our Problems', *Indo Asian Culture*, October 1957, pp 119-124, in G. Ramachandram, *Nehru and World Peace*, Radiant Publishers, New Delhi, 1990, p 15.

150. See E.G. Whitlam, 'Australia's Foreign Policy: New Directions, New Definitions', the Twenty Fourth Roy Milne Memorial lecture on 30 November 1973, Brisbane. Published by the Australian Institute of International Affairs, p 3.

151. CPD, (H of R), Vol. 9, 14 March 1956, pp 804-805.

152. CPD, (H of R), Vol. 84, 24 May 1973, p 2646.

153. Albinski, Henry, 'The Role of Foreign Policy in Australian Electoral Politics: Some Explanations and Speculations', *Australian Outlook*, Vol. 28, No. 2, August 1974. p 123.

154. Nehru, Jawaharlal, *India's Foreign Policy*, p 89 in G. Ramachandram, *Nehru and World Peace*, Radiant Publishers, New Delhi, 1990, p 117.

155. *The Statesman*, New Delhi, 21 March 1956 in S.C. Gangul, *India and the Commonwealth*, Shiva Lal Agarwala, India, 1970, p 35.

156. Lok Sabha Debates, 4 August 1950, Vol. V, Part II, Col. 387.

157. CPD, (H of R), Vol. 61, 5 November 1968, p 2429.

158. *Jawaharlal Nehru's Speeches*, March 1963-May 1964, Vol. V, Ministry of Information & Broadcasting, Government of India, New Delhi, 1968, p 206.

159. See E.G. Whitlam, 'Australia's Foreign Policy: New Directions, New Definitions', the Twenty Fourth Roy Milne Memorial lecture on 30 November 1973, Brisbane. Published by the Australian Institute of International Affairs, p 6.

160. Kamath, M.V., 'Commonwealth overhauled at Ottawa' *Times of India*, 12 August 1973, in Shri Ram Sharma, (ed.) *Indian Foreign Policy Annual Survey: 1973*, Sterling Publishers, New Delhi, 1977, p 147.

161. The Value of the Commonwealth of Nations: Prime Minister Gough Whitlam reports to Parliament on 22 August 1973 on the meeting of Commonwealth Heads of Government in Ottawa, see Neville Meaney, *Australia and the World*, Longman Cheshire, Melbourne 1985, pp 763-764.

162. Ingram, Derek, 'Prospects for Ottawa: The Prime Ministers Prepare', *TRT*, No. 250, April 1973, p 180.

163. King, Jonathan, *Waltzing Materialism*, Harper & Row, Sydney, 1978, p 14.

164. *Jawaharlal Nehru's Speeches*, March 1963-May 1964, Vol. 5, Ministry of Information & Broadcasting, Government of India, New Delhi, 1968, p 149.

165. Freudenberg, *op cit.*, p 82.

166. *Jawaharlal Nehru's Speeches*, September 1946-May 1949, Vol. 1, Ministry of Information & Broadcasting, Government of India, New Delhi, 1949, pp 318.-319. Rajni Kothari comments that in stressing the equality of man and 'the notion of a world order based on the equality of all states ...' Nehru was an early voice. See *Footsteps into the Future*, The Free Press, New York, 1975, p xxi. (Preface)

167. Whitlam, E.G., 'Labor at Home', the 1972, Fabian Winter Lecture Series, Labor in Power-What is the Difference? See Fabian Society Pamphlet 22.

168. Freudenberg, *op cit.* p 80.

169. Fitzgerald, Stephen, *Is Australia an Asian Country*, Allen & Unwin, NSW, 1997, p 22. Also see the editorial comment that Whitlam's 'liberal Socialist image and now foreign policy with an Asian emphasis have an appeal for New Delhi...' , *The Statesman*, Delhi, 7 June 1973, p 6.

170. Whitlam, E.G., 'Nehru Champion of Freedom', Address to an International Seminar- Nehru the Man and His Vision, UNESCO House, Sydney, 27-29 September, 1989.

171. Bruce Grant indicated that it was the one thing that Whitlam was clearly unhappy about India. Interview with Bruce Grant, (Former High Commissioner to India), 19 May 1999, Domain Street, South Yarra, Melbourne.

172. *AFAR*, Senator Willesee's address to the Australian Institute of International Affairs' Conference in Adelaide, 15 June 1974, p 371, in Ian Clark, 'The Indian Ocean', *Australia in World Affairs, 1971-1975*, W.J. Hudson, (ed.), George Allen & Unwin, Sydney, 1980, p 316.

173. Freudenberg, G., 'Gough Whitlam', *The Great: Heroes, Larrikins, Leaders, Visionaries: The Fifty Men and Women Who Shaped Australia*, Leonie Kramer (ed.), Angus & Robertson, Sydney, 1986 p 311.

174. See E.G. Whitlam 'Australia's Foreign Policy: New Directions, New Definitions', the Twenty Fourth Roy Milne Memorial lecture on 30 November 1973, Brisbane. Published by the Australian Institute of International Affairs, p 14.

175. CPD, (H of R), Vol. 56, 17 August 1967, p 220.

176. Ray, Sunanda Datta, 'Where good Anglo-Indians go to die', *The Sydney Morning Herald*, 28 November 1983, p 9.

177. *Ibid*.

178. AA, Despatch No. 2/64 2 June 1964, from Plimsoll to Hasluck, Series A1838/272, Item 169/1/3, Part 3.

179. *The Statesman*, New Delhi, 7 June 1973, p 6

180. *The Times of India*, 8 June 1973, p 8.

# Conclusion

While past writings on bilateral relations have been of considerable value, the logic of enquiry has been largely in terms of how the West's - which included Australia - interests were affected and consequently a Western interpretation of Cold War events and the two countries' responses to them has been advanced. As this analysis argues, the realist orthodoxy became the criterion for measurement of not only super power conduct in the tense Cold War environment, but also for analysing the relationship between non-aligned India and aligned Australia. Thus, the end result tended to suffer from this one-dimensional approach to assessments and interpretations leaving a perceptual gap in the understanding of the bilateral relationship. The impetus for this Indian perspective, was to ensure that the relationship is examined and explained in all its dimensions and nuances enabling a better understanding to be reached.

It should be noted that the two opening chapters provide various international relation concepts and frameworks such as analysis of the doctrine of realism and the critical theory school. In particular, there was an intensive debate on the meaning of bilateralism and an examination of how it operates in the real world of foreign policy operation. Throughout the body of this work there has been a concentrated effort to inform the major interpretive framework with conceptual and theoretical insights relating to the impact of personalities and policies as the key factors in the relationship.

A number of themes examined demonstrate the way in which the relationship developed in each of the three periods, 1947-49, 1949-72 and 1972-75. The examination shows, the relationship over the whole period (1947-75) failed to reach a sustainable level of maturity; except for a fleeting mutuality of interest seen in the 1947-1949 (Nehru/Chifley-Evatt) period, and restored to life two decades later in 1972 with the Whitlam-Indira Gandhi affinity, for most of the twenty-eight years examined it has been largely characterised by indifference on both sides.

Given that there were different and weighty considerations affecting the state of global politics, (a central factor) between 1947-1975, crucial to the effectiveness in bilateral terms of each period was, the personalities of these key players. It embraced personal style, political philosophy and ideological commitment, competing egos and clashing ambitions and, of course, the impact of public opinion on their choice of policies. Public opinion was an important influence but it was not something that was measured with any degree of precision at the time. Newspaper editorials and the media in general represented the best guide to informed public debate. Nehru and Menzies were sensitive to public opinion and would not act against deeply held domestic beliefs such as in 'Non-alignment' and 'White Australia' policies respectively.

The impact of the personality factor is made particularly evident in the discussion of the Nehru-Menzies conflict because of their fundamental divergence over ideology, but was no less a determinant with Chifley, Evatt, Nehru, Casey, Mrs Gandhi and Whitlam where scrutiny of their policies reveals a high level of mental conformity.

For example, while Menzies was not generally averse to the use of force, Nehru searched for peaceful solutions. Nehru was an idealist imbued with a strong sense of nationalism and he was determined to mediate as an independent arbitrator at the international level on behalf of peace and equality. Menzies, a pragmatist, was equally determined to maintain a 'White Australia', Anglophile values, and help protect the Western world from the influence of Communism through subservience to US strategic goals. Crocker underlines this with the observation that, 'America had no more obedient pupil than Australia in learning and intoning the slogans about "the global Communist conspiracy" and "the single Communist enemy".'[1] Consequently, despite Nehru's early interests in drawing Australia closer to Asia and away from its European origins, seen in the discussion of the relationship in the Chifley period (1947-1949) in Chapter Two, Menzies' open Western bias (maintained by his successors) resulted in Australia failing to figure again in India's wider regional and global interests. Against such an individually rigid but bilaterally wobbly framework, there was little scope for improvement until 1972 with the beginnings of an *entente cordiale* in the relationship with Australia seen in a new light. R.G. Neale states:

> So basic were the differences that only major changes in the nature and areas of world conflict, in the internal political and economic structure and the power ratios of the two nations, and in the process of and personnel involved in policy-making, would have been likely to bring them together. In fact none of these changes occurred.[2]

The analysis also demonstrates that the differences between the two countries were fundamentally compounded by the two policies, 'White Australia' and 'Non-alignment.' Considered crucial to his particular view of the world, for Menzies, exclusion of non-Europeans was important to his sense of Britishness and the Empire and entailed in some eyes a suggestion of racial superiority. He allowed this to become the basis for his response to India, failing in the process to understand the importance of India regionally to Australia. For Nehru, racial discrimination was anathema and its abolition became a constant crusade. In the case of non-alignment, it was a natural policy choice for India given the country's colonial experience and its numerous needs after independence (geo-political, economic aid and peace) that it was expected to serve. Menzies' criticism of it was that it helped the cause of the Communist camp, a charge that was difficult to sustain considering that Chou En Lai once called Nehru 'the running dog of imperialism' and Russia's Vyshinsky told India, 'at best you are dreamers and idealists. At worst you... camouflage horrible American policy.'[3]

Another postulate of the study is that the juxtaposition of Pakistan in the India-Australia relationship led to doubts about Australia's evenhanded approach (in the 1950s and 1960s) to the handling of its diplomacy with the two warring nations of the subcontinent. The enquiry demonstrates that the Australian tilt to Pakistan was unambiguous with the reasons traceable, firstly, to the period of the British Raj and the devious methods it employed in the management of Hindu-Muslim differences for its own purposes; and, then, the analysis establishes the crucial consequence of this for the India-Australia relationship when some in Australia inherited British attitudes and with it, the partiality to Pakistan. This bias was particularly evident in Australia's conduct of diplomacy over Kashmir.

The impact of this on India was made worse by the role of SEATO to which Pakistan belonged along with Australia and its allies Britain and the US.

The examination argues that the Colombo Plan, a predominantly Australian initiative, became a two-edged sword failing in its primary aim of achieving a greater level of acceptance in Asia of Australia's interests in its economic well-being because of some doubts about Australia's real motives. For India, while the benefits of Australian aid were not doubted, it carried a note of insincerity. Nehru thought the objective of preventing the spread of Communism by offering aid to poorer nations appeared opportunistic and took away 'the grace of the act.'[4]

The study concludes that the departure of Menzies in 1966 did little to improve the bilateral relationship although some easing of the 'White Australia' Policy did take place soon after. It does this by showing that the Governments of Holt, Gorton, and McMahon that followed, maintained the primary thrust of conservative foreign policy which looked at 'Asia as an arena for action rather than on Asians as actors.'[5] As Datta Ray observed in November 1983, when he offered a retrospective Indian view of Australia (published in *The Sydney Morning Herald*), Menzies was seen not only as a strong supporter of South Africa at Commonwealth Prime Ministers' Meetings, but also as someone who preferred the former 'inner club of the older white dominions, leaving new Asian and African members out in the cold.'[6] An editorial in *The Statesman* observed that Australia's close identification with the West in the twenty-three years of conservative governments (1949-1972) included a continuing commitment to that policy by those who followed Menzies though they were 'not altogether unaware of the absurdity of Australia's "western" pretensions...'[7]. Datta Ray also believed that India's perceptions of the policies of Australia's conservative governments had firmed up by the time of Gorton and McMahon, but there were high expectations that the Whitlam Labor Government of 1972, viewed as a watershed, might free Australia from its British ties and 'follow the Indian precedent' to become another republic.[8]

Another disclosure which springs from the personality theme, is that the Indira Gandhi-Whitlam affinity (1972-1975) was crucial to the future of the relationship. The emergence of Mrs Gandhi as Prime Minister in 1966 with strong views on Vietnam and a continuing commitment to non-alignment, meant a continuation of policy conflict with conservative Australia and indifference in the relationship. Her visit to Australia in 1968, seen as important by the Australian media, had little impact on Prime Minister Gorton preoccupied with the great issue of the period, Vietnam. The book argues that Australia's regional interests and strategic objectives dictated by Cold War imperatives of the Menzies era largely continued until the arrival of the Whitlam Government at the end of 1972. It became the turning point for the bilateral relationship. Whitlam's broader philosophy and his psychological view of the world enabled him to promptly jettison some of Australia's sacred cows of the past: colonialism, support for South Africa and Rhodesia, remnants of the 'White Australia' Policy, involvement in Vietnam, the recognition of China issue and colonial authority over Papua New Guinea. These were no longer matters that tarnished Australia's image in India.

The analysis of the Whitlam-Indira Gandhi period of the relationship bears out the proposition that Whitlam's approach to India was informed by a sensitivity to the country's colonial experience as well as its unique social, economic and geo-political circumstances. His interest in the region and the demonstration of greater independence in foreign policy (although remaining in ANZUS and retaining US bases in Australia) were strong messages to India that Australia was capable of, and serious about, being an equal partner in the Asia-Pacific, conscious of its geography and not shackled by its history. While Whitlam's arrival in 1972 made no significant difference to the strategic divergence of the two countries, *The Times of India* in an Editorial on Whitlam's 1973 talks with Mrs Gandhi and 'his unqualified support for the ... Indian Ocean as a zone of peace' observed that, 'as the years go by Mr Whitlam will perhaps tone down its (Australia's) association with old military alliances.' [9] Whitlam explained the new Government's attitude to the earlier doctrinaire political philosophy:

> Precisely what we are trying to do is to break out of a kind of ideological isolationism which has limited the conduct of our affairs in the past. In our own region, in our dealings with all the countries of that region we think it's time for an ideological holiday. [10]

Unlike in the Holt, Gorton and McMahon led periods of the relationship, the broad Nehruvian policies, which continued under Mrs Gandhi, had a positive impact on the relationship with Whitlam. As the analysis demonstrates, the closeness of Whitlam's views (unequivocally stated during his years as a member of the House of representatives from 1953) with those constantly articulated by Nehru, was an important factor (not previously considered) in the reasons for Whitlam's greater acceptance. The cumulative effect of Whitlam's enlightened philosophy and foreign policy initiatives, and Mrs Gandhi's enthusiastic responses to them, made the Indian media perceive Australia as self-assertive, prepared to transcend its anglophile roots and acquire an independent identity.[11] Also, for India, used to the Nehru-Menzies confrontation and three decades of ideological rigidity, the Whitlam approach was a significant and refreshing change.

There was also the indirect dimension to Whitlam's impact. His greater independence in foreign policy, and the elimination of the remnants of British symbols and protocols, gave Australia a greater sense of pride in being a sovereign nation, less afraid of its Asian neighbours. With the emphasis on a mono-culture population progressively lessened, it is not unreasonable to argue that Australians became more accepting of the idea of a multicultural society with the India-Australia relationship a beneficiary of that readjustment. Of course, any change of this kind has to break through hard-core attitudes and takes time. Dr Mark Lopez in his article in *The Age* of 25 August, 2000 traces Canberra public servant Jim Houston's role in introducing the concept of multiculturalism in the Whitlam period.

> Only a few people promoted multiculturalism at this time, and most of them had seen the election of the Whitlam Government in December 1972, ... as a great opportunity to effect change. [12]

Of importance also was the joint Whitlam-Indira Gandhi role as a catalyst to secure a transition in the India-Australia relationship and its future development with real achievements flowing from the activism of the 1980s and continuing into the 1990s in a more tangible form. In a general overview of the reformist Whitlam Government, Hugh V. Emy says, 'one may argue that, in several ways, the Whitlam era prepared the ground for the Hawke Government.'[13]

It is instructive to stress that the Whitlam-Indira Gandhi Governments' catalytic influence on the relationship is better revealed when examined at many levels and over the longer term; that is to say, when contrasting the pre-1972 era with the post-1972 period of the relationship, it must be in terms of the progress made beyond the purely official bilateral relations between the two Governments. It also needs to be evaluated in the time frame of the decades after the initial policy impact of Whitlam liberalism, the important breakthrough. Examination of these other levels, which take in the post-Whitlam-Indira Gandhi (1972-1975) account of progress in the relationship in its totality, (beyond the scope of this examination), would include the bilaterally constructive activities of organisations such as:

- The Australia India Council
- Australia India Business Council
- Commonwealth activities
- DFAT's Economic, Cultural and Educational initiatives
- The Indian Ocean Centre for Peace Studies
- The National Centre for South Asian Studies
- UN Agencies

In terms of bilateral effectiveness, this work makes out a case for the view that the Whitlam-Indira Gandhi period was a peak in the relationship though limited to three years. However, for the future of the bilateral relationship, it left a positive legacy enabling progressive engagement, initially in the Fraser period because of his commitment to the Commonwealth link and the strong views he shared with India on racial discrimination in Africa; however, because of his anti-Soviet stance and his lack of interest in the Indian Ocean as a zone of peace, there were no great strides made in India-Australia relations in his time. Further initiatives to quicken the pace of improvement in the relationship, (particularly in the area of trade where dramatic increases took place as shown in Figure 3, Chapter Seven) were taken in the Hawke-Rajiv Gandhi Ministries including reciprocal visits. (Rajiv Gandhi visited Australia in 1986 and Hawke to India in 1989).

Also made manifest is that, with India's Congress Party policies in place (under Nehru and Mrs Gandhi) throughout the period (1947-1975) the depth of engagement between the two countries depended on which Australian political party or coalition held office in Canberra. This is achieved by showing that, with Chifley and Nehru, besides the mutual admiration, there was a common interest in some areas of foreign policy absent in any previous Australian conservative government's response to Asia and the sub-continent. The sharp regression in the relationship thereafter with Menzies assuming the Prime Ministership, followed by the excitement restored to it with Whitlam gaining office, leads to the conclusion that there was greater engagement between the two countries during periods when Labor was in office. The book also makes reference to a roundtable discussion, between India and Australia, held in New Delhi in 1995, at which S.A. Mukherjee linked Evatt's ideas to those of Nehru and posits that, 'until Whitlam came Evatt's dreams were never fulfilled ...' [14], further evidence that Labor personalities had greater affinity with India's aspirations and political ethos.

The linking of Labor with periods of India-Australia accord is also reflected in the comments made by Indians at a recent meeting of the two countries. In a publication of the proceedings of a seminar with Indian and Australian delegates, S.K. Bhutani described the post-War relations between India and Australia as characterised by 'drift or discord', the exceptions being, he said, the 1948-1949 years and the latter half of the 1980s. He proceeded to speculate that it 'may be a coincidence that the Australian Labour (sic) Party was in power during these years...' [15]. Bhutani also questioned Australia's inability to collaborate with India on Indo-China agreements and Suez as Canada had done, or agree with India that South Africa's departure from the Commonwealth was beneficial to the Organisation, again a view Canada shared with India. [16] The positive reformist policy initiatives of the Whitlam Government were also mentioned in his paper.[17]

What then is the future for the bilateral relationship?

With its recent economic emphasis, and a range of assets 'backed by one of the most professional military establishments of the world,' [18] India is on course to become a major player in international affairs. India's Minister for External Affairs (1991) M.

Solanski underscores the importance of economic success to India's defence, with his statement that, 'the economic dimension of state power is becoming increasingly important in relation to the military dimension.'[19] Professor Dibb takes the view that provided India is successful with her new economic reforms and is not shackled by politics, a democratic, powerful and secular India may be a major influence regionally and outside it. [20] A confidential paper (written about 1951, probably by the Australian High Commissioner in New Delhi) on India relations with Australia, states:

> not all Indians are happy about the inclusion of Australia in the region (South East Asia), but a considerable body of intelligent comment recognises that India's role in the affairs of Asia can be more effectively discharged in conjunction with Australia than without it. [21] (n.d.)

In 1950, Nehru too observed that despite its European origins, Australia 'finds today inevitably that (its) geography and other things point towards Asia.' [22]

James Plimsoll, in a letter from New Delhi to DEA in Canberra in 1965, refers to a conversation he had with India's T.T. Krishnamachari (the then Minister for Economic and Defence Co-ordination) who thought that he 'could envisage working towards a defence alliance on a regional basis between Australia and India, ...'[23]. In a post-Cold War unipolar world of globalisation and multipolar economic configurations, Australia and non-aligned India, together, could play an important complementary regional role.

The book also points to many areas of common interests between India and Australia, values and experiences that could have brought the two countries together; among them democratic forms of government, independent judiciaries, membership of the Commonwealth of Nations, the speaking of English, not to mention a love of cricket. But there were also those issues that divided and stood in the way of greater engagement such as: ANZUS, 'White Australia' Policy, SEATO, the tilt to Pakistan, South Africa, colonialism and non-alignment. Of the factors of convergence and divergence, the latter, representing what was to each more important Cold War issues, made the difference as illustrated in the India-Australia Strategic Maps, Figure 1, Chapter One. In sum, Australia's motivation was strategic and pragmatic, India's more idealistic and anti-war. The personalities of some leaders such as Nehru, Chifley, Evatt, Whitlam and Mrs Gandhi ameliorated the impact of these differences on the bilateral relationship during their periods in office, as seen in the Matrix, at the end of this Conclusion.

It points to the affinity that prevailed between the leaders of India and Australia when measured against certain variables, and consequently, their impact on the quality of the bilateral relationship.

Maintenance of a strong and sustainable bilateral relationship, however, requires continuing focus on education and understanding on both sides, and a framework that transcends the particular political ideology of incumbent governments in Canberra and New Delhi of the future. Ian Copland in his response to the Report *Australia-India Relations: Trade and Security*, [24] published by the Australian Senate's Committee on Foreign Affairs, Defence and Trade in July 1990, refers to the problem of the negative imagery that has characterised Australian perceptions of India and makes the discerning observation that, 'changing the way the Australian people are accustomed to looking at their world is the real challenge.'[25]

Finally, in the context of the contemporary international environment, two other conclusions may be drawn from this study. As we begin the 21st century with the world poised yet again to engage in a war, an interesting parallel may have emerged between what this study of India-Australia relations (1947-1975) has shown and Australia's current policy response to the war in Iraq. Australia in the 1950s and 1960s was preoccupied with ensuring its security in the region particularly from the Communist threat, by involving itself in a supporting role in US-led wars. The prevailing realist orthodoxy underpinned this policy of remaining within the American sphere of security. Diplomat Crocker attests to Australia's willingness at the time, to speak the American strategic language of the day: 'America had no more obedient pupil than Australia in learning and intoning the slogans about "the global Communist conspiracy" ' and ' "the single Communist enemy." '[26]

Of course, the Communist threat evaporated with the demise of the Soviet Union and also with it, a shift took place from a bipolar to a unipolar world. But, terrorism has replaced Communism and the question is, has Australia resumed Crocker's description of the country as 'America's obedient pupil'?

On the Indian side, this study draws attention to the role of the crusader for international peace played by Nehru in the 1950s. There were those like Einstein, Bertrand Russell and President Eisenhower,[27] who saw Nehru's contribution as probably responsible for much of the peace achieved in a climate of war through his own powers of persuasion, and the *savoir faire* to bring about rapproachment, the triumph of reason and humanity over warring superpower rivalry.

If it is a case of history repeating itself in Australian foreign policy, 2003, can the world hope for a Nehruvian like peacemaker to emerge too.

## Figure 2

*Personalities and Policies: Peaks and Troughs*

| Name | Personality | Philosophy | Policy | Public Opinion |
|---|---|---|---|---|
| **INDIA** | | | | |
| NEHRU | | | | |
| 1947-1949 | + | + | + | + |
| 1949-1964 | – | – | – | – |
| MENON | | | | |
| 1947-1949 | + | + | + | + |
| 1949-1962 | – | – | – | – |
| SHASTRI | | | | |
| 1964-1966 | – | – | – | – |
| MRS. GANDHI | | | | |
| 1966-1972 | – | – | – | – |
| 1972-1975 | + | + | + | + |
| **Australia** | | | | |
| CHIFLEY | | | | |
| 1947-1949 | + | + | ± | – |
| EVATT | | | | |
| 1949-1966 | + | + | ± | – |
| MENZIES | | | | |
| 1964-1966 | – | – | – | – |

(Contd...)

(...Contd...)

| | | | |
|---|---|---|---|
| CASEY | | | |
| 1951-1990 | + | – | ± | – |
| HOLT | | | |
| 1966-1967 | – | – | ± | – |
| GORTON | | | |
| 1967-1971 | – | – | ± | – |
| McMAHON | | | |
| 1971-1972 | – | – | – | – |
| WHITLAM | | | |
| 1972-1975 | + | + | + | ± |

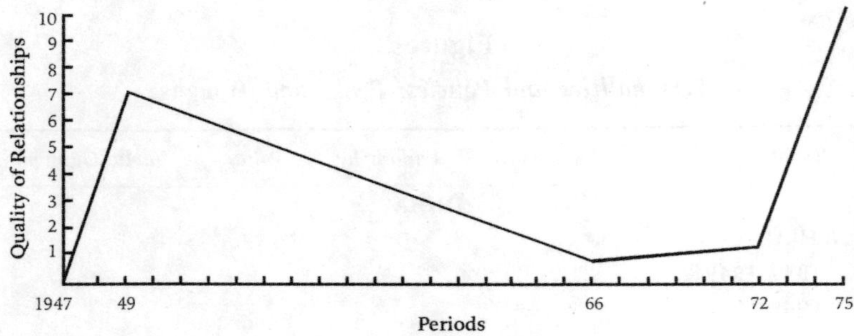

## APPENDIX-A

## A Statement Issued by Jawaharlal Nehru at a Press Conference in New Delhi on 26th September 1946

In the sphere of foreign affairs India will follow an independent policy, keeping away from power politics groups aligned one against another. She will uphold the principles of freedom for dependent peoples and will oppose racial discrimination wherever it may occur. She will work with other peace-loving nation for international cooperation and goodwill without exploitation of one nation by another.

It is necessary that, with the attainment of her full international status, India should establish contact with all the great nations of the world and that her relations with neighbouring countries in Asia should become still closer.

Towards the United Nations Organization India's attitude is that of wholehearted cooperation and unreserved adherence, in both srpit and letter, to the Chapter governing it. To that end, India will participate fully in its varied activities and endeavour to play that role in its Councils to which her geographical position, population and contribution towards peaceful progress entitle her. In particular, the Indian delegate will make it clear that India stands for the independence of all colonial and dependent people and their full right to self determination.

---

The above statement was published in Indian Information, by the Information Bureau of the Government of India, New Delhi, on 15 October 1946

# APPENDIX-B

## *Indian High Commissioners to Australia*

| | |
|---|---|
| Maharaja Shri Duleepsinjhi | 1950 |
| General K.M. Cariappa | 1953 |
| K.R.P. Singh (Acting) | |
| P.A. Menon | 1956 |
| Samar Sen | 1959 |
| B.K. Massad | 1962 |
| D.N. Chatterjee | 1965 |
| A.M. Thomas | 1967 |
| Sambasiva Krishnamurti | 1971 |
| M.J.S. Doddamani (Acting) | |
| Sumal Sinha | 1974 |

## *Australian High Commissioners to India*

| | |
|---|---|
| Iven Mackay | 1944 |
| Hugh Gollan | 1948 |
| Walter Crocker | 1952 |
| Peter Heydon | 1955 |
| Walter Crocker | 1958 |
| James Plimsoll | 1962 |
| Arthur Tange | 1965 |
| Patrick Shaw | 1970 |
| Bruce Grant | 1973 |

# Endnotes


1. Crocker, W.R., *Australian Ambassador: International Relations at First Hand*, Melbourne University Press, Victoria, 1971, p 200.

2. Neale, R.G., 'India', *Australia in World Affairs: 1956-1960*, Gordon Greenwood & Norman Harper, (eds.) F.W. Cheshire, Melbourne, 1963, p 327.

3. 'The Korean Revolution', *TRT*, Vol. XLIII, 1952-1953, p 170.

4. Note to Secretary General, Ministry of External Affairs dated 6 May 1950, File No. 330/CJK/50 in *Selected Works of Jawaharlal Nehru*, S. Gopal (ed.), Vol. 14, Part II, J. Nehru Memorial Fund, New Delhi, 1993, p 438.

5. Stargardt, A.W., *Australia's Asian Policies: The History of a Debate 1938-1972*, The Institute of Asian Affairs, Hamburg, 1977, p 228.

6. Ray, Datta, 'Where good Anglo-Indians go to die', *The Sydney Morning Herald*, 28 November 1983, p 9.

7. *The Statesman*, Delhi, 7 June 1973, p 6. (Editorial.)

8. Ray, Datta, 'Where good Anglo-Indians go to die', *The Sydney Morning Herald*, 28 November 1983. p 9.

9. *The Times of India*, 8 June 1973, p 8. (Editorial.)

10. Meaney, Neville, *Australia and the World*, Longman Cheshire, Melbourne, 1985, p 747.

11. For example, *The Statesman*, Delhi and Calcutta, 3 June 1973, 4 June 1973, 5 June 1973, 6 June 1973, 7 June 1973; *The Times of India*, New Delhi, 3 June 1973, 6 June 1973, 7 June 1973; *The Hindu*, Madras 5 December 1972, p 8.

12. Lopez, Mark, 'The Man who dared to write the m word', *The Age*, 25 August 2000, p 13. A.J. Grassby (Minister for Immigration and Cultural Affairs in the Whitlam Government,) became the first Minister to speak on the concept of multiculturalism with his lecture made in August 1973 on *A Multicultural Society for the Future*. Also see, Robert Wolfgramm, 'Revolution by Stealth', (book review, Mark Lopez, *The Origins of Multiculturalism in Australian Politics 1945-1975*, Melbourne University Press) *The Age*, 11 November 2000, p 8..

13. Emy, Hugh V., *Whitlam Re-Visited: Policy Development, Policies and Outcomes*, Hugh V. Emy *et. al.* (eds.) Pluto Press, NSW, 1993, p 16.

14. Mukherjee, S.A., *A Round Table Discussion on Australia-India Relations* arranged by the Australian High Commission, New Delhi, and the Nehru Memorial Library, February 1995, Published by the Australian High Commission, 1995, p 108.

15. Bhutani, S.K., Paper prepared for a Seminar, in *Towards an Era of Cooperation: Indo Australian Dialogue*, Dipankar Bannerjee, (ed.) Institute for Defence Studies, New Delhi, 1995, p 369.

16. *Ibid.*, p 371.

17. *Ibid.*, p 373.

18. Singh, Jasjit, 'An Indian Perspective', *India Looks East: An Emerging Power and its Asia Pacific Neighbours* , Sandy Gordon & Stephen Henningham, (eds.) Defence Studies Centre, ANU, 1995,pp 47-48

19. Solanski, Madhavsinh, 'India's Foreign Policy Perspectives in the 1990s' Inaugural speech at the India International Centre, New Delhi, 13 August 1991, p 3.

20. Dibb, Paul, *Towards a New Balance of Power in Asia*, Adelphi Paper 295, International Institute for Strategic Studies, Oxford University Press, New York, p 34.

21. AA, Confidential paper on Australia-India Relations, circa 1951, Series A1838/283, Item 169/10/11/3, Part 1.

22. *The National Herald*, Lucknow, 28 December 1950, Nehru's speech on Menzies visit to New Delhi.

23. AA, Interview with Krishnamachari by Plimsoll 20 June 1963, Series A1838/2, Item 169/10/1 Part 6.

24. *Australia-India Relations: Trade and Security*, DFAT, AGPS, Canberra, 1990.

25. Copland, Ian, *Australia and India: The Next Ten Years*, Melbourne South Asian Studies Group, Melbourne, 1991, p 53.

26. Crocker, W.R., *Australian Ambassador: International Relations at First Hand*, Melbourne University Press, Victoria, 1971, p 200.

27. Ramachandram, G., *Nehru and World Peace*, Radiant Publishers, New Delhi, 1990,

## PRIMARY MATERIAL

### Documents: Australian National Archives, Canberra Files covering the period 1946-1965


Series A1838/283. Documents relative to India relations with Australia, Pakistan, the Soviet Union, the USA and China. The Files include the Kashmir dispute, Dr Graham's Negotiations, the Owen Dixon Report, Indo-China, UN peace-keeping forces in Korea, visit of Soviet Leaders to India.

Series A 1838/278. Correspondence, memoranda, letters, cables, savingrams, records of conversations, statements, press conferences, speeches and press clippings on the Korean War, Immigration issues, India relations with Pakistan, Kashmir, US aid to Pakistan and the Colombo Plan.

Series A1838/275. Files refer to Migration from India.

Series A1838/272. Official correspondence between the Australian High Commission in New Delhi and DEA on Australia-India relations.

Series A1838/2, A 1838/263. Diplomatic correspondence and confidential reports relating to External affairs, defence, economic aid and trade. The files deal with Korean prisoners of war issues, the Commonwealth, Apartheid, the 'White Australia' Policy, non-alignment, US-India relations, China border dispute, Pakistan and Kashmir, Goa, visits by the Australian Prime Minister and Minister for External Affairs to India, Indian visitors to Australia.

Series A1838/1. Department of External Affairs documents on India-Canada links, trade enquiries, India cultural agreements.

Series A 67061/1. Message from the Prime Minister of UK on Australia/Canada joint military assistance to India during the China Border War.

Series A4311, A4534/1. Material relative to India and the Commonwealth.

Series CP554/1/1, A9790/1. Documents on India-Australia trade, Colombo Plan aid, Soviet and British assistance to the Indian Steel Industry, imports and exports-India.


### Documents: National Library of Australia


MS 3155 Letter from P. Heydon to J. Plimsoll

MS 4936 Letter from R.G. Casey to R.G. Menzies

Letter from R. G. Menzies to McEwen Letter from R.G. Menzies to Justice Frankfurter


### Documents : National Archives of India, New Delhi


Files F16/102-XPP/53(s), 61-CJK & 1(66) EURII Korean War

File FJ/53/99041/16/70(s) UN Korean repatriation - India's role

File 9(8)-UN11/52 Indian Proposal for the settlement of the Indo-China Dispute

File 1012/IANZ Treatment of Indians

Files 14(2)-AFRI & (25)UNII Treatment of Indians in South Africa

Files 23/1/10-XPP, 7/2/25-XP(P) & 260 IANZ Anti-Indian Propaganda in Australia

File P III/52/19350/1 Pakistan Border Raids

File P III/52/55669/2 Nehru-Liaquat Ali Correspondence

File 16/2-XPP/53 (Parts I & II) (S) Pakistan-US Military Pacts

File P III/52/99147/2 US- Anti Indian Views on Kashmir.

File 35(56)-AMS- India's Continuation in the Commonwealth

File 2/52-AMS (FA) Pt I & II Colombo Plan Meeting - Scholarships

File containing Annual Political Report (1st January 1952 to 31 December 1952) - High Commissioner for India in Australia.

## Manuscripts examined at the Nehru Memorial Library, New Delhi.

Accession No. 49 Document by S.S. Bhatia (Director, Indian Institute of International Understanding)

Accession No. 1097 Record of M.H. Heikal interview with J. Nehru.

Accession No. 952 Review of *Jawaharlal Nehru: A Biography* by Hugh Tinker.

Accession No. 1423 Diary of J. Nehru - Commonwealth Prime Ministers Conference 1960.

Accession No. 656 Record of Dennis Tuohy interview with Lord Mountbatten

## Documents: Public Records Office, London

cp (49) 139 Commonwealth Memoranda

cc 60 (52) Minutes of Unite Kingdom Cabinet Meeting

cc 63 (52) Prime Minister's Statement on the Korean War

cc (52) Minutes of United Kingdom Cabinet Meeting

c (52) 50 Note from the Prime Minister to the Secretary, Ministry of Defence

57/5826 CRS A 462AA Minutes of Meeting of Commonwealth Prime Ministers Conference

Telegram 2731 Commonwealth Relations Office to the United Kingdom High Commission in India.

## Documents: The Commonwealth Secretariat, London.

Minutes of Meetings and Memoranda at the Commonwealth Prime Ministers Meeting, London, 6-15 September 1966, Copy No. 220.

File: SG 131/69/1, Brief re Commonwealth Cooperation - 1966 to 1969.

## Government Records

Commonwealth Parliamentary Debates, (Australia) House of Representatives and the Senate.

Current Notes on International Affairs.

Asia in Australian Higher Education. Report of the Inquiry into the Teaching of Asian Studies and Languages in Higher Education submitted to the Australian Council of Higher Education, 1989.

A National Strategy for the Study of Asia in Australia. Asian Studies Council 1988.

Lok Sabha Debates (India).

Parliamentary (Lok Sabha) Debates.

## Government Publications

*Australian Foreign Affairs Record*

*A Roundtable Discussion on Australia-India Relations* held at the Nehru Memorial Library New Delhi, 14 February 1995. Published by the Australian High Commission, New Delhi, 1995.

DFAT, *Australia-India Relations: Trade and Security*, (Senate Report) Canberra: AGPS, 1990.

DFAT. *In the National Interest, Australia's Foreign Trade Policy*. White Paper 1997. National Capital Printing, Canberra.

East Asia Analytical Unit. *Australia's Economy at the Midnight Hour: Australia's India Strategy*. Canberra: DFAT. AGPS, 1994.

Garnaut, Ross. *Australia and the North East Asian Ascendancy*. Report to the Prime Minister and Minister for Foreign Affairs and Trade, Canberra: AGPS, 1989.

*The ANZUS Alliance*, Paper by the Joint Committee on Foreign Affairs and Defence, the Parliament of the Commonwealth of Australia, AGPS, 1982.

'Treaty Actions.' *US Department of State Dispatch*, Subject: United States Foreign Relations Treaties, Vol. 5, Issue 50, 12 December 1994.

All India Congress Committee. New Delhi, 1973, *Aspects of Our Foreign Policy: From Speeches and Writings of Indira Gandhi*.

Lok Sabha Secretariat, *Foreign Policy of India: Texts of Documents 1947-64*, New Delhi, 1966.

*India 1993- A Reference Annual*, New Delhi, Ministry of Information & Broadcasting, Government of India, New Delhi, 1994.

Chopra, P.N.(ed.), *Whose Who of Indian Martyrs*, New Delhi: Ministry of Education and Youth Services, Government of India, 1969, Vol. I, 1972, Vol. II.

Kashyap, Subash C. (ed.), *Jawaharlal Nehru: His Life, Work and Legacy*, New Delhi, Indian Parliamentary Group, Lok Sabha Secretariat, 1990.

MEA, *Foreign Affairs Record*, Government of India, New Delhi, 1964 to 1973.

## Books and Monograms

Agarwala, A.N. et. al. (eds.), *India: Basic Economic Information*, New Delhi, National Publishing House, 1986.

Aitkin, Don. (ed.), *Surveys of Australian Political Science*, Sydney, George Allen & Unwin, 1985.

Akbar, M.J., *Kashmir: behind the Vale*, New Delhi, Viking, 1991.

Appadorai, A., *Select Documents on India's Foreign Policy and Relations 1947-1972* Delhi, Oxford University Press, 1982, Vol. I.

————. *Political Ideas in Modern India: Impact of the West*, New Delhi, Academic Books, 1971.

Albinsky, Henry., *Australian External Policy Under Labor*, Qld: Queensland University Press, 1977.

Alhuwalia, Shashi., *Nehru: 100 Years*, Delhi, Manas Publications, 1988.

Anderson, D. (ed.), *Australia and Indonesia: A Partnership in the Making*, Sydney, Pacific Security Research Institute, 1991.

Andrews, E.M., *A History of Australian Foreign Policy*, Melbourne, Longman Cheshire, 1979.

Ayoob, M., *India and South East Asia: Indian Perceptions and Policies*, London, Routledge, 1990.

Bain, J.S., *India's International Disputes: A Legal Study*, Bombay, Asia Publishing House, 1962.

Baker, Roy S. and William E. Dodd. *The Public Papers of Woodrow Wilson: War and Peace*, New York, Harper, 1927.

Bandyopadhyaya, J., *North Over South*, New Delhi, South Asian Publishers, 1982.

————. *The Making of India's Foreign Policy*, Delhi, Allied Publishers, 1980.

Bannerjee, Dipankar., *Towards an Era of Cooperation: An Indo-Australian Dialogue*, New Delhi, Institute for Defence Studies, 1995.

Battacharya, N., *India in a Changing World*, Delhi, Orient Longman, 1995.

Bell, Coral. (ed.), *Agenda for the Eighties: Context of Australian Choices in Foreign Policy and Defence Policy*, Canberra, ANU Press, 1980.

Berger, Carl., *The Korea Knot*, Revised Edition, New York, Greenwood Press, 1986.

Bhagwati, Jagdish., *India in Transition: Freeing the Economy*, Oxford, Oxford University Press 1993.

Bhatia, Vinod., *Indira Gandhi and Indo-Soviet Relations*, New Delhi, Panchsheel Publishers, 1987.

Birdwood. C.B., *Two Nations and Kashmir*, London, Robert Hale, 1956.

Bonsal, Stephen., *Suitors and Suppliants*, New York, Prentice Hall, 1946.

Booth, Ken and Steve, Smith., *International Relations Theory Today*, United Kingdom, Polity Press, 1995.

Borrie, W.D., *Immigration: Australia's Problems and Prospects*, Sydney, Angus & Robertson, 1949.

Bowles, Chester., *The Ambassador's Report*, London, Victor Gollancz, 1954.

Bowman, L.W. and I. Clark. (eds.), *The Indian Ocean in Global Politics*, Colorado, Westview Press, 1981.

Bradnoch, Robert W., *India's Foreign Policy since 1971*, Great Britain, Royal Institute of International Affairs, 1990.

Braillard, Phillipe and Mohammad, Reza Djalili., *The Third World and International Relations*, Colorado, Lynne Rienner Publishers, 1986.

Brawley, Sean., *The White Peril*, Sydney, University of NSW Press, 1995.

―――――. *A Century of Labor History Essays*, NSW, Pluto Press, 1992. Vol. 4.

Brecher, Michael., *Nehru: A Political Biography*, (Abridged Edition), London, Oxford University Press, 1961.

―――――. *India and World Politics: Krishna Menon's View of the World*, London, Oxford University Press, 1968.

―――――. *The New States of Asia*, London, Oxford University Press, 1963.

Brett, Judith. (ed.) *Political Lives*, NSW, Allen & Unwin, 1997.

―――――. *Robert Menzies : Forgotten People*, Sydney, Macmillan, 1992.

Buckley, Ken. *et. al.*, *Doc Evatt: Patriot, Internationalist, Fighter and Scholar*, Melbourne, Longman Cheshire, 1994.

Bull, Hedley., *The Anarchical Society* London, Macmillan, 1977.

Burton, J. W., *International Relations: A General Theory*, Cambridge, Cambridge University Press, 1967.

―――――. *The Alternative: A Dynamic Approach to our relations with Asia*, Sydney, Morgan Publications, 1954.

Buzan, Barry., *People, States and Fear*, Hertfordshire, Harvester Wheatsheaf, 1991.

Cain, Frank. (ed.), *Menzies in War and Peace*, NSW, Allen & Unwin, 1997.

Camilleri, J.A., *An Introduction to Australian Foreign Policy*, Fourth Edition, Qld, Jacaranda Press, 1979.

―――――. *Australian American Relations: the Web of Dependence*, South Melbourne, Macmillan, 1980.

Carr, E.H., *The Twenty Years' Crisis: 1919-1939*, London, Macmillan, 1962.

Casey, R.G., *An Australian in India*, London, Hollis & Carter, 1947.

―――――. *The Future of the Commonwealth*, London, Frederick Muller, 1963.

―――――. Lord. *Personal Experiences: 1939-1946*, London, Constable and Company, 1962.

Chandrasekhar, S.(ed.), *From India to Australia*, California, Population Review Books, 1992.

Chanana, C. (ed.), *South Asia: The Changing Environment*, New Delhi, MERB Bookshelf, 1979.

Chopra, P.N.(ed.), *India's Major Non-Violent Movements 1919-1934: British Secret Reports on Indian Peoples' Peaceful Struggle for Political Liberation*, Delhi, Vision Books, 1979.

Chopra, V.D. and M. Rasgotre. (ed.), *Genesis of Regional Conflicts*, New Delhi, Gyan Publishing House, 1995.

Choudary, Ramanarayan.(ed.), *Nehru in His Own Words*, Ahmedabad, India, Navajivan Publishing House, 1964.

Choudary, Subrata Roy., *Military Alliances and Neutrality in War and Peace*, New Delhi, Orient Longman, 1966.

Clark, Claire. (ed.), *Australian Foreign Policy: Towards A Reassessment*, North Melbourne, Cassell, 1973.

Clark, C.M.H., *A Short History of Australia*, London, Heinmann, 1964.

Clark, G., *In Fear of China*, Melbourne, Landsdowne Press, 1967.

Claude, Inis L. (ed.), *Power and International Relations*, New York, Random House, 1962.

Collins, Larry. and Dominique, Lapierre., *Mountbatten and the Partition of India: March 22-August 15, 1947*, New Delhi, Vikas Publishing, 1982.

Copland, Ian., *The princes of India in the endgame of empire, 1917-1947*, Cambridge, Cambridge University Press, 1997.

————. *Europe's Great Game: Imperialism in Asia*, Melbourne, Oxford University Press, 1986.

Crabb, J.C.V., *The Elephants and the Grass*, New York, Frederick A. Praeger, 1965.

Crespigny, de Rafe., *China This Century*, Hong Kong, Oxford University Press, 1992.

Crisp, L.F., *Ben Chifley: A Political Biography*, London, Angus & Robertson, 1977.

Crocker, W.R., *Australian Ambassador: International Relations at First Hand*, Victoria, Melbourne University Press, 1971.

Dalziel, A., *Evatt the Enigma*, Melbourne, Landsdowne Press, 1967.

Department of International Relations, ANU, (Canberra) *Studies in World Affairs*, NSW, Allen & Unwin, 1993.

Dibb, Paul., *Towards a New Balance of Power in Asia*, Adelphi Paper 295. International Institute for Strategic Studies, New York, Oxford University Press, 1995.

Dikshit, Sheila. *et. al.* (eds.), *Jawaharlal Nehru Centenary Volume*, Delhi, Oxford University Press, 1997.

Dougherty, James E. and Robert, L. Pfaltzgraff., *Contending Theories of International Relations*, Second Edition, New York, Harper and Row, 1981.

Dunn, H.A. and E.S.K. Fung. (eds.), *Sino-Australian Relations: The Records 1972- 1985*, Qld., Centre for the Study of Australia-Asia Relations, 1985.

Dutton, G. (ed.), *Australia and the Monarchy: A symposium*, Melbourne, Sun Books, 1966.

Edwards, Michael., *Nehru: A Political Biography*, Harmondsworth, Penguin, 1963.

Edwards, Peter and Gregory, Pemberton., *Crises and Commitments*, Sydney, Allen & Unwin 1992.

Emy, Hugh., *Whitlam Re-Visited: Policy Developments, Policies and Outcomes*, NSW, Pluto Press, 1993.

Evans, Gareth and Bruce, Grant., *Australia's Foreign Relations in the World of the 1990's*, Victoria, Melbourne University Press, 1991.

Evatt, H.V., *Foreign Policy of Australia: Speeches*, Sydney, Angus and Robertson, 1945.

Falk, Richard *et. al.* (eds.), *Towards a Just World Order*, Colorado, Westview Press, 1982.

Farmer, B.H., *An Introduction to South Asia*, London, Methuen, 1983.

Fitzgerald, Stephen., *Is Australia an Asian Country?*, NSW, Allen & Unwin, 1997.

Free, L.A., *Six Allies and a Neutral*, New York, Free Press, 1962.

Freudenberg, Graham., *A Certain Grandeur: Gough Whitlam in Politics*, South Melbourne, Sun Books, 1978.

Gandhi, Sonia. (ed.), *Freedom's Daughter: Letters Between Indira Gandhi and Jawaharlal Nehru, 1922-1939*, London, Hodder & Stoughton, 1989.

Galbraith, J.K., *Ambassador's Journal*, London, Hamish Hamilton, 1969.

Gangul, S.C., *India and the Commonwealth*, India, Shiva Lal Agarwala, 1970.

George, Jim., *Discourses of Global Politics: A Critical (Re)Introduction to International Relations*, Colorado, Lynne Rienner Publications, 1994.

George, Margaret., *Australia and the Indonesian Revolution*, Victoria, Melbourne University Press, 1980.

George, T.J.S. (ed.), *India at Fifty: 1947-1997*, Chennai, India, Express Publications Limited, 1997.

Gilbert, Martin., *Churchill*, Sydney, Books for Pleasure, 1979.

Girard, Michel. *et. al.*, *National Perspectives on Academics and Professionals in International Relations: Theory and Practice in Foreign Policy making*, London, Pinter Publishers, 1994.

Gopal, S., *Jawaharlal Nehru: A Biography 1947-1956*, London, Jonathan Cape, 1979, Vol. II.

————. (ed.), *Jawaharlal Nehru: An Anthology*, New Delhi, Oxford University Press, 1980.

————. (ed.), *Selected Works of Jawaharlal Nehru*, Second Series, New Delhi, J. Nehru Memorial Fund, 1984, Vol. II. .

————. (ed.), *Selected Works of Jawaharlal Nehru*, Second Series, New Delhi, J. Nehru Memorial Fund, 1993, Vol. 14. Part I & Part II.

————. (ed.), *Selected Works of Jawaharlal Nehru*, New Delhi, Orient Longman, 1982, Vol. 15.

————. (ed.) *Selected Works of Jawaharlal Nehru*, New Delhi, J. Nehru Memorial Fund, 1972, Vol. 15, Part I.

————. (ed.), *Selected Works of Jawaharlal Nehru*, Second Series, New Delhi, J. Nehru Memorial Fund, 1993, Vol. 15. Part I.

————. (ed.) *Selected Works of Jawaharlal Nehru*, Second Series, New Delhi, J. Nehru Memorial Fund, 1994, Vol. 16. Part II.

Gordon, Sandy., *The Search for Substance: Australia-India Relations into the Nineties and Beyond*, Canberra, Australian National University, 1993.

Gordon, Sandy. and Stephen, Henningham.(eds.), *India Looks East: An Emerging Power and its Asia Pacific Neighbours*, Canberra, Defence Studies Centre, ANU, 1995.

Govinddas., *On Wings to the ANZACS*, India, Adarsh Publications, 1954.

Graebner, Norman A., *The Cold War: A Conflict of Ideology and Power*, Lexington, Heath, 1976.

Grant, Bruce., *What Kind of Country? Australia and the Twenty First Century*, Victoria, Penguin, 1988.

————. *The Australian Dilemma: A New Kind of Western Society*, NSW, Macdonald Futura, 1983.

————. *Gods and Politicians*, Victoria, Allan Lane, 1982.

Greene, Fred., *Dynamics of International Relations: Power, Security, and Order*, New York, Holt, Rinehart and Winston, 1964.

Greenwood, Gordon and Norman, Harper. (eds.), *Australia in World Affairs: 1950- 1955*, Melbourne, F.W. Cheshire, 1957.

————. *Australia in World Affairs: 1956-1960*, Melbourne, F.W. Cheshire, 1963.

————. *Australia in World Affairs: 1961-1965*, Melbourne, F.W. Cheshire, 1968.

————. *Australia in World Affairs: 1966-1970*. Melbourne, Cheshire Publishing. 1974.

Greenwood, Gordon., *Approaches to Asia: Australian Postwar Policies and Attitudes*, Sydney, McGraw-Hill, 1974.

Grover, Verinder. (ed.), *The Story of Kashmir: Yesterday and Today*, New Delhi, Deep & Deep Publications, 1995.

————. (ed.), *International Relations and the Foreign Policy of India, Great Britain, Commonwealth*, New Delhi, Deep & Deep Publications, 1992.

Gurry, Meg., *India: Australia's Neglected Neighbour? 1947-1996*, Qld, Centre for the Study of Australia-Asia Relations, Griffith University, 1996.

Hall, D.G.E., *A History of South East Asia*, London, Macmillan, 1961.

Harper, Norman A., *A Great and Powerful Friend: A Study of Australian American Relations between 1900 and 1975*, Qld, University of Queensland Press, 1987.

Heesterman, J.C., *The Inner Conflict of Tradition: Essays in Indian Ritual Kingship, and Society*, Chicago, University of Chicago Press, 1985.

Heptulla. Najma., *Indo-West Asian Relations: The Nehru Era*, New Delhi, Allied Publishers, 1991.

Higgott. Richard A. (ed.), *New Directions in International Relations? Australian Perspectives*, Canberra, ANU, 1988.

Hiriyanna, Mysore., *Essentials of Indian Philosophy*, London, George Allen & Unwin, 1985.
*History of the Indian National Congress*, Bombay, Padua's Publications, 1947, Vol. II.

Hobsbawm, Eric., *Age of Extremes: The Short Twentieth Century, 1914-1991*, New York, Pantheon Books, 1995.

Hollis, Martin and Steve Smith., *Explaining and Understanding International Relations*, Oxford, Clarendon Press, 1991.

Holsti, K.J., *International Politics: A Framework for Analysis*, Second Edition, New Jersey, Prentice Hall, 1972.

————. *Why Nations Realign: Foreign Policy Restructuring in the Postwar World*, London, Allen & Unwin, 1982.

Hudson, W.J., *Blind Loyalty: Australia and the Suez Crisis, 1956*, Victoria, Melbourne University Press, 1989.

————. *Casey*, Melbourne, Oxford University Press, 1986.

————. *Great and Powerful Friend, A Study of Australian American Relations Between 1900 and 1975*, Qld, University of Queensland Press, 1987.

————. (ed.), *Australia in World Affairs: 1971-1975*, Sydney, Allen & Unwin, 1980.

Hudson, W.J. and Wendy Way. (eds.), *Documents on Australian Foreign Policy 1937- 1949*, July-December 1946, Canberra, DFAT, AGPS, 1995, Vol. X.

————. *Australia and the Postwar World: Documents 1947*, Canberra, DFAT, AGPS, 1995.

————. *Documents on Australian Foreign Policy 1937-1949*, Canberra, DFAT, AGPS, 1995, Vol. XII.

Indian Council of World Affairs., *Aspects of India's Foreign Policy*, New Delhi, 1964.

Indyk, Martin., *Surveys of Australian Political Science*, Sydney, George Allen & Unwin, 1985.

Ingram, D., *Commonwealth for a Colour-blind World*, London, Allen & Unwin, 1965.

————. *The Commonwealth at Work*, New York, Pergamon Press, 1969.

Jalal, Ayesha., *The Sole Spokesman: Jinnah, The Muslim League and the Demand for Partition*, Cambridge, Cambridge University Press, 1985.

Jayasingh, Hari., *India and the Non-Aligned World: Search for a New Order*, New Delhi, Vikas Publications, 1983.

Jensen, Lloyd., *Explaining Foreign Policy*, New Jersey, Prentice Hall, 1982.

Jha, C.S., *From Bandung to Tashkent*, Madras, Sangam Books, 1983.

Josh, Harcharan Singh. (ed.), *India's Foreign Policy: Nehru to Rao*, Delhi, Indian Council of World Affairs, Surjeet Publications, 1994.

Joske, Percy., *Sir Robert Menzies 1894-1978: A New Informal Memoir*, Sydney, Angus & Robertson, 1978.

Jupp, James. (ed.), *The Australian People An Encyclopedia of the Nation: Its People and their Origins*, NSW, Angus & Robertson, 1988.

Kakar, Sadhiv., *The Indian Psyche*, New Delhi, Viking, 1996.

Karlekar, Hiramay. (ed.), *Fifty Years of Indian Independence*, New Delhi, Oxford University Press, 1998.

Kashyap. Subash C. (ed.), *National Policy Studies*, New Delhi, Tata Mcgraw-Hill Publishing, 1990.

Kak, B.L.(ed.), *Z.A. Bhutto: Diary notes from Death Cell*, New Delhi, Radha Krishnan Prakasham, 1979.

Kaul, T.N., *My Years Through Raj to Swaraj*, New Delhi, Vikas Publishing, 1995.

Keating, Paul., *Engagement: Australia Faces the Asia Pacific*, Sydney, Pan Macmillan, 2000.

Kegley, Charles W. and Gregory A. Raymond., *A Multipolar Peace? Great Power Politics in the Twenty First Century*, New York, St Martins Publishing, 1994.

Kegley, Charles W. & Eugene R, Wittkopf., *World Politics: Trend and Transformation* 7th Edition, New York, Worth Publishing, 1999.

Keohane, Robert O. and Joseph S. Nye. (eds.), *Transnational Relations and World Politics*, Massachusetts, Harvard University Press, 1973.

————. *Power and Interdependence: World Politics in Transition*, Boston, Little Brown & Company, 1977.

Khilnari, N.M., *Socio Political Dimensions of Modern India*, New Delhi, MD Publications, 1993.

King, Jonathan., *Waltzing Materialism*, Sydney, Harper & Row, 1978.

Kothari, Rajni., *Footsteps into the Future: Diagnosis of the Present World and a Design for an Alternative*, New York, Free Press, 1974.

Kumar, Ravinder., *The Making of a Nation: Essays in Indian History and Politics*, New Delhi, Manohar Publications, 1989.

————. *Essays in the Social History of Modern India*, Delhi, Oxford University Press, 1983.

Kumar, Satish. (ed.), *Documents on India's Foreign Policy: 1972*, Delhi, Macmillan. 1976.

Lal, Sham. (ed.), *The Times of India Directory and Year Book, 1978*, Bombay, The Times of India Press.

Lamb, Allastair., *Kashmir: A Disputed Legacy, 1846-1990*, Hertfordshire, Roxford Books, 1991.

Laszlo, Ladamy., *The Communist Party of China and Marxism*, Stamford, Hoover Institution Press, 1988.

Lawrence, James., *Raj: The Making and Unmaking of British India*, London, Abacus, 1998.

Lee, David. (ed.), *Australia and Indonesia's Independence: The Transfer of Sovereignty, Documents 1949*, Canberra, DFAT, AGPS, 1998, Vol. XV.

Lee, David and Christopher, Waters. (eds.), *Evatt to Evans: The Labor Tradition in Australian Foreign Policy* NSW, Allen & Unwin, 1997.

Levi, Werner., *Australia's Outlook on Asia*, Sydney, Angus & Robertson, 1958.

Lipton, Michael and John, Firn., *The Erosion of a Relationship*, London, Oxford University Press, 1975.

London, H.I., *Non-White Immigration and the 'White Australia' Policy*, Sydney, Sydney University Press, 1970.

Lowe, David. (ed.), *Australia and the End of Empires*, Victoria, Deakin University Press, 1996.

————. *Menzies and the 'Great World Struggle': Australia's Cold War, 1948-1954.* Sydney, University of NSW Press, 1999.

Lundestad, Geir., *East, West, North, South: Major Developments in International Politics, 1945-1990*, New York, Oxford University Press, 1999.

Mabbet, I. W., *A Short History of India*, North Melbourne, Cassell, 1968.

Mackerras, Colin. (ed.), *Eastern Asia: An Introductory History*, Melbourne, Longman. 2000.

Macridis, Roy C. (ed.), *Foreign Policy in World Politics*, 5th Edition, New Jersey, Prentice-Hall, 1976.

Mackie, J.A.C. (ed.), *Australia in the New World Order: Foreign Policy in the 1970s*, West Melbourne, Nelson, 1976.

McDougal, D.J., *Studies in International Relations: The Asia Pacific, the Super Powers, Australia*, Melbourne, Edward Arnold, 1991.

Mc Laren John. (ed.), *Towards a New Australia: Under a Labor Government*, Melbourne, Cheshire, 1972.

Mansergh, Nicholas., *Documents and Speeches on Commonwealth Affairs 1952-1963*, London, Oxford University Press, 1963.

Maroof, Raja., *War and No Peace over Kashmir*, New Delhi, Lancer Publishers, 1996.

Martin, A.W., *Robert Menzies: A Life 1894-1943*, Victoria, Melbourne University Press, 1993, Vol. I.

————. *Robert Menzies: A Life, 1944-1978*, Victoria, Melbourne University Press, 1999, Vol. II.

Mathur, P.C., *Political Contours of India's Modernity*, Jayapur, India, Aelekh Publishers, 1994.

Meaney, Neville., *Australia and the World: A Documentary History from the 1870s to the 1970s*, Melbourne, Longman Cheshire, 1985.

Menzies, R.G., *Afternoon Light*, Melbourne, Cassell, 1967.

Millar, T. B., *Australia's Foreign Policy*, Sydney, Angus & Robertson, 1968.

————. (ed.) *Australian Foreign Minister: The Diaries of R.G. Casey 1951-1960*, London, Collins, 1972.

Miller, J.D.B. (ed.), *India, Japan, Australia: Partners in Asia?*, Canberra, ANU, 1968.

Misra, K.P.(ed.), *Studies in Indian Foreign Policy*, New Delhi, Vikas Publications, 1969.

Misra, K.P. & Narayanam, K.R.(eds.), *Non-Alignment in Contemporary International Relations*, New Delhi, Vikas Publications, 1981.

Misra, S.N., *India: the Cold War Years*, New Delhi, South Asian Publishers, 1994.

Morgenthau, Hans J., *Politics Among Nations*, 5th Edition, New York, Alfred A. Knopf, 1973.

Mortimer, R.A., *The Third World Coalition in International Relations*, 2nd Edition, Colorado, Westview Press, 1984.

Mukherjee, Subrata. and Sushila, Ramasamy., *Political Science Annual 1993*, New Delhi, Deep & Deep Publications, 1994.

Mutukumaru, N.(ed.), *Thoughts of Jawaharlal Nehru*, Sri Lanka, Sri-Lanka-India Society, 1994.

Nanda, B.R., *Indian Foreign Policy: the Nehru Years*, New Delhi, Vikas Publishing, 1976.

Narasimha Char, K.T. (ed.), *The Quintessence of Nehru*, London, George Allen & Unwin, 1961.

Nayer, Parameswaran., *India: Year Book of International Affairs*, Delhi, 1962, Vol. XI.

Neeraj., *Nehru and Democracy in India*, Delhi, Metropolitan Book Company, 1972.

Nehru, Jawaharlal., *India and the World*, London, George Allen & Unwin, 1936.

————. *Jawaharlal Nehru: An Autobiography*, London, John Lane The Bodley Head, 1936.

————. *Vision of India*, New Delhi, Indian Council of Cultural Relations, 1981.

————. *Discovery of India*, New York, The John Day Company, 1946.

————. *India and Disarmament: An Anthology*, New Delhi, Ministry of Information & Broadcasting, Government of India, 1988.

————. *Jawaharlal Nehru's Speeches: September 1946-May 1949*, New Delhi, Ministry of Information & Broadcasting, Government of India, 1949, Vol. I.

————. *India's Foreign Policy: Selected Speeches, September 1946-April 1961*, New Delhi, Ministry of Information & Broadcasting, Government of India, 1961.

————. *Jawaharlal Nehru's Speeches: August 1949-February 1953*, New Delhi, Ministry of Information & Broadcasting, Government of India, 1954, Vol. II.

————. *Jawaharlal Nehru's Speeches: September 1957- April 1963*, New Delhi, Ministry of Information & Broadcasting, Government of India, 1964, Vols. II, IV.

————. *Jawaharlal Nehru's Speeches: March 1963-May 1964*, New Delhi, Ministry of Information & Broadcasting, Government of India, 1968, Vols. IV, V.

Nehru, Jawaharlal. & Norman, Dorothy. (ed.), *Nehru: the First Sixty Years*. London, The Bodley Head, 1965, Vol. I, II.

Nicholson, Harold., *Diplomacy*, 2nd Edition, London, Oxford University Press, 1950.

Nihal Singh S., *The Rocky Road of Indian Democracy*, New Delhi, Sterling Publishers, 1993.

Nutting, A., *No End of a Lesson: The Story of Suez*, London, Constable, 1967.

Palfreeman, A.C., *The Administration of the White Australia Policy*, Victoria, Melbourne University Press, 1967.

Panandiker, V.A. Pai. (ed.), *India's Policy Problems: Economic and Political Challenges*, New Delhi, Centre for Policy Research, Konark Publishers, 1996, Vol. I.

Pandey, B.N., *Nehru and India*, London, Macmillan, 1976.

Panikkar, K.M., *Asia and Western Dominance*, New York, Collier Books, 1969.

————. *The Foundations of New India*, London, George Allen & Unwin, 1963.

Patience, Allan and Brian Head. (eds.), *From Whitlam to Fraser*, Melbourne, Oxford University Press, 1979.

Paul, T.V. and John A. Hall. (eds.), *International Order and the Future of World Politics*. Cambridge, Cambridge University Press, 1999.

Perkins, Kevin., *Menzies: Last of the Queen's Men*, Adelaide, Rigby, 1968.

Pettit, D. W. & Anne, Hall., *Selected Readings in Australian Foreign Policy*, Victoria, Sorret Publishing, 1977.

Pettman, R., *International Politics: Balance of Power, Balance of Productivity, Balance of Ideologies*, Melbourne, Longman Cheshire, 1991.

Phillips, D., *Ambivalent Allies: Myth and Reality in the Australian-American Relationship*, Victoria, Penguin, 1988.

Prasad, R., *Colonialism, Lumpenization, Revolution*, Delhi, Ajanta Books, 1995, Vol. I.

Preston, Richard A., *Canada in World Affairs: 1959-1961*, Toronto, Oxford University Press, 1965.

Rais, Rasul B., *The Indian Ocean and the Superpowers*, London, Croom Helm, 1986.

Raja, Mahroof., *War and No Peace over Kashmir*, New Delhi, Lancer, 1996.

Rajan, M.S., *India and the Commonwealth: Some Studies*, New Delhi, Konark Publications, 1990.

————. *India in World Affairs: 1954-56*, New Delhi, Asian Publishing House, 1964.

————. *Studies in India's Foreign Policy*, New Delhi, ABC Publishing House, 1993.

————. *Studies on Nonalignment and the Nonaligned Movement*, New Delhi, ABC Publishing, 1986.

Ramachandram, G., *Nehru and World Peace*, New Delhi, Radiant Publishers, 1990.

Rao, Amiya and B.G. Rao., *Six Thousand Days*, New Delhi, Sterling Publishers, 1974.

Rao, H.S. Gururaj., *Legal Aspects of the Kashmir Problem*, India, Asia Publishing House, 1967.

Ravenhill, John., *No Longer An American Lake*, Sydney, Allen & Unwin, 1989.

Reddy, E.S. and A.K. Damodaran. (eds.), *Krishna Menon at the United Nations: India and the World*, New Delhi, Sanchar Publishing House, 1994.

Renouf, A.P., *The Frightened Country*, Melbourne, Macmillan, 1979.

————. *The Champagne Trail: Experiences of a Diplomat*, Melbourne, Sun Books, 1980.

Reynolds, P.A., *An Introduction to International Relations*, London, Longman, 1971.

Rivett K., *Australia and the Non-White Migrant*, Melbourne, Melbourne University Press, 1975.

Russett, Bruce and Harvey Shaw., *World Politics: The Menu for Choice*, New York, W.H. Freeman & Company, 1996.

Sagar, Vidya., *India in World Affairs: Chronology of Events 1947-72*, New Delhi, Swastik Prakashan, 1973.

Sahgal, Nayantara., *Indira Gandhi: Her Road to Power*, London, Macdonald & Co. 1983.

Sen, S.P. (ed.), *Dictionary of National Biography*, Institute of Historical Studies, India: 1974, Vol. III.

Sengupta, Jayote., *Non Alignment: Search for a Destination*, Calcutta, Nayaprakash. 1979.

Setton, Marie., *Panditji: A Portrait of Nehru*, London, Dennis Dobson, 1967.

Sharma, R.D., *India's Contribution towards World Peace under Nehru*, New Delhi, Segal Publishing Service, 1990.

Sharma Shri Ram. (ed.), *Indian Foreign Policy Annual Survey: 1973*, New Delhi, Sterling Publishers, 1977.

Sheridan, Greg. (ed.), *Living with Dragons*. NSW, Allen & Unwin, 1995.

Silveirab, D.M., *India Book 1996-1997*, Goa, Classic Publishers, n.d.

Singh, K. Natwar. (ed.), *The Legacy of Nehru*, India, Har Anand Publications, 1990.

Sinha, S., *China Strikes*, London, Blandford Press, 1964.

Singh, Jasjit (ed.), *India-China and Panchsheel*, New Delhi, Sanchar Publishing House, 1996.

Smith, Steve *et. al.* (eds.), *International Theory: Positivism and Beyond*, Cambridge, Cambridge University Press, 1996.

Smith, Steve and Ken Booth., *International Relations Theory Today*, Cambridge, Polity Press, 1995.

Spear, Percival., *India, Pakistan and the West*, London, Oxford University Press, 1967.

Spender, Percy., *Exercises in Diplomacy: The ANZUS Treaty and the Colombo Plan* Sydney, Sydney University Press, 1969.

Stargardt, A.W., *Australia's Asian Policies: The History of a Debate 1839-1972*, Hamburg, Institute of Asian Affairs, 1977.

Stevens, C.F., and E.P., Wolfers. (eds.), *Racism: The Australian Experience*. Sydney, Australia & New Zealand Book Company, 1974, Vol. I.

Suter, Keith., *Is There Life After ANZUS?*, Sydney, Pluto Press, 1987.

Taylor, Trevor. (ed.), *Approaches and Theory: International Relations*, London, Longman, 1978.

Teichman Max. (ed.), *New Directions in Australian Foreign Policy: Ally, Satelite or Neutral?*, Harmondsworth, Penguin, 1969.

Thakur, Ramesh., *The Politics and Economics of India's Foreign Policy*, New York, St Martin's Press, 1994.

————. *The Government and Politics of India*, London, Macmillan, 1955.

Tharoor, Shashi., *India: From Midnight to Millennium*, New York, Arcade Publishing, 1997.

Thucydides., *History of Peloponnesian War*, (trans.) Rex Warner, Middlesex, Penguin. 1954.

————. *The Peloponnesian War*, (trans.) Crawley. New York, Modern Library, 1951.

Tinker, Hugh., *Experiment with Freedom*, London, Oxford University Press, 1967.

Tully, Mark. and Jacob, Satish. *Amritsar: Mrs Gandhi's Last Battle*, London, Jonathan Cape, 1985.

Vanaik, Achin., *India in a Changing World*, New Delhi, Orient Longman, 1995.

Vandenbosch, Amry and Mary Belle, Vandenbosch., *Australia Faces Southeast Asia: The Emergence of a Foreign Policy*, Lexington, USA, University of Kentucky Press, 1967.

Varma, Pavan K., *The Great Indian Middle Class*, New Delhi, Viking, 1998.

Varma, Ravinder K., *Australia and South East Asia: The Crystallization of a Relationship*, New Delhi, Abinav Publications, 1973.

Varma, S.N., *Aspects of India's Foreign Relations*, New Delhi, Indian Council of World Affairs, 1957.

Vasquez, J., *The Power of Power Politics*. London, Frances Pinter, 1983.

Varshney, Ashutosh., *India in the Era of Economic Reforms*, New Delhi, Oxford University Press, 1999.

Vicziany, Marika. (ed.), *Australia-India: Economic Links Past, Present and Future*, Perth, Indian Ocean Centre for Peace Studies, University of Western Australia. 1993.

Vicziany, Marika. and Ken McPherson (eds.), *Australia and South Asia: A Blueprint for 2001?*, Melbourne, National Centre for South Asian Studies, 1994.

Viotti, Paul. and Mark R. Kauppi., *International Relations and World Politics: Security, Economy, Identity*, New Jersey, Prentice Hall, 1997.

Wall, Patrick. (ed.), *The Indian Ocean and the Threat to the West*, London, Stacey International, 1975.

Wallace, V. H. (ed.), *Paths to Peace: A Study of War, its Causes and Prevention*, Victoria, Melbourne University Press, 1957.

Walter, James., *The Leader: A Political Biography of Gough Whitlam*, Qld, University of Queensland. Press, 1980.

Waltz, K.N., *Theory of International Politics*, Massachusetts, Addison-Wesley, 1979.

————. *Man the State and War: A Theoretical Analysis*, New York, Columbia University Press, 1959.

Waters, Christopher., *The Empire Fractures: Anglo Australian Conflict in the 1940s*, Melbourne, Australian Scholarly Publishing, 1995.

Watt, Alan., *The Evolution of Australian Foreign Policy: 1938-1965*, London, Cambridge University Press, 1967.

Weigert, Hans and V. Stefanson., *Compass of the World*, New York, Macmillan, 1944.

Whitington, Don. (ed.), *The Liberal Party and the Monarchy*, Melbourne, Sun Books, 1966.

Whitlam, E.G., *The Whitlam Government: 1972-1975*, Victoria, Viking, 1985.

————. *Abiding Interests*, Qld, University of Queensland Press, 1997.

Wight, Martin. *et. al.*, *Power Politics*, Middlesex, Penguin Books, 1979.

Willard, Myra., *History of the White Australia Policy to 1920*, Victoria, Melbourne University Press, 1967.

Wolfers, Arnold. (ed.), *Discord & Collaboration: Essays on International Politics*, Baltimore, Johns Hopkins Press, 1962.

————. (ed.) *Alliance Policy in the Cold War*, Baltimore, Johns Hopkins Press, 1959.

Williams, L.F. Rushbrook. (ed.), *Famous Letters and Speeches*, Bombay, The Times of India & Associated Newspapers of Ceylon, n.d.

Wolpert, Stanley., *Nehru: A Tryst with Destiny*, New York, Oxford University Press, 1996.

————. *India*, New Jersey, Prentice Hall, 1965.

————. *A New History of India*, Fifth Edition. New York, Oxford University Press, 1997.

Yarwood, A.T., *Asian Migration to Australia: the Background to Exclusion 1896- 1923*, Victoria, Melbourne University Press, 1964.

————. *Attitudes to Non-European Immigration*, NSW, Cassell, 1968.

## Articles

Albinski, Henry S., 'The Role of Foreign Policy in Australian Electoral Politics: Some Explanations and Speculations.' *Australian Outlook*, Vol. 28, No. 2. August 1974, pp 118-141.

Andrews, E.M., 'Patterns in Australian Foreign Policy.' *Australian Outlook*, Vol. 26, No. 1. April 1972, pp 31-45.

Aron, Raymond., 'The Commonwealth and the European Community.' *TRT*, No. 244, October 1971, pp 447-454.

Barmon, T., Book Review. *International Affairs, A Quarterly Review*, Vol. 44, No. 1. January 1968, pp 84-85.

Bhandari, Romesh., 'India's Sun in the Ascendant.' *New India Digest*, No. 52, May- June 1996, pp 10-13

Bowles, Chester., 'New India.' *Foreign Affairs*, Vol. 31, October-September 1952- 1953, pp 76-81.

Budania, Rajpal., 'The United States and South Asia.' *Indian Journal of Asian Affairs*, Vol. 8-9, No. 1-2, 1995-1996, pp 55-69.

Budhraj, Vijaya Sen., 'The South Asia Policy of the Soviet Union.' *Australian Outlook*, Vol. 30, No. 1, April 1976, pp 101-119.

Bultjens. Ralph., 'Image and Reality.' *New India Digest*, No. 42, September-October 1994, pp 4-9.

Burns, Gordon., 'An Australian View of British Entry: Economic Gains, Political Dangers.' *TRT*, No. 244, October 1971, pp 527-532.

Candland, Christopher., 'Congress Decline and Party Pluralism in India.' *Journal of International Affairs*, Vol. 51, No. 1, Summer 1997, pp 19-35.

Chakrabarty, D., 'Open Spaces/Public Place: Garbage Modernity and India.' *South Asia: Journal of South Asian Studies*, New Series, Vol. XIV, No. 1, June 1991, pp 15-31.

Cox, David., Book Review. *Australian Journal of Political Science*, Vol. 33, No. 1. March 1998, p 133.

Dodwell, David., Book Review. *Far Eastern Economic Review*, 24 June 1999, p 48.

Donelan, Michael., Book Review. *International Affairs, A Quarterly Review*, Vol. 44, No. 1, January 1968, pp 168-169.

Eayers, James., 'The Overhaul of the Commonwealth.' *TRT*, No. 225 January 1967, pp 48-56.

Fukuyama, Francis., Book Review. *Foreign Affairs*, Vol. 76, No. 4, July-August 1997, p 147.

Garner, Lord., 'Commonwealth Under Strain: Problems of Expansion and Attrition.' *TRT*, No. 258, April 1975, pp 205-214.

Gopal, S., 'The Commonwealth: An Indian View.' *TRT*, No. 240, November 1970, (Diamond Jubilee Number), pp 613-617.

Griffiths, M. and Sullivan, M., 'Nationalism and International Relations Theory.' *The Australian Journal of Politics and History*, Vol. 43, No. 1, 1997, pp 53-63.

Gurry, Meg., Book Review. *South Asia: Journal of South Asian Studies, New Series*, Vol. XVII, No. 2, December 1994, pp 140-142.

————. 'Whose History? The Struggle over Authorship of Australia's Asia Policies.' *Australian Journal of International Affairs*, Vol. 52, No. 1, April 1998, pp 77-88.

Higgott, Richard A. and George, Jim., 'Tradition and Change in the Study of International Relations in Australia.' *International Political Science Review*, Vol. 2, No. 4, 1990, pp 423-438.

Hodson, H.V., 'Earl Mountbatten's Role in the Partition of India.' TRT, No. 277, January 1980, pp 102-106.

Hughes, T.E.F., 'Australia in Free Asia: Both Economic and Military Efforts.' *TRT*, No. 226, April 1967, pp 183-189.

Hunter, R.E. and Windsor, P., 'Vietnam and United States Policy in Asia.' *International Affairs: A Quarterly Review*. Vol. 44, No. 2, 2 April 1968, pp 202-213.

Ingram, Derek., 'Prospects for Ottawa: The Prime Ministers Prepare.' *TRT*, No. 250, April 1973, pp 175-182.

Jetley, Neerja Pawha., 'Political see-saws, red-tape, plain hostility: foreign investors run scared.' *Outlook*, (India) 13 October 1997, p 54.

Kelton, Maryanne and Richard, Leaver, 'Issues in Australian Foreign Policy.' *The Australian Journal of Politics and History*, Vol. 45, No. 4, December 1999, pp 526-543.

Khan, Mohammed Ayub., 'The Pakistan-American Alliance: Stresses and Strains', *Foreign Affairs*, Vol. 24, 1964, pp 195-209.

Krassowski, A., Book Review. *International Affairs Quarterly Review*, Vol. 44, No. 1, January 1968, pp 107-108.

Kumar Dharma., 'The New Community and the Developing Commonwealth-Problems of Trade and Aid.' *TRT*, No. 244, October 1971, pp 475-484.

Leslie, S.C., ' British Attitudes to the Commonwealth: Dreams and Daylight.' *TRT*, No. 251, July 1973, pp 363-375.

Lougheed A.L. and Roy, K.C., "India's Export Trade with Australia: Problems and Prospects,' *Australian Outlook*, Vol. 28, No. 2. August 1974, pp 179-186.

Lowe, David., Book Review. *Australian Journal of Political Science*, Vol. 32, No. 1. March 1997, p 130.

————. 'Australia at the United Nations in the 1950s: The paradox of Empire.' *Australian Journal of International Affairs*, Vol. 51, No. 2, 1997, pp 171-181.

Lyons, Peter., 'The Indian Bomb: Nuclear Tests for "Peaceful Purposes"?' *TRT* No. 256, October 1974, pp 403-410.

McClelland, J.R., 'The Australian Political Scene.' *TRT*, No. 246, April 1972, pp 253-258.

Macleod, Alexander., 'The New Foreign Policy in Australia and New Zealand.' *TRT*, No. 255, July 1974, pp 287-298.

Mathews, Jessica., 'Power Shift.' *Foreign Affairs*, January/February 1997, pp 50-66.

Meaney, Neville., 'The End of "White Australia" and Australia's Changing Perceptions of Asia, 1945-1990.' *The Australian Journal of International Affairs*, Vol. 49, No. 2, November 1995, pp 171-189.

Mediansky, F.A., 'Conservative Style in Australian Foreign Policy.' *Australian Outlook*, Vol. 28, No. 1, April 1974, pp 50-56.

Menzies, Robert., 'Australia and Britain Drift Apart: the Need for Common Purpose.' *TRT*, No. 232, October 1968, pp 365-368.

Millar, T.B., 'The Australia-Britain Relationship: Where Has It Come To?' *TRT*, No. 266, April 1977, pp 191-201.

————. 'Changes in the Formal Structure of Foreign Policy Consideration.' *Australian Outlook*, Vol. 37, No. 1, April 1983, pp 26-28.

Miller, J.D.B., 'The Development of International Studies in Australia 1933-83.' *Australian Outlook*, Vol. 37, No. 3, December 1983, pp 138-142.

Mitra, Subrata K., 'Nehru's Policy Towards Kashmir: Bringing Politics Back in Again.' *The Journal of Commonwealth and Comparative Politics*, Vol. XXXV, No. 2, July 1997, pp 55-74.

Nanda, B.R., 'Father and Daughter.' *New India Digest*, No. 42, September-October 1994, pp 17-22.

Narayanan K.R., 'New Perspectives in Indian Foreign Policy.' *TRT*, No. 248, October 1972, pp 453-464.

Nautiyal, Anupurna., 'India Pakistan and the United States in the Post-Cold war Era.' *Asian Studies*, Vol. XV, January-June 1997, No.1, pp 1-9.

Palmer, Norman D., 'Some Personal Impressions.' *New India Digest*, No. 42, September-October 1994, pp 13-14.

Price, Charles., 'Beyond White Australia: The Whitlam Government's Immigration Record.' *TRT*, No. 260, April 1975, pp 369-377.

Purnell, Leigh., 'Australia Reviews Foreign Policy Priorities.' *Asian Business Review*, November 1996, p 66.

Raote, Dilip., 'The queue as democracy.' *New India Digest*, No. 46, May June-1995, pp 15-17.

Sen, Amartya., 'Indian Development: Lessons and Non-Lessons.' *Mainstream*, Vol. XXXVI, No. 44, 24 October 1998, pp 11-21.

Spence, J.E., 'South Africa and the Defence of the West: Liability or Asset to the Free World?' *TRT*, No. 241, January 1971, pp 15-23.

Subramaniam, V., 'Unity and Diversity in India: the Strength of the Indian Union.' *TRT*, No. 248, October 1972, pp 509-518.

Tow. William T., 'Western Defence in the Asian-Pacific Region.' *TRT*, No. 270, April 1978, pp 156-165.

Vatkiotis, Michael., 'Case Closed.' *Far Eastern Economic Review*, Vol. 23, Issue. 51, December 1993, p 13.

Vivekanandan, B., 'Naval Power in the Indian Ocean: A Problem In Indo-British Relations.' *TRT*, No. 257, January 1975, pp 59-72.

Wariavwalla, B.K., 'The Indo-Soviet Treaty: The Sub-Continent Reconstructed.' *TRT*, No. 246, April 1972, pp 199-208.

Zinkin. T., 'Indian Foreign Policy: An Interpretation of Attitudes.' *World Politics*, Vol. 7, 1954-55, p 180.

'A Leaf Falls: South Africa Outside the Commonwealth.' *TRT*, No. 203, June 1961, pp 219-223.

'Australia Faces Asia.' *TRT*, No. 177, December 1953, pp 57-63.

'Australia: A Debate on Foreign Policy.' *TRT*, No. 155, June 1949, pp 281-287.

'Australia and the Colombo Plan', *TRT*, No. 190, March 1958, pp 202-204.

'Commonwealth Relations: The Coronation Conference.' *TRT*, Vol. XLIII, December 1952-September 1953, pp 359-363.

'Commonwealth, South Asia and the Enlarged Community: The Continued value of the Commonwealth Link.' *TRT*, No 244, October 1971, pp 507-510.

'India: The Sun also Sets.' *TRT*, No. 190, March 1958, pp 177-182.

'British Interests in the Commonwealth.' *TRT*, No. 234, April 1969, pp 170-171.

'India: Aid from America.' *TRT*, Vol. XLIII, December 1952-September 1953, pp 169-171.

'India and Her Neighbours: Hostility on Right and Left.' *TRT*, No. 184, September 1956, pp 337-347.

'India: Bandung Balance Sheet.' *TRT*, No. 179, June 1955, pp 278-281.

'India: Lessons for a Neutral.' *TRT*, No. 173, December 1953, pp 78-81.

'India: Retreat from the West.' *TRT*, No. 177, December 1954, pp 69-74.

'Mr Nehru's Views on South African Incidents' *Indian Panorama*, Vol. IV, 4 April 1960.

'Pakistan: The Presidents Travels: Alliances or Neutralism.' *TRT*, No. 202, March 1961, pp 186-189.

'The Commonwealth, An Indian View: The Pioneer Republic.' *TRT*, No. 200, September 1960, pp 371-378

'The Foreign Policy of Mr Nehru.' *TRT*, No. 176, September 1954, p 363-368.

'The Korean Revolution.' *TRT*, Vol. XLIII, December 1952-September 1953, p 170.

'The Reconstruction of the Sub-Continent.' *TRT*, No. 247, July 1972, p 275-282.

## Newspapers and Magazines

The Australian.

*The Age,* Melbourne.

*The Australian's Review of Books,* (published bi-monthly in *The Australian)*

The Sydney Morning Herald.

*Times Higher Education Supplement,* 12 October 1993.

*The Bulletin.*

*India Today,* (Special Issue 1947-1997)

*The Hindu,* Madras.

*The Hindu Weekly Review,* Bombay.

*The Hindu Weekly, Madras.*

*The Hindustan Times,* New Delhi.

*The Indian Express.*

*The Leader,* India.

*The National Herald,* Lucknow.

*The Sunday Leader,* Allahabad.

*The Sunday Times of India,* New Delhi.

*The Statesman,* Calcutta.

*The Statesman,* Delhi.

*The Times of India,* New Delhi.

*The Tribune,* Simla.

*The Tribune,* Lucknow.

Indian Panorama.

*The Daily News,* Ceylon.

*The Daily News,* Sri-Lanka.

*The Observer,* Ceylon.

*The Sun,* Ceylon.

*The Sunday Times,* Sri-Lanka.

*The Times,* Ceylon.

*Look Japan,* Vol. 43, Issue 495, June 1997.

## Learned Societies/Institutes Publications, Conference/Seminar Papers, Reports and Lectures

*Australia and India: The Next Ten Years,* Papers presented at a Seminar, October 1990, Melbourne. (Responding to the Senate Report, *Australia-India Relations: Trade and Security.* AGPS. Canberra. 1990).

Bruce, Robert H.(ed.), *Prospects for Peace: Changes in the Indian Ocean Region,* Papers presented at a seminar 14-16 January 1991, published by the Indian Ocean Centre for Peace Studies, Perth, 1992.

Chopra V.D., 'Indo-Pak Relations: A Historical Perspective' Paper presented at a Seminar, *Studies in Indo-Pak Relations,* 24-25 April, 1984 New Delhi, published by the Centre for Regional Affairs, New Delhi.

Grassby A.J., *A Multicultural Society for the Future,.* Lecture at the 'Strategy 2000: Australians for Tomorrow ', Symposium, AGPS, Canberra, 1973.

Jayasuriya, L., *The Australian-Asian Connection: Retrospect and Prospect*, revised edition of paper first presented to the University of Third Age, Perth published by H.V. Evatt Research Centre, Sydney, 1988.

Malik, Ifthikar H., 'The Continuing Conflict in Kashmir: Regional Detente in Jeopardy', *Conflict Studies* 259, Paper published by the Research Institute for the Study of Conflict and Terrorism (risct), March 1993, Delhi.

Marshallsay, Z., (ed.) *Australia-Malaysia Relations: New Roads Ahead*, Proceedings of a Conference organised by the Centre of Malaysian Studies, 20 April 1995, Clayton, Victoria, published by the Monash Australia-Asia Institution, 1996.

Smith, Kate Darian., (ed.) *Working Papers in Australian Studies*, No. 88-96, Sir Robert Menzies Centre for Australia Studies, London, 1994.

Viviany, Nancy., (ed.) *The Abolition of the White Australia Policy: The Immigration Reform Movement Revisited*, Australia-Asia Paper No. 65, Centre for the Study of Australia-Asia Relations, Griffith University, Qld. 1992.

Viviany Nancy., (ed.) *Asia and Australia: The Capricornia Papers*, presented to a Seminar on 'Asia and Australia' at the Capricornia Institute of Advanced Education, Rockhampton, 29/30 March 1980.

Lowe, David., Abstract of 'Menzies Memory and Britain: Australian Perspectives on International Affairs in the 1950s', Paper for discussion at Seminar, Sir Robert Menzies Centre for Australian Studies, London, 1997.

'Labor in Power: What's the Difference?', Essays delivered at the 1972 Fabian Winter Lecture Series, Pamphlet No. 22.

'Australia in a World Economy', Proceedings of a Seminar by the Evatt Foundation, 15 October 1988.

'Nehru Champion of Freedom' Lecture by E.G. Whitlam at an International Seminar 'Nehru: the Man and His Vision' arranged by UNESCO. Sydney, 27-29 September 1989.

'Australia's Foreign Policy: New Directions, New Definitions', Twenty Fourth Roy Milne Memorial lecture by E.G. Whitlam, 30 November, 1973.

'Australia's Role in Asia', Eighteenth Roy Milne Memorial Lecture by McMahon Ball, November 1967, Australian Institute of International Affairs.

'Australia's Foreign Policy: Responding to Change.', (Sir Hermann Black Lecture, University of Sydney) by Gareth Evans, 10 September, 1990.

'Australia in a World Economy.' Impact Series. Proceedings of a Seminar 15 October 1988, Evatt Foundation, Sydney.

'Indira Gandhi A Dynamic Decade of Progress.' Address by Inderjit Kaur Sandhu, (Vice-Chancellor) at a symposium held at Punjab University, Patiala, 1976.

'India's Foreign Policy Perspectives in the 1990s.' Speech delivered by Madhavsinh Solanski, on 13 August 1991, at the India International Centre, New Delhi.

National Strategy for the Study of India and Indian Languages, Melbourne: Melbourne South Asian Studies Group for the Asian Studies Council, 1991.

Performance Evaluation of the National Centre for South Asian Studies, Don Plimer Consultancies Report, June 1996.

## Theses

Gurry, Meg., 'No Will or No Way? Australia's Relations with India, 1947-1993.' Ph. D. Thesis Latrobe University, Bundoora, Victoria, 1993.

Zacharial, George, 'Britain and the Sino-Indian Border War of 1962.' B.A. Thesis. University of Oxford, Oxford, 1994.

Ngoc, Nguyen., 'The Miracle of Vietnam: The Establishment and Consolidation of Ngo Dinh Diem's Regime 1954-1959.' Ph. D. Thesis, Monash University, Victoria, 1997.

## Television Programmes

- *Portrait of H.V. Evatt.*, Southern Cross Programme, 18 June 2000, Discovery Channel, Foxtel T.V.
- *Suez Crisis*, 31 October 1998. Presented by Jeremy Bennet, Australian Broadcasting Corporation.
- *Indo-Pakistan conflict over Kashmir*, Sunday Programme, 27 March 2000, Melbourne, Channel Nine.

## Interviews

- Mrs. Aurora, Lok Sabha Library, New Delhi, 20th October, 1997.
- C.R. Bain, Research Officer, Ministry of External Affairs, New Delhi, 18th November, 1997.
- V.K. Jain, Director Library and Information, Ministry of External Affairs, New Delhi, 10th October, 1997 and 27th January, 1999.
- Arul Kumar, Policy Planning and Research Division, Ministry of External Affairs, New Delhi, 27th January, 1999.
- S. Tripathi, Deputy High Commissioner for India, Colombo, Sri Lanka, 10th February, 1999.
- B.B. Tyaji, Deputy High Commissioner for India in Australia, Telephone interview, Canberra.
- Bruce Grant, Author/Diplomat, Melbourne, 9th May, 1999.
- Professor D. Markwell, Visiting Professor of Political Science, Victoria University of Technology, Melbourne, 24th June, 1996.
- M. Teichman, Author, Melbourne, 9th October, 1998.
- Professor Marika Vicziany, Director National Centre for South Asia Studies, Monash University, Asia Institute, Melbourne, 15th December, 1998.
- Dr. J. Karunasekera, Commonwealth Capital Secretariat, London, 22nd and 23rd September, 1997.